Poverty in the Midst of Affluence

Poverty in the Midst of Affluence

How Hong Kong Mismanaged Its Prosperity

Leo F. Goodstadt

香港大學出版社
HONG KONG UNIVERSITY PRESS

Hong Kong University Press
The University of Hong Kong
Pokfulam Road
Hong Kong
www.hkupress.org

ISBN 978-988-8208-21-0

British Library Cataloguing-in-Publication Data
A catalogue record for this book is available from the British Library.

10   9   8   7   6   5   4   3   2

Printed and bound by Paramount Printing Co. Ltd. in Hong Kong, China

Contents

Preface

This book is the last of a trilogy which I have written in gratitude to the people of Hong Kong with whom I have spent my life since 1962. The first book, *Uneasy Partners: The Conflict Between Public Interest and Private Profit in Hong Kong,* investigated the collusion and cooperation between government and the business and professional elite. It described how the community defeated the rampant corruption within both the public and the private sectors. It traced the development of a political maturity and social discipline which made Hong Kong the most stable society not only within China but by comparison with the whole of Asia. It charted the rise of a manufacturing sector that dominated the world's textile market despite decades of global protectionism. At the same time, Hong Kong overcame 'Cold War' embargoes and worldwide currency controls to provide China with an outstanding international financial centre.

The second book told a similar story of Hong Kong's triumph over its political and economic handicaps. *Profits, Politics and Panics: Hong Kong's Banks and the Making of a Miracle Economy, 1935–1985* recounted how a city ruined first by the Japanese invasion and then by the Korean War blockade of China managed to replace its lost Mainland markets almost overnight as its factories boosted their exports by 136 per cent a year in the 1950s. High-speed economic growth continued in the decades that followed, financed almost entirely by the local banking system despite repeated bank failures, market collapses, corporate scandals, currency crises and government mismanagement. By the end of the last century, this talented community had won for itself a new lease of life because of what China's Prime Ministers in this century have described as its 'irreplaceable' role in the nation's modernisation.

Hong Kong had also emerged from the global financial crisis of 2007–09 with an enhanced reputation for financial stability and well-regulated financial institutions. So much so that I felt obliged to interrupt the trilogy to write *Reluctant Regulators: How the West Created and China Survived the Global Financial Crisis,* which highlighted how impressive Hong Kong's recent performance has been by world banking standards.

This, the final book in the trilogy, presents a very different experience of Hong Kong's prosperity. Research into housing conditions was what brought me to the University of Hong Kong. When I first arrived in 1962, most families had to make their homes in housing that was barely fit for human habitation in both the public and the private sectors. I quickly discovered that despite the squalor and lack of amenities, people were unfailingly positive, pleasant and helpful, even in the worst tenement slums. Streets were safe and crime was low. Adults were clean and healthy, and schoolchildren were immaculate. There was a confidence among ordinary men and women about finding new jobs as old industries failed and giving their children a decent chance in life, no matter what the shortfalls in educational and other social services. Most striking of all was the robust confidence that political uncertainties and economic setbacks would not halt the rise of prosperity and that the future would be even better for the next generation.

The grounds for such optimism were highlighted by the first Legislative Council proceedings that caught my attention that summer. The government declared that Hong Kong had eradicated hunger among its largely refugee population and, as a result, welfare agencies should tell their foreign donors that food relief was no longer needed. In 2008, history was reversed when the second Chief Executive asked the public to support food relief programmes.

In 1962, the government was insisting that standards of public hygiene and fire safety should be kept at the lowest possible levels for the 580,000 people living in squatter huts in order to deter families from leaving their filthy, over-crowded tenements and building shanties for themselves on the hillsides. In 2011, a senior minister adopted a similar strategy. She announced that individuals living in dangerous, dirty and usually illegally subdivided buildings would have to put up with these dreadful conditions: to relocate them would be to create an incentive for other families to move into such accommodation in the hope of being rehoused by the government.

In this century, poverty has reappeared in new forms. The supply of public housing has shrunk, and private property prices have soared. Access to social services has become more expensive, and their supply has fallen far below the community's needs. The labour force has become even more efficient than in previous decades but earnings have failed to match the improved productivity; and for the lower-paid workers, wages have declined. Instead of 'trickle down' to the community at large from the sustained economic growth, inequality of incomes (as measured by the Gini Coefficient) has increased and is now among the worst in the world.

This reversal in the fortunes of the average family demands explanation. When I first came to Hong Kong, it was a model of high-speed, sustained industrial takeoff which was unsupported by international aid and confronted by determined efforts overseas to block the expansion of Hong Kong's exports. Half a century later, life in this world-class economy has become harsher for the deprived, the disadvantaged and the disabled. Destitution has reappeared, and ordinary families have been left struggling to pay for reasonable accommodation, decent education and proper treatment for serious illnesses. The origin of these new hardships is to be found in the pursuit of fiscal austerity, the adoption of business models and other misguided and misinformed government policies and the dominant role played by business interests, this book will show.

The investigation of Hong Kong's 'new poverty' has not been completely disheartening. This book highlights how the 'economic miracle' that was formerly Hong Kong's boast has been matched by a contemporary 'social miracle'. The community is more stable and self-reliant than in the previous century despite the erosion of living standards, mistreatment of the workforce and the government's retreat from responsibility for the community's social wellbeing. Doctors, nurses, teachers and social workers have managed to raise standards even after their budgets have been squeezed and working conditions have deteriorated. The quality of public services as a whole improved significantly in this century despite the strains caused by the poor performance of so much of the government's leadership and its denigration of the civil service and its efficiency.

'Of all things in the world, people are the most precious,' said Mao Zedong in 1949, 'as long as there are people, every kind of miracle can be performed.' Hong Kong's 7 million people are very special, and they have not yet run out of miracles. They have kept their city a haven of hope today not just by comparison with the rest of Asia — as was the case 50 years ago — but when measured against the quality of life in most of the world's leading cities.

Hong Kong has been made all the more pleasant for me in the 21st century by the kindness and hospitality which my friends and former colleagues at the Central Policy Unit so generously offer me. Among those I can acknowledge here with gratitude are Barry Cheung, Helen Cheng, T. L. Tsim, Dr Rikkie Yeung, Professor Cecilia Chan and their families who take such good care of me.

It is a pleasure to renew my thanks to Dr Christopher Munn of Hong Kong University Press. Once again, he has been the best kind of editor: patient, pleasant and with all the academic expertise that a book on Hong Kong public affairs needs most.

Acknowledgments

In the course of writing this book, I was fortunate enough to be selected for a substantial award from the WYNG Foundation Ltd, for which I am most grateful. The Trustees and their team have been a constant source of encouragement and support throughout the last two years, which I found invaluable. I deeply appreciate the commitment which the Foundation has shown to the needy and the vulnerable of Hong Kong. Its 'Poverty Project' has been both innovative and inspirational in raising awareness of social responsibility within the community, and I am proud to be associated with it.

I am indebted to the Hong Kong Institute for the Humanities and Social Sciences at the University of Hong Kong which has provided me with generous use of its facilities. The Institute is the ideal environment in which to do research, which enabled me to complete this volume between October 2011 and March 2013. My special thanks are due to the Director, Professor Angela Leung Ki Che, for all her help and for her personal interest and kindness. I must also thank the Institute's staff for looking after me so patiently.

My research on the historical development of Hong Kong's housing programmes and its social services would have been impossible without the assistance of the Government Records Service. The professionalism and efficiency of Mr Bernard Hui Sung-tak and his colleagues in the Public Records Office have provided me with an outstanding quality of research support over many years.

I am, as always, indebted to the School of Business Studies, Trinity College, University of Dublin, and in particular to my friend, Professor Gerard McHugh, for their interest and encouragement, as well as for their facilities, throughout my stays in Ireland.

None of the institutions or individuals referred to in these acknowledgments has any responsibility for any part of the contents of this book or the views which it expresses.

Hong Kong
July 2013

Introduction: Pain, Panic and Poverty

Nothing had prepared the people of Hong Kong for the abrupt reversal in their fortunes that was to overtake them in this century. Adversity began with the 1997–98 Asian financial crisis but the economic downturn did not create the calamity that followed. The worst damage was social, where disaster was to be deep and prolonged. For the first time in decades, poverty became widespread. The numbers of workers who 'despite working hard', the government admitted, 'consistently cannot earn reasonable salaries to satisfy the basic needs of themselves and their families' was to reach almost 200,000.[1]

Panic and helplessness paralysed policy-makers, who were convinced that budget austerity was the appropriate remedy despite the protracted and unparalleled deflation that was shrinking the economy.[2] By 2005, the government reluctantly conceded that more than a million individuals (15 per cent of the population) were living in poverty.[3] The business and professional elite was convinced that the new poor had had only themselves to blame. Past prosperity had 'spoiled' Hong Kong people and made them unwilling to help themselves, claimed one prominent business spokesperson.[4]

The average family had no escape from distress. From the 1960s, the people of Hong Kong had been conditioned to expect that their living standards would steadily advance, while the government — however grudgingly, as later chapters will explain — undertook to provide public housing, schooling, more and better medical services and a basic social welfare programme. Above all, there were ample work opportunities, and employment was indeed the best form of welfare. Even the older worker and individuals with disabilities had a reasonable chance of finding paid employment, such was the chronic labour shortage.

There had seemed every chance that this happy state of affairs would continue, especially since China's leaders had promised to leave Hong Kong's systems unchanged after 1997. With its long record of prosperity and abundant jobs, there seemed no reason to complain that the Basic Law — China's constitutional blueprint for the new Special Administrative

Region — had made the welfare of society so subordinate to business interests. Of the Basic Law's 159 articles, 34 were devoted to entrenching the pro-business, laisser-faire policies of the colonial era, together with its financial and commercial structures. The social rights set out in the Basic Law were far vaguer and less comprehensive than its economic prescriptions. On even the most generous interpretation of the document, only seven articles could be described as relating to the provision of social services, while workers' rights were referred to in another three.[5] The government-business nexus which had long ensured that official policies did not encumber business profits remained in control. Hong Kong, it seemed, was to be a world with little regard for welfare.

The absence of welfare suddenly began to matter in 1998. Now, for the first time since the Japanese Occupation ended in 1945, parents could not take it for granted that their children would enjoy better job prospects, rising wages and more secure and rewarding careers. Younger citizens — the '80s generation' — were the best-educated in Hong Kong's history, according to a government-sponsored study. But they faced worse employment opportunities, lower earnings and grimmer lifetime prospects than any previous generation.[6]

There was to be no relief from the distress caused by inadequate social services which the most vulnerable groups had to endure. By 2009, for example, some 2,700 individuals with severe physical or mental disabilities faced an average delay of almost five years for admission to the residential facilities which they urgently needed. The government declined to set a target for ending these distressing waiting times.[7]

Government Blunders, Past and Present

The collapse of the general prosperity that the community had previously been able to take for granted had not been the inevitable consequence of the Asian financial crisis. On the eve of the crisis, the economy was not dependent on the rest of the region (excluding Japan and the Mainland).[8] Hong Kong's economy was driven by two external trade cycles: the North American/European Union and the Chinese Mainland. Both were still positive, with China's growth particularly healthy. In the past, furthermore, Hong Kong had emerged unscathed from far worse turmoil in the region. What made the events that followed 1997 so traumatic was an unhappy conjunction of adverse circumstances. As international business sentiment and investor confidence in Asia slumped, misjudgements by the new Special Administrative Region's government and business leaders aggravated the liabilities accumulated through reluctance under colonialism to finance the modernisation of Hong Kong's social services.

Business leadership

Leadership failed during the initial crisis and the decade that followed. The first Chief Executive, Tung Chee Hwa, claimed that ruling Hong Kong had become more difficult after colonialism ended in 1997. He had not foreseen, he stated, that 'social and political behaviour' would alter so much. The media were more difficult to manage, he went on, while the government faced a more demanding community. He and his team were taken by surprise and did not 'have the necessary experience to respond appropriately', he confessed.[9]

Inexperience of public affairs was his own, crucial weakness. Tung was a businessman whose principal achievement had been the rescue of the family shipping firm from bankruptcy in 1986. Once owner of the world's biggest fleet, its debts had reached an estimated US$2.5 billion. He saved the company through brutal cost-cutting and asset disposal, together with substantial Mainland help.[10]

Tung frequently referred to his business experience as a guide to the management of Hong Kong's recession.[11] He seemed blind to the difference between corporate and public finance. For corporations, responsibility is first and foremost to the shareholders, which usually means slashing payroll and negotiating write-offs with debtors when liquidation threatens. Governments are different. Their duty is to protect the community, including its workers. Tung chose financial stringency, nevertheless, which matched the mindset of the entire government-business nexus. Unfortunately, austerity budgets, civil service redundancies and wage cuts, all aggravate deflation when an economy goes into recession, as do constraints on social security and on the supply of social services.

Business models

Tung and the upper ranks of the civil service also believed that the 'business model' was the best guide to managing the public sector. From at least 1989, senior officials in Hong Kong had been impressed by the 'New Public Management' philosophy which had become fashionable worldwide.[12] Posts were deleted, and an attempt was made to freeze the overall size of the civil service.[13] Despite media and business community approbation, the colonial administration realised that there must be limits to the concept of 'zero growth' for public sector employment, which it described as 'a severe discipline'. 'New schools, new housing estates, and new hospitals' would need new staff, the Chief Secretary pointed out, and they could only be made available under a 'zero growth policy' by 'cutting back on existing services'.[14] As the drive to adopt business values and practices within the civil service gathered momentum, however, the potential constraints on the supply and the quality of social services were increasingly disregarded. The colonial administration became convinced that the civil service should follow the international trend and adopt business values and practices. Consultants were hired from the private sector in the 1990s, and their recommendations on trimming staff and cutting wage costs through outsourcing and privatisation were warmly embraced by the Housing and the Social Welfare Departments, among others.[15] These initiatives were endorsed by Christopher (later Lord) Patten, the last colonial Governor, despite his reputation as a welfare populist. He was, after all, a former Conservative Cabinet Minister under Margaret Thatcher who had been a leading proponent of public sector reform through learning from business. The measures taken to promote a business-based culture at the end of the colonial era laid the foundations for the drastic changes in policy which Tung and his senior officials imposed on public housing and the social services at the beginning of this century.

Financial savings achieved through cutting staff were seen as the acid test of the new efficiency. The social services were to suffer heavily because health, education and welfare are all labour intensive. Once staff were laid off, social services programmes lost momentum because government departments were now operating with the minimum personnel to maintain existing services. They had little scope for expansion, although social services were the government programmes most needed by the community during the economic turndown. There was a constant temptation, too, to cut back on staff not directly involved in delivering current services — quality control and forward planning, for example — with damaging consequences for the future. Long-term targets to end shortfalls in existing programmes were no longer set. Potential gaps between the supply of services and current and future needs were not quantified. Finance was allocated on a short-term basis, which disrupted the organisation of programmes to build new premises, train more professional staff and modernise existing facilities.[16]

Little attention was paid to evidence that the business model was no panacea. For example, in 1995, the Housing Authority had switched from using a professional fee scale in negotiating contracts to a form of competitive tendering. Henceforward, contracts were approved 'even if the tender prices were considered too low for the works required'. The justification offered by officials was that 'tenderers might have their own way to make their tenders financially viable'. In reality, there was no way to make an honest profit, and malpractice mushroomed as a result.[17]

No part of the administrative machine seemed safe, not even its statistics, the raw material of policy-making. Allegations surfaced in 2013 that over the previous ten years, Census and Statistics Department personnel had been fabricating survey data.[18] A subsequent investigation revealed that as the government's demand for more economic and social data increased in this century, staff resources did not rise in tandem. In 2003, the dedicated fieldwork team for a key survey programme had been disbanded as part of a campaign to increase management flexibility and enhance productivity. Statistical staff stated that this and similar 'efficiency' measures had jeopardised the quality of the information collected. Increased workloads and the employment of temporary personnel were identified as other threats to maintaining professional statistical standards.[19]

Past neglect

The crisis faced by Tung and his team was worsened by past complacency on the part of the colonial administration and its collaborators among the business and professional elite before 1997. During the previous decades of unbroken economic growth and a constant shortage of workers, Hong Kong had deliberately delayed investment in social development. Immigrants, reared and educated on the Mainland, had finished their schooling before they arrived. These young people needed little medical care and could tolerate miserable living quarters. As for Hong Kong's own youngsters, unqualified teachers and inferior school facilities had seemed no great handicap. Demand for workers remained intense, and labour productivity rose year after year. Employers themselves were opposed to free, compulsory education, Chapter 4 will explain.

Before the 'one-child' family became the Hong Kong norm in this century, households were big enough to be able to operate as largely self-sufficient economic units. They could pool incomes and savings to start small enterprises, to raise a mortgage or to cover the medical and other costs of life's accidents. The sort of social insurance common in other advanced economies to provide retirement, unemployment and sickness benefits seemed unnecessary. The average household size has now fallen to below three, and life spans have grown longer. The family's traditional self-reliance has gone. The people of Hong Kong now face the bills for social insurance that have been long postponed.

The unemployment created by the recession that began in 1997 drastically reduced the jobs available for the older and the poorly educated worker. Claims on the non-contributory, tax-financed social security system rose sharply. At the same time, Hong Kong's ageing population became a challenge that could no longer be ignored. Facilities for the elderly and the disabled were already inadequate, and the government took fright at the potential costs of making good the past under-spending on medical and welfare facilities. The caring professions were left to struggle to overcome the shortfalls, while the government rationed access to services through waiting lists and increased charges.

A New Poverty

A new era had started, and with it came a new kind of poverty. Earnings and incomes were no longer buoyant, in contrast to the 1980s and 1990s, which have been depicted as a golden era for the workforce.[20] In 2010, the average household income of HK$18,000 a month was no higher than it had been in 2000. The lowest-income groups fared worst, and the number of households with less than HK$6,000 a month rose from 13 per cent to 17 per cent of the total. Employees did not deserve this treatment. Their efficiency had continued to improve despite the lack of monetary incentives. Between 2002 and 2011, labour productivity rose by 3.4 per cent a year, faster than Singapore (2.4 per cent), the United States (1.4 per cent) and Germany (0.8 per cent).[21]

The new poverty brought unfamiliar hardships for the average household. The wellbeing of families that hitherto had been financially secure was now in jeopardy. Earnings stagnated, hours of work grew longer and job prospects were uncertain. The supply of public housing was slashed, and private sector prices surged. The pressures on the typical family's budget intensified as hospital charges and school and university fees were increased. For most families, the situation was uncomfortable but not unbearable if they scrimped and saved.

Some, however, were in imminent danger of impoverishment (as Chapter 5 will explain in detail). The government's efforts to limit Hospital Authority spending and to push patients towards the private sector meant that for families with a seriously ill relative, there was an agonising dilemma. Even a comfortably-off family could be driven heavily into debt in a bid to ensure immediate diagnosis and care for a relative in a private hospital rather than queuing in the public sector when a life-threatening illness was suspected. A family could also impoverish itself through buying the drugs of choice for cancer and other illnesses when these were rationed by price in the public sector. Less heart-breaking but still distressing were the choices to be made about education by families with limited incomes. How could parents afford the fees for the better schools or for university or other post-secondary courses when the annual charges per student could amount to the equivalent of four months' earnings for the average employee? Government loans were available, but the worsening career prospects of new graduates and school-leavers made their repayment an intimidating burden.

There was another category of victim whose financial and physical distress was intensified by official policies. In the drive to imitate business and to achieve 'value for money', programmes for the most vulnerable groups lagged well behind demand for their facilities. Waiting times remained scandalously long in almost every sector, no matter how small the numbers to be cared for or how difficult it was for them to survive without residential or other essential facilities. Age made no difference: pre-school children with disabilities and elderly people with dementia waited and suffered, as this book later explains in detail.

The distress for the families affected was aggravated in this century because it became an article of faith that 'welfare' was unaffordable. The government refused to make specific commitments for the solution of shortfalls and the improvement of facilities. And there was no escape from the government's demeaning message: only the destitute should have any right to public services. Everyone else should be self-supporting, both as an individual and as a member of a 'Confucian' family unit.

Blaming the Victims

Life was made harsher for the average family principally because of policy decisions made by officials who closed their eyes to the grim consequences for the community at large. Tung Chee Hwa suggested that Hong Kong had brought financial disaster on itself. For many years, he declared, Hong Kong had lived in 'a bubble economy'. His government started to preach financial stringency, which intensified the deflation. 'The bubble needed correction and it's now being corrected,' was his standard message, '[o]f course there is government sympathy for those people who will be unemployed in the near future, and of course it's all part of the fortunes we have to go through,' he said.[22] He had little practical comfort to offer. 'What we had to do,' the Chief Executive later explained, 'was make our people accept the inevitability of the need for the adjustment, however painful it might be.'[23]

As his government failed to halt the decline in the community's wellbeing, he pleaded his helplessness in the face of external forces. 'Globalisation has aggravated poverty generally in many places around the world and we are no exception,' Tung complained in 2004. His remedy was a suggestion that those in need could rescue themselves from poverty.[24] His social policy innovations sounded remote from the painful realities of everyday life. He was determined, for example, to resurrect elitism long 'trodden down in thoughtless media vilification', he complained. He chose as a major goal of his education plans at the height of the recession the establishment of 'more private schools to meet the diverse quality needs of different parents and students'.[25]

The second Chief Executive, Donald Tsang Yam-kuen, was also ready to leave those in need to solve their own problems because he was opposed to 'assisting the poor by giving them financial assistance'.[26] While Tsang was emphatically denying the government's ability to relieve poverty, the unequal distribution of wealth in Hong Kong was described as 'the worst among developed nations'. Its extraordinary record of economic growth had not eradicated poverty but, rather, appeared to have widened the gap between rich and poor.[27]

Those in power were reluctant to accept that in Hong Kong, poverty was not a social failing which could be remedied by moral encouragement or by learning to be enterprising. 'The idea of "aid for the poor" is not relevant to Hong Kong, which is an affluent society whose annual GDP per head is US$24,000,' a leading business daily declared.[28] The community at large was discouraged from regarding the poor as 'deserving' in any way. Poverty was depicted as an imported contagion and an almost genetic condition. Hong Kong could not expect to be any different from other international financial centres like New York, London and Tokyo, Tsang insisted, where the gaps between rich and poor are also large. 'The wealthiest people are gathered in such cities,' he asserted, 'but the poorest people also make their way to such cities.' Tsang was adamant that attempts to close the gap were bound to do more harm than good.[29]

The third Chief Executive, Leung Chun-ying, attempted to redirect this debate over the gap between rich and poor and focus it, instead, on the hardships inflicted by poverty. The wealth gap itself was not the issue, he stated, and his concern was with 'the living conditions of the lower strata of society'.[30] Despite the rhetoric, he did not break with his predecessors' misgivings about spending on social services. Leung took care to allay potential anxiety among the business community about social expenditure. The wealth gap had widened dramatically in the 12 years from 1997, he pointed out to a business forum.

> . . . the income of the group having the highest 10 per cent per capita household income increased by 64.7 per cent, while the income of the group having the lowest 10 per cent per capita household income dropped by 22 per cent.

Nevertheless, his administration would not adopt radical remedies to reverse this trend, he promised his business audience. 'Many see redistribution and not economic growth as the only way to move forward,' he said. His own conviction, he frankly stated, was that redistribution 'could be the major obstacle to our pro-growth policies'.[31] The traditional government-business nexus remained intact.

A peculiarity of contemporary Hong Kong is the narrow view which Hong Kong's rulers have taken of poverty. The poor have been seen, almost entirely, as an economic problem: unemployment or low-paid jobs prevented them from being financially self-supporting.[32] The government, therefore, almost always made 'economic growth' 'the key to tackling poverty' through creating more work opportunities.[33] Leung bracketed a fall in the number of Comprehensive Social Security Assistance (CSSA) recipients with a rise in GDP as a leading indicator of economic wellbeing.[34] Yet, the jobless have represented only a small proportion of those in financial need. For them, the CSSA scheme provided subsistence support until their employment situation improved (as Chapter 6 will show). Far more numerous were the elderly and those with disabilities. These could never become self-supporting, so there was no 'cure' for their poverty. The government ignored the fact that their lives could not be made tolerable by social security benefits alone. They needed healthcare, special housing and, often, residential services in order to live as free as possible from mental and physical distress. But these were programmes to which the government, this book will demonstrate, was reluctant to commit adequate resources.[35]

The refusal of those in power to recognise how a new poverty was being created through service shortfalls was highlighted by the third Chief Executive's decision to revive his predecessor's Commission on Poverty. Its members were advised to accept 'the findings of local academics' who had produced a vaguely worded definition of the primary causes of poverty: 'structure, system, culture, and personal and socio-economic status'. The Commission's agenda would be 'to mitigate causes of poverty and promote upward social mobility of the grass roots' even though, this book will show, the inadequate supply of government services is the primary cause of poverty in contemporary Hong Kong.[36]

A Siege Mentality

The retreat from social responsibilities and the pursuit of budget cuts were not forced on Hong Kong by falling tax revenues and fiscal crises. The public sector's finances were more than adequate. By 2011, the government had accumulated net assets that totalled HK$1.4 trillion. Yet, in the government's long-standing campaign to reject all but a minimal obligation to those in need, it did not shrink from fomenting public prejudice against social expenditure. To alarm the better-off, officials claimed that a commitment to improved social security benefits would be beyond the Hong Kong's financial resources and could lead to budget deficits.[37] 'Welfare-based relief measures on a long-term basis', it was alleged, would lead to changes in Hong Kong's low-tax regime.[38] All governments, the second Chief Executive declared, face unaffordable 'public pressure to spend more, on welfare, on spending on education, a whole range of services' which must be resisted. As evidence, he invoked the fiscal challenges of 'Western Europe'.[39] These, in fact, were the outcome of a failure to regulate financial markets effectively. (Canada and Australia provide generous social services but had escaped financial disaster in the 2007–09 global financial crisis because their banking regulation before 2007 — like Hong Kong — had been vigorous.)

Austerity was not imposed on government spending by deteriorating business conditions. On the contrary, the economy proved remarkably robust, and GDP was 47 per cent higher in 2012 than it had been at the start of the century. Hong Kong was ranked fifth after New York, London, Paris and Tokyo as an international business centre by a well-known global survey in the same year. Singapore was listed in eleventh place, with Beijing and Shanghai even lower.[40] Nevertheless, there were constant predictions that a resurgent Shanghai would render Hong Kong redundant, even though China's leaders repeatedly insisted that Hong Kong retained an 'irreplaceable' role in the nation's economy. For example, Prime Minister Li Keqiang declared that as 'an international free port city and a major financial, trade and shipping center, Hong Kong is one of the world's most open, vibrant and competitive economies'. It was 'China's need,' he acknowledged, 'that Hong Kong continues to bring out the unique advantages it has developed over the years and play its irreplaceable role in the mainland's reform, opening-up and modernization drive.'[41] Such accolades were justified by Hong Kong's astounding performance in providing half the total foreign direct investment for China's modernisation since 1978 as well as by its achievements as an international financial centre.

With a record of unbroken annual GDP growth, which averaged 7.5 per cent from 1961 to 1997, Hong Kong seemed to have an inexhaustible capacity to succeed as a capitalist society.[42] The people had made the transition from poverty to prosperity faster, it has been claimed, than any other society in history.[43] In 1949, national income per head was a mere quarter of the United Kingdom level.[44] By the end of British rule, Hong Kong GDP per head had caught up with the United Kingdom, thanks to breakneck industrial expansion which relied almost entirely on local funding, with no significant foreign aid.[45]

In the process, Hong Kong's manufacturers had to overcome efforts by the United Kingdom, North America and Western Europe to protect their domestic markets against Hong Kong exports. A hostile political and economic environment throughout much of the 20th century forced Hong Kong to adopt a growth model which was self-financed and self-sustaining.[46] A siege mentality developed, and, as a result, business and its wellbeing took absolute precedence in official policy-making, regardless of the social costs to the community.[47] The perception grew that crises would never end.[48] Within the government-business nexus, paranoia about the future intensified in the 1990s, fuelled by what leading business people believed to be an imminent danger of increased social expenditure and 'welfare state' policies.[49]

China's leaders did their best to allay unease and uncertainty for business by entrenching the survival of capitalism and protection of privileged priority for business interests as prominent features of the Basic Law, and business representatives dominated the new political system that was being created for the post-colonial era. By 1995, nevertheless, 59 per cent of the local firms listed on the Hong Kong Stock Exchange were reported to have taken the precaution of obtaining overseas incorporations, double the figure when the Basic Law had been promulgated in 1990. There was ample evidence, too, of how wealthy individuals were transferring sizeable portions of their wealth overseas because of uncertainty about future prospects.[50]

While political risk receded in 1997, the Asian financial crisis provided what the government and the business community viewed as incontrovertible evidence of Hong Kong's economic fragility. These gloomy apprehensions marked an important boundary between the ruling elite and the rest of the community Society as a whole retained 'a pervasive sense of wellbeing', which was regarded as among the most important building blocks of Hong Kong's social stability, even though political risk was a serious anxiety for most families.[51]

Fragile Prosperity

Both before and after the end of British rule in 1997, economic survival thus provided the standard excuse to justify government hostility towards social expenditure and indifference to the plight of the poor, the elderly, the disabled and the infirm, as later chapters will recount. The colonial administration and its collaborators from the business and professional elite refused to introduce education for all children until late in the last century. Housing conditions were deliberately kept squalid and insanitary to an extent that, in retrospect, seems unbearable. Social insurance, retirement protection and unemployment benefits were bitterly opposed and postponed for as long as possible. Public housing and social services lagged well behind the expectations of this sophisticated, post-industrial society and were far from adequate in 1998 to meet the community's needs during Hong Kong's worst-ever recession in over 60 years.

Obsession with economic vulnerability seemed boundless. Despite the evidence cited earlier of Hong Kong's financial strength and economic prowess, there were repeated warnings in this century of impending catastrophe.[52] The target was always the same: to prove to the public 'how welfare populism destroys prosperity', to quote the title of a presentation by the Financial Secretary in 2012.[53] There was almost no debate about the assumption that welfare spending had to be constrained. The government's claims that welfare was unaffordable and that expansion of social services was unsustainable had long become articles of faith, while the case for giving priority to business interests was taken for granted.[54]

Hostility towards social expenditure intensified in this century, whether for public housing, health, education or welfare programmes. The public now had to pay for services previously provided either free or at minimal cost. The supply of these services was also rationed, leading to severe shortfalls in the facilities on which depended the health, comfort and future wellbeing of the most vulnerable groups in the community. Those who turned to the government for assistance were defamed without justification, especially those households which could only survive by applying for CSSA benefits. An extensive propaganda campaign sought to convince the community that social security was leading to a dependency culture in which the able-bodied voluntarily quit their jobs and the younger generation turned their backs on Confucian filial piety and abandoned their elderly relatives to the care of the state. (These allegations will be shown to have been entirely without foundation in Chapter 6.)

Counting the Costs

In the past, as long as the economy managed to create additional wealth and new jobs year after year no matter how adverse the political or business environment, there had seemed no great urgency about programmes to transform the housing stock and upgrade the social services. Retirement and care for the elderly were challenges on the horizon but seemed still remote to a community which had been so recently largely young and immigrant. As long as the economy constantly reinvented itself and matched world best practice, first in manufacturing for export and then in financial services, the Third World legacy of slum housing conditions and limited social services seemed tolerable. That complacency was dangerously misleading because it left for future decades serious shortfalls that would prove extremely costly to solve in this century.

A comparison of social expenditure in Hong Kong with economies of similar affluence offers a guide to how large the outstanding bill to be paid for the elimination of these deficiencies was. At the start of this century, Hong Kong was 'forty years behind' the rest of the world's advanced economies in terms of its public spending on social services, an academic study reported. Hong Kong's social expenditure in 2001 was at the same level as the average for OECD members in 1960. But since that date, the OECD average had almost doubled to 22 per cent of GDP.[55]

The damaging effects of the Third World heritage are rarely recognised, even though the long-term social consequences have shaped the lives of those who arrived in Hong Kong or grew up here before 1980. Indeed, some commentators have applauded the inadequate social services. Their deficiencies were 'an important component of [Hong Kong's] ticket to prosperity', it has been stated, because 'if food and shelter are easy to come by, then people will not work hard'.[56] In addition, an unconscious assumption persisted that the community should be able to overcome its future challenges with much the same sort of self-help and social improvisation as in the past.

The government continued to believe that Hong Kong could defer payment to remedy the social handicaps inherited from its recent Third World origins. The examples that follow indicate that this complacency was misplaced.

Housing

Private sector housing offered the most dramatic evidence of the bills now becoming payable for ignoring the legacy of the past. The average concrete multi-storey building in Hong Kong has a design life of 50 years. Construction in the 1950s and 1960s was cut-price. Maintenance was neglected in every subsequent decade. Overcrowding was gross and facilities minimal. In consequence, dilapidation was more rapid than anticipated, and renovation to meet health and safety standards became very expensive. Homes turned into slums, especially when these multi-storey structures had multiple owners anxious to maximise rental profits and to hold down expenses.

A 2006 United Nations report stated that the proportion of Hong Kong's population classified as 'slum dwellers' had grown at an annual rate 150 per cent faster than the overall average for the world's developed regions The situation in Hong Kong was expected to worsen significantly by 2020. Meanwhile, Singapore had no measurable slum population.[57]

Education

Educational neglect was, arguably, the biggest Third World handicap that the average individual suffered because a full system of free, universal and compulsory schooling had been postponed until 1978. Much of the school teaching in the 1980s was carried out by untrained staff and took place in overcrowded and unsuitable premises. An official report by overseas experts suspected that the government deliberately tolerated these unsatisfactory standards.[58] The harm done to those deprived of adequate schooling became apparent as soon as recession got underway in 1998. Official data showed that in the years that followed, workers born too early to benefit from free and compulsory education accounted for more than half the unemployed receiving CSSA, while another 31 per cent of the claimants had only had partial access to free schooling.[59]

Less immediately obvious but very damaging long-term was 'financial illiteracy' which could be traced to the low standards of many schools until the start of this century. The 2007–09 global financial crisis highlighted the heavy costs inflicted by 'low levels of financial literacy' on individuals as well as on financial markets and society as a whole, a senior financial official warned, with less sophisticated customers more easily misled by financial institutions.[60]

The need for 'financial literacy' was of special relevance to reforming the Mandatory Provident Fund (MPF). Current employees would have to wait another 20 years at least before their MPF accounts were large enough to make a significant contribution to their retirement incomes. In the meantime, MPF accounts were managed commercially by financial institutions whose fees were generally excessive and returns poor, the financial services minister complained.[61] The government's solution was to suggest that employees should be given greater control over the management of their personal MPF accounts. The extent of the 'financial illiteracy' that had to be overcome to make this change practical was highlighted by the large-scale public education campaign launched by the MPF Scheme Authority in 2010.[62]

Healthcare

Very serious, too, were the consequences of the government's underspending on medical and health services. Official arguments that Hong Kong was over-dependent on the public sector were misleading. The private sector enjoyed a larger share of the health market than in other affluent economies. At the start of the century, furthermore, Hong Kong's total health spending as a share of GDP had been well below the average of other advanced economies, which indicated that funding for healthcare fell far short of what was required to match world best practice.[63] The Hospital Authority, nevertheless, was forced to make financial cutbacks after the Asian financial crisis started.

The treatment of Hong Kong's 187,000 patients with mental illnesses brought into especially sharp focus both the disturbing consequences of the Third World legacy and the physical distress caused by the government's austerity drive. The health minister argued that cuts in the budgets for psychiatric services were too small to reduce the standards of patients' care.[64] Quality did decline, however. Between 2000 and 2012, the queues to enter the system lengthened, and the average waiting time for a first appointment with a psychiatrist rose from three to seven weeks.[65] Once accepted as a patient, there was no guarantee that treatment would match world standards. The government's insistence that the Hospital Authority suppress demand for modern drugs was particularly damaging to mental patients. They were prescribed older versions of anti-psychotic drugs whose side-effects could involve a level of distress and discomfort that deterred patients from taking the regular dosages needed to control their symptoms and to lead normal lives.[66]

The medical profession complained in vain about this 'price rationing' imposed as a result of budget cuts.[67] The policy resulted in cruel discrimination. Low-income mental patients could only keep their illness under control with sub-standard medication which could cause significant suffering. Patients who could afford to pay for First World medication were not subject to such pain.

Welfare

Perhaps the most striking reminder of Hong Kong's Third World origins was the revival in 2008 of government-funded, food relief schemes. When post-war Hong Kong had been flooded with refugees, a considerable quantity of food and other relief in kind was provided both by the colonial administration and by religious organisations and overseas welfare agencies, with the United States a conspicuous donor.[68] In 1962, the colonial administration claimed that hunger was no longer a problem and declared that these aid programmes should be halted.[69] In 1971, the government itself finally ceased to provide the destitute with food and other relief in kind because the Social Welfare Department had won a protracted battle to establish the Public Assistance Scheme which provided the needy with cash allowances.[70] (Chapter 4 traces this reform.)

Hunger returned to Hong Kong in this century, and in 2008, the Chief Executive was urging support for food programmes to help individuals in 'dire need'.[71] The severity of the new poverty was highlighted by this return to a distant and barely remembered era when destitution had not yet been eliminated. The new generation of the hungry included 'the unemployed, low-income earners, new arrivals, street sleepers and individuals or families encountering sudden . . . financial hardship'. They did not receive social security benefits, according to the welfare minister, even though they had 'proven difficulty coping with daily food expenditure'. These unfortunates were victims of glaring gaps in the CSSA 'safety net' which officials had long described as the guarantee that those unable to support themselves would be provided with an income to meet their basic needs.[72] Food aid also pandered to the sceptics who believed the poor could not be trusted with cash benefits.[73] By 2012, some 75,000 individuals were being rescued from hunger and malnutrition through the government's food programme, 40 per cent of them in low-paying jobs.[74]

This food relief was also linked to official efforts to restrict the government's welfare expenditure. When food prices rose, there were demands for CSSA benefits to be improved immediately. Cash was not the only solution, officials indicated. Hunger could be relieved with food donated by hotels and other firms as well as by charitable organisations and individuals, a practice which the government was keen to encourage.[75]

History came full cycle in 2011 when the welfare minister visited the United States, the original home of food kitchens and food banks to help the destitute and also the principal source of food aid for Hong Kong's original refugee population. He was highly impressed by the San Francisco Food Bank's operations and spoke warmly about how successfully these had been financed by private donations of food and cash.[76] Sadly, welfare cutbacks were a global phenomenon, and the San Francisco programmes were to be badly hit by subsequent curbs on federal funding.[77]

Haunted by History

This book will show how costly is the legacy of past policies that chose to restrict social expenditure in the erroneous belief that spending on welfare would automatically mean lower business profits and slower economic growth. In referring to this historical heritage, the term 'Third World' is used throughout this book to refer to the sort of economic and social conditions that prevailed when Hong Kong first began its ascent to prosperity after World War II. The term sums up the acute shortage of financial, physical, social and human resources at that period.

It covers the squalid slums and squatter huts that were homes for the bulk of an immigrant population. It includes the acute shortage of hospital, education and welfare facilities and the absence of social insurance and similar schemes to provide the individual with financial cover when retired, unemployed or ill. The term embraces the beginnings of Hong Kong's takeoff as a successful manufacturer. But it ceased to be an accurate description of industry after Hong Kong industrialists became a global force in the 1960s. Also excluded from the term's coverage are financial services because Hong Kong was a major international financial centre throughout the last century.[78]

Third World refers to conditions, not to people. Although the squalor and overcrowding under which so many lived and worked were often not vastly different even as late as in the 1980s from conditions three decades earlier, Third World was a label which the people of Hong Kong themselves had shed. 'The mere act of immigration achieved with great abruptness an economic and social transition which in other underdeveloped countries may take years,' a pioneering economist argued in 1971. The immigrant was forced to seek survival by adapting virtually overnight to the demands of an open, competitive, modern economy.[79]

The term has fallen out of fashion in academic circles.[80] But it is still common in China's official news media which frequently use 'Third World' in articles on the Mainland's own economic transition in the last four decades and on the performance of nations with which the Chinese government is on good terms.[81] Third World is too convenient a shorthand for the experiences of Hong Kong and its people to be discarded in a book of this sort. The term offers a generalisation that sums up a past which the community had proudly put behind it only to discover in this century that remnants of Hong Kong's Third World history had become a serious current liability.

The Unseen Victims

The vulnerable were often unrecognised and sometimes invisible even to caring people.

- The largest and best publicised group are the elderly. Barely perceived, nevertheless, is that old age is 'incurable'. As individuals get older, they face loss of mobility and failing memory. Their illnesses become serious and more crippling. Many will become incapable not only of caring for themselves physically but, because of mental deterioration, will become even more dependent than a child.
- Among those with disabilities, the most fortunate appear to be those able to lead lives on what seem equal terms with everyone else if they are given suitable education and training facilities. The paraplegic executive or professional in a wheelchair, for example, seems to suffer no special disadvantage. But life is 'different' when there is no feeling or function below the waist. Rarely realised is the continuous fatigue and the endless struggle to overcome the medical complications and threats to health that the paraplegic must endure.
- Hidden from view are groups who live close to death. These include boys with genetic deficiencies who cannot expect to live much beyond their twenties. Often academically gifted, they rarely reveal their fears about their limited life expectancies. Another group are the young people who cannot breathe independently

and are kept alive on ventilators. They are in constant danger of choking and should live close to an intensive care unit. Yet their parents are under pressure from the government's economy measures. They are urged to ignore the daily danger of choking to death and accept funding to employ a domestic helper and to care for the vulnerable individual at home instead of occupying space in a more expensive specialised unit close to emergency facilities.

- Parents live with unperceived distress when they have to face their inability to protect a vulnerable child.
  - Long-term prospects for a child with autism are enhanced through intensive pre-schooling treatment starting as early as possible. The average waiting time for admission to such pro-grammes increased by 50 per cent between 2008 and 2012. What chance had a family of being able to fill the gap through its own caring efforts when the average standard of living in Hong Kong required both parents to work?
  - A mother later in life may have a child with Down's syndrome who has limited intellectual ability and cannot live completely independently. When the child reaches 30, the mother is probably over 70. What arrangements can she make to ensure a secure future for her child when residential care is so scarce?

The potential list of examples is endless. They all involve prolonged hardship. Only the seriously wealthy can meet the cost of providing the quality of care and the living environment that those with disabilities need to live with the minimum discomfort and anxiety and with the maximum opportunity to achieve as fulfilling a life as their personal abilities permit. In the absence of personal affluence, a decent and com-fortable existence is only possible with the state's assistance, direct or indirect. In Hong Kong, the government has retreated from this respon-sibility for reasons which this chapter and the rest of the book shows were misinformed or misguided.

Anatomy of Poverty

The book begins with a review of the economic environment. The government made the Asian financial crisis the rationale for introduc-ing austerity measures and reducing its own social responsibilities. These decisions intensified the initial downturn and delayed economic recovery. For low-income groups and the sick in particular, means-testing and price-rationing for access to social services were to become severe. Both the Asian and the global financial crises were also used as the excuse for introducing new measures to promote business interests and protect profits. These often proved ineffectual and wasteful. This state of affairs was neither sound economics nor sensible budgetary management.

The second chapter deals with the peculiar politics of Hong Kong. Distribution of incomes is grossly unequal. Taxation favours the rich. The government constantly expresses a fear of public unrest, while treating the community with little respect and its elected representatives with contempt. The people of Hong Kong are fully aware of how the political system gives business a dominant role. Yet, there is little political discontent and no serious social envy. The public's trust in the government and the civil service is an important feature of the political scene. Nevertheless, the community's docility cannot be taken for granted, and it has proved its power to call Chief Executives to account.

There follows a chapter about housing, on which the quality of life for families so largely depends in every society. The aim of the colonial administration's housing programmes was to provide basic shelter rather than homes. The private sector, for its part, was free initially to build what quickly became slums. The emergence of large-scale developers raised the quality and design of new buildings but created monopolistic conditions in the property sector. In this century, the government decided to leave the property market entirely at the developers' mercy. Supply slumped, while prices surged. Meanwhile, dilapidation and neglected maintenance created extensive squalor and threats to public health and safety, which officials have been slow to tackle.

The next two chapters focus on the major social services: housing, education and welfare. Chapter 4 recounts the colonial administration's protracted efforts, in collaboration with the business community, to block the development of modern social services. The caring professions were able to slowly circumvent this opposition, and social expenditure became 'respectable'. The increased budget allocations were too little and too late, however. The community was left with a Third World legacy that was to affect service standards in contemporary Hong Kong. Chapter 5 examines the government's retreat from social responsibility in this century and the dismantling of reforms introduced in the previous one.

Hong Kong's social security system was always a target for hostility among senior officials and has aroused considerable public mistrust, Chapter 6 explains. The colonial administration and its business collaborators successfully delayed the introduction of CSSA until 1993. The economic downturn of 1997 was followed by a concerted campaign to convince the community that families receiving CSSA were the 'undeserving poor'. The chapter reveals how successful this campaign of denigration was in deterring the unemployed and the elderly from applying for social security. In fact, over the last two decades, more than three-quarters of the unemployed and over 80 per cent of the elderly received no CSSA benefits, according to the official data presented in this chapter.

The final chapter responds to the obvious question: why has welfare so few advocates? The major political parties were not without compassion, yet they condoned the government's neglect of the social services. Non-governmental organisations (NGOs) and pressure groups ceased to be powerful forces. Trade unions made political elections their priority in place of workers' welfare. The explanation is to be found in the special political situation of Hong Kong. The dividing line in electoral politics has been neither wealth nor welfare but a party's commitment or otherwise to publicly championing Hong Kong interests against Mainland pressures.[82]

Conclusions: Flawed Policies and Defective Decisions

This book does not review the causes of poverty in the same way that a development economist might. Hong Kong had escaped from community-wide poverty typical of the Third World by the 1960s. Nor do the chapters that follow investigate such issues as intergenerational poverty or poverty among immigrants and single mothers in a way that a sociologist might. The focus will be on how, at the end of the 20th century, poverty reappeared so unexpectedly in one of the world's most stable and prosperous cities, and was allowed to intensify in the years that followed. The overwhelming conclusion from every chapter is that the decline in the economic and social wellbeing of the average family can be traced directly to government decisions.

This book does not seek to assess Hong Kong by international practice and performance.[83] The Hong Kong community's problems of poverty cannot be properly understood or tackled realistically unless they are examined in the Hong Kong environment. A theme in every chapter is how unique have been the economic, political and social circumstances of the people of Hong Kong and how successful they have been in overcoming the crises which have been such a conspicuous feature of its history. Despite the deterioration in the provision of decent housing and social services in this century, Hong Kong is still close to being the ideal city in which to live in terms of the social behaviour and civic responsibility of its people. It is by the standards of Hong Kong's achievements in so many fields and by its past progress in the face of great odds that the current plight of its more vulnerable members can most fairly be judged.

It is noteworthy that Nobel Laureate, Friedrich Hayek, declared that he had sought in vain 'to discover the meaning of what is called "social justice" for more than ten years'. 'The phrase has no meaning whatever,' he insisted.[84] This and the chapters that follow show that, tragically, there is no difficulty in identifying social *injustice* in contemporary Hong Kong. Evidence abounds of neglect and mistreatment of the vulnerable. In consequence, this book does not seek to assess the rise of the new poverty or the plight of the social services by such criteria as United Nations conventions on human rights.

The facts and the data for this book are drawn overwhelmingly from official publications, and the explanations for government decisions are quoted from official sources.[85] What is uncovered is generally so lacking in compassion and so self-incriminating as to challenge belief. Hence, the source of each fact and assertion is given in full. There is one exception. In the case of basic statistics which are published routinely, the reader can assume that they are taken from the monthly and the annual *Digests of Statistics* unless otherwise indicated.[86]

This book offers a review of what went wrong with the government's policy-making and its management of both financial and social affairs, and which resulted in a new form of poverty. It also attempts to identify the costs to the community and the impact on vulnerable individuals of flawed policies and defective decisions. Hopefully, by the end of the book, the 'new poor' will have defined themselves not just in terms of low incomes but of the specific distress they suffer because their housing, health, educational or welfare needs have been neglected by the government's flawed social programmes.

At the outbreak of the Asian financial crisis, a prominent social scientist explained how in what Hong Kong regarded as an uncertain world, social costs were regarded as irrelevant in the struggle to achieve prosperity, and so business came first.[87] This attitude was entirely predictable. As a distinguished economist, Robert Heilbroner, remarked, 'a society where economic activities are ruled by the market will be an attentive servant of the rich, but a deaf bystander to the poor.'[88] This book will indicate how valid this prediction has been in the case of Hong Kong.

Notes

1. There were 176,000 employees in this category in 2001, 6 per cent of the workforce. They had risen to 195,800 by 2007. Commission on Strategic Development, 'An Overview of the Opportunities and Challenges of Hong Kong's Development' (CSD/6/2008, October 2008), p. 6 and 'Table 2: Characteristics of Working Poor in Hong Kong, 2001–2007', p. 24.
2. One senior official quoted Adam Smith to justify austerity as the proper prescription in laisser-faire Hong Kong. Dr Yeoh Eng-kiong, Secretary for Health and Welfare, *Hong Kong Hansard* (*HH* hereafter), 21 November 2001, p. 1834.
3. Economic Analysis and Business Facilitation Unit, 'Legislative Council Subcommittee to Study the Subject of Combating Poverty. Indicators of

Poverty — An Update for 2005' (CB(2) 2727/05–06(03), July 2006), 'Annex 2: Indicators of Poverty — An Update for 2005', p. 3.

4.   Hui Cheung-ching, *HH*, 10 May 2000, p. 6266.

5.   See Yash Ghai, *Hong Kong's New Constitutional Order: The Resumption of Chinese Sovereignty and the Basic Law* (Hong Kong: Hong Kong University Press, 1997), pp. 406–10.

6.   Xiaogang Wu, 'Hong Kong's Post 80s Generation: Profiles and Predicaments. A CPU Commissioned Report', Centre for Applied Social and Economic Research, Hong Kong University of Science and Technology (Central Policy Unit, May 2010), p. 40.

7.   Legislative Council Secretariat, 'Pilot Scheme on Home Care Services for Persons with Severe Disabilities' (CB(2)1986/09–10(03), 7 July 2010), p. 2.

8.   In 1996, Asia (excluding the Chinese Mainland and Japan) accounted for 19 per cent of total merchandise trade. The share had not altered much in the previous decade. Census and Statistics Department, *Hong Kong Annual Digest of Statistics. 1997 Edition* (Hong Kong: Government Printer, 1997), pp. 37–8.

9.   Tung Chee Hwa, Chief Executive, *HH*, 12 January 2005, p. 3262.

10.   Tung's considerable achievement in saving the family firm is clear from the coverage in the *Far Eastern Economic Review*. Robert Cottrell and Nick Seaward, 'Shipping: A Slip of the Tung: Major Hongkong Shipping Group in Financial Straits', 12 September 1985; Nick Seaward and Bruce Roscoe, 'Companies: Creditors on Deck: Estimates of the Tung Group's Debts Are Ballooning', 28 November 1985; Emily Lau and Nick Seaward, 'Shipping: Chinese Maritime Roulette: Peking Appears to Be Backing the Rescue of a Hongkong Company', 10 April 1986.

11.   Examples of his business-based approach are Tung, *Government Information Services* (*GIS*, hereafter), 10 June 1998, 6 and 14 December 1999.

12.   In 1988, the Governor, Sir David (later Lord) Wilson, revealed that growth in the civil service was to be restricted and its 'ministerial' structure was being reviewed by international management consultants. Wilson, *HH*, 7 October 1987, p. 46.

13.   Sir Piers Jacobs, Financial Secretary, *HH*, 7 March 1990, p. 958.

14.   Sir David Ford, Chief Secretary, *HH*, 9 May 1990, 29 May 1991.

15.   This account draws heavily on the analysis (but not the assumptions) of Anthony B. L. Cheung, 'Civil Service Reform in Post-1997 Hong Kong: Political Challenges, Managerial Responses?', *International Journal of Public Administration*, Vol. 24, Issue 9 (2001), pp. 930–3, 939, 940–1.

16.   The practical difficulties created by abandoning the former five-year planning exercises were summarised in Hong Kong Council of Social Service, 'Response to SWAC's 2nd Stage Consultation Exercise on Long Term Social Welfare Planning in Hong Kong', pp. 3–4.

17.   Select Committee on Building Problems of Public Housing Units, *First Report January 2003: Volume I Main Report* (Hong Kong: Legislative Council, 2003), pp. 42, 46; Chapter IX 'Conclusions and Recommendations', especially pp. 192, 194–5. It should be noted that the Select Committee did

not make a direct connection between the scandals and the Management Enhancement Programme and similar initiatives.

18. *Ming Pao Daily*, 7 and 24 January 2013.

19. 'Report of Investigation Task Force on Statistical Data Quality Assurance', pp. 28–9. This investigation did not find evidence of significant fabrication of survey data. But the report highlighted the need for the Census and Statistics Department to deal with the threats to the professional quality as well as the integrity of its operations which the department's professionals had identified.

20. Chak Hung J. Cheng and Michael K. Salemi, 'Feast and Famine: Explaining Big Swings in the Hong Kong Economy between 1981 and 2007', *HKIMR Working Paper No. 37/2009* (December 2009), p. 1.

21. Economic Analysis Division, *First Quarter Economic Report 2012* (May 2012), 'Chart 1: Hong Kong's labour productivity growth outperformed many other economies', p. 13.

22. Tung, *GIS*, 15 June 1998.

23. Tung, *GIS*, 22 July 1999.

24. Tung, *HH*, 7 January 2004, p. 2500.

25. Tung, *GIS*, 18 December 2001.

26. Donald Tsang Yam-kuen, Chief Executive, *HH*, 27 June 2005, pp. 8944, 8945.

27. Zhao Xiaobin et al., 'Income Inequalities under Economic Restructuring in Hong Kong', *Asian Survey*, Vol. 44, No. 3 (May–June, 2004), p. 443.

28. Editorial, *Hong Kong Economic Journal*, 26 January 2006.

29. Donald Tsang, *HH*, 12 January 2006, p. 3881.

30. Leung Chun-ying, Chief Executive-elect, *GIS*, 19 June 2012.

31. Leung, Chief Executive, speech at Annual Hong Kong Business Summit, Hong Kong General Chamber of Commerce, *GIS*, 29 November 2012.

32. This preoccupation is apparent even in impressive critiques of the government's misguided policies. See, for example, Professor Wong Hung's analysis, which focuses on 'the working poor' and on 'social exclusion' and mentions only in passing the inadequate access to public housing and social services which this book will argue are the main causes of poverty in Hong Kong. Wong Hung, 'Misled Intervention by a Misplaced Diagnosis: The Hong Kong SAR Government's Policies for Alleviating Poverty and Social Exclusion', *China Review*, Vol. 7, No. 2 (Autumn, 2007), pp. 123–47.

33. Labour and Welfare Bureau, 'Legislative Council Panel on Welfare Services: Definition of Poverty' (CB(2)179/09–10(07), November 2009), p. 5.

34. 'Gross Domestic Product (GDP) grew by 2.8% in real terms year-on-year in the first quarter of 2013. Total employment reached a new high . . . The seasonally adjusted unemployment rate remained low at 3.4%. The Comprehensive Social Security Assistance caseload dropped to . . . the lowest [level] in the past 10 years'. Leung Chun-ying, Chief Executive, 'Seek Change Maintain Stability Serve the People with Pragmatism. Report on the Work of the Current-term Government in its First Year June 2013', p. 5.

35. This narrow focus was very evident in Matthew Cheung Kin-chung, Secretary for Labour and Welfare, 'Poverty in Hong Kong: Our Challenges and

Responses', speech to Hong Kong Democratic Foundation, 22 September 2010. URL: www.hkdf.org/newsarticles.asp?show=newsarticles&newsarticle=282

36. 'Commission on Poverty convenes fourth meeting', *GIS*, 24 May 2013.

37. Donald Tsang, Chief Executive, *HH*, 15 October 2009, p. 94.

38. Donald Tsang, Chief Executive, *HH*, 14 October 2009, p. 42.

39. Donald Tsang, Chief Executive, *GIS*, 2 November 2011.

40 A. T. Kearney, '2012 Global Cities Index and Emerging Cities Outlook' (2 April 2012), p. 3. URL: www.atkearney.com/images/global/pdf/2012_Global_Cities_Index_and_Emerging_Cities_Outlook-FINAL3.pdf

41. At the time, he was still Deputy Premier. Li Keqiang reported in 'Set up Cooperation for Development and Prosperity', *New China News Agency*, 17 August 2011.

42. Ho Lok-sang, 'Housing as a Mover of the Domestic Economy', in Joseph Y. S. Cheng (ed.), *The July 1 Protest Rally: Interpreting a Historic Event* (Hong Kong: City University of Hong Kong Press, 2005), p. 307.

43. Gordon Redding, 'Culture and Business in Hong Kong', in Wang Gangwu and Wong Siu Lun (eds.), *Dynamic Hong Kong: Business & Culture* (Hong Kong: Centre of Asian Studies, University of Hong Kong, 1997), p. 102.

44. Ronald Ma and Edward F. Szczepanik, *The National Income of Hong Kong 1947–1950* (Hong Kong: Hong Kong University Press, 1955), p. 14.

45. On self-financing, see Leo F. Goodstadt, 'Dangerous Business Models: Bankers, Bureaucrats and Hong Kong's Economic Transformation, 1948–86', *HKIMR Working Paper No.8/2006,* June 2006, pp. 4–8. On foreign aid, see M.2 Acting Financial Secretary to Governor, 10 September 1968. Hong Kong Public Records Office (HKRS hereafter) 229–1-807, 'Financial Aid (Including Loans) Received from the United Kingdom and Other Governments record of . . .'; (10) Governor to Secretary of State for the Colonies, 28 March 1962. HKRS163–1-1007 'Finance Estimated Capital Investment in Hong Kong'.

46. Business leaders, however, urged the government to adopt the interventionist model which was in vogue in other Asian 'capitalist' economies. See Leo F. Goodstadt, 'Crisis and Challenge: The Changing Role of the Hongkong & Shanghai Bank, 1950–2000', *HKIMR Working Paper No.13/2005,* July 2005, p. 3.

47. David Mole, 'Introduction', in David Mole (ed.), *Managing the New Hong Kong Economy* (Hong Kong: Oxford University Press, 1996), p. 4; David C. Chaney and David B. L. Podmore, *Young Adults in Hong Kong: Attitudes in a Modernizing Society* (Hong Kong: Centre of Asian Studies, University of Hong Kong, 1973), p. 186; Ahmed Shafiqul Huque, 'Understanding Hong Kong', in Paul Wilding et al. (eds.), *Social Policy in Hong Kong* (Cheltenham: Edward Elgar, 1997), p. 20.

48. Gertrude Williams, *Report on the Feasibility of a Survey into Social Welfare Provisions and Allied Topics in Hong Kong* (Hong Kong: Government Printer, n.d.), p. 11.

49. Ernest Wing-tak Chui, 'The 1995 Legislative Council Election: Inefficacious Opposition Characterized by Fragmentation', in Kuan Hsin-chi et al. (eds.),

The 1995 Legislative Council Elections in Hong Kong (Hong Kong: Hong Kong Institute of Asia-Pacific Studies, Chinese University of Hong Kong, 1996), p. 413.

50. Bruce Giley, 'Hong Kong's Future: A Red Flag Over Hong Kong', *Far Eastern Economic Review*, 7 December 1995; Michael J. Enright et al., *The Hong Kong Advantage* (Hong Kong: Oxford University Press, 1997), p. 286.

51. This characteristic was indentified in a study of pre-1989 attitudes by Wong Siu-lun and Shirley Yue, 'Satisfaction in Various Life Domains', in Lau Siu-kai et al. (eds.), *Indicators of Social Development Hong Kong 1988* (Hong Kong: Hong Kong Institute of Asia-Pacific Studies, Chinese University of Hong Kong, 1991), p. 22. Polling data indicated that it survived until the Asian financial crisis. See, for example, Home Affairs Bureau public opinion survey, *GIS*, 6 August 1997; Hong Kong Transition Project, 'Will the People Speak? And What Will They Say? Preparing to Go to the Polls for the First SAR election' (May 1998), 'Table 2. Are you currently satisfied or dissatisfied with life in Hong Kong?', p. 5.

52. See, for example, Donald Tsang, Chief Executive, *GIS*, 2 November 2011.

53. John Tsang Chun-wah, Financial Secretary, *GIS*, 7 November 2012.

54. Paul Wilding, 'Social Policy and Social Development in Hong Kong', *Asian Journal of Public Administration*, Vol. 19, No. 2 (December 1997), pp. 263–4; James K. C. Lee, 'Balancing Collectivization and Individual Responsibility: Hong Kong Social Policy under the Chinese Regime', in Kwok-leung Tang (ed.), *Social Development in Asia* (Dordrecht: Kulwer Academic Publishers, 2000), p. 25.

55. Chack Kie Wong, 'Squaring the Welfare Circle in Hong Kong: Lessons for Governance in Social Policy', *Asian Survey*, Vol. 48, No. 2 (March–April 2008), 'Table 1 Social Expenditure as Percentage of GDP in Selected OECD Countries and Hong Kong (selected years)', pp. 329, 330, 341.

56. Lau Chi Kuen, *Hong Kong's Colonial Legacy* (Hong Kong: Chinese University Press, 1997), p. 69.

57. UN-Habitat, *The State of the World's Cities Report 2006/2007: 30 Years of Shaping the Habitat Agenda* (London: Earthscan, 2006), 'Table 1: Population of slum areas at mid-year, by region and country; 1990, 2001 and slum annual growth rate', pp. 181–2; 'Table 2: Slum population projections, 1990–2020', p. 193.

58. Visiting Panel, *A Perspective on Education in Hong Kong. November 1982* (Hong Kong: Government Printer, 1983), p. 49.

59. On age distribution of the unemployed, see 'Statistics on Comprehensive Social Security Assistance Scheme, 1996 to 2006', *Hong Kong Monthly Digest of Statistics July 2007*, 'Table 4 Percentage distribution of unemployed CSSA recipients by sex and age group as at end-2006', p. FA10. On their inadequate educational backgrounds, see Dr York Chow Yat-ngok, Secretary for Health, Welfare and Food, *HH*, 29 June 2005, 'Table 3 Number of CSSA Recipients by Educational Attainment, 2001 to 2004', p. 9066.

60. Eddie Yue, Hong Kong Monetary Authority Deputy Chief Executive, 'Evolution of Financial Consumer Protection and Education in Asia', *Hong Kong Monetary Authority*, 13 December 2012.

61. Officials find it hard to defend MPF providers, e.g., 'MPF fees and charges have come down to 1.74 per cent, representing a 17 per cent reduction [since 2008]. Clearly, to the general public this is too little and too slow,' Professor K. C. Chan, Secretary for Financial Services and the Treasury, *GIS*, 14 December 2012.

62. The Mandatory Provident Fund Schemes Authority's attack on 'financial illiteracy' began with the 'MPF Investment Education Campaign "Making Informed Decisions for Your MPF Life"' (replete with pop personalities and media icons) in 2010. *GIS*, 21 May 2010.

63. Hospital Authority, *Hospital Authority Annual Plan 2006–07* (Hong Kong: Hospital Authority, 2006), p. 4.

64. Chow, Secretary for Health and Welfare, *HH*, 18 October 2006, pp. 141, 143.

65. Chow, Secretary for Health and Welfare, *HH*, 25 May 2005, p. 7612; Dr Ko Wing-man, Secretary for Food and Health, *HH*, 19 December 2012.

66. The costs involved of switching to the modern drugs would have been relatively small to judge from Chow, Secretary for Health and Welfare, *HH*, 18 October 2006, p. 145.

67. See the submission from the Hong Kong College of Psychiatrists in Hospital Authority, 'Mental Health Service Plan for Adults 2010–2015', pp. 30, 69. URL: www21.ha.org.hk/files/PDF/mental%20health%20platform/ MentalHealthServicePlan_Pamphlet_ENG_Final.pdf

68. A summary of the foreign relief programmes is available in Hu Yueh, 'The Problem of the Hong Kong Refugees', *Asian Survey*, Vol. 2, No. 1 (March 1962), pp. 33–4.

69. Claude B. Burgess, Colonial Secretary, *HH*, 13 June 1962, pp. 219–20.

70. The historical background is recorded in HKRS890–1-15 'Subsistence Level' and HKRS307–3-15/17 'Social Security in Hong Kong'.

71. Donald Tsang, Chief Executive, *GIS*, 31 October 2008.

72. Eva Cheng Yu-wah, Secretary for Transport and Housing, *HH*, 27 May 2009, pp. 8212–3; Cheung, Secretary for Labour and Welfare, *HH*, 23 February 2011, pp. 5861–2. Eventually, almost 10,000 of the recipients of food aid were also CSSA beneficiaries in apparent breach of the rule that they would not be eligible. Franco Kwok, Labour and Welfare Bureau to Candice Lam, Panel on Welfare Services Clerk, letter, 4 January 2012. LWB CR 2/1136/07.

73. A prominent banker, Legislative Councillor and National People's Congress Deputy put forward a proposal to replace cash payments with coupons for clothing, food, accommodation and transportation to check 'abuse of public resources and . . . prevent recipients from using the assistance not on basic necessities'. Ng Leung-sing, *HH*, 11 February 2004, pp. 3524–5.

74. Cheung, Secretary for Labour and Welfare, *GIS*, 15 March 2012. For the makeshift as well as the demeaning features of this scheme, see Legislative Council Secretariat, 'Finance Committee of the Legislative Council Minutes of the 7th meeting . . . 16 December 2011 (FC70/11–12, 16 March 2012); and 'Report of the Panel on Welfare Services for submission to the Legislative Council' (CB(2)2468/11–12, 4 July 2012), pp. 12–3.

75. Legislative Council Secretariat, 'Short-term food assistance' (CB(2)248/11–12(04), 8 November 2011), pp. 2–3; Tsang Tak-sing, Secretary for Home Affairs, *GIS*, 1 August 2012.
76. Cheung, Secretary for Labour and Welfare, *GIS*, 15 September 2011.
77. www.sfgate.com/bayarea/article/Federal-funding-cut-hurts-S-F-Food-Bank-3929513.php
78. On the early emergence as an international financial centre, see Leo F. Goodstadt, *Profits, Politics and Panics: Hong Kong's Banks and the Making of a Miracle Economy, 1935–1985* (Hong Kong: Hong Kong University Press, 2007), p. 169.
79. Nicholas C. Owen, 'Economic Policy', in Keith Hopkins (ed.), *Hong Kong: The Industrial Colony. A Political, Social and Economic Survey* (Hong Kong: Oxford University Press, 1971), p. 152.
80. B. R. Tomlinson, 'What Was the Third World?', *Journal of Contemporary History*, Vol. 38, No. 2 (April, 2003), pp. 307–21.
81. Examples include such articles as: *New China News Agency*: 'China an example for third world: Cuban media', 9 October 2010; 'Singapore needs foreigners to complement resident workforce: minister', 25 September 2012; Cao Kai, Cheng Zhiliang and Cai Min, 'U.S. sets bad model by blocking Huawei, ZTE: experts', 18 October 2012; *China Daily*: 'Getting "tough" with China won't help US', 19 May 2011; Fulong Wu 'Urbanization and its discontents', 6 February 2012; 'Africa must follow China's example', 8 January 2013.
82. Joan Y. H. Leung, 'Political Parties: Public Perceptions and Implications for Change', in Ian Scott (ed.), *Institutional Change and the Political Transition in Hong Kong* (London: Macmillan, 1998), pp. 102–9.
83. The book contains a dozen or so unavoidable international comparisons (of which half refer to Hong Kong's superior performance). The limited relevance to Hong Kong of welfare policies elsewhere has been well expressed by a distinguished British academic. Wilding, 'Social Policy and Social Development in Hong Kong', pp. 270–1.
84. F. A. Hayek, *New Studies in Philosophy, Politics, Economics and the History of Ideas* (London: Routledge and Kegan Paul, 1985), p. 57.
85. This reliance on official sources should not be understood to imply in any way a lack of appreciation for the research undertaken by academics and NGOs, especially in tackling the government's data deficits. A notable example is Oxfam, 'Research on the Living Conditions of Tenant Households Who Have Been on the Waiting List for Public Rental Housing for Over 3 Years'. URL: http://www.oxfam.org.hk/filemgr/2040/OHKstandpointsonhousing_editedeng_final.pdf
86. The Census and Statistics Department revises many of its statistical series from one edition of its publications to another. An effort has been made to use the latest, revised figures that are accessible.
87. Wilding, 'Social Policy and Social Development in Hong Kong', pp. 263–4.
88. Robert Heilbroner, *Twenty-First Century Capitalism* (London: UCL Press, 1993), p. 86.

1
Crisis Economics: Private Profits, Public Pain

Hong Kong did not deserve to suffer disaster in 1997. Its economic environment remained as attractive as ever, and it was underwritten by an excellent infrastructure, much of it technically breath-taking, a firmly pro-business government and an honest and efficient administration. Hong Kong stood high in global rankings as an international financial centre, as a source of manufactured products and as a telecommunications and transport hub. Its people seemed ideally suited to a capitalist regime.

Hong Kong's fortunes collapsed during the 1997–98 Asian financial crisis, nevertheless, and its government and business leaders never recovered from the trauma. A World Bank survey of 5,550 public-listed corporations in nine East Asian economies covering the period 1988–96 indicated that the collapse in 1997 had been a disaster waiting to occur. It had been created by excessive optimism among international financial institutions and investors about the region's growth potential. No limits had been seen to Asia's prosperity. The 'poor performance and risky financing structures of East Asian corporates' between 1988 and 1996 were generally ignored, this World Bank report complained, although they 'involved investment with high risks'.[1] 'Even the most sophisticated operators in global financial markets' were prepared to go on lending 'well after the increased risks in the region were generally apparent', a prominent economist noted.[2] By mid-1997, the business realities could no longer be disregarded, and foreign capital took flight. The Thai baht collapsed, and the region's currencies came under severe pressure. Unlike the rest of the region, Hong Kong's financial system suffered from none of these defects, and its financial institutions and its currency survived the Asian crisis unscathed.

The recession that overtook Hong Kong had very different origins. The damage was mostly self-inflicted, this chapter will argue, although the Chief Executive, Tung Chee Hwa insisted that the economic misfortunes of 1997–98 were the proper penalty for past economic transgressions.

If the pain were bravely endured, he and his team promised, the community would emerge chastened but strengthened for future economic growth.

The Asian financial crisis convinced Tung that government spending had to be reduced and the government workforce cut, which hit the social services severely because health, education and welfare programmes are heavily labour intensive. This chapter will show that Tung's decisions were based on serious errors of judgment about the robustness and resilience of the Hong Kong economy, its export competitiveness and the efficiency of its labour force. His austerity programme aggravated social distress because it intensified deflation and prolonged the economic downturn. Also damaging, this chapter will explain, was the long-term fallout from the misguided campaign within the public services for privatisation, outsourcing and promotion of a private sector culture. These administrative 'reforms' led to price-rationing for health and education services and created a new group of low-wage, vulnerable workers in the public sector. Shortfalls in the supply of social services were to remain acute for the next decade.

The Mainland was the setting for another, less publicised 'crisis', this chapter will explain, which did not lead to catastrophe but, nevertheless, had painful implications for the Special Administrative Region's long-term economic development. It also had an unfortunate effect on employers' attitudes to labour reforms in Hong Kong.

These adverse events were triggered by a long, uncertain and often unpleasant readjustment in business relations with Guangdong Province in particular. By the start of this century, China's economy had generated considerable wealth for Hong Kong since 1978 thanks to Deng Xiaoping's reforms. These had given Hong Kong privileged access to what seemed endless profit opportunities, especially in Guangdong. But after 2000, the national reform process changed in both pace and priorities, to which the Special Administrative Region adapted with difficulty.

- The Mainland became much less hospitable to Hong Kong's industrialists who had relocated to Guangdong (and other provinces). While the Special Administrative Region government steadfastly resisted expansion of its own social responsibilities, the Mainland authorities became increasingly determined to introduce social and environmental reforms and a new deal for their workforce. From 2003, stricter enforcement of new Mainland labour and anti-pollution laws drove down Hong Kong manufacturers' profits.
- In the financial services sector, misconceptions among Hong Kong officials in 2007 about the nation's financial reforms led to a boom in Hong Kong share prices followed by a crash which shook

investor confidence just as the global financial crisis was gathering momentum.

- The Special Administrative Region's strategy for participating in the nation's 12th Five-Year Programme (2011–15) was badly conceived and poorly managed, leading to wasteful budget subsidies and strains on Hong Kong's social services.

This chapter will review the social as well as the economic consequences of these Mainland developments.

Self-inflicted Punishment

As the first recession in half a century overtook Hong Kong, Tung and his team had no solutions to offer the public — nothing, in fact, but deflation, disinvestment and retrenchment. And Tung himself made repeated references to 'pain' which, it seemed, the community was supposed to embrace without discussion, let alone objection. The government's sense of helplessness was summed up by a future Chief Executive. There is 'no economic Promised Land', said Donald Tsang Yam-kuen, then Financial Secretary, and if there were, 'I am not the Moses who can lead our community to it.'[3]

The pain was very significant. 'Evaporation of personal wealth' was widespread, Tung said, as 'job losses and reduced income' hit 'almost 90 per cent of our working families'.[4] These traumatic experiences had been foreseen, he admitted, but he had chosen not to halt the downturn.

> It would have been easier for all of us, in the short run, to ease back into another [pre-1997] bubble economy built on asset price inflation, and supplementing them with heavy doses of Keynesian fiscal and monetary stimulus. But let me tell you, we are definitely not taking that route. Instead we have embarked on another that will perhaps take longer, involve more hard work, and certainly more learning, one that perhaps imparts more pain in the short term as well, but is ultimately healthier.[5]

The reference to the English economist, Keynes, and his theories was bizarre. The Chief Executive had completely misunderstood Hong Kong's unique financial and fiscal situation. For almost any other government, a 'Keynesian' solution would involve boosting demand through larger budget deficits funded by increased government borrowings. Hong Kong, however, had only token public debt, and its reserves were more than sufficient to cover government stimulus programmes in a crisis. In 2000, the government's fiscal reserves were enough to finance government spending for 22 months without collecting any taxes, rates, fees or other revenues. In 2013, these reserves were equivalent to 23 months

government spending and to 36 per cent per cent of GDP. It was hard
to imagine any crisis striking Hong Kong that would prevent the government raising even a dollar in revenue for two years. Yet, official financial
contingency plans in this century were based on a disaster scenario of
this unlikely magnitude. As a later Financial Secretary explained, even
the five years of budget deficits that followed the Asian crisis had left the
government with reserves equivalent to 13 months of expenditure.[6]

The obvious health of Hong Kong's finances gave the lie to the repeated
warnings about how spending on the social services would destroy the
low tax regime. Even business got tired of this alarmist rhetoric. There
was no danger 'that the Government might be running out of money', a
leading business representative eventually pointed out in the Legislative
Council, or that it will have 'to ask the rich to pay more'.[7]

Tung had decided to let the recession rip regardless because he had
completely misread the economy and grossly underestimated its basic
strengths. He ignored the economic information which was available to
him from his own government agencies. Tung was convinced that the
economy had deteriorated so much in the 1990s that recession 'would
have come sooner or later anyhow'. 'For years we have been troubled by
high land prices, soaring inflation and negative interest rates,' he stated,
'with the result that our competitiveness has gradually lagged behind
that of our competitors.'[8]

Tung's assertions were hopelessly wrong. Official statistics showed
that the economy had not faltered or fallen behind its overseas rivals in
the 1980s and 1990s.

- Hong Kong had become the world's seventh largest trading centre
  by 1995, outranked in Asia only by Japan. (In 1990, it had been in
  tenth position.)[9]
- The efficiency of the workforce had risen dramatically. Labour
  productivity grew at an annual average of 4.1 per cent between
  1980 and 1996, far outstripping the annual increase of 1.2 per cent
  in real wages.[10]
- Inflation was increasing at an annual rate of 3.5 per cent in the world's
  advanced economies and 8 per cent in Hong Kong. Hong Kong
  exporters, nevertheless, managed to remain competitive, holding the
  increase in their prices to an annual average of 3 per cent.[11]

Struck by Amnesia

Ignorance made Tung Chee Hwa fall victim to invincible pessimism.
Wiped out from the collective memory of the government-business nexus
was Hong Kong's astonishing track record, which ought to have been an

effective antidote to despair. Neither the 1997–98 Asian financial crisis nor the 2007–09 global financial crisis should have caused serious disruption of the Hong Kong economy. Its financial systems survived both events without any of the currency instability, bank failures and corporate scandals that had regularly accompanied economic downturns in every previous decade until the mid-1980s. The economy, nevertheless, went into recession in 1998.

The shock was all the more severe because Hong Kong had routinely overcome more serious threats to its prosperity in the past. It had achieved unbroken real GDP growth from one year to the next for almost half a century, an unparalleled record in modern history. During the Korean War, the economy had survived the embargoes imposed by the United States and United Nations that in 1950 had destroyed the China trade on which Hong Kong had been totally dependent. Less than a year later, a boom was underway, with the textile industry moving towards three-shift production to meet soaring export orders.[12] Throughout the 1950s, profits surged, and the demand for land and labour was insatiable as the manufacturing sector's exports grew at an average annual rate of almost 140 per cent.[13]

There were to be occasional troughs in the business cycle during the decades that followed. But as one sector withered, another sprang up. Wigs and plastic flowers gave way painlessly to fashion wear and electronic products. Textiles weathered every storm, and at the end of the century, Hong Kong was described as 'the de facto control centre of the world's textile and garment trade'.[14] From the 1980s, nevertheless, manufacturing had been in retreat while the services sector took over as the mainstay of the economy. China's adoption in 1978 of Deng Xiaoping's 'open door' policies had allowed Hong Kong to recover its traditional role as entrepôt and international financial centre for the Mainland.

A Crisis of Confidence

For Tung Chee Hwa, austerity was the only strategy if the economy were not to collapse.[15] The business and professional elite shared his despondency. With no advocates of a better-informed and more hopeful analysis, public confidence evaporated. In January 1998, an official poll found the public's dissatisfaction with the government had risen to 35 per cent, a level higher than any previously recorded since this poll began in 1983. This rating was worse than during any of the political and economic shocks of the previous 20 years, including the collapse of the exchange rate in 1983; the crushing of the Beijing democracy movement in 1989; and the confrontation with China's leadership over Christopher (later Lord) Patten's 1992 constitutional reform package.

Public dissatisfaction with the government was to reach a high of 61 per cent in July 1998.[16]

Tung had lost touch with the people of Hong Kong, and his attempts to repair public morale were an embarrassing mixture of unconvincing rhetoric and meaningless platitudes.

> I want to assure you that we understand the pain and the government is determined to do whatever we can do to reduce the pain and to revive our economy and to improve our competitiveness . . . I therefore would like to urge the entire community not to be depressed, not to be pessimistic . . . Let us not forget, one of the key features of a free market economy is that it can go down fast — it can also come up very fast.[17]

There followed repeated doomsday messages from Hong Kong's leadership which destroyed the community's long-standing conviction that the economy would always manage to create additional wealth and new job opportunities, no matter how adverse the political or business environment. The collapse in public confidence was followed by a slump in both domestic consumption and in investment. The economy lost momentum, and recession accelerated.

The confidence factor was to show up very rapidly in the GDP figures. The Chief Executive and his Financial Secretaries emphasised repeatedly that the government was expanding its own investment plans to boost economic recovery.[18] In practice, however, the government believed public sector expenditure was a 'burden' on the economy that must be cut.[19] The results were to be disastrous and long-lasting.

- Government investment remained consistently below the 1997 level in every year (except 1999) until 2011.
- Private sector investment slumped and did not revive until 2006. It remained below the 1997 level until 2012.
- Total investment (as measured by gross fixed capital formation) plunged by 14 per cent in 1998 and by a further 16 per cent the following year. In 2006, total investment was still 29 per cent below 1997 and did not recover to its 1997 level until 2012.

The long delay in the revival of both public and private investment had serious implications for Hong Kong's wellbeing. The recession was deeper and recovery was slower than necessary. Over the longer term, the backlog of investment postponed, infrastructure not modernised and outdated facilities unreplaced were inevitably considerable.

Consumer spending showed much the same forlorn pattern although the declines in private consumption expenditure were not as severe as for investment. (Households in general had much less room to slash their spending.) Consumption fell by a total of 8 per cent in 1998–99, enough to hurt businesses across the economy. It declined again by almost the same percentage in 2002 and 2003, in tandem with falls in GDP per head. Private consumption remained below its 1997 level until 2006.[20]

The downturn in consumer spending could have been cushioned by measures to offset the drop in earnings and the increased unemployment. When wages were falling and jobs were disappearing, the government declined to utilise the available income-support programmes (i.e., by maintaining Comprehensive Social Security Assistance (CSSA) benefits and the subsidies to the social services). Instead, officials attacked the rise in the numbers of unemployed receiving CSSA as unaffordable and labelled the claimants as work-shy.[21] (The data presented in Chapter 6 will show that less than a quarter of the unemployed received CSSA.) This hostility towards social security remained intense even after the end of the Asian financial crisis. 'Increases in social welfare benefits will not only make our welfare system unsustainable but also undermine the community's resilience in the face of adversity,' an official pronouncement declared in 2006, and thus 'create a culture of dependency'.[22]

Workers' Pain, Business Gains

In 1998, the government started to act as if it were a business enterprise going through hard times which needed to shrink its payroll.[23] But there was also a determination to encourage the private sector to share in the delivery of public services because of the government's assumption that private firms operated with 'more flexible and hence less costly practices'.[24] Civil Service pay and benefits were cut for new entrants. Extensive outsourcing and privatisation began, and existing staff were replaced with contract workers.[25] The damage done by the cost-cutting and privatisation measures imposed on the public sector was not simply 'economic' as measured by reduced consumer spending and increased deflation. The profit margins of private contractors, the government knew, depended very heavily on squeezing wage rates.[26] As a result, officials found that in fostering the role of the private sector, they had to close their eyes to illegal and improper business practices.

Very quickly, evidence emerged of widespread abuse of contract workers, together with extensive disregard of labour legislation and outright fraud by government contractors.[27] Hong Kong was suffering the same sort of abuses which have accompanied privatisation and outsourcing in other advanced economies according to a study by the International Labour Office (ILO).[28] In 2005, the senior official responsible for labour matters admitted that exploitation of workers by service contractors was extensive. He insisted, nevertheless, that 'enforcement action should be the last resort' in dealing with contractors who flouted their legal and contractual obligations.[29] The Chief Executive responded to the reports of abuses with a promise of 'zero-tolerance for unscrupulous employers'.[30] But they remained free to breach their contractual obligations up to six times in any 12-month period before being blacklisted by the government.[31]

Three years later, a government-commissioned study uncovered widespread breaches of contract as well as of the law in the public housing sector. The report indicated that initially, these workers' wages had been in 'free fall'. Private firms 'would extract profits by lowering workers' wages, forcing them to work without rest days, refusing to give paid statutory holidays or intensifying their workload'. Little was done to deter unscrupulous employers. As many as 'half of the officially recognised cleaning contractors eligible to work for the Housing Authority had been convicted of violating provisions of labour legislation', the report pointed out.[32]

Repeated pledges from the highest levels of government that workers would be protected from unfair wages proved to be no more than empty promises. A minimum wage law was included in the second Chief Executive's 2005 election manifesto.[33] Vigorous business opposition meant that the law came into effect only in 2011. When the legislation was finally enacted, the labour minister announced that 'over half' of the '40,000 non-skilled workers engaged under government service contracts' — equivalent to 25 per cent of the regular civil service — would need a 20 per cent pay increase to reach the statutory minimum wage, with a significant number requiring a 45 per cent rise.[34]

The economy was supposed to benefit from downsizing the civil service and from a reduction in the public sector's payroll. The GDP figures told a different story, this chapter has argued, one of deflation intensified and recovery delayed, together with unconscionably low earnings for large numbers of workers. When these men and women had been thrown out of work by the government during Hong Kong's worst recession for half a century, they had to accept drastic pay cuts in the struggle to find jobs. Their sudden transfer to the private sector during a recession also helped to undercut wages for low-skilled labour across the entire labour market.

Property Protection

Some forms of special treatment for business were entirely proper. In 1998, speculators were actively trying to engineer a collapse of Hong Kong's exchange rate and/or the stock market. Should Tung and his team defy the then prevailing worldwide consensus that governments must not intervene to prevent markets from falling? Was it prudent to risk Hong Kong's financial reserves in the attempt? The government rightly decided in August 1998 to gamble HK$118 billion — 27 per cent of the reserves — on defending the financial system, and it won.[35] The profit from its unprecedented market intervention came to HK$119 billion.[36] Among the biggest (albeit indirect) beneficiaries of this brilliantly managed rescue operation were the property developers because 'property stocks account[ed] for nearly 20% of the [stock exchange's] market capitalization and about 25% of its turnover'.[37]

Much less easy to justify was another exercise in government intervention, this time to rescue an individual business sector under monopolistic control. Tung Chee Hwa had come into office with an unconditional pledge to meet the community's aspiration of a decent, affordable home for every family. To this end, he promised to boost the number of new flats to 85,000 a year.[38] His ambitious plan led to immediate speculation that the increased supply would be more than the market could absorb and that, in consequence, property prices would collapse. In a bungled attempt to allay fears about the market's fragility, Tung confirmed in 1997 that catastrophe was also on his mind. 'If the market drops 40, 50 per cent, 60 per cent, the damage to the economy will be unthinkable,' he warned.[39] Within nine months, the fall in property prices was to reach 40 per cent.[40]

Tung now found himself under assault from the property sector to which he quickly capitulated. In early 1998, the housing programme was abandoned. The government next suspended the sale of new housing sites, which relieved the pressure on the value of the private developers' extensive land banks. Then, the government agreed to suspend the production of public housing for sale through the Home Ownership Scheme and similar programmes.[41]

The developers had snatched an astonishing victory from the market crisis. The government had abandoned its involvement in the supply of housing New public housing would be provided only for the lowest income groups who could not afford to buy or rent private accommodation. It had imposed severe restrictions on its own freedom to sell public land. The Housing Authority — the government's statutory housing agency — lost control of its own land bank. When the Authority's older buildings were demolished for redevelopment, the sites would be made available to the private sector instead of remaining exclusively for its own use. (This last concession had long been a major target for the developers.)[42]

Ordinary households were given neither government bailouts nor even official sympathy. Families buying their homes with a mortgage were left to fend themselves when residential property values plunged.

By late 2003, their flats had lost 70 per cent of their 1997 value.[43] The government refused help for those struggling with negative equity. 'The [government] upholds the principle of free economy, and will allow the private property market to operate freely without unnecessary intervention,' the official responsible for housing announced, '[t]he Government will not consider setting up any funds or loan schemes to assist owners of negative assets.'[44] The public bore the strain uncomplainingly, and mortgage delinquency rates never exceeded 2.5 per cent.[45]

The community was now left at the mercy of a market in which the developers enjoyed monopoly advantages. Tung's building programme had increased the annual output of public housing by 137 per cent between 1997 and 2000. By 2011, however, the annual supply had shrunk to a mere 17 per cent of the 2000 total. The drop in the public supply allowed private sector property prices to rise by 55 per cent between 2000 and 2011 although monthly household incomes remained firmly below the 1997 level in every year until 2011.

Mainland Shocks

In 2003, the Hang Seng Index had slumped to 12,500, with a daily turnover of around HK$13 billion. But when Tung Chee Hwa was replaced by Tsang Yam-kuen in 2005, economic recovery was well under way. The index broke through the 30,000 level for the first time in late 2007, with daily turnover at almost HK$110 billion, the commerce minister boasted. Deflation was now 'a distant memory', he proudly proclaimed, and 'more people now have jobs than ever before'.[46] Another crisis was looming, nevertheless, whose dimensions were difficult to measure and whose origins were barely discussed in public. The threat would come not from global turmoil but from Mainland policies.

The commerce minister's pride in the stock market's recovery was to prove an ill omen. The surge and subsequent collapse of the Hang Seng Index in 2007–08 was a dramatic revelation of Hong Kong's growing vulnerability to changes in the Mainland business environment. The index rose 50 per cent in the first ten months of 2007 to reach an historic high of 31,958 before shedding all its gains within the next four months. The index had still not recovered to its 2007 peak by 2013. This downturn was far more severe than the Dow Jones, which rose 14 per cent in the first ten months of 2007 and shed all these gains in the next four months but in 2013 was back to its 2007 high.

The collapse in Hong Kong's share prices had been triggered by Mainland events. In 2007, the public had been told that a 'through train' was about to arrive loaded with investors from Tianjin eager to buy Hong Kong stocks and shares. The market took off. The Financial Secretary,

John Tsang Chun-wah, confirmed that China's State Administration of Foreign Exchange had approved a pilot 'free walk' scheme to allow Mainland residents to use their own foreign currency to trade on the Hong Kong Stock Exchange.[47]

Then rumours swept Hong Kong that the 'through train' would not be authorised although, for a time, China's official news media continued to claim that the 'train' would shortly arrive.[48] It turned out that the views of Premier Wen Jiabao had not been solicited before the announcement had been made. His role in the decision-making was only discovered by the second Chief Executive when he visited Beijing in November 2007. Tsang Yam-kuen told the press that he had learnt from a deputy governor of the People's Bank of China 'that Premier Wen Jiabao had made a decision and the ["through train"] arrangement would take effect after policy measures were rationalized. However, no timetable was given.'[49] The 'train' had been derailed.

End of the Guangdong Boom

This incident was only one element in the mounting challenges to Hong Kong in managing its business affairs as its Mainland privileges diminished. The largest threat came from the complex readjustments that Hong Kong firms were being forced to make in response to Mainland policies. The origins of this menacing development were barely discussed in public because of political sensitivities which the Special Administrative Region's leaders always found hard to manage in responding to Mainland developments.

By 2002, the Guangdong authorities had already made clear to the Hong Kong business community that the manufacturing boom in the province was over and that state policy was about to render the Mainland's most advanced industrial bases increasingly inhospitable to offshore manufacturing subsidiaries.[50] Tung Chee Hwa had not been much concerned by these 'policy' difficulties which Hong Kong firms were encountering. For him, continuing integration into the Mainland economy must be the priority because he believed it to be a guarantee of future prosperity. He was determined to silence calls to proceed with caution.[51]

His successor, Tsang Yam-kuen, was enthusiastic about economic integration although, by the time he took office, Guangdong's enforcement of the new reform policies was causing serious distress. 'Immense pressure' was being exerted on Hong Kong firms, he confessed in 2006, after the Central People's Government introduced new, radical measures to protect the environment, eliminate low-tech, low-wage industries and to give the labour force a better deal.[52] The Special Administrative

Region government could not convince the Mainland authorities to ease the tax, labour and other burdens they were imposing on Hong Kong firms. Thus, 'most of the problems' facing Hong Kong, Tsang declared in 2008, were still 'right there in Guangdong Pearl River Delta'.[53]

There were an estimated 56,000 Hong Kong-owned factories in Guangdong with a labour force of over 10 million.[54] Because of the new Mainland policies, a 2008 Hong Kong Trade Development Council research report stated, profits had been badly hit, with 'one-third' of these firms preparing to close down or reduce production.[55] The danger that this huge industrial base might falter had grave implications. The flow of profits remitted to their Hong Kong owners would shrink. Demand for the financial and other services provided by Hong Kong would slump.[56]

There seemed little prospect of relief, however. In the wake of a desperate shortage of labour in Guangdong and other manufacturing areas, there were double digit increases in the Mainland's legal minimum wages. The role of the official trade union movement was strengthened, and there was a rise in worker activism.[57] Guangdong's leaders were not wholly unsympathetic to the plight of Hong Kong investors but the financial help which the province offered to firms in trouble was modest. There was no backing down from the new policies, however, nor was there any valid reason for the province to put Hong Kong firms and their profits ahead of a cleaner environment and better protection of the workforce.[58]

The Special Administrative Region government felt able to offer only limited support to struggling Hong Kong factories in Guangdong as their situation worsened. In 2011, the Special Administrative Region set up a HK$1 billion fund to help Hong Kong firms expand Mainland market sales 'through developing brands, upgrading and restructuring operations'. This was no more than a gesture given the large number of firms at risk. In desperation, officials allowed these firms access to a loan guarantee programme for small and medium-sized enterprises (SMEs).[59] (This scheme was deeply flawed, the analysis below will demonstrate.)

Mainland Plans, Hong Kong's Priorities

Tsang Yam-kuen had failed to grasp the economic realities behind the stresses on Hong Kong manufacturers operating in Guangdong and elsewhere on the Mainland. They could not escape from the risks that any 'capitalist' enterprise must face in China. The nation has abolished central planning and, with it, the command economy. But the state remains deeply involved in managing economic affairs, directing investment and deciding on growth priorities. The planners frequently override market forces to meet what the leadership decides is the national interest. The more that individual sectors of the Hong Kong economy operated within the Mainland, the more exposed they were to changes in the economic environment dictated by the state rather than led by the market.[60]

The Mainland challenge became more acute in 2008 when state planners examined Hong Kong's potential contribution to China's modernisation. The National Development and Reform Commission published a blueprint for Guangdong's Pearl River Delta in the period up to 2020 which sought to identify Hong Kong's future growth sectors.[61] This document's impact on economic policy was dramatic. Economic integration was 'clearly and comprehensively laid down on the Central Government's policy agenda' for Hong Kong, the Chief Secretary explained.[62] Hong Kong now announced that it had downgraded reliance 'on established core industries of financial services, trade and logistics, tourism and professional services' which accounted for 60 per cent of total GDP.[63]

The government's own strategy would be to promote six new 'development industries': 'testing and certification; medical services; innovation and technology; cultural and creative industries; environmental industry; and educational services.' Practical problems arose at once. The commercial merits of these sectors were far from clear. At best, the six accounted for 8 per cent of GDP and 11 per cent of total employment. These figures, however, over-stated their status as key 'growth' industries. For example, the bulk of the health and educational services were in the public sector (and included subsidised care for the elderly and non-profit-making kindergartens).[64] The 2010 Budget provided the chosen six with subsidies even though their prospects were unimpressive. The projected expansion of 'innovation and technology', for example, turned out to be mostly a matter of faith.[65] An official report on 'cultural and creative industries' in 2013 described them as 'among the most dynamic sectors' of the economy. But their share in total GDP was only 4.7 per cent in 2011, and their net contribution to the balance of payments was negative.[66] And the film industry already had a poor record in managing its previous government grants.[67]

This Mainland-orientated strategy disregarded the costs to the community of attempting to transform segments of the social services — health and education — into high-growth 'development industries'. 'Medical services' proved a political disaster and had to be abandoned because of public anger in 2012 after fee-paying Mainland patients had overwhelmed local maternity facilities.[68] Education was also unpromising. As Chapter 5 will explain, there were already serious complaints about the quality of self-financed post-secondary education. An attempt to expand this quasi-commercial sector into an international education hub could only succeed at the expense of the already limited facilities available for the local student population. After the third Chief Executive, Leung Chun-ying, took office, his team showed little enthusiasm for Tsang's selection of development industries.[69] Leung himself attacked the choice of education and health services which were already over-stretched in trying to meet local demand.[70]

The selection of the six growth industries had been dictated by priorities set out in a Mainland planning document. Unlike the rest of China, however, Hong Kong officials could not enforce government development programmes. It was perhaps fortunate that the first attempt to select and subsidise growth sectors to meet Mainland planning goals had demonstrated so quickly the complex and costly contradictions that arise if a state planning exercise is extended to an economy as open and free from government direction as Hong Kong. Nevertheless, Leung Chun-ying's team found it hard to jettison the commitment to 'development industries'. Their numbers were reduced to three in 2013 and relabelled 'new industry heroes' by the Financial Secretary, with a promise to find additional candidates for this superior status and the government support that would go with it.[71]

China's leaders themselves seemed to understand the obstacles to planning Hong Kong's development very well. In 2011, Tsang Yam-kuen had been fulsome in his gratitude to the country's leadership for giving Hong Kong its own chapter in the nation's 12th Five-Year Programme. Premier Wen Jiabao, however, emphasised that the Mainland was not the driving force behind the initiatives to promote economic integration. The Mainland, he insisted, had no intention of imposing an economic plan on Hong Kong: the Basic Law made the Special Administrative Region responsible for its own development arrangements, he made clear.[72]

The third Chief Executive promised to make use of 'internal diplomacy' to promote Hong Kong's interests with the Mainland authorities. But Leung's preferred formula for improved economic relations with the Mainland seemed little different from that of his immediate predecessor: active participation in the national planning process.[73] His priority, he stated soon after taking office, was financial relations. 'Our most important function today, with relation to our country,' he declared, 'is to dovetail our financial system with that of the Mainland.' He would break with both his predecessors, however, by dramatically increasing the time he would spend in Beijing visiting 'Central Government commissions and ministries'.[74]

Light-touch Taxation

In resisting calls for increased social expenditure, officials claimed to be acting in defence of Hong Kong's low-tax traditions. Taxation arrangements had been deliberately 'anti-welfare' from the very beginning, a former Financial Secretary, Sir John Cowperthwaite, recalled in 1970. When the current system was introduced in 1947, expatriates and 'the whole upper and middle income groups' were regarded as 'the only really permanent elements in our society', he said. It was generally accepted that they should not be taxed 'on any substantial scale to provide benefits or services for the general population'.[75] As a result, the tax system incorporated no sense of social responsibility, and it seemed designed to minimise the burdens on the rich.

The reluctance to use direct taxation to finance social expenditure in 1947 persisted into the current century. The continuing commitment to the traditional taxation arrangements which were so protective of the better-off was illustrated in 2006 during the government's abortive campaign to introduce a regressive consumption tax in the form of a goods and service tax (GST). Only cursory attention was paid to proposals that salaries and profits tax might be increased or made more progressive. The suggestion that dividends and capital gains might be taxed was dismissed out of hand. Even for Hong Kong, however, a GST was hard to stomach, and the business community could not be induced to endorse the proposal despite claims that introduction of a GST was the ideal way to prevent future increases in profits and salaries taxes.[76]

The GST proposal and the debate it provoked was, nevertheless, a reminder that Hong Kong taxes are vintage Third World, which have not changed in half a century.[77] Capital gains, dividends and inheritance — key sources of wealth for the affluent — are entirely untaxed. The concept of a comprehensive, worldwide, income tax is anathema. Profits and salaries are subject to tax but only if earned in Hong Kong. The standard rates of profits and salaries tax have been kept astonishingly low: 10 per cent in 1947; 15 per cent in 1966; 16.5 per cent for corporate profits by 2010 but still only 15 per cent for salaries.[78] It is wrong to assume that contemporary rates of taxation represent the maximum that business firms and affluent individuals will tolerate without fleeing to some friendlier (and so far mythical) tax jurisdiction. In the mid-1980s, for example, corporate profits tax reached 18.5 per cent, while the high for the 1990s was 17.5 per cent. The economy was in a flourishing condition in both decades despite the perceptions of mounting political risk as Sino-British tensions over Hong Kong intensified. See Table 1.1.

Table 1.1
Profits tax, 1980–98

Year of Assessment	Corporate Profits Tax Rate (per cent)	Profits Tax Rate for Unincorporated Businesses (per cent)
1980–81 to 1983–84	16.5	15
1984–85 to 1986–87	18.5	17
1987–88	18	16.5
1988–89	17	15.5
1989–90 to 1991–92	16.5	15
1992–93 to 1993–94	17.5	15
1994–95 to 1997–98	16.5	15

Source: Finance Bureau, *Profits Tax Review Consultation Document* (Government Secretariat, July 1997), Appendix A: 'Changes in Profits Tax Rate'.

When faced with a cogent case for increased financial support for vulnerable groups in this century, officials have fought back by appealing to the doctrine of 'a low tax regime' which, they assert, gives the economy 'a competitive edge'.[79] The chairman of the first Commission on Poverty buttressed his opposition to social expenditure with an appeal to the self-interest of the salaried classes. 'Welfare expenditure alone,' he told a business community forum in 2006, accounted for 'more or less the same as the revenue we receive from salaries tax.'[80] The third Chief Executive, Leung Chun-ying, expressed his own reservations about social expenditure. He lamented how in this 'generally affluent society', many 'live a hand-to-mouth existence'. It would not be 'a viable option', nevertheless, to have more welfare if it involved 'heavy taxation', he stated in his 2013 Policy Address.[81]

The government generally proffered a misleading analysis about the tax system and its narrow base. Officials complained that around 60 per cent of the workforce did not pay salaries tax (because their wages were below the tax threshold). The 40 per cent who were liable paid on average only 8 per cent of their total earnings in 2012, well below the standard rate of salaries tax.[82] The highest earners were in much the same position. Between 1996 and 2011, the top 20 per cent of Hong Kong's earners consistently paid less than 10 per cent of their incomes in tax. Yet, they took home over 55 per cent of the total incomes paid to Hong Kong households.[83] These figures show how unjustified were suggestions from Chief Executives and Financial Secretaries that Hong Kong taxation was close to an unbearable level for any group.

One Law for the Rich

When the Asian financial crisis got under way, officials had looked around for measures that would boost investor confidence. These provided a study in contrasts as the government's financial resources were deployed to underwrite business ventures while austerity was being imposed on the rest of the community.

- In 1999, the government allocated HK$7.8 billion towards the controversial Cyberport project, which was supposed to put Hong Kong on the global IT and services map. The terms of the deal were so generous that they were widely denounced as 'crony capitalism' despite the government's formal denial of a 'secret deal'.[84]
- In the same year, the Hospital Authority's budget for drugs and medical instruments was HK$2.2 billion, not enough to provide all its patients with the medication and appliances that their medical conditions warranted and which formerly had been free of charge.[85]

Similar but much more startling contrasts were to occur in the wake of the later global financial crisis. 'Business populism' had been a growing influence on economic policy since 1998, and SMEs had been showered with financial largesse and other favours.[86] Under Tsang Yam-kuen, this constituency's priority was raised to new heights. In 2008, the Chief Executive promised that the government would provide HK$100 billion to expand the programme to underwrite bank loans for SMEs in order to help them to survive the global financial crisis.[87]

This special treatment was undisguised political patronage from the very start, with little pretence that there was concrete evidence that the banks were refusing loans to SMEs for any viable business projects.[88] Schemes to assist SMEs had begun as a method of subsidising the cost of lending to enterprises with unacceptable credit ratings, higher loan delinquency rates and poorer standards of book-keeping and management. They were, therefore, unable to qualify for ordinary bank loans, the Hong Kong Monetary Authority reported.[89] The justification offered for such subsidies has been a vague combination of economics and welfare. Officials, year after year, repeated that 'these firms are very important to the health of our economy because they account for over 98 per cent of our firms and half of our total employment'.[90]

The waste of public money that the subsidised funding involved has been largely overlooked. SME schemes have been established and run with a reckless disregard for the normal standards of bank lending and of the control of public finances. Their performance has been attacked in two scathing reports by the Director of Audit. Warnings from the banking industry, the Hong Kong Monetary Authority and even the Treasury about the threat of fraud and misuse of public funds were ignored. The loans did not appear to create significant new employment, and the economic and social gains they generated for Hong Kong were unclear, the Director of Audit reported.[91]

In 2012, the Financial Secretary based his case for the further extension of the HK$100 billion commitment to the SME loan guarantee programme on two generalisations:

- Business sentiment: 'SMEs may suffer financial hardship as a result of credit crunch in the coming year' and 'they are the backbone of Hong Kong's economy'.
- Business lobbying. There were 'growing demands from the business sector' for 'swift and effective measures'.

There was no suggestion that, at best, this guarantee programme would do more than protect existing jobs and benefit a relatively small number of firms and employees.[92] And there was no assurance that the funds would be spent in Hong Kong. Indeed, the government's efforts to support the business community embraced Mainland and overseas subsidiaries.[93]

The scheme's ultimate justification was, of course, the plight of Hong Kong's industrialists who had created China's largest export manufacturing base in Guangdong Province (discussed earlier in this chapter). The economic and social benefits to post-industrial Hong Kong from subsidising factory production in Guangdong were hard to quantify, all the more so since the firms had encountered credit problems because they were not efficient enough to meet the standards set by national and provincial labour and environmental legislation.[94]

It was probably not coincidental that the mounting threat to profitability posed by tougher Mainland labour laws, especially enforcement of minimum wage legislation, was paralleled by increasing opposition from the business community to a statutory minimum wage and maximum working hours in Hong Kong, with the campaigners claiming to be anxious to safeguard SMEs. The experience of their Mainland subsidiaries had convinced many Hong Kong firms that better wages and working conditions — and welfare generally — were a recipe for ruin.

Tougher Laws for the Poor

Perhaps the most striking contrast between the generosity shown towards business interests and the harsh financial discipline imposed on the vulnerable was the funding of healthcare. The mentally ill were probably the largest group to suffer avoidable distress and a delayed return to health because of financial constraints. In 2009, the Hospital Authority

drafted a five-year plan for the mental health services. No financial commitments were laid down for the future. Under the heading, 'Need/
Demand Assessment', the planners presented no statistics on the gap
between demand and supply, the costs of proposed improvements or
projected future budgets, information which normally would be a major
feature of such a document. However, it contained a damning indictment of the existing deficiencies and defects created by financial stringency. These included the open scandal that to save money, the Hospital
Authority treated mental patients with older versions of anti-psychotic
drugs whose side-effects could cause such distress that patients disconin-
ued treatment (as the 'Introduction' already pointed out).[95] The additional cost of supplying modern drugs would not have been excessive.[96]

This mistreatment of the vulnerable was in open breach of the government's public pledge: 'One fundamental role of the public health
care system in Hong Kong is to protect the citizens from potentially
huge financial risks arising from catastrophic or prolonged illness.'[97] As
Chapter 5 will show, the government rationed treatment by insisting that
access to the more expensive 'new' drugs must be self-financed, while
claiming to offer exemptions from fees to the needy. The arrangements
for such waivers proved complex, however, and far from satisfactory at
the patient level.[98]

There was little pretence that the vulnerable would be exempt.
'People with low incomes and the chronically ill and the elderly with
limited resources,' admitted the health minister, would still have to pay
some part of the charges. In any case, an effective system for linking
charges to an individual's ability to pay was almost impossible to devise,
he stated, 'because in Hong Kong we don't have a mechanism to know
what people's incomes are'.[99] Officials faced mounting public anxiety
about the costs of drugs for the seriously ill. A new health minister
pledged that the Samaritan Fund administered by the Hospital Authority
would act 'as a safety net to offer assistance to ensure that no one will be
denied treatment because of lack of means', which was, in any case, its
statutory obligation.[100]

The Samaritan Fund had no credibility as a safety net, however. It had
been set up in 1950 when the colonial administration was denying its
social responsibility for the immigrant community. The Fund's current
assistance criteria have been drafted to exert the maximum pressure on
a patient's relatives to pay for the more expensive drugs.[101] In 2008, the
Financial Secretary responded to public complaints by making a HK$1
billion donation to the Samaritan Fund to fund its operations until
2013.[102] This lump-sum payment in advance meant that the adequacy or
otherwise of the financial assistance the Fund offered to patients requiring the most expensive forms of treatment would not automatically

come under the legislature's review in the annual Budget debate. The Financial Secretary used exactly the same stratagem in 2012 to refinance the Fund, with a donation of HK$10 billion to cover funding for the next ten years.[103] In the case of both donations, there were few details of how they had been calculated or of what the rationing imposed by the Samaritan Fund meant in terms of untreated patients.[104]

Double standards were also shamelessly evident in the supervision of financial assistance provided by the government. Earlier in this chapter, it was stated that business firms were knowingly allowed to exploit every possible loophole in the loan guarantee and similar schemes to aid SMEs. As the Director of Audit recorded, the government's defence was that nothing should be done to deter potential borrowers or subject them to bureaucratic controls. CSSA applicants and hospital patients, however, were confronted with every possible obstacle to obtaining benefits. They were subject to strict means testing and residence quali-fications. In addition, 'outcomes' in terms of 'welfare dependency', for example, were under regular scrutiny.

Conclusions: A Painful Legacy

This chapter has illustrated how the community has been forced to endure considerable economic hardship since the 1997–98 Asian finan-cial crisis. The most obvious damage done by misconceived economic policies was the collapse in consumer spending and the prolonged decline in investment. In addition, the budgetary strategy tried, as far as possible, to deny the public any specific entitlements to services or enforceable rights to social benefits.[105] There was also misconceived and wasteful management of budgetary resources. The funding provided for SMEs was the most obvious example of money allocated without proper regard for the value it generated. It would be easy to demon-strate a similar situation with the government's showpiece infrastructure projects almost all of which were justified by officials as a contribution to increased employment opportunities. They turned out to be extremely costly in terms of the number of jobs created.

Social services generally were seriously disrupted by the pursuit of value-for-money targets which became in practice excuses for attacking social expenditure and left the quality of the services themselves seri-ously endangered. When civil servants were called on to operate as if running business ventures, they were urged to acquire 'the skills to suc-cessfully make the transition from being service providers to perform as contract managers'.[106] Assessments of performance became based on business criteria and on how to cut costs. Quality of care and the adequacy of supply in relation to society's needs were demoted to secondary considerations.[107]

> Social values of justice, equality, fairness, and social needs are replaced by market values such as competitiveness, efficiency, productivity and profitability. The principles of public service are rapidly being eroded as commercial values and market forces are fast becoming the dominant operational criteria.[108]

Even Tung Chee Hwa came to realise how wide was the difference between business incentives and the motivation called for in providing public services. On the eve of his departure from office, Tung warned the business community that to claim that public sector efficiency could be raised by 'making it more salary oriented' was a 'purely theoretic' assertion which he did not share.[109] His conversion came too late to reduce the pain suffered by the community and especially its most vulnerable groups. Worse still, his successors and their ministers preferred to stick to the business-based model he had promoted for the public sector and for the social services in particular. So the pain continued.

Notes

1. Stijin Claessens and Simeon Djankov, 'Publicly-Listed East Asian Corporates: Growth, Financing and Risks', paper presented to the Regional Conference on Asian Corporate Recovery: Corporate Governance, Government Policy (World Bank, 15 March 1999).
2. J. A. Kregel, 'Derivatives and Global Capital Flows: Applications to Asia', *Cambridge Journal of Economics*, Vol. 22, No. 6 (November 1998), p. 678.
3. Donald Tsang Yam-kuen, Financial Secretary, *Government Information Services* (*GIS* hereafter), 12 February 1998.
4. Tung Chee Hwa, Chief Executive, *GIS*, 29 May 2004.
5. Tung, *GIS*, 10 August 2000. That this choice was a considered decision is borne out by his very different statement in 1999 that earlier on, 'we deliberately but uncharacteristically went for budget deficit which is not the way we do things . . . with a view really to help stimulate the economy'. Tung, *GIS*, 6 December 1999.
6. John Tsang Chun-wah, Financial Secretary, *GIS*, 10 March 2013.
7. James Tien Pei-chun, *Hong Kong Hansard* (*HH* hereafter), 24 January 2007, p. 4190.
8. Tung, *GIS*, 9 February 1998. His personal conviction on this issue was demonstrated by the fact that similar comments were made in other speeches, e.g., *GIS*, 7 December 1998. Interestingly, Tung's choice of a well-known banker to take over as Financial Secretary in 2001 was followed by a more nuanced explanation of the 'bubble', including a reference to 'the restriction on land supply' imposed by the 1984 Sino-British Joint Declaration which prevented the sale by the government of more than 50 hectares a

year until 1997. Antony Leung Kam-chung, Financial Secretary, *HH*, 6 March 2002, p. 4142.

9. Census and Statistics Department, *A Comparison of the Economic and Social Situation of Hong Kong with Eleven Selected Economies* (Hong Kong, 1997), p. 30.

10. A more extensive review of productivity data can be found in John Dodsworth and Dubravko Mihaljek, *Hong Kong, China: Growth, Structural Change, and Economic Stability During the Transition* (Washington: International Monetary Fund, 1997), pp. 6, 54–64.

11. Norman Chan Tak-lam, Hong Kong Monetary Authority Deputy Chief Executive, *GIS*, 4 December 1997.

12. Attitudes were very different in facing up to the expected economic collapse and large-scale unemployment at the start of the Korean War. The colonial administration's emergency measures and the business community's reactions are recorded in HKRS1017–3-4 'Unemployment Relief' and HKRS1017–2-6 'Committee to Review the Unemployment Situation in the Colony'.

13. Leo F. Goodstadt, *Profits, Politics and Panics: Hong Kong's Banks and the Making of a Miracle Economy, 1935–1985* (Hong Kong: Hong Kong University Press, 2007), p. 67.

14. Henry Wai-chung Yeung, *Transnational Corporations and Business Networks: Hong Kong Firms in the Asian Region* (London: Routledge, 1998), pp. 130, 206–7.

15. On the case made for reducing social expenditure, see Eliza W. Y. Lee, 'Governing Post-Colonial Hong Kong: Institutional Incongruity, Governance Crisis, and Authoritarianism', *Asian Survey*, Vol. 39, No. 6 (November–December 1999), pp. 445–6.

16. *GIS*, 2 February 1998 and 3 August 1998; Home Affairs Branch, *Report on a Telephone Opinion Poll in March 1999*, (March 1999), Question 11.

17. Tung, *GIS*, 29 May 1998.

18. 'Fiscal measures were devised in both the 1998 and 1999 budget with a view to, on the one hand, providing short-term stimulus for economic recovery and, on the other hand, investing in our long-term future. Substantial tax cuts were granted to stimulate demand. Simultaneously, many infrastructural projects for railways, highways, protection of environment, and schools were committed as a long term investment in our future'. Tung, *GIS*, 22 July 1999.

19. Leung, Financial Secretary, *GIS*, 27 November 2002.

20. As the Financial Secretary, Donald Tsang, rightly observed, it was 'sentiment' which linked Hong Kong to the East Asian crisis. *GIS*, 24 November 1997.

21. Dr Yeoh Eng-kiong, Secretary for Health and Welfare, *GIS*, 9 December 1998. In the end, the SAR Government decided not to reduce the level of benefits although administrative measures had been taken to curtail entitlement to social security. *GIS*, 14 June 1999.

22. Health, Welfare and Food Bureau, *GIS*, 17 May 2006.

23. See Finance Bureau, *Information Note for Legislative Council Panel on Public Finance. Short Term Phase of the Enhanced Productivity Programme* (December 1998); Efficiency Unit, *Paper for Briefing to LegCo Panel on Public Services Second Phase of the Enhanced Productivity Programme* (December 1998).

24. See Anthony B. L. Cheung, 'Civil Service Reform in Post-1997 Hong Kong: Political Challenges, Managerial Responses?', *International Journal of Public Administration*, Vol. 24, Issue 9 (2001), pp. 930–3, 939, 940–1.

25. Civil Service Bureau, *Civil Service Reform: Consultation Document* (March 1999).

26. Efficiency Unit, 'Survey on Outsourcing of Government Activities in 2004', slides 5, 8. URL: www.eu.gov.hk/attachments/english/psi_out_sg/survey2004.pdf

27. For a striking instance of government failure to police dishonest and exploitative contractors, see Michael Suen Ming-yeung, Secretary for Housing, Planning and Lands, *HH*, 6 July 2005, pp. 9521–4.

28. Andrew Bibby, 'Responsible contracting: An approach aimed at improving social and labour practices in the property services sector', Working Paper No. 282 (Geneva: International Labour Office, 2011), p. 4.

29. Matthew Cheung Kin-chung, Permanent Secretary for Economic Development and Labour, *GIS*, 8 March 2005.

30. Donald Tsang, Chief Executive, *GIS*, 29 April 2005.

31. 'Standard employment contract for Government service contractors', *GIS*, 29 April 2005.

32. Public Policy Research Centre, *Low-Wage Workers in Hong Kong: Final Report* (Hong Kong: Institute of Asia-Pacific Studies, Chinese University of Hong Kong; Central Policy Unit, September 2008), pp. 50, 142.

33. Joseph Li, 'Trade Union Booster to Tsang Nomination', *China Daily*, 13 June 2005.

34. Matthew Cheung, Secretary for Labour and Welfare, *GIS*, 11 April 2011.

35. The scale and sophistication of the government's market intervention were applauded by Charles Goodhart and Lu Dai, *Intervention to Save Hong Kong: Counter-Speculation in Financial Markets* (Oxford: Oxford University Press, 2003).

36. Donald Tsang, Financial Secretary, *GIS*, 12 April 2001.

37. Paul B. McGuinness, *A Guide to the Equity Markets of Hong Kong* (Hong Kong: Oxford University Press, 1999), p. 22.

38. The potential weaknesses of Tung's strategy were obvious even in an otherwise positive report of his first weeks in office. Alkman Granitsas, 'Land's End: Hong Kong Chief Outlines Real Estate Policy in First Speech', *Far Eastern Economic Review*, 17 July 1997.

39. Tung, *GIS*, 12 September 1997.

40. Anson Chan Fang On-sang, Chief Secretary, *GIS*, 5 June 1998; Tung, *GIS*, 4 December 2004.

41. Wai-chung Lo, 'A Review of the Housing Policy', in Joseph Y. S. Cheng (ed.), *The July 1 Protest Rally: Interpreting a Historic Event* (Hong Kong: City University of Hong Kong Press, 2005), pp. 348–9; Lok Sang Ho, 'Policy Blunder of the Century Threatens Hong Kong's Economic Future', in Lau

Siu-kai (ed.), *The First Tung Chee-hwa Administration: The First Five Years of the Hong Kong Special Administrative Region* (Hong Kong: Chinese University Press, 2003), especially pp. 179–81; Bowen Leung Po-wing, Secretary for Planning, Environment and Land, *GIS*, 9 February 1998; Dominic Wong Shing-wah, Secretary for Housing, *GIS*, February 11 1998; Donald Tsang, Chief Secretary, *GIS*, 3 September 2001.

42. Adrienne La Grange, 'Housing (1997–2007)', in Joseph Y. S. Cheng (ed.), *The Hong Kong Special Administrative Region in Its First Decade* (Hong Kong: City University of Hong Kong Press, 2007), pp. 722–3.

43. Tung, *GIS*, 17 October 2003.

44. Wong, Secretary for Housing, *HH*, 21 February 2001, p. 3581.

45. Hong Kong Monetary Authority, 'Survey of residential mortgage loans in negative equity — June quarter', *GIS*, 14 August 2003.

46. Frederick Ma Si-hang, Secretary for Commerce and Economic Development, *GIS*, 22 October 2007.

47. John Tsang, Financial Secretary, *GIS*, 20 August 2007.

48. *Hong Kong Economic Journal* and *Hong Kong Economic Times*, 5 September 2007; *New China News Agency*, 13 September 2007.

49. Editorial, *Hong Kong Economic Journal*, 5 November 2007; *China Daily*, 22 November 2007; *New China News Agency*, 28 February 2008.

50. On early business awareness of the poor prospects for manufacturing and Guangdong's retreat from low-wage, low-tech industry, see "Vision for Hong Kong" Study Group, *To Be the Services Metropolis of the Pearl River Delta: A Blueprint for Hong Kong* (Hong Kong: Hong Kong General Chamber of Commerce and Hong Kong Coalition of Service Industries, 2002), pp. 18, 23.

51. Tung referred to his long struggle against 'a lagging mindset . . . concern that closer economic ties with the Mainland would undermine our autonomy'. Tung, *GIS*, 9 January 2003.

52. Donald Tsang, Chief Executive, *HH*, 18 May 2006, p. 7609.

53. Donald Tsang, Chief Executive, *GIS*, 17 October and 12 November 2008.

54. These factories were located in the Pearl River Delta. Ma, Secretary for Commerce and Economic Development, *HH*, 28 November 2007, p. 2219.

55. HKTDC Research, 'Economists' Pick', 5 September 2008. URL: www.hktdc.com/business-news/article/Economic-Forum/Beyond-Cheap-Labour-Building-a-Competitive-Edge-through-Adding-Value/ef/en/1/1X000000/1X0041HG.htm

56. The potential losses were hard to quantify because the government did not collect comprehensive data. Rita Lau Ng Wai-lan, Secretary for Commerce and Economic Development, *HH*, 14 January, 2009, p. 3877.

57. Federation of Hong Kong Industry, 'Hong Kong Enterprises in the Pearl River Delta: Current Situation and Future Prospects' (〈珠三角港資企業現況與前景問卷調查報告〉), Report, 2012, p. 11; 'The Pearl River Delta: Hong Kong Business Executives' Current Drive to Transform and Upgrade' (〈珠三角港商轉型升級已是大勢所趨〉), Press Release, 23 May 2012.

58. For useful discussions of Guangdong's policies, see Chris King-chi Chan, 'Labour Policies under Hu-Wen's Regime: Transformation and Challenges'

and Alvin Y. So, 'New Labour Law and Its Implication for the Human Rights Regime in China', in Joseph Y. S. Cheng (ed.), *China: A New Stage of Development for an Emerging Superpower* (Hong Kong: City University of Hong Kong Press, 2012).

59. The limited range of assistance offered was described in some detail by Gregory So Kam-leung, Secretary for Commerce and Economic Development, *HH*, 2 May 2012, pp. 8943–8 and p. 8946 especially.
60. For the background to this subordination to Mainland planning, see Leo F. Goodstadt, 'Hong Kong: Market or "Command" Economy?', *Hong Kong Economic Journal Monthly*, No. 414 (September 2011), pp. 68–71.
61. NDRC, *The Outline of the Plan for the Reform and Development of the Pearl River Delta (2008–2020)*, pp. 29, 65, 95 (Civic Exchange version based on: http://en.ndrc.gov.cn/policyrelease/P020090120342179907030.doc).
62. Henry Tang Ying-yen, Chief Secretary, *GIS*, 1 December 2009.
63. These statistics are from Census and Statistics Department. URL: www.censtatd.gov.hk/hong_kong_statistics/statistical_tables/index.jsp?subjectID=12&tableID=188 (and 189, 190, 191)
64. These drawbacks were canvassed in Census and Statistics Department, 'The Situation of the Six Industries in Hong Kong in 2010', *Hong Kong Monthly Digest of Statistics March 2012*, pp. FB8–9.
65. See John Tsang, Financial Secretary, *GIS*, 1 March 2011.
66. Census and Statistics Department, 'The Cultural and Creative Industries in Hong Kong, 2011', *Hong Kong Monthly Digest of Statistics May 2013* (Hong Kong: Census and Statistics Department, 2013), pp. FB2, 6, 11–2.
67. Audit Commission, *Report No. 59*, 'Chapter 5: Create Hong Kong. Government's financial support to film industry' (26 October 2012).
68. 'Medical Services Dumped as Pillar Industry, Says Minister Ko Wing-man', *South China Morning Post*, 5 September 2012.
69. Their rejection was signalled clearly by Julia Leung Fung-yee, Secretary for Financial Services and the Treasury, *HH*, 31 October 2012, pp. 1067–9.
70. Leung Chun-ying, Chief Executive, *HH*, 17 January 2013, p. 4983.
71. John Tsang, Financial Secretary, *GIS*, 18 March 2013.
72. Donald Tsang, Chief Executive, *GIS*, 16 March 2011; Premier Wen Jiabao quoted in '12th Five-Year Plan not to replace HK's own development plan', *New China News Agency*, 14 March 2011.
73. Leung has stated that he has expanded considerably the Special Administrative Region's participation in the national planning process, as well as agreeing on measures to monitor Hong Kong's implementation of current five-year plan commitments. Leung, Chief Executive, *GIS*, 6 December 2012 and 11 June 2013.
74. Leung, Chief Executive, *GIS*, 22 March 2013.
75. Sir John Cowperthwaite, Financial Secretary, *HH*, 25 February 1970, pp. 366–7.
76. 'Reforming Hong Kong's Tax System Consultation Document' (2006), pp. 4, 6, 16, 25; Financial Services and Treasury Branch, 'Public Consultation on Tax Reform Final Report' (June 2007).

77. Under British rule, London made several, abortive efforts to get Hong Kong to modernise the tax system from 1922. The salient facts are recorded in HKRS41–1-2769(1) 'Inland Revenue Ordinance 1. General question of imposing etc . . . ' and HKRS41–1-1233 'Taxation General Policy regarding . . . in the Colony'.

78. Property taxes and rates, together with minor excise duties, were lightly fixed. (Tobacco was the exception in modern times and for health reasons.) On the tax system and its history, see Michael Littlewood, *Taxation without Representation: The History of Hong Kong's Troublingly Successful Tax System* (Hong Kong: Hong Kong University Press, 2010).

79. Very notably by Health, Welfare and Food Bureau Spokesperson, *GIS*, 17 May 2006.

80. Tang, Financial Secretary, Joint Business Community Lunch, *GIS*, 2 March 2006.

81. Leung, Chief Executive, *HH*, 16 January 2013, p. 4922.

82. These tax data are from Professor Anthony Cheung Bing-leung, Secretary for Transport and Housing, *HH*, 19 December 2012, p. 3841.

83. Census and Statistics Department, *2006 Population By-Census: Thematic Report: Household Income Distribution in Hong Kong* (Hong Kong: Census and Statistics Department, 2006), 'Table 6.6 Percentage Distribution of Original Monthly Household Income . . .', p. 77 and 'Table 7.21 Summary Statistics on Households in the 9th and 10th Decile Groups', p. 106; *2011 Population Census. Thematic Report Household Income Distribution in Hong Kong* (Hong Kong: Census and Statistics Department, 2012), 'Table 5.6: Percentage Distribution of Original Monthly Household Income . . .', p. 91 and 'Table 7.4 Summary Statistics on Households in the 9th and 10th Decile Groups', p. 122.

84. *GIS*, 3 August 2000; Rahul Jacob, 'Hong Kong in Cyberport deal', *Financial Times*, 17 May 2000; 'Secret Deal on Cyberport Dismissed', *GIS*, 16 March 1999.

85. Hospital Authority, 'Spending on "Specialist Supplies and Drugs"', *Hospital Authority Statistical Report 1999–00*, 'Table 9.1: Expenditure for 1999/00'.

86. Government schemes to aid SMEs were summarised by Maria Kwan Sik-ning, Trade and Industry Director-General, *GIS*, 21 February 2012.

87. Donald Tsang, *GIS*, 8 December 2008.

88. See the absence of serious economic analysis in Tung, *GIS*, 2 December 1999.

89. These risks as seen by the banks were reported in Market Research Division, 'Survey of the Financing Situation of Small and Medium-Sized Enterprises', *Hong Kong Monetary Authority Quarterly Report*, October 2000, p. 38.

90. John Tsang, Financial Secretary, *GIS*, 30 August 2012.

91. The determination to meet requests for loans regardless of the borrowers' merits was documented on almost every page of Audit Commission, *Report 39*, 'Chapter 5: Special Finance Scheme for Small and Medium Enterprises' (Hong Kong, 15 October 2002). The persistence of abuses was well illustrated in Audit Commission, *Report No. 47*, 'Chapter 4: Four Small and Medium Enterprise Funding Schemes' (Hong Kong, 23 October

2006), especially pp. 13, 15, 31–2. The Audit Commission reports uncovered abuses not only in schemes guaranteeing bank loans but throughout a range of business support initiatives.

92. An estimated 29,800 enterprises, each employing an average of four workers each, might benefit from the HK$100 billion loan guarantee according to Commerce and Economic Development Bureau, *Item for Finance Committee*, HEAD 152 Subhead 700, 'New item "SME Financing Guarantee Scheme — Special Concessionary Measures"' (FCR(2012–13)12, April 2012), pp. 2, 7.

93. Legislative Council Secretariat, 'Background Brief on Funding Schemes for Small and Medium Enterprises' (CB(1)1873/06–07(03), 11 June 2007), pp. 2, 5; Commerce and Economic Development Bureau, 'Legislative Council Panel on Commerce and Industry. Progress Update on the Support Measures for Small and Medium Enterprises' (CB(1)389/10–11(06), November 2010), p. 4.

94. The efficiency factor had been recognised as the underlying issue early on. See 'GPRD Business Council and HKTDC Seminar on Guangdong's Economic Restructuring', *GIS*, 13 November 2006.

95. The five-year plan made this point clearly, and it was reinforced by the submission from the Hong Kong College of Psychiatrists. Hospital Authority, 'Mental Health Service Plan for Adults 2010–2015', pp. 30, 32–3, 69.

96. On the pace and costs in previous years of providing the modern medication, see Dr York Chow Yat-ngok, Secretary for Health and Welfare, *HH*, 18 October 2006, p. 145.

97. Health and Welfare Bureau, *Lifelong Investment in Health: Consultation Document on Healthcare* (Hong Kong: SAR Government, 2001), p. 51.

98. From early on, official explanations of the waiver system were almost incomprehensible, e.g., Yeoh, Secretary for Health and Welfare, *GIS*, 8 November 2002.

99. Ibid.

100. The minister was quoting almost verbatim the requirements set out in the Hospital Authority Ordinance (cap. 113), s. 4(d). Chow, Secretary for Health, Welfare and Food, *HH*, 8 November 2006, pp. 1649–50.

101. Legislative Council Secretariat, 'The Samaritan Fund' (CB(2)1640/11–12(04), 10 April 2012), p. 3.

102. Food and Health Bureau, 'Legislative Council Panel on Health Services. Grant for the Samaritan Fund' (CB(2) 208/08–09(05), November 2008), pp. 2, 3, 8, 10.

103. Food and Health Bureau, 'Legislative Council Panel on Health Services. Samaritan Fund' (CB(2)1640/11–12(03), April 2012), p. 3.

104. Legislative Council Secretariat, 'The Samaritan Fund' (CB(2)1640/11–12(04), 10 April 2012), p. 4.

105. See Ahmed Shafiqul Huque, 'Understanding Hong Kong', in Paul Wilding et al. (eds.), *Social Policy in Hong Kong* (Cheltenham: Edward Elgar, 1997), p. 20.

106. Steve Barclay, Efficiency Unit Assistant Director, *GIS*, 30 June 2005.

107. For important examples of the sidelining of quality issues, see *Enhanced Productivity Programme 2002–03* (Hong Kong SAR Government, 2003); Yeoh, Secretary for Health and Welfare, *HH*, 20 December 2000, pp. 2036–43, 2256–7.
108. Jermain T. M. Lam, 'Enhanced Productivity Program in Hong Kong: A Critical Appraisal', *Public Performance & Management Review*, Vol. 27, No. 1 (September, 2003), p. 63.
109. Tung, *GIS*, 17 October 2005.

2
The Business of Government: Less Politics, No Welfare

Hong Kong has always been a deeply 'pro-establishment' society. Support for democratic reforms has never meant a call for radical change. Most people share the same commitment to 'small government, low taxation' as officials and the business and professional elite. The average household would rather go hungry than seek Comprehensive Social Security Assistance (CSSA) when they lose their jobs (as the data in Chapter 6 will show). And the elderly have been even more reluctant to rely on social security benefits (as Chapter 6 will also show). The public have deep respect for the law and the courts, for the police and the Independent Commission Against Corruption (ICAC). Almost everyone cooperates spontaneously with government departments and their rules and regulations, whether in renewing an identity card or in applying for school places for their children. This chapter will present the polling and other indicators that reveal how conservative this community has been in its attitudes towards social as well as political issues.

Hong Kong has been exceptional for the lack of serious public pressure on the government to accept responsibility for the wellbeing of vulnerable members of the community. In the absence of universal suffrage, the community could impose no direct political sanctions on incompetent or uncaring members of the government, although the public has also shown a surprising capacity to veto the survival of those in power. The legislature has had only limited powers to alter official policies or to allocate public expenditure, and throughout this century, those in high office were able to reduce the provision of public housing and social services with impunity. Yet, political stability and social harmony, if anything, strengthened, as this chapter later explains. This combination of polite politics and social maturity reflected Hong Kong's historical realities, and these qualities were openly acknowledged by the Mainland authorities in the last century.[1] Over the years, the community had been conditioned to accept that there were sacrifices and compromises which must be made in order to ensure Hong Kong's survival. In particular, a 'high degree of autonomy' and the principle of 'Hong Kong people ruling Hong Kong' could only be achieved through unconditional compliance with the Basic Law, the 1990 constitutional blueprint for post-colonial Hong Kong.

The Basic Law was intended to put an end to controversy about the role of democracy in Hong Kong. Political reform would be carefully controlled. Universal suffrage in the selection of the chief executive and legislators was 'the ultimate aim', and political change would be 'gradual and orderly'. Social reform would be even more restricted. 'The development and improvement' of social welfare was made subject first to 'economic conditions' and linked to 'social needs' only second (Article 145). The vaguest mention was made of rights to social services, and no entitlements were bestowed on the needy and the vulnerable. By contrast, the Basic Law elaborated in detail the rights and freedoms of business, and it pledged commitment to unrestricted capitalism and the most conservative budgetary policies.[2]

China's leaders had decided that it would be harmful to the national interest if Hong Kong's capitalist system did not continue to flourish after 1997, and it was generally believed that the co-option of business leaders into the political structure had been a key factor in the economy's impressive performance in the past.[3] At the same time, Mainland officials shared the business community's misgivings about increased social expenditure because they were genuinely alarmed that the colonial administration would seek to dissipate the government's financial reserves through spending on social services.[4] Leading Mainland officials joined forces with the business and professional elite to denounce increased welfare spending, thus providing a practical demonstration of how the pro-business commitments of the Basic Law would be implemented after it came into effect in 1997.[5] An eloquent statement of intent was made in 1994 by the highest ranking Mainland official in Hong Kong at a prestigious business forum. He issued a dire warning about welfare expenditure. 'We see disconcerting signs of attempted [policy] changes, proposed in the name of lofty causes,' he said. 'It is true,' he went on, that 'the poor and the old should be taken care of.' But they should expect only limited state help because of the costs involved: 'the cost to tax-payers . . . to budgetary balance . . . to Hong Kong's overall economic structure and its free market orientation.' It was unfortunate that the one, concrete example he cited of a potentially unaffordable welfare initiative was a pension scheme, the absence of which has continued to burden Hong Kong's ageing community into this century.[6] By contrast, the Mainland was to tackle the nation's pension gap with increasing determination from 1997 despite its much lower levels of income per head and the shortage of social services generally by comparison with Hong Kong.[7]

The Basic Law ensured that the protection of business interests would be the first priority for official policy-makers and made it 'extremely difficult for [the legislature] to pass any bill against the interests of the business class'.[8] These constitutional arrangements fixed the balance of political power and reduced potential competition between rival economic and social interests. The Central People's Government retained overriding control and maintained a considerable presence in the Special Administrative Region, with an average of 7,756 new arrivals with official status each year between 2009 and 2011.[9] Beijing's intervention in local affairs was limited but decisive, especially in the selection of the Chief Executive and the approval of ministerial and other senior appointments.

Within Hong Kong, the Special Administrative Region government was the most powerful political actor. There were three other contestants for influence over government policies and spending: the business and professional elite, the legislature and the community. This chapter will explore this balance of power and its consequences for social development. It will also review the community's relationship with its rulers and seek to explain the public's tolerance of the large gap between its expectations and the behaviour of both government and business.

Business Takes the Lead

The Basic Law made business pre-eminent in the political system, and the government's subsequent deference to business interests seemed almost limitless. The government's propensity to favour business was, however, far more a matter of political convenience than is usually thought, this chapter will argue. On the whole, the collaboration was voluntary, and when officials believed they had been threatened or pressured in negotiations with tycoons, they were free to publicly disclose the facts, if they chose, without fear of retaliation.[10]

Relations between government and business were made all the easier by the background of the first Chief Executive, Tung Chee Hwa. He had spent his entire career in business, and his approach to economic affairs was shaped very largely by his commercial experiences.[11] The Chief Executive had been selected for office by a small body of individuals dominated by business interests, and he depended heavily on the same group for his re-selection in 2002. In managing the government, business support was essential for Tung because his private-sector background had not equipped him to mobilise the bureaucracy, develop a political coalition or rally the public's support.[12] Hence, he and his ministers needed the backing of the business community and its functional constituency representatives in the Legislative Council to get the government's legislative and financial proposals through the legislature unscathed.

Tung's successor, Donald Tsang Yam-kuen, was a career civil servant. His diligent efforts to bond with Hong Kong's business leaders eventually left him battling to refute allegations about improper acceptance of 'hospitality involving yachts and private jets' and his arrangements for a luxury post-retirement residence. His defence of this conduct before the Legislative Council included a naive account of his relations with tycoons. 'The several people with whom I travelled on private jets or returned to Hong Kong from Macao on yachts are ordinary friends of mine,' he declared, 'not friends close enough to affect my impartiality when handling official business.' As Chief Executive, he needed the know-how of business leaders, he stated, and he was not to blame when 'the frequency of socializing' with them rose from 'one or two evenings a week' to 'several evenings' plus 'luncheon and breakfast meetings'.[13]

The third Chief Executive, Leung Chun-ying, was widely regarded as being more distant from the business and professional elite, many of whose most prominent members had endorsed his election rival, Henry Tang Ying-yen. But Leung proved no less enthusiastic about the government-business nexus than the two earlier Chief Executives. His 2013 Policy Address, for example, provoked instant controversy by setting up a Financial Services Development Council, which was to be formed as a private company and not subject to the legislature's scrutiny as advisory bodies normally were. Almost 20 per cent of its members were reported to be executives of Mainland enterprises with close ties to the national leadership. The Council was attacked as adding a new dimension to cronyism through its co-option of Mainland business representatives into the Hong Kong power structure.[14]

The Rise of Cronyism

Political reforms between 1985 and 1995 had offset business influence within the political system through the introduction of elected (especially directly-elected) legislators.[15] The Basic Law tilted the political balance back in favour of business, which helps to explain the widespread feeling among the community from the late 1990s that the doors had been opened wide to cronyism. In the post-1997 environment, access and influence have been the most visible evidence of the privileged status of the business community and its leaders even though there were personal rivalries within the business community and frequent conflicts between individual firms and the government.[16] Hong Kong now had its 'princelings', the tycoons' sons and daughters who were routinely co-opted into the power structure.[17] Directors of the six largest development conglomerates were appointed in rapidly rising numbers, the media reported, to influential statutory bodies and advisory committees.[18] The government-business nexus was fulfilling its traditional function: providing business leaders with opportunities to benefit personally from public status and political access in return for their cooperation with the government to offset public opposition.

In post-colonial Hong Kong, the danger of cronyism at first caused more concern overseas than locally. In 1998, Tung announced that the government had redefined the traditional economic policy of 'non-interventionism'. In future, it would identify growth industries and create new profit opportunities for the private sector.[19] The International Monetary Fund reviewed Hong Kong's economic performance and declined to endorse Tung's initiative.[20] In 1999, the public was alarmed by the controversial Cyberport deal. This project combined a world-class IT hub with a residential complex on 26 hectares of public land and was to be a partnership between the government and a member of the Li Ka-shing family.[21] Rival property tycoons claimed that if the site had been sold by competitive tender, the terms would have been far less favourable to the project's developer, and there was a flood of allegations of cronyism.[22] The criticism was persistent, and the technology minister was still battling seven years later to convince the community that Cyberport was worth the money.[23]

A flagrant example of prolonged favouritism for business as a whole was the official resistance to a proposed competition law. For three decades, the government had knowingly left the public vulnerable to exploitation because of restricted competition in many sectors, from supermarkets to housing. Officials were brazen in their defence of price rigging and restrictive practices, both before and after the British departure.[24] The government's intransigence provoked mounting community resentment, and from 2005, the second Chief Executive made repeated promises to end market abuses. The government and the business community managed, however, to delay reforms for several years with the unlikely argument that legislation would jeopardise the survival of small and medium-sized enterprises (SMEs). The legislation was finally passed in 2012 by which date 'over 120 economies worldwide' — including the Mainland — had already enacted competition laws, the commerce minister admitted.[25]

The most determined resistance came from the property sector. Developers had long refused to supply basic information about the size and facilities of new flats, and they had been left free to circulate misleading price information. This scandalous behaviour had first aroused criticism in the 1980s, and legal remedies had been under discussion since 1992. Even after legislation had finally been passed, developers were threatening court action to block the new law.[26]

The Case for Competition

Collusion between government and business to prevent legal measures to enforce competition has been interpreted as proof that officials have abdicated the power to interfere with profit-seeking even if it leads to overt exploitation of the public. That conclusion would be misleading. Concessions to business were not forced on the government but were generally made by ministers and senior officials who shared the same economic preconceptions as the business elite.

The telecommunications industry, for example, was dominated by property-related interests. When developers entered the industry in this century, they accepted the draconian regulations enacted in 1995 to promote competition and which had been modelled on United States, European and Australian practices. Significantly, officials took the credit for the substantial benefits which consumers obtained as a result of the competitive market.[27] Similarly, the colonial administration had severely restricted competition in the banking industry from 1965 on the grounds that excessive competition had led to that year's banking crisis. The government enforced an interest-rate cartel and imposed restrictions on foreign banks seeking to enter Hong Kong until 2001, when the cartel was wound up and barriers to foreign bank branches removed. Banks were no longer protected against free and open competition in the domestic market, and the banking industry flourished as never before.

The government's intervention in this century to protect the community's interests in telecommunications and banking deprives the government-business nexus of the excuse that restrictions on business profits inevitably jeopardise the economy and undermine investor confidence. On the contrary, the impressive progress of the telecommunications industry and the exceptional stability of banking during the Asian and global financial crises indicated how economic performance can be enhanced by measures to protect the public from monopolies and unfair trading practices.

The government retained its autonomy in dealing with the property sector even though the first and second Chief Executives bowed to its demands for the government to withdraw from the housing market (except for the lowest income groups) and to restrict the supply of new building sites in order to minimise pressure on property values. But concessions had important limits. From 1991, Hong Kong bank regulators had imposed tight restrictions on the freedom of the banking industry to lend to the property sector. These loan ceilings were imposed in defiance of the worldwide trend to abolish controls of this sort. The restrictions reduced the earnings of both the banks and the property sector. The banks could not freely expand the volume of their lucrative mortgage business. The developers could not maximise their profits by pumping up speculation and exploiting bubble markets.

The government from 1998 intervened at will to halt whatever it judged to be unhealthy property price surges. In 2009, the restrictions on mortgage lending were raised to record levels to counter an incipient bubble.[28] In 2012, the government responded to claims that an influx of Mainland buyers was driving up prices to irrational heights by imposing a penal rate of stamp duty on all property purchases, from which Hong Kong 'permanent residents' alone were exempt.[29] Such discrimination against offshore investors was unprecedented. Property developers were bitterly resentful of the exceptional severity of this intervention in their sector.[30] The government could not be budged, however. Financial stability had to come first.

Mainland Partners

From the Mainland's standpoint, the choice of business leaders to be the Chinese Communist Party's partners in Hong Kong paid off handsomely. Their political loyalty was demonstrated in the aftermath of the 500,000-strong march in 2003 to protest against the formula put forward by the government 'to discharge its responsibility to protect the state by implementing Article 23 of the Basic Law, to ensure that national security is not threatened by serious criminal offences'.[31] This demonstration had gone ahead despite a personal plea to the public from Premier Wen Jiabao on the eve of the march to trust the Special Administrative Region's government.[32] Business leaders, however, responded promptly to his request for loyal support.[33] Their fidelity to China's leaders did not waver in subsequent controversies over Mainland proposals which the general public opposed. (This issue is dealt with at greater length in Chapter 7.)

The large family conglomerates also earned the patronage of China's leadership because of their willingness to underwrite major development projects on the Mainland and the massive IPOs floated in Hong Kong by state-owned enterprises.[34] Not that the Hong Kong tycoons could take their profits for granted. Many encountered well-publicised difficulties with local governments over property, transport, power and retail projects. These investors, however, had ample access to Mainland power-holders at both national and regional level. They did not need Special Administrative Region government officials to intercede on their behalf.

Another group of businesses emerged in this century, which was less favourably placed in dealing with the Mainland's bureaucracies. These were the 56,000 firms which had set up enterprises in Guangdong Province where they had 10 million workers on their payroll by 2007.[35] They were being crippled, they complained, by the costs of complying with new national as well provincial policies to halt pollution and improve workers' welfare. Hong Kong officials had been able to do little to protect these businesses.[36] As the previous chapter explained, the Mainland authorities regarded these firms as low-tech, low-wage producers which had no place in Guangdong's modernisation programme.

In the wider Hong Kong context, these Mainland measures intensified business mistrust of all social reforms. Mainland initiatives were bankrupting Hong Kong firms in Guangdong, the second Chief Executive publicly stated.[37] A substantial number of Hong Kong entrepreneurs and investors thus had first-hand experience of how better protection for the labour force, the environment and the consumer could trim profit margins. Their Mainland tribulations seemed to justify unrelenting business opposition whenever proposals surfaced in Hong Kong for minimum wages, shorter workings hours, tougher environmental controls, competition legislation and new taxes.

At the Mainland's Mercy

The inability of Hong Kong's first two Chief Executives to protect the interests of its entrepreneurs and investors who, since the 1980s, had responded to the Mainland's calls to take a leading role in the industrialisation of Guangdong Province was a major turning point, politically as well as economically. It marked an important break with the past and revealed unanticipated limits to the Special Administrative Region's political authority.

Historically, in dealings with the rest of the world, Hong Kong officials had mounted uninhibited campaigns to maintain Hong Kong's access to its overseas markets and to defend Hong Kong firms against trade discrimination. Among the two most important historical examples were direct confrontations with Washington and London.

- Hong Kong officials induced Washington to lift the ban that it had imposed — with the agreement of the British Foreign Office — on all United States shipments to Hong Kong as part of its 1950 economic and financial blockade of China. Despite the Cold War obsessions of American political leaders, Hong Kong won a special status which indirectly enabled China to obtain access to international trade and financial markets via Hong Kong until the embargo was lifted in 1971.[38]

- Hong Kong officials were so ruthless in fighting restrictions on Hong Kong textile exports to the United Kingdom that the senior British negotiator commented in 1961: 'Crudely stated, the position of the Hong Kong Delegation was that, if [Britain] was going to be ruined, it might as well be at the hands of Hong Kong as those of third countries.'[39]

In the contemporary world, Hong Kong officials continued to boast of their vigour in defending external business opportunities. Their efforts ranged from active involvement in international and regional arrangements for banking supervision and currency cooperation to legal and tax agreements with foreign governments, as well as unrestrained comment on the policies of the United States and the European Union.[40] When it came to the Mainland, however, Hong Kong felt it had to be more diplomatic. Officials claimed that they had no right to interfere with the decisions made by Mainland authorities. Even the business community shared this reluctance to express disagreement. For example, the new national labour and environmental policies discussed earlier aroused strident protests in Beijing from foreign businesses which were in marked contrast to the more muted complaints from Hong Kong's trade associations.[41]

The Special Administrative Region government had only limited scope to intervene on behalf of Hong Kong firms. The third Chief Executive, nevertheless, was willing to declare that 'I see it as my responsibility to safeguard the interests of Hong Kong'. 'We need more support' from the Mainland authorities, he went on, identifying in particular a need for 'clearer procedures' and 'better co-operation at the regional level'.[42] Unfortunately, even the Central People's Government itself had serious difficulties in achieving goals of this sort, while the Special Administrative Region had little bargaining power when dealing with local Mainland leaders. Among the more notorious examples of local authorities' insubordination has been their defiance of both national law and the financial regulators in raising bank loans for unauthorised business and investment projects. These illegitimate borrowings totalled USD 1.66 trillion at the end of 2010.[43]

Thus, there was a significant difference between what Hong Kong officials traditionally achieved in defending Hong Kong's global export markets and what they could deliver for Hong Kong investors and manufacturers on the Mainland. The balance within the government-business nexus shifted in response to this development. In the past, the business community was not just the government's political partner. It was also a 'client' whose profits depended directly on the performance of trade and financial officials in negotiating market access for Hong Kong exports, which gave business a powerful incentive to support the government's policies in general. For post-industrial Hong Kong with the export trade operating under liberal World Trade Organisation (WTO) rules, business profits were no longer at the mercy of quotas, tariffs and trade restrictions. The direct link between business survival and the government's trade and financial policies had gone.

The targets for market exploitation altered in consequence.

- Until 1978 and Deng Xiaoping's 'open door' policies, Hong Kong could exploit world markets with a clear conscience. Manufacturing for export generated burgeoning profits and higher wages at the expense of protectionist Western economies.
- From 1978, Hong Kong manufacturers could maintain their export competitiveness by relocating to the Mainland. Here, they were free to exploit the low wages, cheap land, tax and tariff privileges and the wide exemption from labour and environmental regulations offered by Guangdong and other provinces. From 2003, Guangdong sought to halt this exploitation.
- In this century, Hong Kong itself became the main market for exploitation. Here, the principal targets were the residential property market, the labour force and the retail consumer. Government policies, as the last chapter made clear, created new opportunities to exploit home-buyers and low-skilled workers, and there was no competition law to protect consumers until 2012.

The business ethic of contemporary Hong Kong was summed up by a leading property tycoon.

> The world is unfair and we want to make sure the advantage becomes more and more unfair. That's the nature of the game.[44]

Beleaguered Legislators

The Legislative Council ranked third in the power structure, but legislators themselves hardly seemed to count. They were belittled and derided by the government, business and the community. They were made scapegoats for the government's inability to administer effectively. Pro-democracy Legislative Councillors especially were denounced as more intent on empty protests than on tackling Hong Kong's problems. Business leaders continued to fear politicians: elections were seen as creating an irresistible temptation for political parties to compete for power through populist welfare programmes and anti-business measures.[45]

Government ministers led the campaign against the legislature. When Tung Chee Hwa took office, Hong Kong's prospects had never seemed so promising. 'A colonial administration gave way to a Special

Administrative Region Government, which embodies the principle of "Hong Kong people ruling Hong Kong" and enjoys a high degree of autonomy,' Tung recalled, 'We, finally, became our own master.'[46] The conflicts and contradictions of the colonial era would evaporate. Confrontations with Beijing which had dominated public attention would disappear, he believed, and with them political rancour. The community would be able to unite behind a government made up of individuals who had been shaped by the same experiences; who treasured the same Chinese heritage; and who shared the same future.

The electoral system was designed to create a legislature dominated by business and professional interests and by the organisations which had shown loyalty to the Chinese Communist Party during the colonial era.[47] Electoral politics would become of secondary importance.

- Political activism would decline. The community would become less 'politicised' and thus easier to govern because 'populist' political parties which advocated universal suffrage would be sidelined.
- The economic environment would improve. Investors would respond positively to the decline in political 'populism' and removal of the threat of higher taxes to pay for improved social services and the danger of new employment legislation which would raise labour costs.[48]

There was also an assumption that public protests and hostile media reporting suffered by the pre-1997 administration had been the natural response to colonialism. The community would abandon such disruptive activities when ruled by their compatriots to whom they could give their trust. In consequence, there would be no need to buy off public discontent with social programmes.

Tung Chee Hwa was soon to be disappointed, and his team quickly lost patience with the community and its politicians. In 2000, the Secretary for Security issued a warning to 'would-be demonstrators'. She referred to the way 'freedom fighters' discredited their cause — as if there could be any comparison between Hong Kong's tradition of orderly protests and the violence associated with 'freedom fighters'. The 'mass media' were accused of having 'become too prone to take things at face value; to jump to conclusions and to pass judgment without an objective inquiry'. She attacked legislators who 'seem to be more interested in seeing heads roll rather than establishing the facts'. 'To those at the receiving end of their attack,' she went on, 'it would appear as though all they want is "blood"; to pin down culprits in the absence of a thorough investigation.'[49]

The first post-1997 President of the Legislative Council, Rita Fan Hsu Lai-tai, later expressed dismay at the damage done by this sort of official hostility towards legislators. During a confidential discussion at the United States Consulate after she stepped down from her Legislative Council post in 2008, she reportedly identified the source of political conflict in Hong Kong as the arrogant mentality shared by business leaders and senior bureaucrats (who dominated the political system). They expected their decisions to be implemented without question, and they saw no need to mobilise political support for their proposals. In the past, she declared, officials had been happy to acknowledge the input from legislators, which generated goodwill. When Tsang Yam-kuen was Financial Secretary, she went on, he had used this tactic successfully. If as Chief Executive, he had started 'showing respect and acknowledging the contribution of legislators to proposals the government ultimately adopts, [he would] go a long way in improving LegCo-[SAR government] relations'.[50]

The low status accorded to legislators as a class was well illustrated in the public consultation on the 2011 Policy Address and the 2012 Budget. The Chief Executive met with 17 groups. The arrangements for these meetings signalled the political standing of the participants.

- First to be consulted were those with national status: National People's Congress Deputies, followed by members of the Chinese People's Political Consultative Conference.
- Then came the 'pro-government' groups: the Democratic Alliance for the Betterment and Progress of Hong Kong (DAB) and then the Federation of Trade Unions (FTU).
- Next in line were the 'pro-business' legislators (newly-founded Economic Synergy first, followed by the less reliable government ally, the Liberal Party).
- Only then were other legislators invited.

Neither the Democratic Party nor the Civic Party was mentioned by name in the official schedule. It was as if they had no formal status as legitimate organisations in Hong Kong's political arrangements.[51]

The Legislative Council's second post-1997 President, Jasper Tsang Yok-sing, was among the most ideologically respectable public figures in Hong Kong who met all Beijing's criteria for 'politically correctness'. Yet, he publicly derided allegations that the government's work was sabotaged by a recalcitrant legislature. He explained that 'it would be a gross misconception to think that the legislators spent most of their time trying to obstruct the government's work'. 'What is the worry,' he asked, since 'government-friendly legislators, or "government-loyalists", form a majority in the legislature,' and 'even the parties which the government has labelled "the opposition" . . . supports 95% of all government proposals.'[52]

Nevertheless, the government continued to regard political activists with serious mistrust. The unelected government insisted on dividing the world into friends and foes: 'people who are pro-establishment and people who are pan-democratic', as the Chief Secretary put it in 2011.[53] The third Chief Executive, Leung Chun-ying, was alleged to have gone a stage further. He was accused of labelling the pan-democrats as belonging to a category of political foes whom Mao Zedong had relentlessly attacked.[54]

The government's mistrust was not reciprocated by politicians in the routine conduct of the legislature's business. There were occasional 'pantomime' protests by a handful of legislators causing brief, theatrical disruptions of proceedings and their even rarer filibusters, which the Council's President kept within reasonable bounds. The majority of Legislative Councillors were 'conservative', both in their behaviour and their views. They were not particularly populist nor advocates of radical welfare reforms. Except for Mainland-related issues, they assumed that the government's intentions were good and that the civil service was honest and professional. Monitoring was the principal role played by legislators. The good faith assumed by legislators in their dealings with government agencies was also resilient. They tended to believe, for example, that the accuracy of official statements could be largely taken for granted even though this trust has proved misplaced in recent years.

- Direct Subsidy Scheme (DSS) schools received the same government financial support as the rest of the subsidised school sector but were allowed to charge fees, and they operated with considerable autonomy. In return, they had to provide scholarships or fee remission schemes so that needy students were not excluded from access to this elite education. In 2009, allegations that the schools were breaking the rules were denied in detail by the government.[55] The following year, a damning report from the Director of Audit showed that the Education Bureau had misled the Legislative and Executive Councils about DSS schools. Among other irregularities uncovered, at least 40 per cent of the schools did not offer the financial assistance to needy students that they were contracted to provide.[56]
- Private hospitals enjoyed a similar 'light-touch' relationship with their official regulators. In 2010 and again in 2011, the Legislative Council was given blanket assurances that potential problems had been remedied and that the government was effectively policing private hospitals.[57] In 2012, the Director of Audit uncovered irregularities in handling complaints about professional misconduct in the private sector. Patients were in danger of exploitation because of the lack of transparency about fees. He also showed how justified

legislators' questions had been about whether or not the private hospitals which had been granted free public land had complied with their commitment to operate on a not-for-profit basis and to provide a quota of free or low-fee beds for the needy.[58]

In neither case did legislators launch a witch-hunt into why they — and the community — had been so grossly misinformed by the government. (These two incidents are discussed in more detail in Chapter 5.)

A World without Welfare

The Basic Law's restrictions on the legislature's powers made it 'impossible to push for welfare reforms'. As a result, it has been observed, 'social provision is secondary to economic development and the former must give way to the latter whenever they are in conflict'.[59] The Basic Law was designed for a world without welfare. Mainland officials, it was noted earlier, chose to support business interests in denouncing expansion of the social services in the 1990s despite the risk of alienating both the general public and those trade unions which were a major source of political support for Mainland policies.[60] Limited social services did not seem an urgent priority because until the 1990s, the youthful immigrant population needed relatively little medical care or social support and could survive squalid housing. Nor did education seem to matter much, with sustained economic growth and a chronic labour shortage.

In the very different conditions of this century, a world without adequate welfare has caused considerable distress. Austerity measures during the recession and privatisation of public services led to the public sector being scaled back. Its costs were transferred increasingly to sick patients, needy students and welfare recipients. Long-term financial commitments to social service development were abandoned. The elderly, the mentally ill and the children and adults with disabilities had to endure agonisingly protracted waiting times for access to residential care (which Chapter 5 will describe). Yet, there were no mass protests against the government's retreat from the social responsibilities which it had previously accepted.

This passivity was not due to ignorance or apathy. The community understood very well the consequences of the government's new policies. In 2006, the Hong Kong Transition Project uncovered extensive evidence of the gap between government policies and community priorities. The public strongly disapproved of increased charges for social services (medical care, for example). Opposition to privatisation of government services was considerable. There was overwhelming support for increased government spending on medical services and education (especially at the primary and secondary levels). The community strongly favoured minimum wage legislation, shorter working hours and mandatory health insurance.[61] The public's views were not heeded, yet Hong Kong's governability remained in no danger.

Public Protests Surge, Social Harmony Improves

Chief Executives and their teams, nevertheless, lived in trepidation about the threat to 'social harmony' which they expected to emerge with the growing burdens imposed on the public by their misguided policies. Tsang Yam-kuen produced an explicit list in 2005 of the public's causes for complaint:

> . . . employment difficulties for workers with low academic quali-
> fications and skills; declining real pay levels in certain jobs; the
> polarisation of the middle class; a widening income gap; an ageing
> population . . .[62]

By 2010, Tsang was warning that 'social division and confrontation' had intensified, aggravated by political controversies and the wealth gap.[63] But the anticipated breakdown of social order never happened. Public protests did not become more dramatic in this century by comparison with the 1980s, for example.

- In 1986, a popular campaign collected 230,000 signatures in favour of the early introduction of direct elections.
- In 1987, some 700,000 signatures were obtained for a petition to halt the Daya Bay nuclear power station planned for neighbouring Guangdong Province because of public fears about its safety.[64]
- In 1989, over a million people marched in Hong Kong to demonstrate support for the pro-democracy movement in the Chinese capital.

There were only two comparable incidents in this century.

- In 2003, 500,000 people marched in protest against Article 23 legislation and in defence of Hong Kong's values (to quote Tsang Yam-kuen).[65]
- In 2012, a campaign against the proposed National Education syllabus was supported by 100,000 signatures as well as hunger strikes and repeated mass protests around the Central Government Offices.

The community was prepared to take to the streets far more frequently in this century. But Hong Kong's 'polite politics' remained the norm.

- Between 1975 and 1995, there were on average 182 public protests, processions or demonstrations a year.
  Less than 1.5 per cent led to even minor violence.[66]
- From 2002 to 2012, the total number of public protests, processions and demonstrations each year increased from 2,303 to 7,529. The number of participants prosecuted was trivial: 29 in 2002 and 31 in 2012.[67]

Other indicators of social conflict showed no deterioration in this century (see Table 2.1). The overall crime rate actually dropped. Industrial disputes remained rare and were only occasionally large in scale, regardless of stagnant wages and the level of unemployment. The dispute which has attracted the most public attention so far in this century was a 40-day stoppage by 450 workers at a container terminal in 2013. The rest of the port was unaffected, and the overall economic costs were marginal.[68] Polite politics and social discipline were very much in evidence, and a striking feature of the dispute was that much of the battle was conducted in the courts over the right of strikers and their supporters to picket the business premises of the terminal's ultimate owner.

Table 2.1
Social harmony indicators

Year	2001	2006	2011
Average monthly earnings	HK$10,000	HK$10,000	HK$11,300
Unemployment rate (per cent)	5.1	4.8	3.4
Industrial disputes (total days lost)	780	54	590
Crime rate (reported crime per 100,000)	1,087	1,183	1,084

The people of Hong Kong continued to display exemplary political maturity and social discipline. Personal dissatisfaction at flawed government policies which caused a shortage of modern social services and their increased costs to the public noted earlier in this chapter did not turn into collective disorder in retaliation against the ruling elite or its property. The traditional political 'conservatism' was conspicuous even among the younger age groups, a government-commissioned research project found in 2010, despite government and media concern about the rise of political activism and social protest among the so-called '80s generation'. Its members were, if anything, less resentful of the influence of big business and more optimistic than older groups with whom, overall, they shared common political attitudes. This research project also noted that the younger generation 'have not developed distinctive attitudes towards social justice or opportunities' nor did they identify themselves as supporters of either 'the pan-democratic camp or the government'.[69]

Nevertheless, nothing, it seemed, could convince the government-business nexus that Hong Kong was not about to become ungovernable. A member of the government's prestigious Commission for Strategic Development claimed in 2010, for example, that an 'outright "uprising" and "liberation"' was being planned by 'dissidents' and that 'some of our officials still insist they are obliged by law to fund and assist these seditious acts'.[70]

Badge of Shame

Surprisingly, it was the unequal distribution of incomes rather than poverty itself which caused the most serious political embarrassment for the government-business nexus. The publication every five years of the latest Gini Coefficients and the related census data showing how incomes had grown still more unequal was not easily shrugged off (see Table 2.2). The statistics became a badge of shame as Hong Kong was found to rank 'worst among developed nations' for income inequality.[71]

Table 2.2
Gini Coefficients: Household income disparity, Hong Kong and Mainland 1971–2011[72]

Year	1971	1981	1991	2001	2006	2011
Hong Kong Gini Coefficients	0.430	0.451	0.476	0.525	0.533	0.537
Mainland Gini Coefficients	N.A.	0.288	0.282	0.412	0.487	0.477

N.A.: not available

Hong Kong government economists argued that the very high levels of income disparity were an unavoidable consequence of changes in the population structure and of the shift from manufacturing to services.[73] Their professional analysis did not placate a society which was highly sensitive to its international reputation. A 2008 United Nations study rated income distribution in Hong Kong as the most unequal among Asian cities and 'relatively high' by world standards.[74] The embarrassment to the ruling elite was all the greater since comparisons with Korea, Singapore and Taiwan and their Gini Coefficients indicated that a highly unequal distribution of incomes was not an inevitable feature of Asian capitalism or of 'Confucian' societies.[75]

The government sought to discredit the arithmetic of inequality by disputing the relevance of the Gini Coefficient to Hong Kong's circumstances.[76] Officials got considerable support from the business community. A prominent business member of the legislature, for example, argued that it was misleading 'to include the wealth generated by the city at the international level in the computation of its Gini Coefficient'.[77] With great reluctance, a Commission on Poverty was established in 2005 headed by the Financial Secretary who was personally very doubtful about whether poverty could be measured.[78] The Commission's endeavours seem to have brought little improvement to the lives of the most deprived and disadvantaged.

Tsang Yam-kuen appealed for the public to realise that the gap between rich and poor was one of the 'inevitable phenomena' of capitalist societies, something that cannot be avoided except 'in a socialist state in which everyone receives the same wages'.[79] Ironically, the Mainland's experience indicated that a return to 'socialism' was not the only way to reduce the Gini Coefficient. The Chinese nation had experienced a very sharp rise in income inequality during the break-neck growth after the adoption of Deng Xiaoping's 1978 economic reforms. In response, the Mainland authorities in this century had described a Gini Coefficient of 0.45 as the 'international alert line for wealth gap', and they tried to adjust policies when this danger point was reached.[80] Nevertheless, the Mainland Gini Coefficient rose from 0.479 in 2003 to a peak of 0.491 in 2008. Meanwhile, the process of dismantling the remaining state controls and reducing the state-owned sector continued uninterrupted, and the Gini Coefficient had fallen back to 0.474 by 2012. This level was still too high for comfort as far as the nation's leaders were concerned, and they continued to tackle the income gap by making urgent efforts to raise the earnings of low income groups.[81]

By contrast, Table 2.2 shows, Hong Kong's Gini Coefficient had been well above 0.5 from the start of this century. But pious hope was literally all that the second Chief Executive had to offer when challenged about income inequality and the rise in poverty. 'We hope that people who are living at the grass-roots level this year will be able to enjoy better lives in five years,' he stated in 2007. In addition, he declared, education to prevent intergenerational poverty is of 'paramount importance'.[82] His remedies failed. Life for the less well-off had not been materially improved by 2012, the 'Introduction' pointed out. As for education, Chapter 5 will show that the quality of schooling that a child could enjoy had come to depend on family income more than ever before in this century. The gap between rich and poor actually widened dramatically in terms of access to university education between 1991 and 2011.[83]

The Gini Coefficient continued to trouble Hong Kong's rulers. It seemed so unlikely that the community could continue to tolerate passively the economic and political arrangements that allowed the rich to take an increasing share of Hong Kong's wealth while the government enforced queues and rationing on the users of essential social programmes. The third Chief Executive made the revival of a Commission on Poverty a high priority although its agenda did not suggest that its deliberations would reduce poverty and cure its causes any more successfully than its 2005 predecessor.

Political Risk Crowds out Class Conflict

Why, it must be asked, have Hong Kong politics remained so polite and social hardships been so patiently endured? The conventional explanation has long been that, in the last resort, the Chinese community was uninterested in conventional politics and concerned solely with its financial wellbeing.[84] In reality, the community has been obsessed with political risk since the 1980s: the fear that Hong Kong's very special way of life could be brought to an abrupt end. Society knew that its separate identity depended on the tolerance of China's leaders and their confidence that Hong Kong was contributing substantially to the national interest.

The dividing line in local politics was not class conflict or inequality but the stand that individual politicians and parties took on the implementation of 'one country, two systems' and Hong Kong's 'high degree of autonomy'.[85] The statistics quoted earlier in this chapter on major public demonstrations indicate how dominant has been the Mainland factor in the political consciousness of Hong Kong. Little room has been left for lobbying on behalf of the deprived, the disabled and the destitute in the last three decades, as Chapter 7 will discuss.

As a result, the community took a pragmatic view of the superior benefits attainable under the present political arrangements and which would be in danger if the current system were abolished. In this sophisticated society, it was the efficiency of the system that counted. But the public was also very aware of the areas of government in which personal incompetence was dangerous. Most conspicuously, economic and financial management. The community grasped at once how perilous were the economic decisions being made by the Tung Chee Hwa administration in response to the downturn in 1997. Public trust in the government collapsed, as Chapter 1 explained, and so did consumer and investor confidence. But the underlying resilience of the economy and the robustness of the financial system gradually offset the despondency preached by Tung and his team. Confidence had revived by the end of 1999, when it reached the point of 'general bullishness' (except for jobs), according to the official polls.[86]

Shortly before 1997, the Hong Kong Transition Project had found a general acceptance of the existing system of public finances, with its principles of low taxation and small government. A decade later, attitudes were much the same. There was no indication that calls for political reforms were linked to ambitions 'to open up the treasury to buy favor with the populace'. Indeed, a striking feature of the results of the Transition Project's research was how little support existed for improving CSSA benefits. The public was sceptical about the provision of more generous welfare payments for the most vulnerable and disadvantaged groups in society. (Chapter 6 will show how much of this scepticism had been generated by government misinformation.) Less than 30 per cent of those surveyed were in favour of increasing CSSA payments, while a quarter of the respondents thought that benefits should be cut.[87]

Tolerating the Tycoons

A Hong Kong Transition Project survey in 2010 showed that distrust of the ruling elite had not become universal and that the poorest members of society were not the most resentful of the pro-business bias of decision-makers. Of those with monthly family incomes below HK$5,000, 36 per cent felt that official policies were fair (compared with an average of only 27 per cent for all income groups). On the issue of political reforms, the richest members of society were the most optimistic that more democracy would lead to more equitable policies. Among those with monthly family incomes of HK$60,000 and above, some 60 per cent believed that political reforms would lead to fairer policies (compared with an average of only 50 per cent for all income groups).[88]

A 2011 Chinese University survey showed that Hong Kong was still not an envious society. The report's authors pointed out that hostility to the rich was much less widespread than was generally assumed, and the community remained far from radical in its views on the growing gap between rich and poor. Indeed, the public's attitudes towards unequal incomes, social spending and 'welfare' generally would be classified as 'conservative' in Western democracies and closer to 'Republican' in the United States and 'Thatcherite' in the United Kingdom than to 'socialism'. More than half those surveyed believed that income distribution was unfair, and 59 per cent believed that the interests of the rich were the priority concern of the government. But less than half believed that the unequal distribution of wealth was harmful. In addition, considerable scepticism had developed by 2011 about the statutory minimum wage as a measure to relieve poverty.[89]

'Local big business leaders' had been regarded in 2002 as having 'too much' influence, but 49 per cent of those polled described that influence as either 'reasonable' or 'small'.[90] Resentments were rising, however, and according to a 2010 survey by the Hong Kong Transition Project, well over 60 per cent of the community believed that the government was guilty of favouritism and generally made policies 'unfairly'.[91] The property conglomerates had long been identified by the community as the biggest beneficiaries of government generosity. A Chinese University survey the following year reported that 66 per cent of those questioned believed that developers exercised 'hegemony' over the government. An almost identical number felt that developers pursued profits regardless of any social responsibilities.[92]

In general, nevertheless, dissatisfaction with the rich and their privileged position in the political system had risen relatively slowly despite the widening wealth gap, the decline in the government's performance, the deterioration in the economic prospects of the young in particular and the increased costs to ordinary families of housing and key social services. Which helps to explain why social conflict has not been a feature of Hong Kong life.

Conclusions: The Masses Are the Real Masters

The irony of Hong Kong's political situation was that the community remained the ultimate judge of whether its rulers should survive. The Basic Law allocated power and influence in greatest measure to the rich and left little room for either political change or social reform. Power within the administration was centralised in the hands of the Chief Executive. Formal accountability to the people of Hong Kong was limited. Nevertheless, the rulers who lost the community's trust suffered an ignominious fate.

When Tung Chee Hwa was making his final bid to avoid leaving office in 2005, he publicly confessed that his government had ignored the public's needs. He acknowledged that 'shortcomings and inadequacies have undermined the credibility of our policymaking capability and our ability to govern'.

> In formulating policies, we fell short of 'thinking what people think' and 'addressing people's pressing needs'. Second, we were not sufficiently mindful of the impact of some policies on the community's capacity to bear and the potentially controversial nature of these policies. We introduced too many reform measures too hastily, putting heavy burdens on our people. We also lacked a sense of crisis, political sensitivity as well as the necessary experience and capability to cope with political and economic changes. We were indecisive when dealing with emergencies.[93]

Tsang Yam-kuen replaced him as Chief Executive with a promise to avoid Tung's mistakes. 'It is very important to know what citizens are concerned about the most and what their needs are,' Tsang told the

People's Daily shortly after taking office, '[o]nly people-first governance can win extensive support from citizens.'[94] By 2008, he was making his own self-criticism after he realised that public trust was ebbing.

> People have doubts about certain issues: Have the core values of the HKSAR Government changed? Is the Government trustworthy? Is the Government fair and impartial? Is it less capable than before? Does the Government still adhere to the principle of meritocracy? Does it take into account public opinion in formulating policies?[95]

His term ended with him standing shamefaced before the Legislative Council acknowledging his intimate links with the wealthy and his remoteness from the standards of behaviour demanded by the people of Hong Kong.

> The mass media have recently disclosed that I accepted my friends' hospitality involving travels on private yachts and private jets, and that I have rented a private property in Shenzhen with the intention of using it as my residence after retirement. Such media reports have led the public to question my integrity and conduct as Chief Executive . . . my 45 years of experience in public service . . . has created 'blind spots' that make me overlook the fact that as times change, public expectations have also changed and people have turned more demanding towards public officers.[96]

The third Chief Executive was always going to face a serious challenge to his political credibility. He had been a member of the Executive Council, the Special Administrative Region's highest policy-making body, since 1997 and, as Convenor, the Council's most senior member since 1998. It was not that he never expressed dissatisfaction with the performance of the previous Tung and Tsang administrations. His occasional public criticism could be biting although always discreetly presented.[97] But Leung's role as Convenor obliged him to publicly praise the contents of the annual Policy Addresses and Budget Speeches, year after year. He was left thoroughly identified with official policies. Not until the eve of his election campaign for Chief Executive did he manage to distance himself significantly from Tsang Yam-kuen through an attack on the government's defective housing and anti-poverty measures.[98]

Leung's bid to win the public's trust was further handicapped from the very start of his term of office when confronted with a wave of allegations which grew increasingly serious. They began with media reports of illegal or unauthorised building works at his luxury residences in the exclusive Peak area. Allegations mushroomed in spite of his explanations.[99] Then came sensational reporting about the role of business contacts in mobilising support for his successful election campaign and their expectations of prestigious appointments, locally and nationally.[100]

Leung's standing was further shaken as Executive Councillors and ministers were forced to step down to deal with personal and business embarrassments within months of their appointment.

When a political system is as dominated by business interests as it is in Hong Kong and where, as a matter of official policy, social expenditure is not permitted to hinder the pursuit of profits, the credibility of both the policy-makers and their decisions must always be in danger. This chapter has shown that the community possessed considerable reserves of patience in the face of unsympathetic treatment by the government-business nexus. The public's preference for polite and tolerant politics had its limits, nevertheless, and, even in the absence of universal suffrage, the people of Hong Kong were well able to hold political leaders to account when they forfeited public trust.

The most striking conclusion of this chapter is that the community does not judge the government and its merits by the social benefits which it provides. Income inequality does not provoke unrest, and the affluent do not arouse envy, however unfairly the workforce is rewarded for its sustained high productivity and its resilience. Incompetence is criticised but is not politically fatal. The real test for Chief Executives and their ministers turns out to be mostly about their ethics. As Tsang Yam-kuen confessed to the legislature, a lengthy period in high office can unfortunately blunt one's sensitivity to the rules that society assumes apply to all. On this analysis, the real threat to the governability of Hong Kong starts with misconduct by those in power.

Notes

1. Lu Ping, Hong Kong and Macao Office Director, *New China News Agency*, press release, 30 May 1996.
2. Yash Ghai, *Hong Kong's New Constitutional Order: The Resumption of Chinese Sovereignty and the Basic Law* (Hong Kong: Hong Kong University Press, 1997), especially pp. 139, 270, 406–10, 465 and 468.
3. The Mainland's pre-1997 view of 'capitalist' Hong Kong was recorded in the two-volume study, *Hong Kong's Economy*, in the official Chinese research series on 'The Return of Hong Kong'. The second volume is simply a directory of 109 of Hong Kong's leading tycoons. Chen Duo and Cai Chimeng, *Xianggang de Jingji Yi* and Yin Chongjing and Cao Huanguang (eds.), *Xianggang de Jingji Er* (Beijing: Xinhua chubanshe, 1996). On the role of business in the pre-1997 political system, see Ambrose Yeo-chi King, 'Administrative Absorption of Politics in Hong Kong: Emphasis on the Grass Roots Level', in Ambrose Y. C. King and Rance P. L. Lee (eds.), *Social Life and Development in Hong Kong* (Hong Kong: Chinese University Press, 1981), pp. 129–30.

4. The strength of these suspicions was illustrated by a national figure quoted as accusing the colonial administration of clandestine activities to disrupt Hong Kong's political environment, to despoil its economy and to impoverish to public finances. Bao Xin, 'Letter from Hong Kong', *Liaowang*, 28 March 1994. See also Joseph Y. S. Cheng, 'Towards the Establishment of a New Order', in Beatrice Leung and Joseph Cheng (eds.), *Hong Kong SAR: In Pursuit of Domestic and International Order* (Hong Kong: Chinese University Press, 1997), pp. 293–4.

5. For example, *Wen Wei Po*, 4 March 1993; *New China News Agency*, 8 March 1994; Sammy W. S. Chiu, 'Social Welfare', in Nyaw Mee-kau and Li Si-ming (eds.), *The Other Hong Kong Report 1996* (Hong Kong: Chinese University Press, 1996), p. 431.

6. Zhou Nan, New China News Agency Hong Kong Branch Director, speech at the Hong Kong Management Association annual fellowship dinner, *Zhongguo Xinwen She*, 16 November 1994.

7. The initial challenges which the national pension initiatives encountered were reported in *Renmin Ribao*, 14 June and 14 August 2000. On the leadership's commitment to pension reforms, see Labour and Social Security Minister, Zhang Zuoji, *Renmin Ribao*, 22 June 2000, and former Prime Minister, Li Peng, *New China News Agency*, 25 August 2000.

8. Benny Tai Yiu-ting, 'The Development of Constitutionalism in Hong Kong', in Raymond Wacks (ed.), *The New Legal Order in Hong Kong* (Hong Kong: Hong Kong University Press, 1999), p. 73.

9. These 'arrivals' were 'working in the Liaison Office . . . the Office of the Commissioner of the Ministry of Foreign Affairs . . . Chinese enterprises . . . set up in Hong Kong with the approval of the Mainland authorities'. Excluded were members of the People's Liberation Army. Raymond Tam Chi-yuen, Secretary for Constitutional and Mainland Affairs, *Hong Kong Hansard* (*HH* hereafter), 18 January 2012, p. 4689.

10. See the complaints by Donald Tsang Yam-kuen, Chief Secretary, reported in *Hong Kong Economic Journal*, 13 November 2003.

11. Tung Chee Hwa was far more relaxed addressing business audiences than in discussing social issues. Compare, for example, his speeches recorded at *GIS*, 8 April 2000 and 1 June 2001 with those of 4 May and 4 August 2000 and 29 March 2001.

12. Lau Siu-kai, 'Government and Political Change in the Hong Kong Special Administrative Region', in James C. Hsiung (ed.), *Hong Kong the Super Paradox: Life after Return to China* (London: Macmillan, 2000), pp. 49–51.

13. His friendships were explained in Donald Tsang, Chief Executive, *HH*, 1 March 2012, pp. 6926, 6942, 6950, 6052.

14. Details of the controversy were recorded in *Ming Pao Daily*, 18 and 21 January 2013 and *Hong Kong Economic Journal*, 21 January 2013.

15. The government-business nexus, its origins and its operations, are discussed at length in *Uneasy Partners: The Conflict Between Public Interest and Private Profit in Hong Kong* (Hong Kong: Hong Kong University Press, 2009), second edition.

16. An excellent analysis of the relationships is Tai-lok Lui, 'How a Fragmented Business-Government Alliance Has Helped Change Hong Kong's Political Order', *Hong Kong Journal*, No. 10 (April 2008), pp. 1–9.
17. Over 100 had been appointed to statutory bodies and advisory committees regardless of experience or qualifications according to an editorial in *Ming Pao Daily*, 9 August 2010.
18. Data were published by Gary Cheung, *South China Morning Post*, 12 April 2010.
19. Tung, *HH*, 8 October 1998.
20. Dubravko Mihaljek et al., *People's Republic of China — Hong Kong Special Administrative Region: Recent Economic Developments* (Washington: International Monetary Fund, 1998), pp. 60, 67.
21. *GIS*, 17 May and 3 August 2000.
22. *GIS*, 29 April 1999.
23. Editorial, *Ming Pao Daily*, 27 January 2005; John Tsang Chun-wah, Secretary for Commerce, Industry and Technology, *GIS*, 12 January 2006.
24. Trade and Industry Bureau, *Government Response to Consumer Council's Report Entitled "Competition Policy: The Key to Hong Kong's Future Economic Success"* (November 1997) and Economic Services Bureau, *Legislative Council Panel on Economic Services. Development and Competitiveness of the Hong Kong Container Port* (November 1998).
25. Gregory So Kam-leung, Secretary for Commerce and Economic Development, *GIS*, 10 December 2012.
26. A history of the protracted campaign to delay the competition legislation and the unconvincing case made by its opponents can be found in Leo F. Goodstadt, 'Hong Kong — Business Friendly but Not Competitive', *Hong Kong Economic Journal* (October 2011), pp. 72–6.
27. Communications and Technology Branch, *Public Consultation Paper on 2004 Digital 21 Strategy* (Hong Kong: CITB, 2003), pp. 1–4; OFTA, *Report on the Effectiveness of Competition in Hong Kong's Telecommunications Market: An International Comparison June 2003* (Hong Kong: Spectrum Strategy Consultants, 2003).
28. *GIS*, 25 October 2009; Norman T. L. Chan, Hong Kong Monetary Authority Chief Executive, *Hong Kong Monetary Authority*, 14 December 2009.
29. Professor Anthony Cheung Bing-leung, Secretary for Transport and Housing, *GIS*, 28 October 2012.
30. The developers' grievances were well aired in the media. See, for example, *Hong Kong Economic Times*, 7 and 24 November 2012; *Ming Pao Daily*, 7 December 2012; *Hong Kong Economic Daily*, 19 November 2012.
31. Security Bureau, 'Proposals to Implement Article 23 of the Basic Law. Consultation Document' (Hong Kong, September 2002), p. 4.
32. Premier Wen Jiabao reported in *Renmin Ribao*, 30 June 2003.
33. The unhesitating business support was all the more striking because some prominent members of the professional elite argued that Hong Kong officials were to blame as they had mishandled the whole affair. See, for example, the comments of Yang Ti-lang, former Chief Justice and member

of Tung Chee Hwa's first Executive Council, interviewed in *Ming Pao Daily*, 9 September 2003.

34. For examples of the financial support, see Vice-Premier Wen Jiabao, *New China News Agency*, 17 November 2000; Vice-President Zeng Qinghong quoted in Tony Chan, *China Daily*, 7 June 2004; *Financial Times* 21 May 2004; editorial, *Ming Pao Daily*, 12 May 2006.

35. Frederick Ma Si-hang, Secretary for Commerce and Economic Development, *HH*, 28 November 2007, p. 2219.

36. Some indirect assistance was made available through financial support and other schemes to assist mainly small and medium-sized enterprises, as the previous chapter explained.

37. Donald Tsang, Chief Executive, *GIS*, 12 November 2008.

38. *Hong Kong Annual Report* 1951 (Hong Kong: Government of Hong Kong, 1952), pp. 7, 9; Wenguang Shao, *China, Britain and Businessmen: Political and Commercial Relations, 1949–57* (Basingstoke: Macmillan, 1991), p. 106; Frank M. Cain, 'Exporting the Cold War: British Responses to the USA's Establishment of COCOM, 1947–51', *Journal of Contemporary History*, Vol. 29, No. 3 (July 1994), p. 515.

39. Sir Lesley Robinson (Board of Trade) quoted in (12) Appendix C, draft minutes of a meeting by the Financial Secretary (J. J. Cowperthwaite) and Board members with the Board of Trade in London on 16 August 1961. HKRS270–5-56 'Cotton Advisory Board. Minutes of Meeting'.

40. See, for example, Carrie Lam Cheng Yuet-ngor, Chief Secretary, *GIS*, 14 November 2012; John Tsang, Financial Secretary, *GIS*, 7 and 26 November 2012.

41. See Chris King-chi Chan, 'Labour Policies under Hu-Wen's Regime: Transformation and Challenges' and Alvin Y. So, 'New Labour Law and Its Implication for the Human Rights Regime in China', in Joseph Y. S. Cheng (ed.), *China: A New Stage of Development for an Emerging Superpower* (Hong Kong: City University of Hong Kong Press, 2012).

42. Leung Chun-ying, Chief Executive, *GIS*, 29 November 2012.

43. This total was equivalent to RMB 10.72 trillion. 'China's local government debts exceed 10t yuan', *New China News Agency*, 27 June 2011. The continuing scale of this daunting breakdown in central control at the lower levels of state administration can be judged from 'China to further check local government financing', *New China News Agency*, 31 December 2012.

44. Raymond Kwok, vice chairman of Sun Hung Kai Properties interviewed by Bruce Gilley, 'Smooth Operator', *Far Eastern Economic Review*, 25 May 2000.

45. On business opposition to political reform, see Sonny Shiu-Hing Lo, *The Dynamics of Beijing-Hong Kong Relations: A Model for Taiwan?* (Hong Kong: Hong Kong University Press, 2008), pp. 15, 75.

46. Tung, *HH*, 12 January 2005, p. 3262.

47. Ghai, *Hong Kong's New Constitutional Order: The Resumption of Chinese Sovereignty and the Basic Law*, pp. 260–1.

48. Academics grasped the significance of these issues at an early stage. For example, Byron S. J. Weng, 'The Hong Kong Model of "One Country, Two Systems": Promises and Problems', in Peter Wesley-Smith and Albert Chen

(eds.), *The Basic Law and Hong Kong's Future* (Hong Kong: Butterworths, 1988), p. 81; Lau Siu-kai, 'Political Reform and Political Development in Hong Kong: Dilemmas and Choices', in Y. C. Jao et al. (eds.), *Hong Kong and 1997: Strategies for the Future* (Hong Kong: Centre of Asian Studies, University of Hong Kong, 1985), pp. 30–1.

49. Regina Ip Lau Suk-yee, Secretary for Security, *GIS*, 23 August 2000.

50. Mrs Fan enjoyed the confidence of China's leaders and had a long record of service at the highest levels of Hong Kong's political system both before and after 1997. Wikileaks, 'Former Legco President Discusses Hong Kong's Political Challenges', 8 December 2008. URL: cable/2008/12/08HONGKONG2213.html

51. The data are from '2011–12 Policy Address and 2012–13 Budget consultation sessions already conducted', 30 August 2011. URL: www.policyaddress.gov.hk/consultation/eng/sessions.html. See also, Leo F. Goodstadt, 'Government and the People: Friends or Foes?', *Hong Kong Economic Journal Monthly*, 10 December, 2011, pp. 50–3.

52. Jasper Tsang Yok-sing, Legislative Council President, 'Can the LegCo-ExCo Relationship Be Improved?', speech to Hong Kong Democratic Foundation, 5 February 2010. URL: www.hkdf.org/newsarticles.asp?show=newsarticles&newsarticle=263

53. Stephen Lam Sui-lung, Chief Secretary, *GIS*, 3 October 2011.

54. The implications of this label in the context of Chinese Communist Party history were set out by Frank Ching, *South China Morning Post*, 30 January 2013.

55. Education Bureau, 'Legislative Council Panel on Education. Monitoring of Direct Subsidy Scheme (DSS) Schools' (CB(2)2073/08–09(01), June 2009), pp. 1–6.

56. Audit Commission, *Report No. 55*, 'Chapter 1 Education Bureau: Administration of the Direct Subsidy Scheme' (25 October 2010), pp. 16–20, 26–7, 33–6, 41–4, 48.

57. Dr York Chow Yat-Ngok, Secretary for Food and Health, *HH*, 27 January 2010, pp. 4706–8; 9 November 2011, pp. 1692–7.

58. Audit Commission, *Report No. 59*, 'Chapter 3: Food and Health Bureau, Department of Health. Regulatory control of private hospitals', (26 October 2012), pp. v, vi, 44–8; 'Chapter 4: Food and Health Bureau, Department of Health, Lands Department. Land grants for private hospital development', pp. v, vi, 5–7.

59. Eliza W. Y. Lee, 'The Renegotiation of the Social Pact in Hong Kong: Economic Globalisation, Socio-economic Change, and Local Politics', *Journal of Social Policy*, Vol. 34, Part 2 (April 2005), pp. 302–3.

60. These officials also supported greater importation of Mainland workers in direct conflict with their ally, the Federation of Trade Union, which was struggling to maintain credibility among the labour force. John P. Burns, 'Civil Service Systems in Transition: Hong Kong, China and 1997', in Ming K. Chan (ed.), *The Challenge of Hong Kong's Reintegration With China* (Hong Kong: Hong Kong University Press, 1997), p. 40. In the event, the Federation faithfully followed the official line.

61. Hong Kong Transition Project, 'Parties, Policies and Political Reform in Hong Kong' (Hong Kong Transition Project and National Democratic Institute for International Affairs, May 2006), pp. 46–7.
62. Donald Tsang, Chief Executive, *HH*, 12 October 2005, p. 24.
63. Donald Tsang, *HH*, 13 October 2010, p. 47. His predecessor also expressed concerns about social harmony though less colourfully.
64. Charles F. Emmons, *Hong Kong Prepares for 1997: Politics and Emigration in 1997* (Hong Kong: Centre of Asian Studies, University of Hong Kong, 1988), pp. 12, 103.
65. Donald Tsang, Chief Secretary, *GIS*, 19 September 2003.
66. The data and conclusions presented here are based on the statistics and analysis presented in Anthony Bing-leung Cheung and Kin-sheun Louie, 'Social Conflicts in Hong Kong: 1975–1986', and Lau Siu-kai and Wan Po-san, 'Social Conflicts in Hong Kong: 1987–1995', in Lau Siu-kai (ed.), *Social Development and Political Change in Hong Kong* (Hong Kong: Chinese University Press, 2000).
67. Lai Tung-kwo, Secretary for Security, *HH*, 19 December 2012, 'Annex', p. 3861; 27 March 2013, 'Annex: Figures on Arrest and Prosecution during Public Order Events from 2004 to the first two months of 2013', pp. 7999–8002.
68. See the initial estimate of the strike's costs to the work force and its impact on the port's operations given by Matthew Cheung Kin-chung, Secretary for Labour and Welfare, *HH*, 8 May 2013.
69. Wu Xiaogang, 'Hong Kong's Post 80s Generation: Profiles and Predicaments. A CPU Commissioned Report', Centre for Applied Social and Economic Research, Hong Kong University of Science and Technology (Central Policy Unit, May 2010), pp. 35–8.
70. This individual's name was not disclosed by the official Mainland publication. 'Full-scale Showdown', *China Daily*, 2 February 2010.
71. Zhao Xiaobin et al., 'Income Inequalities under Economic Restructuring in Hong Kong', *Asian Survey*, Vol. 44, No. 3 (May–June, 2004), p. 443. For a careful analysis of the earlier data, see Hon-Kwong Lui, *Income Inequality and Economic Development* (Hong Kong: City University of Hong Kong Press, 1997), pp. 1–2, 6–7 and Chapter 3.
72. Economic Analysis Division, *Half-Yearly Economic Report 2012* (Hong Kong: SAR Government, 2012), 'Chart 1: Household income disparity of Hong Kong widened most appreciably during 1980s–90s', p. 86; *Renmin Ribao*, 19 June 2003 and 20 July 2006; *New China News Agency*, 18 January 2013.
73. Economic Analysis Division, *Half-Yearly Economic Report 2012*, 'Box 5.2: The Gini coefficient of Hong Kong: trends and interpretations'.
74. UN-Habitat, *State of the World's Cities 2008/2009 Harmonious Cities* (London: Earthscan, 2008), p. 24.
75. Kui-Wai Li, *The Hong Kong Economy: Recovery and Restructuring* (Singapore: McGraw-Hill Education (Asia), 2006), 'Table 1.4: The Gini Coefficients of Four Asian Economies', p. 14.
76. See, for example, Henry Tang Ying-yen, Financial Secretary, *HH*, 8 February 2006, p. 4198.

77. Sophie Leung Lau Yau-fun, *HH*, 29 October 2009, pp. 964–7.
78. Henry Tang, Financial Secretary, *HH*, 15 February 2006, p. 4498.
79. Donald Tsang, Chief Executive, *HH*, 12 January 2006, pp. 3880–1.
80. On the Mainland's policy responses to growing inequality, see *Renmin Ribao*, 19 December 2005. A report of a 'keynote speech' by President Hu Jintao appeared to set 0.40 as the danger zone. *New China News Agency*, 15 October 2007.
81. *New China News Agency*, 18 January 2013.
82. Donald Tsang, Chief Executive, *HH*, 5 July 2007, p. 10167.
83. 'The university degree enrolment rate of young people (aged 19 and 20) living in the top 10% richest families (48.2%) is now 3.7 times that of those living in poverty (13%), a much wider gap than 20 years ago (1.2 times)'. Professor Chou Kee-lee, 'HKIEd Study: Disparity in Higher Education Attainment Is Widening between Rich and Poor', Hong Kong Institute of Education (31 January 2013). URL: www.ied.edu.hk/media/news. php?id=20130131
84. Michael E. DeGolyer and Janet Lee Scott, 'The Myth of Political Apathy in Hong Kong', *Annals*, Volume 547 (September 1996), p. 69.
85. This feature of the political landscape was already very visible in the early 1990s. Leung Sai-wing, 'The "China Factor" in the 1991 Legislative Council Election: The June 4th Incident and Anti-Communist China Syndrome', in Lau Siu-kai and Louie Kin-sheun (eds.), *Hong Kong Tried Democracy. The 1991 Elections in Hong Kong* (Hong Kong: Hong Kong Institute of Asia-Pacific Studies, Chinese University of Hong Kong, 1993), p. 192.
86. *GIS*, 6 December 1999.
87. Hong Kong Transition Project, 'Parties, Policies and Political Reform in Hong Kong', 'Table 58: Would you support or oppose the SAR Government to adopt the following policies? FEB Ranked by combined support level', p. 47; 'Table 59: Which of these areas of government expenditure would you cut or increase spending on? FEB Ranked by Combined Increase', pp. 48–9.
88. Hong Kong Transition Project, 'Calm after the Storm? Hong Kong People Respond to Reform', 'Chart/Table 19 Does government make policies fairly by income?', p. 24; 'Will reforms make government policies fairer by income?', p. 25.
89. Hong Kong Institute of Asia-Pacific Studies in cooperation with the Hong Kong Professionals and Senior Executives Association, 'Disparity of Wealth Research Project Findings', 1 December 2011.
90. Hong Kong Transition Project, *Winter of Despair. Confidence and Legitimacy in Crisis in the Hong Kong SAR (December 2001)* (Hong Kong: Hong Kong Baptist University, 2002), pp. 19, 26, 27.
91. Hong Kong Transition Project, 'Calm after the Storm? Hong Kong People Respond to Reform', 'Chart/Table 1 Do you think government currently makes policies in general fairly, helping or hurting all parties equally, or unfairly, favoring the interests of some over others?', p. 14.
92. Hong Kong Institute of Asia-Pacific Studies, 'Summary of survey of Hong Kong people's views on "real estate hegemony"', 10 August 2011.
93. Tung, *HH*, 12 January 2005, p. 3263.

94. Donald Tsang, Chief Executive, 'Hong Kong Dream' interview, *Renmin Ribao*, 1 July 2005.
95. Donald Tsang, Chief Executive, *HH*, 15 October 2008, p. 56.
96. Donald Tsang, Chief Executive, *HH*, 1 March 2012, pp. 6926–7, 6929.
97. A notable example was a formal speech on the declining fortunes of the lower-income groups since 1997. The prepared text pointed no fingers at members of the government. But when Leung departed from his prepared script, he denounced the failure under the first two Chief Executives to match the performance of the last decade of colonial rule. He left it to the media representatives present to report his biting observations. Leung Chun-ying, 'The Real Hong Kong and the Real Politics', speech to the Hong Kong Democratic Foundation (24 September 2009). URL: www.hkdf. org/newsarticles.asp?show=newsarticles&newsarticle=238; 'Exco Chief Says City's Development Has Slowed', *South China Morning Post*, 25 September 2009.
98. Tsang dismissed Leung's criticism as an attempt to curry favour with the community. Donald Tsang, Chief Executive, *HH*, 15 July 2011, pp. 14689–90.
99. Leung Chun-ying, Chief Executive, *GIS*, 23, 24 and 26 November 2012.
100. The original allegations were published in 〈劉夢熊爆料「倒梁」〉 ('Lew Mon-hung's anti-Leung "reverse exposé"'), 《陽光時務週刊》 (*iSun Affairs Weekly*), 24 January, 2013, 26–35. Reactions and implications were summarised in *Ming Pao Daily*, 25 January 2013. For the Chief Executive's threat of legal action in response to these allegations, see *Hong Kong Economic Journal*, 8 February 2013.

3
Housing: Unending Crisis

A family's quality of life depends very heavily on the comfort and convenience of its housing. Hong Kong's misfortune is that its homes are where its Third World legacy is most intractable. The housing stock's defects are often so serious that they threaten health and safety. They have grown beyond the ability of individual families to remedy. The bill to be paid by contemporary society for past neglect has become both onerous and inescapable. Housing is also the challenge which Hong Kong's rulers have consistently underestimated in the past. The third Chief Executive, Leung Chun-ying, called Hong Kong 'a modern, safe, convenient and liveable metropolis'. The disagreeable truth is that this boast does not apply to the home of the average family, as he pointed out.

> Shortage in the supply of housing has pushed up property prices and rental substantially. Many families have to move into smaller or older flats, or even factory buildings. Cramped living space in cage homes, cubicle apartments and sub-divided flats has become the reluctant choice for tens of thousands of Hong Kong people.[1]

These unfortunates are the victims of the refusal by previous administrations over the last half century to frame policies in terms of homes fit for an increasingly prosperous society.

Hong Kong entered this century with a housing heritage that was shameful. Average living density was 150 square feet per person. For families buying their own flats in 1998, the average mortgage absorbed 33 per cent of the household's income.[2] In addition, 235,000 individuals were still living in squatter huts.[3] Housing conditions were to get worse. A 2006 United Nations study found that the relative size of Hong Kong's slum population was increasing at a far higher rate than the average for advanced economies.[4] In 2013, households living in public housing had to have less than 59 square feet per head before being classified as 'overcrowded families' who could seek rehousing.[5]

For such a prosperous community, the housing data were shocking enough. These statistics did not uncover, however, the full inadequacy of the housing stock, much of which had never been fit for human habitation, as this chapter will show. It provided shelter of a sort for most families rather than homes with a decent quality of life for all. The average size of accommodation was so small that privacy was a luxury even though in this century, the 'one-child family' became the norm. Everyone's living standards were depressed by the limited space for furniture and consumer durables. In addition, the average student lacked personal study space. Families could not provide comfort and safety for their elderly or disabled members. The average bathroom and toilet was not easily converted for safe as well as convenient use by those with limited mobility. Narrow corridors and doorways obstructed the use of wheelchairs.

Leung Chun-ying set housing at the heart of his agenda for winning hearts and minds. He was following a well-established but ill-fated tradition. The first Chief Executive, Tung Chee Hwa, had made a dramatic building programme the centrepiece of his plans for the transformation of Hong Kong (and he had appointed Leung as housing overlord in 1997).[6] Tung's ambitious vision was to prove his downfall, as Chapter 1 recounted. Tung had been following the example of a colonial governor, Sir Murray (later Lord) MacLehose, who continues to be lauded for the visionary housing programme launched after his arrival from London in 1971. That too had failed to meet its targets although MacLehose proved better at managing his public image than Tung.[7]

Leung was also to discover soon after taking office that the chances of any rapid increase in the amount of affordable housing were remote. He conceded in his 2013 Policy Address that the supply of new public housing would remain flat for the next four years. After that date, the rate of annual construction was expected to expand by 28 per cent.[8] Leung was trapped by the legacy of Tung's decisions at the start of the century when the government terminated its land and housing programmes. The cumulative consequences of past housing neglect and favouritism towards property interests had become a formidable barrier against any ambitious remedial action.

The New Slums

It was not just the chronic shortfall in the supply of new homes that confronted Leung. He also faced, as he said in his first Policy Address, a daunting legacy of housing that had been built at the cheapest cost and to the lowest specifications in previous decades and mostly neglected by the owners ever since. Officials had long been aware of the threat of dilapidation in high-rise concrete buildings. In 1988, the Housing Authority had started to upgrade the 560 buildings which it had erected before 1973. Because of the complexity of this sort of renovation programme, its final stage was not reached until 2009, by which time, it had been necessary to launch a new monitoring and renovation scheme.[9]

The private sector was in worse straits, and schemes launched under previous administrations had not halted the deterioration of the housing stock. Private owners had mostly been unaware that the maximum design life of their concrete flats was only 50 years. In addition, the government had left unresolved for decades the obstacles to adequate management and maintenance of the average block of flats when under multiple-ownership.

By 2011, the private sector had become a time bomb. Its alarming dimensions had been uncovered by the Urban Renewal Authority (URA), whose public statements on social deprivation were remarkably frank and far-sighted for a public body in contemporary Hong Kong. Altogether, 110,000 families were already living in 'homes that are neither healthy nor safe', the URA reported. In these slums, life was made 'miserable by the dirt, decay and lack of amenities that the rest of the community takes for granted'. No less serious was 'the risk from the disease and dangers' in 4,000 buildings erected 50 or more years earlier. They had reached the end of their design life, according to another URA survey, which identified 2,600 of these buildings as 'already substandard'. Typically, three or more families were packed into the average living unit of around 500 square feet. The common areas were filthy and prone to flooding, and there was a constant threat of fires caused by defective electrical wiring and fittings. The total number of 'dilapidated, over-crowded and neglected' buildings with their 'dreadful standards of accommodation' was forecast to rise rapidly because by 2030, Hong Kong would have 16,000 buildings that were 50 or more years old.[10]

For vulnerable groups, the housing crisis of modern Hong Kong was part of the new poverty. Increasingly, the elderly, the unemployed and low-wage individuals and households were forced to seek shelter in the worst of the housing stock, where rents were high, amenities sparse and squalor abounded. The government insisted that these conditions had to be tolerated. In 2012, despite Leung's condemnation of such housing quoted at the start of this chapter, his ministers rejected a call for more humane policies, it is explained below. Instead of a permanent home, housing has been viewed almost universally either in terms of minimal shelter or as an investment asset that would be freely traded in the future.

The Market's Chronic Failure

The government, it was explained in Chapter 1, had withdrawn from the housing market by 2002 (apart from homes for low-income groups), and the private sector was freed from effective competition from the public sector. That move followed an earlier claim by Donald Tsang Yam-kuen when still Financial Secretary, that market forces had ceased to operate 'fairly and freely'. The government was determined, he proclaimed in 2001, to reduce its 'intervention in the housing area, and to restore the proper role of the private residential property market'.[11]

This decision should be seen in the wider context discussed in earlier chapters of the enthusiasm among senior officials for shrinking the public sector as a matter of principle and regardless of social costs. The dominant role of the government in housing was 'an unfortunate thing', Tsang had already observed in 1998, 'In all [other] sectors of the market we are totally free.'[12] His comments ignored the Consumer Council's research into the cost to the community of the lack of competition within the private property sector especially, and the International Monetary Fund's endorsement of calls for a competition law to remedy such abuses.[13]

In practice, the withdrawal of the government from the housing market proved disastrous for the community. A long-term shortage of accommodation became impossible to avoid.

- The annual supply of new public housing fell by 62 per cent: from an annual average of 38,900 units for the period 1997–2002 to 14,600 for the period 2007–12.
- The annual supply from the private sector fell by 45 per cent: from an annual average of 21,900 units for the period 1997–2002 to 9,900 units for the period 2007–12.

A Modern Tragedy

As a dramatic signal of the better world to which the new Special Administrative Region could look forward, Tung Chee Hwa had declared in 1997: 'To me and to the community as a whole, housing is the number one priority.' 'To be able to build these 85,000 [new housing] units is the absolute priority,' he went on.[14] Tung had at his command a public housing model that had been tried and tested in economic fluctuations and political crises for over four decades. His housing policy carefully incorporated this expertise.[15] His intention was not a revolution in the public sector but to make it function faster and more efficiently. His blueprint openly relied on the findings of the colonial administration's Long Term Housing Strategy Review published in early 1997, which had been well publicised and thoroughly discussed by the legislature.[16] From this document was borrowed the main title for Tung's 1998 White Paper on housing, *Homes for Hong Kong People.*[17] Almost immediately, however, his ten-point programme to build 85,000 new homes a year and lift the ratio of home-owners to 70 per cent of the population came under fierce attack.

Initially, his Financial Secretary and future successor, Tsang Yam-kuen, brushed aside any suggestion that Tung's targets might prove over-ambitious, insisting that 'if there is anything which obstructs the target of 85,000, it has to be removed'.[18] Nevertheless, Tung later faced allegations that he had set these daunting targets against the advice of his officials and even before a feasible programme had been drafted. He was accused of adopting a populist strategy designed to dramatically increase the housing supply and bring down market prices.[19] He was blamed for the 40 per cent drop in residential property prices during the first nine months of his programme. By 2003, prices were to have fallen by a full 70 per cent.[20]

Tung was so overwhelmed by this disaster that he ended his involvement in housing policy. In 1997, his responses to personal briefings from the Housing Authority had been lengthy and demonstrated keen personal interest. By the end of 1998, they had been reduced to a formal, two-sentence acknowledgement from his private secretary of receipt of the briefing documents.[21] The public housing programme was virtually abandoned in 2001.[22] Thus ended the government's traditional commitment to ensuring an adequate supply of public housing, both for rent and for sale, to families which could not afford to look for homes in the private sector. This policy had been the showpiece of government social programmes since 1954 and was widely credited with enabling the government to reduce potential social unrest through providing low-rent homes which could help to offset the low wages of the labour force.[23]

The tragedy was that Tung had got off to an excellent start in the public housing sector. The reforming momentum of 1997 was so dynamic that by 2002, some of the community's worst housing problems inherited from the colonial era had been finally overcome and at an even faster rate than Tung had originally planned.[24]

- Average waiting time for public rental housing was reduced from almost seven years to just over three years and, in the case of elderly applicants, from just over three years to 16 months.
- 'Inadequately housed' households were reduced from 170,000 to 100,000.
- Some 68,000 households from older Resettlement Estates were rehoused in modern units.

- Public housing tenants in overcrowded units fell from 8.4 per cent of the total residents to 2.1 per cent.
- The 24 squalid, often rat-infested Temporary Housing Areas and Cottage Areas were finally cleared, and their 12,600 households rehoused.[25]

These were goals which had eluded the last Governor, Christopher (later Lord) Patten. But the achievements only made good shortfalls created by past neglect. They were not enough to offset the calamitous consequences for the future of Tung's decision to hand over responsibility for the supply of housing to the private sector.

A Squalid Heritage

One of Hong Kong's most harmful Third World legacies was the way that the people of Hong Kong had been conditioned continuously since World War II to endure living conditions that were at the very margins of what could be considered fit for human habitation. The community came to take for granted a lack of living space and amenities so acute that quality of life was constrained to an unpleasant degree. The failure to provide decent homes for Hong Kong families can only be fully understood in the context of this historical experience which led the community to tolerate the intolerable for some 70 years.[26]

From the early 1950s, an astonishing surge in the supply of housing got underway in the public and private sectors. But the quality of accommodation in both seems unbearable in retrospect. Public housing standards were kept as low as possible as a matter of official policy, despite complaints from the government's own medical adviser. In the private sector, slum conditions were the norm for existing tenements and for newly built multi-storey buildings, officials complained. They made it plain that families living in squatter huts were far better off.

Squatters: Neither safe not healthy

In 1963, some 585,000 people — 17 per cent of the total population — were still living in squatter huts.[27] They were expected to survive despite health and safety facilities that were outright inhuman. The government provided squatters with only the minimum amenities and services required on 'basic humanitarian, security and public grounds', to quote an official policy document. Any steps 'to introduce or provide services beyond the barest essentials', officials argued, 'would be to run the very real risk of attracting great numbers of people from our pre-war and post-war slums'.[28]

Government policy was to provide only minimal protection against fire hazards in squatter areas, while health and sanitation standards were of the lowest.[29] Thus, in the 1960s, water was supplied on the basis of '1 tap for 500 people' while the allocation of latrines was '1 compartment to 100 people'.[30] Reluctance to improve these levels persisted into the 1970s.[31]

Public housing: Barely tolerable

The public housing programme has been compared by one academic to the state planning of 'some socialist countries'.[32] By 1963, some 463,000 squatters had been moved into permanent housing in the new resettlement estates, which provided homes for 13 per cent of the total population. [33] These families had been freed from life in makeshift shanty huts and from the dangers caused by fires in the dry winters and from the typhoons and landslides of the summer months. But standards in the first Resettlement Blocks were tolerable only by comparison with the grim conditions for the rest of the community.

Densities of occupation were alarming. When the first Resettlement Blocks became available, the Director of Medical and Health Services had protested that 'the standards of accommodation accepted for resettlement are probably the lowest in the world so far as cubic space is concerned'.[34] The statutory minimum was 35 square feet of living space per person, which was not very different from the average in Mainland cities around 1960.[35] The colonial administration discarded this requirement for Resettlement Blocks, however, and an allocation of 24 square feet per adult was approved. But by 1963, this standard was 'being officially depressed', a government report admitted, and average living space of '16 sq.ft. for an adult and 8 sq. ft. for a child' was being tolerated.[36]

There was little privacy either within or outside the home, and initially, there was complete disregard for family comfort and personal dignity. Latrines and washing facilities were communal and shared by all the tenants on a floor. Families had to do their cooking in the corridors. Squalor was a constant threat.[37] In 1965, the government accepted that these primitive standards were no longer tolerable. Construction of 'Mark IV' Resettlement Blocks began, and each flat had its own toilet which freed families from sharing communal latrines for the first time. Public housing projects continued to upgrade facilities and improve living space thereafter.

The colonial administration was determined to exclude 'welfare' from its criteria for allocating public housing. The programme was to be no more than a land clearance exercise to remove squatters from building sites. Social grounds were not approved as a qualification for public housing until 1964, and then on a very limited basis although the government did not face a shortage of funds.[38] Public housing, nevertheless, made possible a major expansion of Hong Kong's social services. Resettlement Estates provided space for rooftop schools and a variety of welfare non-governmental organisations (NGOs) and relief agencies, including facilities for children with impaired hearing, for example. Nothing so convenient and well-organised was available in other urban neighbourhoods.

In 1985, the government faced the first housing bill for its Third World tolerance of corruption which had been allowed to flourish until the creation of the Independent Commission Against Corruption (ICAC) in 1974. Twenty-six Resettlement Blocks built between 1964 and 1973 were found to be so dangerous that 15,000 families were moved out at a cost of HK$800 million to the government. A further 577 blocks built before 1983 were found to be sub-standard as a result of a corrupt conspiracy between civil servants and construction companies.[39] These revelations obliged the government to accept that the earlier Resettlement Blocks were unsatisfactory homes, and it began to rebuild them.[40]

Private sector: Better off as squatters

The private sector underwent a transformation of its housing stock comparable in scale to the early resettlement programme. Between 1956 and 1963, it was officially estimated, 310,500 persons had been evicted from private sector buildings that were to be redeveloped. Many of these families sought shelter in other, increasingly over-crowded premises in the private sector which 'through sheer pressure of demand started turning into near slums' Here, rents were high and key money was demanded for new tenancies.[41]

The demolished tenements were described by the Director of Social Welfare as having been often worse than squatter areas: 'more cramped, insanitary, dark and unhealthy'.[42] Conditions in the new buildings that replaced them were just as dreadful according to a 1963 official Working Party, and tenants would have been better off as squatters.

> . . . it is not unknown for 60 or 70 persons to be living in a three-room flat . . . the W.C.s are as few as the builder could get away with installing; and on many if not most floors the water taps can stay empty even in a good water year because of the inadequacy of the internal supply pipes. The people in these buildings may well present a more serious health hazard, and bring up their children mentally, socially and physically more handicapped or stunted than if they had been in . . . squatter shacks on the hillsides.[43]

If the public sector could not prevent outright swindling by contractors and shoddy work by sub-contractors aided and abetted by extensive corruption (even after the ICAC was set up in 1974), what hope was there for a better performance in the private sector?[44] Indeed, the government stated openly that private construction standards were far lower.[45]

Contemporary Hong Kong: Squalor survives

The drastic reduction in the government's public housing programme in this century made it extremely difficult to rescue families from even the most dangerous and squalid living conditions. There was a lack of spare capacity in the public sector, which meant that private sector tenants were not rehoused even when they were living in rack-rented slums which were in breach of health and safety requirements or which involved illegal sub-division of residential units.

The government tried to pacify critics of the official tolerance of this dangerous and illegal accommodation with sentimental appeals. Many of the owners of 'old and dilapidated buildings' were 'elderly themselves', the legislature was officially informed in 2010, and 'their poorly maintained flats are probably their only assets'. Illegally sub-divided flats should also be viewed, it was suggested, as an understandable — and, by implication, acceptable — response by the property market to 'a growing demand for affordable housing'.[46] The minister responsible for handling this problem was asked by a legislator in 2011 why she did not 'ban sub-divided units across the board' or 'immediately revise the public housing allocation system to enable existing tenants of sub-divided units to be allocated public housing'. Her reply included a repetition of her colonial predecessor's excuse in 1963 for the grim conditions of squatter areas (quoted earlier in this chapter). If public housing were provided on a priority basis for those living in this illegal accommodation, she said, it might result in 'encouraging people to move into sub-divided flats which would worsen the problem'.[47]

Throughout the government's efforts to play down the scale of the scandal, the numbers at risk were seriously underestimated. There was a dearth of statistics which, the government claimed in 2012, would be virtually impossible to overcome. A mere six months later, an officially-sponsored survey revealed that 171,000 individuals were living in subdivided buildings. Almost half their 'homes' lacked one or more 'of the essential facilities (i.e. kitchen or cooking place/toilet/water supply)'.[48]

The URA was left to find a solution. It had launched its original slum clearance programme with a substantial government injection of capital. Its projects depended very heavily, nevertheless, on commercial partnerships with developers. These business deals aroused constant public suspicion that the URA must put the profits of its partners ahead of the public interest.[49] The controversies distracted attention from the urgent need to rehouse over 100,000 families living in the slums which the URA proposed to clear and whose plight it consistently highlighted.

Supply Crisis: The Government Stands Idly By

As private sector supply shrank instead of expanding to fill the gap left by the government's retreat from the housing market, officials stuck to the role of bystanders. In future, the government's only fixed commitment would be to ensure that qualified applicants from low-income families on the list for public housing tenancies would have to wait no more than three years to obtain a flat, the housing minister explained. Public housing targets were no longer set in terms of new residential units. They had become 'assisted housing opportunities'. There would be no more annual production targets, it was revealed, and the government would allow the number of 'assisted housing opportunities' to fluctuate from one year to another.[50]

In effect, property developers were being given a long-term guarantee that a future government could not re-enter the housing market except with great difficulty. The need for the Housing Department's professional, technical and managerial teams had disappeared, and by 2002, the last of them were being dispersed or disbanded.[51] Half a century's experience and expertise had been jettisoned. It was now impossible to resurrect public housing programmes at short notice, as Tsang Yam-kuen himself had foreseen in 2001.[52] When the government finally bowed to public dissatisfaction in 2011 and decided to re-enter the housing market on a limited scale, it no longer had the professional teams capable of organising the funding, design and tendering for the new projects.

Nor did the government have the building sites.[53] In 2000, the senior official responsible for housing had confidently declared that his team had an inventory of about 1,000 sites, enough to build up to 730,000 public and private housing units by 2008.[54] For the developers, this land bank represented a major barrier to maximising their profits, and they argued that these were assets which ought to be liquidated to ease pressure on public finances in a time of economic recession. It was claimed, for example, that by selling off the 38 sites allocated for new Home Ownership Scheme (HOS) flats, the government would generate HK$46.8 billion, equivalent to 27 per cent of the total budget revenue for 2001–02. Developers had been particularly anxious to get hold of Housing Authority sites which were located in the core urban areas and ideal for private residential projects. They won, and the Housing Authority surrendered its freedom to manage its land bank independently.[55] The long-term consequences were calamitous. In 2011, another minister confessed 'that the major housing policy review in 2002 had resulted in a shrinkage in land supply' not just for housing but to meet the needs of new industries.[56]

The Asian financial crisis has been made the scapegoat for these radical changes in traditional policy. They were, in fact, the outcome of the adoption by senior officials in the 1990s of an agenda to shrink the public sector and to adopt business values and practices. The Housing Department had begun this process in 1995, with the initial goal of improving its image with the public, its residents and its staff. The following year saw consultants hard at work on a plan to make the organisation as similar as possible to a business enterprise.[57]

This approach was misguided. It ignored the department's role of 'town manager' and how its staff were more than rent-collectors. They were the guardians of the tenants' quality of life in terms of cleanliness, respect for common areas and facilities and the early identification of causes of dissatisfaction. These traditional responsibilities were not endorsed by the department's new 'Management Enhancement Programme', however, whose primary concern was cost-cutting. The consultants who had advised on the department's future had fostered the belief that 'much of the bureaucratic apparatus which previously services these families' housing needs will need to be dismantled'. The ultimate objective was that 'the bottom third of the market' — public housing tenants — were to be 'released from bureaucratic control'. They would own properties that they would be free to trade at 'real market prices', and 'the economy [would be] stimulated by the freeing up of resources inefficiently deployed'.[58]

This vision of the future for the lower segment of the market was pure fantasy. In early 1997, the Director of Housing had publicly promoted large-scale privatisation of public housing as the solution to a host of management problems. Yet, for those at the bottom of the housing market, he had admitted, the choice was stark. 'There is almost no private sector accommodation for rent other than in the oldest, most dilapidated properties, in bed-space apartments and the like, or in squatter shacks. That is where most of our tenants come from.'[59] How could it be imagined that this group could benefit from commercialisation of the Housing Authority and the Housing Department? A decade later, the failure of business-based policies could no longer be concealed. The numbers living in unsafe and illegal premises were increasing, as was earlier explained, which the minister responsible attributed, at least in part, to market forces. The enthusiasm among officials for private sector solutions had always been unrealistic. The private sector was simply incapable of replacing the government, as Tung Chee Hwa himself had admitted in 2001.[60]

Protecting Investors

The long-term housing problems of Hong Kong involved 'market failure'. Bank of China senior economist, Wang Chunxin, had warned in 2003 of long-term 'market malfunctioning'.[61] Furthermore, the private sector had already shown itself incapable of providing the community with better homes. Their quality had barely improved, he noted, no matter how high property prices rose or how fast the economy grew. Between 1989 and 2001, per capita GDP doubled, he pointed out, but the average private flat recorded only 'a meager increase' in size.[62]

Officials, nevertheless, liked to justify their decision to get out of the housing market as a measure to protect investors. The sentiment 'always on our mind when we frame our housing policy', said Tsang Yam-kuen while still Financial Secretary, is that 'for the ordinary family including mine, the purchase of a home is the single most important investment made in a lifetime'. As a result, he went on, 'We want to feel confident that this home will be a good investment for our own future and a store of value which we can pass onto our children.'[63] As a result, he decided that the HOS scheme should be abolished although it had proved an invaluable ladder in enabling families to move from being public tenants to owner-occupiers, first in the public and then in the private sector.

In 2001, he declared the HOS was a threat to property values. His statement was to form the basis of housing policy for the next ten years. He wished to end 'a situation where government subsidised ownership housing competes unfairly with the private sector market' and adversely affected 'the wealth of all home-owners who represent half of the households in Hong Kong'. The time had come, he declared, for 'ridding ourselves of inefficient and interventionist elements in our public housing programmes'.[64] The data produced in support of this attack on public housing were not convincing.[65] Not surprisingly, therefore, the announcement that 'heavily subsidised HOS' would no longer 'crowd out private housing in a slow market' did not provide an instant cure for the property sector's woes.[66]

The public did not accept the government's condemnation of HOS as a threat to property values. With the greatest reluctance, officials eventually conceded that the community wanted the programme reinstated, and in 2010, it was announced that 'on balance, there was support for subsidising home ownership'.[67] The following year, the first tentative steps were taken to revive this policy.

Limited Quality Control

Poor quality is a legacy from which both the public and private sectors have suffered. When officials were called to account for the construction scandals in public housing estates recounted above, they claimed that quality control had been an unrealistic goal in the 1960s and sub-standard construction had been almost impossible to avoid. 'The building industry suffered from severe water restrictions, shortage of cement, a temporary ban on the use of explosives and a shortage of skilled construction workers,' a senior official stated. The government's overriding aim had been 'to produce the largest possible number of units to meet the pressing housing need within the limited resources then available'. 'The tender prices for these buildings were . . . substantially lower than those for other building works,' he went on, and 'one gets what one pays for,' although he denied that it had ever been 'the Government's intention that safety should be compromised'.[68]

Subsequently, maintenance of public housing started to deteriorate once privatisation measures got underway. In 1999, Housing Authority tenants were made responsible for hiring their own contractors to carry out repairs with the result 'that many tenants had allowed defects inside their flats to deteriorate' and 'minor items' became 'major maintenance issues'. A significant problem was that tenants often faced 'difficulties in procuring [repair] services in the market', an official explained. In the case of the elderly and tenants with disabilities, the Authority accepted that they could not be expected to take responsibility for maintenance. The market, once again, had failed to provide a solution, and in 2006, the Authority resumed responsibility for repairs.[69]

The private sector fared far worse. This century's crisis started with a decision 50 years earlier to lift the restrictions on erecting buildings with more than five storeys.[70] Hong Kong's familiar multi-storey, mass housing then got underway, and by 1959, a single development project was offering for sale almost 1,000 units as small as 517 square feet.[71] These early buildings had no specific design life, a URA report stated, and 'they are more prone to rapid deterioration' because they 'contain low strength concrete'. The indications were that at least 30 per cent of the properties built in the 1950s were in 'poor' condition by 2009.[72]

The government's building professionals had become seriously alarmed about the private sector in the 1990s, and a number of schemes were launched from 1998 onwards to eradicate dangerous and illegal conditions in privately owned buildings.[73] These efforts were very limited, however, as the minister responsible later confessed.[74] The underlying strategy was sensible but underestimated the scale of deterioration that would need government intervention to overcome.[75] In parallel, a separate campaign was launched to counter dilapidation by tackling what were regarded as the most dangerous hazards:

- 'unlawful building works', since these evaded statutory require-ments and government monitoring and were often undertaken by individuals with no trade or technical qualifications; and
- illegal rooftop structures, especially where these provided no safe escape routes in case of fire.

Between 2001 and 2011, some 400,000 unlawful building works had been removed, and the most dangerous illegal roof top structures had gone. But another 400,000 had been identified and still remained to be remedied, while legal orders to remove a further 52,000 had been ignored by property owners. In the meantime, a new hazard had ben created: the growing trend to sub-divide and rent out premises in older buildings with no regard for health and safety standards. The result was accidents with serious loss of life.[76] Multiple-ownership proved a serious obstacle to enforcing basic fire safety measures, especially in buildings not designed originally for exclusive use as living accommodation, and the government felt unable to rigorously enforce the legislation despite the potential danger to their occupants.[77]

These campaigns removed only the most visible dangers and promoted the most urgent repairs and immediate maintenance. The full dimensions of the mounting crisis only started to receive the official exposure that they warranted when the URA began a protracted drive to expose the desperate conditions which Hong Kong's slum popula-tion was forced to endure. By 2010, the government had followed the URA's lead and was denouncing 'dilapidated concrete', 'illegal altera-tions to internal building structure' and general disregard for building legislation as 'urban time bombs waiting to strike and cause injuries and fatalities'.[78]

Buyers Beware

The property sector was a glaring example of how business came first in Hong Kong with no regard for social costs. Developers had long enjoyed extraordinary market advantages which were reinforced by the absence until 2012 of a competition law. In 1987, the nine largest developers had supplied 48 per cent of new private residential housing. By 1991, their share had risen to 84 per cent. The industry was also becoming dominated by the largest firms. Between 1991 and 1994, four developers supplied 55 per cent of the new units, with a single developer producing 26 per cent of the total.[79]

The price of private sector flats rose so rapidly that they were 'beyond the reach of the average family', the colonial administration had admitted.[80] Between 1985 and 1994, the annual average price increase was 23 per cent, far outstripping the annual inflation rate of 8 per cent. The property market was in the hands of a very small number of players who were able to generate exceptional profits by the standards of other listed companies. The only countervailing force in this monopolistic situation was the public housing programme. After the government had finally withdrawn from the property market in 2002, the annual increase in property prices until 2011 was 19 per cent. The annual inflation rate in this period was less than 2 per cent.

Developers have enjoyed an additional advantage in protecting their interests in this century. They were able to block the introduction of statutory measures to protect the consumer. The legal right to full disclosure of all the information that a buyer needed in order to make an informed choice was taken for granted for everything from insurance policies and financial products to vegetables and air-conditioners. But not for new flats. In Hong Kong, sales of uncompleted residential properties have been standard practice and a crucial source of funding for developers since the 1950s. After a 1958 scandal, the government introduced measures to protect purchasers of uncompleted properties from fraud and insolvency on the part of developers and lawyers,[81] and attempts by developers to circumvent these procedures were not tolerated.[82] Some 30 years later, a new danger surfaced for prospective buyers because of what a Legislative Council document called 'rampant' problems such as 'inaccurate size of the property, misleading descriptions of fittings and finishes, sketchy layout and location plans'.[83]

In the 1990s, a campaign began to stamp out these abuses and introduce modern legislation to protect the public. Draft legislation emerged in 2000 but was not enacted.[84] In 2005, the government excused its inactivity on the grounds that 'the self-regulatory regime had struck a proper balance between protecting consumers' interests and providing an environment conducive to business development'.[85] The public was being asked to trust the property developers.

Officials continued to reject calls for legislation despite substantial evidence that the buyers were still at serious risk. The government entrusted the Real Estate Developers Association (REDA) with the enforcement of voluntary self-regulation even though not all developers were members of REDA, which, in any case, lacked the power to eject members for malpractice or misconduct. The Financial Secretary tried self-regulation again in 2009 with 'nine new enhancement measures' for the sale of new residential property. Complaints about abuses mounted, however, and the government was finally forced to legislate. But the developers managed to postpone the date on which legislation would finally come into force until 2013. And even then, several displayed considerable reluctance to comply with the new regulations.[86]

The truly shocking feature of this reluctance to protect home-buyers was the ample evidence of how vulnerable the public were to exploitation in the Hong Kong property market. The community was deliberately left unprotected by the government for almost 20 years after the costs to the community of the monopolistic state of the market had been revealed.[87] The Law Reform Commission had identified how to end the abuses in 2001.[88] It was not just the consumer who was at risk from the lack of competition in the property sector. Hong Kong's financial system was in danger. The Chief Executive of the Hong Kong Monetary Authority warned in 2005 that 'the structure of the market itself, in which there is a virtual oligopoly in the supply of property' endangered the stability of Hong Kong's financial markets.[89]

Conclusions

Nowhere is the community more at the mercy of history than in its housing. The mistaken policies of the past and the defects in quality and design were literally built to last, even in the construction of the cheapest accommodation. This chapter has illustrated how Hong Kong's current housing standards are tolerable only by comparison with the dreadful conditions in which much of the adult population grew up. Squalor and high densities of occupation, however, become less and less tolerable for any ageing population no matter how primitive was the sanitation and how squalid the living environment endured by the elderly during their childhoods.

Most of the housing stock was built originally to accommodate individuals who were fit, active, mobile and away at work or school for much of the day. For individuals whose mobility is limited and for whom privacy is essential for sleep, for toilet and self-care, the average housing unit in this century — in both the public and private sectors — is uncomfortable and sometimes dangerous. The younger generation is also at risk. As they enter their teens, they too need space and a measure of privacy, partly because of the social expectations of this century but also for them to function effectively under the modern education system with its emphasis on self-study. Young people who wish to set up their own homes face additional obstacles. So scarce has been the available supply of public housing that the best the government could suggest in 2011 was to encourage NGOs to expand the supply of hostel places at reasonable rentals for the under-30s. This short-term remedy was endorsed by the third Chief Executive in 2012. The hostel places, it was made clear, 'were not meant to provide permanent accommodation'.[90]

A principal defect in official policy-making was the failure to see housing in terms of people's homes, this chapter has argued. Instead, housing was all about assets, values and prices. Private owners were assumed to have a strong financial incentive to maintain their property. Similarly, it was assumed by the Housing Authority that comparable incentives could be created in the public sector. Maintenance has proved unsatisfactory in both sectors. The damaging consequences of these mistaken assumptions are conspicuously on view in the dilapidated state of so many buildings.

The focus should have been on ensuring the quality of the home. The case for insisting that building maintenance and repair were treated as urgent priorities could then have been made in terms of providing a safe and healthy living environment. Instead, the priority was how to maintain orderly queues for the limited supply of public rental housing, for which the principal qualification was low income rather than the need to be removed from unfit living accommodation. The definition of need was subordinated in this century to political convenience, this chapter has shown, just as it was when squatters were denied adequate water and sanitation half a century earlier. Individuals and families have been permitted to remain in buildings which were unhealthy and dangerous because, after 2002, officials found it inexpedient to give them priority over others with low incomes whose applications to join the Housing Authority's waiting list for tenancies had already been approved. This policy was maintained, this chapter has recounted, because private sector accommodation, however dangerous, was seen as an appropriate market solution for the personal situations of these individuals.

There was an obsession within the government about the market's merits and a reluctance to perceive its limitations or to recognise its failures. It was astonishing that the government in this century has been so insistent that the solution of Hong Kong's housing problems (except for the needy) should be left to market forces without 'unfair' competition from the government. And yet, officials intervened in the stock market to rescue developers (and other listed companies) when values slumped in 1998. Furthermore, developers benefited from delays in enacting legislation to ensure that the property sector conformed to the same principles of fair competition and consumer protection that applied to almost every other business in Hong Kong.

The inescapable conclusion of this chapter is that market failure has overtaken the property sector. The property market has yet to show that it will ever be able to ensure that supply and demand at least approach equilibrium. In addition, the market cannot be trusted to operate in an orderly manner that will not endanger Hong Kong's financial stability. Hence, the frequent intervention by monetary officials to limit mortgage business.

The other unhappy conclusion is that there can be no early end to Hong Kong's housing crisis, either in terms of supply or maintenance. The government's exit from housing was so total that nothing was left of the machine that had formerly provided public housing for over three million people and had created a reserve land bank sufficient to meet demand for several more years. This structure had been denounced as 'bureaucracy' by senior officials and laid waste. It was not to be mourned until a decade later when the third Chief Executive hoped to revive the housing vision of his original mentor, Tung Chee Hwa. In 2013, Leung Chun-ying discovered that starting from scratch, the process of 'land planning and consultation procedures, as well as design and build' would take five years to complete so that the annual output of public housing would be more or less static until 2018 at 'the earliest'.[91]

Notes

1. Leung Chun-ying, Chief Executive, *Hong Kong Hansard* (*HH* hereafter), 16 January 2013, p. 4907.
2. MDR, 'Survey of Housing Aspirations of Households (1999) Prepared for Planning Department. Executive Summary' (Hong Kong: 1999), pp. 3–5.
3. *Homes for Hong Kong People into the 21st Century* (Hong Kong: SAR Government, 1998), p. 31.
4. UN-Habitat, *The State of the World's Cities Report 2006/2007: 30 Years of Shaping the Habitat Agenda* (London: Earthscan, 2006), 'Table 1: Population of slum areas at mid-year, by region and country; 1990, 2001 and slum annual growth rate', pp. 181–2; 'Table 2: Slum population projections, 1990–2020', p. 193.
5. There were relatively few public housing tenants with less than 59 square feet per head by 2012. The criterion itself is significant as an indication of the minimalist standards still used to define adequate housing in this century. Transport and Housing Bureau, 'Panel on Housing, Subcommittee on the Long Term Housing Strategy, Measures to Maximize the Rational Use of Public Rental Housing Resources' (CB(1)600/12–13(03), February 2013), p. 4.
6. Tung Chee Hwa, Chief Executive (designate), *Government Information Services* (*GIS* hereafter), 21 March 1997.
7. Examples of MacLehose's detractors, critics and admirers are Mary Lee, 'Hongkong: And the Plans Came Tumbling Down', *Far Eastern Economic Review*, 30 March 1979; Joseph Y. S. Cheng, 'Goals of Government Expenditure in a Laissez-Faire Economy: Hong Kong in the 1970s', *Asian Survey*, Vol. 19, No. 7 (July 1979), pp. 697–8, 701, 704; Paul Wilding, 'Social Policy and Social Development in Hong Kong', *Public and Social Administration Working Paper Series 1996/3*, City University of Hong Kong, p. 13; Ahmed Shafiqul Huque et al., *The Civil Service in Hong Kong. Continuity and Change* (Hong Kong: Hong Kong University Press, 1998), p. 143.

8. Leung, Chief Executive, *HH*, 16 January 2013, p. 4911. For a fuller analysis of his team's plans to maximise output before 2018, see Transport and Housing Bureau, 'Panel on Housing Subcommittee on the Long Term Housing Strategy Measures to Maximize the Rational Use of Public Rental Housing Resources' (CB(1)600/12–13(03), February 2013).

9. Professor Anthony Cheung Bing-leung, Secretary for Transport and Housing, *HH*, 14 November 2012, pp. 1892–3.

10. Barry Cheung Chun-yuen, Urban Renewal Authority Chairman, *Urban Renewal Authority: New Strategy New Focus for Urban Renewal. Annual Report 2010–11*, pp. 5–6. See also Steering Committee on Review of the Urban Renewal Strategy, 'Report on the Building Conditions Survey' (SC Paper No.18/2009, 30 June 2009).

11. Donald Tsang Yam-kuen, Chief Secretary, *HH*, 24 October 2001, pp. 809–10.

12. Donald Tsang, Financial Secretary, transcript of BBC interview, *GIS*, 23 June 1998.

13. See Consumer Council, *Competition Policy: The Key to Hong Kong's Future Economic Success* (Hong Kong: Consumer Council, 1996). The IMF's endorsement of the Consumer Council's approach was published in *GIS*, 4 December 1997.

14. Tung, *GIS*, 12 September 1997.

15. 'Each of the elements of our strategy . . . take into consideration the results of a public consultation exercise carried out in the first half of 1997.' A footnote adds that the colonial administration's consultation document 'contained 41 specific recommendations'. *Homes for Hong Kong People into the 21st Century. A White Paper on Long Term Housing Strategy in Hong Kong February 1998* (Hong Kong: SARG, 1998), p. 2.

16. The range and detail of the public and professional discussion may be gauged from Legislative Council records. Legislative Council Secretariat, LegCo Panel on Housing, Subcommittee on Long Term Housing Strategy Review: 'Minutes of meeting . . .': 20 February 1997 (CB(1) 1317/96–97, 17 April 1997); 9 April 1997 (CB(1) 1518/96–97, 9 May 1997); 22 April 1997 (CB1/PS/10/95/1, 11 June 1997); 24 April 1997 (CB(1) 1519/96–97, 9 May 1997); 13 May 1997 (CB(1) 1830/96–97, 11 June 1997).

17. Housing Branch, *Homes for Hong Kong People: The Way Forward. Long Term Housing Strategy Review Document January 1997* (Hong Kong: Government Printer, 1997).

18. Donald Tsang, Financial Secretary, *GIS*, 16 July 1997.

19. See Alkman Granitsas, 'Land's End: Hong Kong Chief Outlines Real Estate-Policy in First Speech', *Far Eastern Economic Review*, 17 July 1997.

20. Tung, *GIS*, 17 October 2003; Joseph Yam Chi-kwong, Hong Kong Monetary Authority Chief Executive, *GIS*, 14 October 2003.

21. Dr Rosanna Wong Yick-ming, Executive Councillor and Chairperson of the Hong Kong Housing Authority, had previously sent the colonial governor a personal report on the Authority and housing issues every six months. She continued this practice after 1997. See Wong, letter to Governor, 16 June 1997 HD (CR) 1/247 XII and Governor's reply, 21 June 1997; Wong, letter to Chief Executive, 20 November 1997 HD/SAO/A 37 and Chief

Executive's reply, 31 December 1997; Wong, letter to Chief Executive, 3 December 1998 HD/SAO/A 37, and Joshua C. K. Law, Private Secretary, letter of acknowledgement, 19 December 1998.

22. Donald Tsang, Financial Secretary, *GIS*, 3 September 2001.

23. M. Castells et al., *The Shek Kip Mei Syndrome: Economic Development and Public Housing in Hong Kong and Singapore* (London: Pion Limited, 1990), pp. 87–95.

24. Shorter waiting times for public housing for example for which a 2005 deadline had been adopted originally. Tung, *GIS*, 16 December 1998.

25. *Review of the Institutional Framework for Public Housing: The Report June 2002* (Hong Kong: SAR Government, 2002), pp. 40–1.

26. Such long-term acceptance of housing conditions grossly inferior to the standards that economic growth brought to everyday life as a whole was deemed almost inconceivable 50 years earlier. See Leo F. Goodstadt, 'Urban Housing in Hong Kong, 1945–63', in I. C. Jarvie (ed.), *Hong Kong: A Society in Transition* (London: Routlege and Kegan Paul, 1969), p. 270.

27. (4) Memorandum for the Working Party on Housing, 'The Resettlement Programme: 1963 Review', Paper No. WPH3/63, pp. 2, 4, Appendix F. HKRS934–9-40 'Working Party on Housing'.

28. 'Report of the 1963 Working Party on Government Policies and Practices with regard to Squatters, Resettlement and Low Cost Housing' (mimeo 1963), p. 23. HKRS163–3-219 'Working Party on Squatters, Resettlement and Government Low Cost Housing'.

29. Roger Bristow, *Hong Kong's New Towns: A Selective Review* (Hong Kong: Oxford University Press, 1989), pp. 40, 50.

30. (32) 'Note for Executive Council: Provision of Facilities in Resettlement Cottage Areas and Licensed Areas', p. 1; Annex A 'Provision of Facilities in Resettlement Cottage Areas and Licensed Areas', XCR(68)302, 14 June 1968. HKRS394–20-8 'Resettlement Policy Committee'.

31. 'Minutes of 72nd Meeting of the Housing Board . . . 17th January 1973', pp. 3, 4. HKRS156–3-95 'Squatters on Land Not Required for Development'.

32. The Hong Kong government's provision of industrial sites as well as housing was included in this comparison. Leonard K. Cheng, 'Strategies for Rapid Economic Development: The Case of Hong Kong', *Contemporary Economic Policy*, Vol. 13. No. 1 (January, 1995), p. 30.

33. (4) Memorandum for the Working Party on Housing, 'The Resettlement Programme: 1963 Review', Paper No. WPH3/63, pp. 2, 4, Appendix F. HKRS934–9-40.

34. (72) D. J. M. Mackenzie, Director of Medical and Health Services, memo to Colonial Secretary, 'Resettlement Programme', 25 November 1958. HKRS163–3-64 'Squatter Clearance and Resettlement 1. General Questions of . . . 2. Programmes of . . . '.

35. Nevertheless, in Mainland cities undergoing high-speed industrialisation during the 1950s (as Hong Kong itself was), living space fell to half the national average or less (in Lanzhou for example). Kang Chao, 'Industrialization and Urban Housing in Communist China', *Journal of Asian Studies*, Vol. 25, No. 3 (May 1966), especially pp. 382, 393, 395.

36. 'Report of the 1963 Working Party on Government Policies and Practices with regard to Squatters, Resettlement and Low Cost Housing', pp. 8–9. HKRS163–3-219.
37. Aggravated by the absence of a communal garbage system which meant that rubbish proliferated in the open areas. See Castells, *The Shek Kip Mei Syndrome: Economic Development and Public Housing in Hong Kong and Singapore*, p. 19.
38. *Review of Policies for Squatter Control, Resettlement and Government Low-Cost Housing 1964* (Hong Kong: Government Printer, 1964), pp. 6, 10, 11.
39. Pang Yuk-ling, Acting Secretary for Housing, *HH*, 18 December 1985, pp. 436, 439; *South China Morning Post*, 28 April 1988.
40. Chan Nai-keong, Secretary for Land and Works, *HH*, 18 December 1985, p. 443.
41. (22) J. C. McDouall, Secretary for Chinese Affairs, 'The Landlord and Tenant Ordinance, Cap. 255 and the Effects of the Operation of Sec. 31 on the Problem of Housing', p. 3. Paper No. WPH21/63, 29 June 1963. HKRS934–940 'Working Party on Housing'.
42. (65) DSW memo to CS, 'Resettlement Programme', 6 September 1958, p. 2. HKRS163–3-64.
43. 'Report of the 1963 Working Party on Government Policies and Practices with Regard to Squatters, Resettlement and Low Cost Housing', p. 8. HKRS163–3-219.
44. On the complex corruption involved, see ICAC, 'Landmark Cases: 26 Public Housing Blocks Case'. URL: www.icac.org.hk/new_icac/eng/cases/26p/26p.htm
45. Chan, Secretary for Land and Works, *HH*, 18 December 1985, p. 444.
46. Legislative Council Panel on Development, 'Subcommittee on Building Safety and Related Issues: Measures to Enhance Building Safety in Hong Kong', Annex: 'Legislative Council Brief, Measures to Enhance Building Safety in Hong Kong (File Ref: DEVB(PL-CR) 12/2010)', (Development Bureau, CB(1)681/10–11(01) December 2010), p. 3.
47. Carrie Lam Cheng Yuet-ngor, Secretary for Development, *HH*, 7 December 2011, p. 2956.
48. Paul Chan Mo-po, Secretary for Development, *HH*, 7 November 2012, pp. 1491–2; Cheung, Secretary for Transport and Housing and 'Seventh Meeting of Long Term Housing Strategy Steering Committee', *GIS*, 27 May 2013. For other surveys, see Diana Wong, 'Subdivided flats in Hong Kong: Information Note' (IN22/12–13, 28 May 2013).
49. See Carrie Lam, Chief Secretary, *GIS*, 6 March 2013.
50. Michael Suen Ming-yeung, Secretary for Housing, Planning and Lands, *HH*, 13 November 2002, pp. 1152–4.
51. For details of this process, see Housing Department, 'Information Paper for the Legislative Council Panel on Housing, Greater Private Sector Involvement in Housing Authority's Estate Management and Maintenance Services 4th Report on the Progress of Implementation (November 2001 to April 2002)' (CB(1) 1947/01–02, May 2002); 'Panel on Housing Greater Private Sector Involvement in Housing Authority Estate Management and

Maintenance Services Final Report on the Progress of Implementation (November 2002 to April 2003)' (CB(1) 1877/02–03, May 2003).

52. Donald Tsang, Chief Secretary, 'Statement on Housing', 3 September 2001. URL: www.info.gov.hk/gia/general/200109/03/0903236.htm

53. Panel on Housing, 'Updated Background Brief on Land Supply for Housing (Position as at 25 July 2011)' (CB(1) 2805/10–11(01), 25 July 2011).

54. Dominic Wong Shing-wah, Secretary for Housing, 'LegCo Panel on Housing, Minutes of Meeting . . . 17 October 2000' (CB(1) 121/00–01, 4 November 2000), p. 2.

55. The private sector's struggle to win control of the Housing Authority's land bank is analysed in Adrienne La Grange, 'Housing (1997–2007)', in Joseph Y. S. Cheng (ed.), *The Hong Kong Special Administrative Region in Its First decade* (Hong Kong: City University of Hong Kong Press, 2007), pp. 722–3.

56. Carrie Lam, Secretary for Development, Legislative Council Panel on Development, 'Minutes of Special Meeting . . . 14 October 2011' (CB(1)798/11–12, 12 January 2012), p. 4.

57. The role of consultants was crucial. Overlooked by the Housing Authority and Housing Department was that they were receiving advice from firms the bulk of whose expertise was acquired from auditing and advising commercial firms whose wellbeing depended on maximising profitability. The public sector had to meet a very different objective: to provide a universal service for all those who met statutory or similar criteria, regardless of the 'convenience' of doing so. Public sector agencies also had to meet much higher standards of public accountability than a corporation's shareholders were entitled to. For a typical example of consultants' influence in shaping housing reorganisation, see Hong Kong Housing Authority, Memorandum HA 31/99, 'Management Enhancement Programme: Next Steps for Corporate Reform', (HD(CR)MEP/8, 30 April 1999).

58. Tony Miller, 'Management Enhancement Programme in the Housing Department', in Anthony B. L. Cheung and Jane C. Y. Lee (eds.), *Public Sector Reform in Hong Kong: Into the 21st Century* (Hong Kong: Chinese University Press, 2001), pp. 139, 151–2, 153–4.

59. Tony Miller, Director of Housing, 'Becoming Stakeholders of Hong Kong: Home Ownership', Speech to the Hong Kong Institute of Real Estate Administration (19 February 1997). URL: www.housingauthority.gov.hk/en/about-us/news-centre/speeches/1435.html

60. Tung, *HH*, 23 June 2000, p. 8368, with editing based on the government's translation of the Chinese original in 'CE's statement at Legislative Council', *GIS*, 23 June 2000.

61. This was a long-standing and well-known problem. The private sector's annual output had been highly volatile in the decade before 1997, and 'the discrepancy between estimated and actual supply from one year to another ranged from +7% to –35%, a Legislative Council study six years earlier had shown. Eva Liu et al., *Supply of Flats* (Research and Library Services Division, RP09/96–97, 3 April 1997), pp. 4, 7, 9–10.

62. Wang Chunxin, Senior Economist, *Economic Review Monthly* (Bank of China (HK) Ltd, May 2003), pp. 1–2.

63. Donald Tsang, Financial Secretary, *GIS*, 23 November 2000.

64. Donald Tsang, Chief Secretary, 'Statement on Housing', 3 September 2001; Press Conference, *GIS*, 3 September 2001.

65. The claim was made in 2002 that following the Asian financial crisis, there was 'a significant overlap between the target group of the Government's subsidised home ownership programmes and that of the private sector residential market', although no evidence was produced. 'This short term problem did not affect the Government's long term housing goals', it was promised, a pledge that had already been discarded. *Review of the Institutional Framework for Public Housing. The Report, June 2002*, p. 13. Tsang's assertions were contradicted by data and analysis that had been presented in 1999 in MDR, 'Survey of Housing Aspirations of Households (1999)'.

66. See Rating and Valuation Department, 'Hong Kong Property Review 2002 preliminary findings', *GIS*, 3 May 2002; Rating and Valuation Department, 'Property Market Statistics, Private Domestic — Average Prices by Class (from 1982)'. URL: www.rvd.gov.hk/doc/en/statistics/his_data_2.xls

67. This reality could not be concealed despite considerable efforts in the final official report of a public consultation exercise to demonstrate that 'this view was not universal as there were also opposing views from some contributors with strongly held views'. Transport and Housing Branch, 'Report on Public Consultation on Subsidising Home Ownership' (October 2010), p. 6.

68. The rebuilding programme to remedy past sub-standard construction in the public sector began in 1972 and by 1980 had rehoused 'more than 100,000 people in modern, self-contained accommodation'. Donald Liao Poon-huai, Secretary for Housing, *HH*, 19 November 1980, p. 173.

69. Lau Kai-hung, Deputy Director of Housing, *GIS*, 30 January 2006.

70. K. M. A. Barnett, Census Commissioner, 'Introduction', in W. F. Maunder, *Hong Kong Urban Rents and Housing* (Hong Kong: Hong Kong University Press, 1969), p. 1.

71. *Hong Kong Annual Departmental Report by the Registrar General 1959–60* (Hong Kong: Government Printer, n.d.), p. 3.

72. Steering Committee on Review of the Urban Renewal Strategy, 'Report on the Building Conditions Survey' (SC Paper No. 18/2009, 30 June 2009), p. 2.

73. Full details of these measures were set out in Development Bureau, 'Panel on Development Subcommittee on Building Safety and Related Issues: Consolidation of Financial Assistance Schemes for Building Maintenance and Repair' (CB(1)2087/10–11(02), May 2011).

74. Suen, Secretary for Housing, Planning and Lands, *GIS*, 25 October 2003.

75. See the relatively modest projections in Planning and Lands Bureau, *People First — A Caring Approach to Urban Renewal. Urban Renewal Strategy* (Consultation Paper, July 2001), pp. 1, 2–3.

76. Legislative Council Panel on Development, 'Subcommittee on Building Safety and Related Issues: Measures to enhance building safety in Hong Kong', Annex: 'Legislative Council Brief, Measures to Enhance Building Safety in Hong Kong (File Ref: DEVB(PL-CR) 12/2010)', (Development Bureau, CB(1)681/10–11(01) December 2010), pp. 2–3.

77. John Lee Ka-chiu, Acting Secretary for Security, *HH*, 20 March 2013, pp. 7530–2.

78. Development Bureau, 'Legislative Council Panel on Development Subcommittee on Building safety and Related Issues: Measures to enhance building safety in Hong Kong', Annex: 'Legislative Council Brief Measures to Enhance Building Safety in Hong Kong (File Ref: DEVB(PL-CR) 12/2010)', (CB(1)681/10–11(01), December 2010), p. 1.

79. Consumer Council, *How Competitive Is the Private Residential Property Market?* (Hong Kong: Consumer Council, 1996), pp. 2–4, 5, 8, 3–9, 5–3, A 3–2, Annex 4.

80. Planning, Environment and Lands Branch, *Report of the Task Force on Land Supply and Property Prices* (June 1994), p. 1.

81. Salient details of this scandal can be found in HKRS 70–3-13 'Building Control. Peony House — Failing by completion'; HKRS 54–10-1(406) 'Documents handed in by Mr Turnbull of Messrs Deacon & Co'.

82. See E. B. Teesdale, Colonial Secretary, *HH*, 26 March 1964, p. 147.

83. Except where otherwise indicated, the analysis that follows, and its quotations, are drawn from the very full history of the developers' successful campaign to block the introduction of legislation to protect the public against misinformation when buying their homes in the Legislative Council document, Panel on Housing, 'Meeting on 4 April 2011 . . . Updated Background Brief on Regulation of Sales of First-hand Private Residential Properties (Position as at 29 March 2011)' (CB(1) 1738/10–11(04), 29 March 2011).

84. Elaine Chung Lai-kwok, Acting Secretary for Housing, *GIS* 10 July 2001.

85. Suen, Secretary for Housing, Planning and Lands, *HH*, 18 May 2005, p. 7394.

86. It seemed almost as if some developers believed — wrongly, as things turned out — that the regulations would not be vigorously enforced from the start. See *Sing Tao Daily*, 8 May 2013.

87. Consumer Council, *How Competitive is the Private Residential Property Market?*

88. Description of Flats on Sale Sub-committee, *Local Completed Residential Properties: Sales Descriptions and Pre-contractual Matters* (Hong Kong: Law Reform Commission, 2001), pp. 46–8.

89. Joseph Yam, Hong Kong Monetary Authority Chief Executive, 'Viewpoint', *Hong Kong Monetary Authority,* 3 March 2005.

90. The limitations of this initiative were frankly admitted from the start. Legislative Council Secretariat, 'Youth Hostel Scheme' (CB(2)612/12–13(07), 7 February 2013).

91. Chief Executive's Spokesman, *GIS*, 30 January 2013.

4
Social Reforms: Too Little, Too Late

Contemporary Hong Kong is paying a heavy price for the misguided government decisions on social expenditure made decades ago. In the 1940s and 1950s, the colonial administration and its partners in the business and professional elite insisted that the million people who flooded into Hong Kong after World War II had no right to health or welfare services. They were transients, not even refugees, the colonial administration argued, and they would return to the Mainland once the civil war was over and a stable government was in power.

As a result, officials tried to delay as long as possible the drafting of policies to introduce decent health, education and welfare programmes. The colonial administration was prepared to perpetuate Third World standards for these three major social services no matter what the risks in terms of public health, child welfare or outright destitution. Grudgingly, in the 1960s, the government expanded its spending in these areas. In this and subsequent decades, nevertheless, senior officials openly opposed proposals for Hong Kong to escape from its Third World shortcomings and adopt modern standards for welfare and other social services. Throughout, the business community supported the government's parsimony towards social expenditure.

The government-business nexus's 'anti-welfare' consensus marked a sharp break with history. In the 1930s, officials and the business and professional elite had increasingly accepted a duty to provide decent working and living conditions for Hong Kong families regardless of economic and fiscal constraints. At the height of the severe economic recession in that decade, for example, an official report declared that Hong Kong could afford to pay for improved social services through increased taxation.[1] This sense of social obligation seems to have been inspired in part by a widespread conviction throughout China during this era that social reform was an imperative that could not be denied. Sun Yat-sen, the father of modern China, had fostered a belief that social welfare should be regarded as 'a hallmark of the modern nation state'.

'The idea of the "welfare state" began to be widely disseminated through the writings of many Chinese intellectuals,' a Hong Kong historian has pointed out, and 'so did the discipline of social work.' Even the warlord Chen Jitang who ruled Guangzhou from 1929 to 1936 launched ambitious housing and social welfare programmes because he felt that he 'could not afford to ignore the needs of society'.[2]

The start of all-out Japanese hostilities in 1937 strengthened the sense of social responsibility since the destitute and disabled now included large numbers who were the victims not of personal misfortune or family failures but of enemy action. Hong Kong, like the rest of the country, saw a huge rise in the number of voluntary aid and relief organisations. The colonial administration could have remained aloof on the grounds that the United Kingdom was not involved in Sino-Japanese hostilities. Instead, the Governor, Sir Geoffry Northcote, who arrived in 1937, refused to close his eyes to the way 'malnutrition and slum housing conditions dominate . . . the lives of a very large majority of Hong Kong's population'.[3] Their misery was intensified during 1938 and 1939 when 650,000 war refugees poured into a city whose normal population was only a million.[4] The colonial administration chose this moment in history to launch reforms to tackle the acute deficiencies 'in primary education, in facilities for sick poor, and sick children, in housing of the poorer class'.[5] The new programmes' costs were to be borne by the taxpayer, and direct taxation was imposed for the first time in Hong Kong's history.[6]

When British rule was re-established after the Japanese occupation, the Chinese community's leading spokesman, (later Sir) Man-kam Lo, took it for granted that the pre-war commitments would continue to drive social reforms. Indeed, he believed that the community's entitlement to adequate housing and social services had 'received a tremendously added emphasis from the common effort, common toil and common suffering of the war years'. He prophesied that with the democracy which the United Kingdom had promised to its colonial empire in 1945 would come the tax reforms to finance 'adequate hospitalisation, medical and sanatorium care, universal education, old age pensions, unemployment insurance, workmen's compensation, etc.'[7]

The pledge of political reform was to evaporate after 1948, and the vision of social progress was erased from Hong Kong's collective memory.[8] Its post-war rulers later confessed that they had felt overwhelmed by the new tide of desperate and largely destitute humanity. 'When one reads of one million homeless exiles [i.e., Hong Kong's refugee population], all human compassion baulks,' the official *Annual Report* was to assert in 1956, 'and the great sum of human tragedy becomes a matter of statistical examination'.[9] Compassion was replaced by resentment. The Social

Welfare Department, for example, was to become 'an expensive luxury which Hong Kong can ill afford' in the eyes of senior officials.[10]

People Are the Problem

At the end of World War II, the colonial administration had returned to a ruined city whose prospects of recovery looked grim. Meeting the daily survival needs of its population seemed an almost impossible task. In August 1945, 'the economic life of Hong Kong was dead', an official publication recorded, 'there was no food, no shipping, no industry, no commerce', and the Japanese military occupation had reduced the population to 600,000, a third of its pre-invasion level.[11] Wartime destruction had diminished the colony's already inadequate capacity to provide decent homes and essential health and other social services. Hong Kong, nevertheless, became a haven for a rising tide of refugees from civil war and economic chaos on the Mainland. In early 1946, the population had reached 900,000. It had doubled to 1.8 million by the end of 1948.[12] By 1950, it was estimated to be 2.3 million.

The newcomers seemed destined to eke out a miserable living in their makeshift squatter huts. But an extraordinary industrial take-off got underway, and growth of the export-driven manufacturing sector averaged 136 per cent a year between 1950 and 1960.[13] Demand for labour from the new factories was so high that squatter households became self-supporting almost immediately on arrival.[14] The colonial administration, however, seemed blind to everything except the immigrant headcount. Refugees and squatters were continually portrayed as threats to Hong Kong's survival and governability. Officials insisted that any welfare or similar assistance provided for the newcomers would encourage further influxes. That anxiety became an article of faith, and to minimise the attractions for would-be immigrants, the standards of public services were to be kept at the lowest possible levels.[15]

The influx did not prove unlimited. The Mainland authorities imposed tight controls on entry into the colony after the Chinese Communist Party came to power. Until the late 1970s, relatively few, and only the fittest and the most daring individuals, managed to make the dangerous crossing into Hong Kong.[16] In consequence, 'from 1950 onwards immigration ceased to be the main factor in Hong Kong's population growth'.[17]

No Shortage of Funds

Throughout the second half of the 20th century, finance was never a barrier to social programmes. In 1952, the Governor had informed the

Colonial Office in London that there was no 'real shortage of funds for social development or for building up adequate [fiscal] reserves'.[18] Sir John Cowperthwaite, the much-vaunted financial overlord of the 1960s, and his widely praised successor, Sir Philip Haddon-Cave, were prepared occasionally to drop all pretence that expansion of the social services meant financial ruin.[19] In 1982, another Financial Secretary, Sir John Bremridge confessed that 'the true shortage is of resources including people — and not of money'.[20] In the background was an unstoppable economy. Real GDP per head grew by an annual 6.3 per cent in the 1960s and 1970s; 5.8 per cent in the 1980s; and 3.4 per cent between 1990 and 1997.[21] Yet, the health, education and welfare services were starved of funding for decades, and their development remained firmly Third World till the closing years of British rule.

The colonial administration has largely escaped blame for this past neglect thanks to an abiding belief among the general public, as well as the business community, that government finances were limited and unstable because of Hong Kong's political and economic vulnerability. Officials carefully nurtured this illusion in order to justify their hostility to social expenditure, and they discredited proposals for social expenditure by raising fears about budget deficits and higher taxes. Cowperthwaite was a master of this ploy. He attacked calls for free education in 1964, for example, on the grounds that families could and should contribute substantially to their children's schooling. To clinch his case, he presented the public with a doomsday scenario. This initiative, he declared, would require direct taxation to more than double.[22] The claim was shameless scaremongering, and no such budget crisis occurred after free, compulsory education up to the age of 16 was introduced in 1978.[23]

Within the upper echelons of the colonial administration, opposition to social expenditure was 'ideological' rather than the product of rational financial analysis. Officials were convinced that without firm resistance from the colonial administration, 'socialism' would prevail, and the community would come to view social services in terms of rights and entitlement, as in Western democracies.[24] The passion with which the colonial administration clung to this dogma was illustrated by the senior official who, from 1957, did most to block welfare spending. In 1971, he expressed some regret for his obstructive tactics in the past but went on to warn his colleagues not to relax their vigilance. He wrote on file:

> We are becoming more affluent and public attitudes are changing. . .
> The danger is that we might creep into a social welfare system which
> is not contributory (this is almost upon us in medical services), a
> system which not even Britain has envisaged.[25]

Cultural sensitivities were also invoked to reinforce the government's case against social reform. During the British era, colonial officials endorsed Chinese traditional culture and institutions as a superior form of social assistance provided by the 'Confucian' family. Although there was an element of political expediency in these declarations of respect for Chinese values, the origins of this desire to rely on what the colonial administration regarded as the special social strength of the Chinese community were sincere.[26]

An official definition of the social services and their role, 'tentatively' adopted in the early 1950s, showed the remoteness of the policy-makers from everyday life. Social services were seen as a sort of civic education, whose goal was 'to enable every member of the community to develop into a reliable neighbour and a useful and well-informed citizen'. 'Successful social work,' the definition went on, meant 'fewer social misfits, more individual self-reliance and less dependence on "charity" . . . and perhaps most important of all, less gullible material for subversively-minded persons to work on.'[27] Welfare as a defence against sedition then disappeared as an incentive for the government to improve the social services, this chapter will make clear. The colonial administration discovered that it lost nothing politically by leaving the community to overcome its own social challenges.

In addition, the colonial administration had seen no need to provide facilities for the sick, the elderly or the unemployed. These unfortunates voluntarily removed themselves from Hong Kong and returned to their native villages, the government believed, 'where social convention demands that their families care for them'.[28] But the stricter border controls which the Mainland authorities introduced after the Chinese Communist Party's victory meant that parents could no longer send children with impaired sight or intellectual disabilities back to the countryside. As a result, the available facilities to care for these children in Hong Kong were stretched to breaking point by 1951.[29]

By 1957, a serious welfare gap had emerged, and government departments in direct contact with the community were reporting that those in need could no longer rely for support on the family and the family firm.[30] Senior officials more distant from society as a whole continued to believe in the abiding influence of Chinese traditions and that provision of social relief could be left to the Kaifongs and other traditional charitable organisations in Hong Kong.[31] A proposed welfare programme was savaged by the Financial Secretary who complained in 1962 that 'the draft [is] curiously detached from local or Chinese social structure and traditions'. 'It is "relief" that worries me most,' he went on, 'particularly so because it takes the place of family assistance.'[32] This refusal to

recognise how Hong Kong society was changing had distressing consequences for the needy and deprived.

The Health Miracle

With the post-war influx of a million homeless and impoverished newcomers, the control of disease seemed the most obvious priority. The
government, however, saw the protection of public health as less important than doing everything possible to deter further immigration. Life
was to be made as uncomfortable as possible for the new arrivals, and the
previous chapter set out the horrifying details of the minimal health and
sanitary facilities provided for the growing tide of squatters.[33] These newcomers from the Mainland 'brought with them a variety of infectious,
parasitic and deficiency diseases'. They arrived not only destitute but 'in
a poor physical condition . . . being near starvation'. The result should
have been a disastrous surge in death rates, with epidemics spreading
out of control. Instead, the mortality rate from infectious and parasitic
conditions fell sharply: from 24 per cent of total deaths in 1951; to 16
per cent in 1961; and to 4 per cent by 1975.[34] Medical historians have yet
to clarify why epidemics were so rapidly tamed.[35]

The business model fails

The government's anti-immigrant measures were not the only threat
to the community's health. The survival of 19th-century arrangements
for public hospitals hindered Hong Kong from achieving the quality
of healthcare that its people deserved and which its growing prosperity could have financed. The community was trapped by a Third World
heritage which was not finally discarded until the end of the 20th century.

The role of non-governmental organisations (NGOs) in delivering
social services has been vigorously promoted in contemporary Hong
Kong. This development repackaged what, historically, had been the
major source of Hong Kong's medical and social facilities. Originally,
they had been provided by traditional charitable institutions in which
business people played the dominant role. Particularly prominent was
the Tung Wah Group of Hospitals (TWGH) which supplied a large share
of hospital care.

These philanthropic activities had an important political dimension
from early in colonial history. Generous business people enjoyed social
prestige and community respect, which made them ideal candidates for
co-option into the colonial power structure in return for their endorsement of the colonial administration and its policies. Their performance
in providing health and social services after World War II was inadequate,

it will be shown. The government tolerated their deficiencies, nevertheless, because officials put political convenience ahead of the public's health needs.

These Third World arrangements had already been ripe for reform in the 1930s when Northcote, an unusually progressive Governor, had introduced measures to expand and modernise the social services, including the hospitals (discussed above).[36] After World War II, business philanthropy was seen to be a less than ideal formula for supplying medical care, especially when large government subventions were needed to keep these hospitals going.[37] United Kingdom plans for self-government in all colonial territories were expected to lead to an elected municipal council for Hong Kong which would take over responsibility for public health and other social services. The TWGH and similar bodies were seen as likely to be nationalised.[38]

But Hong Kong managed to avoid the political reforms that took place in Singapore, Malaya (later Malaysia) and other British territories. The TWGH and similar charitable organisations survived as an invaluable source of political support for the colonial administration regardless of how satisfactory or otherwise their managements were in providing social services. The government donated the bulk of the funding but left the administration of these traditional institutions in the hands of business leaders. The TWGH offered repeated examples of the limitations of a business background as a 'welfare' qualification.

- In 1948–49, the TWGH vigorously resisted a proposal to help the University of Hong Kong (then Hong Kong's sole medical school) to increase the supply of qualified doctors through training students in the Group's hospitals. It paid no attention to the potential benefit to its own performance from having access to the University's superior medical talent and facilities. Among the delaying tactics adopted by the TWGH directors was the demand for a guarantee that those involved from the University would be exclusively of Chinese race.[39]
- In the 1950s, nurses in one of the Group's hospitals admitted that 'most of the abandoned children are not properly attended; some small babies are not even fed regularly'.[40] To help TWGH to improve its inadequate standards of surgery, the government was forced to offer its own surgical staff.[41]
- In 1971, in spite of extensive reprovisioning of one of the Group's major hospitals, it remained Third World. Its pathology laboratory was inadequate, and there were no physiotherapy, occupational therapy or medical social work services.[42]

- In 1979, TWGH medical staff were alarmed about restructuring plans 'whereby control would be surrendered to lay administrators'. They requested 'that the Government should take over the management of the Tung Wah hospitals'.[43]

Progress postponed

The colonial administration's political dependence on the business and professional elite — especially those with philanthropic credentials — was not the only factor which enabled the TGWH and similar bodies to retain their historical role in spite of their shortcomings. The highest echelons of the government had no interest in replacing them with direct public services. As a result, senior officials did nothing to overcome the administrative weaknesses of the government departments responsible for social services. Indeed, their bureaucratic blunders were exploited to delay the drafting of policy blueprints and to enable the colonial administration to postpone making financial commitments to social reform.

The development of medical and health services was seriously obstructed by piecemeal planning in an unsympathetic environment. Not until 1957 was a long-range programme devised for medical services, and this plan failed to win government approval. In 1959, a small medical planning unit was established, which produced a five-year plan. In 1964, a White Paper was issued on the development of services in the following decade.[44] In 1974, a second White Paper was issued setting out the goals to be achieved over the next ten years.[45]

After 1974, however, the government produced no further policy documents, despite severe criticism of its silence from the medical profession, political and pressure groups and the media.[46] Progress had come to a halt, and reforms designed to create a modern healthcare service seemed blocked by an insuperable bureaucracy.[47] By the end of the 1970s, not surprisingly, there were still serious shortfalls in the quality of hospital services. 'From a clinical point of view', for example, 'average durations of [in-patient] stay' even in the best hospitals were 'far too short', an official report complained, being 19 to 25 per cent below what was 'preferred for most of the specialities'.[48]

Hong Kong's public health was, nevertheless, another example of this community's astonishing capacity to transform its own standards and, through the social discipline and resourcefulness of its families, to overcome the most daunting obstacles. Despite the low levels of household incomes, the community had achieved rapid improvements in life expectancy and effective control of epidemic diseases in the 1950s and 1960s which were remarkable by comparison with the rest of the Asian region. Among the considerable obstacles that Hong Kong overcame, according to an authoritative study of child health, were dietary and child-rearing customs which normally would be hazardous for both mothers and infants. These health risks ought to have been aggravated by the over-crowded and insanitary living conditions that were described in the previous chapter.[49]

It is often assumed that the traditional culture of Guangdong Province, especially its emphasis on personal hygiene, had enabled its families to adjust 'to the health aspects of industrialisation as well as or better than most of the world's population'.[50] This view would be only partially correct. Individual efforts were not enough to defeat the most serious threats to public health. Government funding was indispensable, as the successful immunisation campaigns to eradicate polio and TB from the early 1960s demonstrated dramatically. Similarly, the virtual eradication after 1980 of deaths from infectious diseases among children must be credited to an official programme to improve drinking water and sanitation facilities for the average household.[51] These achievements serve to highlight how the delay in financing modern health standards and adequate public amenities had permitted an earlier generation to suffer unnecessary disease and disability.

When the Hospital Authority was set up in 1990, it faced a legacy of past neglect. It was taking over a health system which hitherto had not been given clearly defined goals or provided with adequate management.[52] As in other areas of social policy, efforts to improve the delivery of services were deliberately sabotaged. An authoritative academic study concluded in 1991 that the programmes provided by the colonial administration had not matched the standards of OECD countries.[53]

The new Hospital Authority transformed hospital care. The gap between the high-quality government-operated hospitals and the much lower standards in the traditional 'charity' (but heavily subsidised) sector came to an end, a reform which had been both possible and desirable 50 years earlier. New hospitals were built, and existing ones refurbished. Patients were given a new deal, thanks to improved accountability. Management was modernised.[54] The Authority became the most transparent organisation within the public sector, and the public was provided with detailed annual plans based on a clear overall strategy and specific targets.[55]

Financial fears

These improvements had been made despite the influence on the Hospital Authority's reform model of the colonial administration's enthusiasm for importing business values and practices into the public sector during the 1990s. There were complaints that the Authority was operating like a business corporation and giving priority to cost-effectiveness rather than clinical concerns.[56] At the same time, however, the government was becoming uneasy about the high standards of care provided by the new Authority, with which, reportedly, the private sector was finding it difficult to compete. The implication was that the improvements in the public hospitals were viewed by senior officials as having gone too far and that funding would be more tightly rationed in the future.[57] The last British Governor, Christopher (later Lord) Patten, personally discussed plans to curtail the pay packages of medical staff.[58]

There was also a sense of foreboding about post-1997 funding because of the Basic Law's requirement that taxes be kept low. In the future, it would be difficult to maintain 'the same level of quality and accessibility, let alone improve quality' to make up for past under-spending, it was predicted.[59] The government floated suggestions about introducing a 'user pays' formula in setting fees in the hope that charges for previously free treatment would help to suppress demand. Since almost 70 per cent of hospital in-patients were not wage-earning, this proposal made little sense to the public.[60]

The obvious solution was to establish a system of public health insurance. Senior officials were opposed to such an innovation on the grounds that it would create a 'hypothecated health tax' which could not be diverted to any other purpose, thus reducing the government's budgetary autonomy. Among the ruling elite, there was a predictable repugnance towards a measure which was viewed as 'a threat to the low-tax policy' and a major step towards the social insurance systems that were alleged to have introduced 'collectivism' and 'welfarism' and undermined Western economies.[61] A series of consultation documents was issued, but the government either took issue with its consultants' recommendations or failed to mobilise community-wide support for its own proposals. The failure to bring forward coherent policy proposals on the funding of healthcare was to persist after the British departure in 1997.[62]

Education: Pledges Postponed

Education was late in emerging as a serious priority. In 1948, the colonial administration publicly declared its commitment to the principle that 'elementary education should be free and universal' in compliance with the United Nations International Declaration on Human Rights.[63] A decade later, officials were still arguing about whether this pledge would be honoured in the near future, and the Financial Secretary declared: 'Surely it is wrong to fix fees to suit the poorest?' The Governor, Sir Robert Black, personally intervened in 1959 to condemn a proposal to reduce teaching standards in government schools 'to make them less attractive' (for example, by reducing the numbers of qualified staff) and thus give an indirect boost to the private sector.[64] His directive made little difference in practice. The overall supply of school places was expanded by turning a blind eye to illegal and unsatisfactory private sector establishments.[65]

In the 1960s, officials and their business partners maintained their resistance to increasing the education budget despite growing public pressure for free primary education for all. Affordability was not the obstacle because the government had ample resources, as was explained earlier in this chapter. Officials simply insisted that free schooling was neither necessary nor desirable. The Governor, Sir David Trench, did not believe that compulsory schooling would work in Hong Kong and declared: 'I personally have residual doubts about the wisdom of making [education] free anywhere.'[66]

At the time, the decision to do as little as possible appeared to do no great harm. The average family showed considerable determination in obtaining access to education for their children. As early as 1957, just over 70 per cent of children under 14 years of age, were estimated to be attending some form of school (only a quarter of which received government funding). The community by 1961 had achieved a major improvement in literacy rates compared with the pre-war period, and the urban male population was almost entirely literate, despite high school fees and a gross under-provision of primary school places. The 1966 By-Census recorded 85 per cent of children aged 6–14 as enrolled in an educational institution. By 1971, enrolment had reached 92 per cent, although primary education was still neither free nor compulsory. Even children not attending school tended to have become literate before they dropped out of the educational system.[67]

Cheap and nasty

The colonial administration saw no compelling economic reason to boost public spending on education.[68] Its business collaborators not only feared tax rises and budget deficits if education were both free and compulsory, they also saw secondary schooling as a threat to their profits. In 1978, when free schooling for all up to the age of 16 was about to be made compulsory, the measure was condemned by a textile representative in the legislature because of 'a danger that more young people than ever before will choose to continue full-time education rather than employment'.[69] This objection was inspired by business dogmatism rather than reality. Child labour was no longer freely available anyway because the Labour and the Social Welfare Departments had waged a successful campaign to keep youngsters from poor families at school. The introduction in 1971 of the Public Assistance Scheme (explained below) and the arrangements to remit school fees had proved effective in persuading even the worst-off parents to send their children to school rather than to factories.[70]

When the government finally introduced three years of free secondary schooling in 1978, the new policy was implemented on the most penurious basis possible. Visiting international experts seemed shocked in 1982 by the Third World state of Hong Kong's schools. 'Learning conditions for children and working conditions for staff, both at school and home, are hardly satisfactory,' their government-commissioned report stated, '[m]ost of the schools we visited were spartan to say the least.' The visitors expressed special alarm about overcrowding and noise pollution.[71] They came close to accusing the government of wilfully perpetuating poor quality education.

> Ironically, the resource allocation formulae seem to provide the least government resources to the schools which are regarded by the public as of the lowest quality. Moreover, the schemes of aid are not designed to improve the quality of lower-funded/lower-quality schools but essentially to leave them at their current level.[72]

A major obstacle to improvement of educational standards was the continuing reliance on the private sector to fill the gaps in the supply of school places. For-profit education was already failing commercially in the 1970s. Yet, in 1982, the government was buying 146,000 places from private sector schools (a third of the total secondary supply). Their quality was known to be inferior, and many were seen as unlikely to improve their performance sufficiently to qualify for membership of the fully subsidised sector.[73]

Astonishingly, the last of these private sector establishments were still part of educational system at the start of this century (albeit on a very small scale). The government in 2002 bought 7,300 places in these schools even though their quality was often low, their buildings and facilities sub-standard and ample places were available in regular schools to absorb their students. Education officials were in no hurry to bring to an end this relic of the Third World era.[74]

Resources allocated to the school system continued to fall far short of what was required to create a truly modern system by international standards. The government claimed that its education budget was the maximum that could be reasonably afforded. But its spending on schools did 'not compare favourably with countries of comparable economic strength and development in education', a leading Hong Kong education expert pointed out. 'Hong Kong has lost its competitive position in educational spending in the past decade, while neighbouring countries [had] caught up' by the late 1980s, his careful study of the available data concluded.[75]

Breakneck reform

From 1985, the government launched a number of ambitious initiatives which were intended to drastically alter the long-standing balance of priorities within the educational system. But by 1990, a review of the education field was warning that policy-making was in chaos. There was 'no concise or comprehensive statement of education policy or strategy, by way of which guidance could be given to the [Education] Department on operational priorities and allocation of resources', an education official complained.[76] An unconvincing excuse offered for the dysfunctional decision-making was the complexity of Hong Kong's adjustment to its future as a post-industrial economy under Chinese rule.[77]

The drive for change reached reckless proportions. A 'massive expansion of higher education' was announced, for example, with the output of graduates planned to almost treble between 1989 and 1995. The striking feature of these new measures was an almost complete absence of consultation, either with the community at large or even with the government's own advisory bodies. One well-regarded educational specialist denounced this new style of decision-making as transforming 'a rational, consultative mode to one of autocracy and secrecy'.[78]

The Education Department in the 1990s accelerated the pace of change to breakneck speed. Radical alterations were made to the goals and the teaching model of primary schools, which teachers were expected to master at two- or three-day seminars. This programme was announced before the targets to be achieved had been defined; new textbooks had been designed; or the funding issues had been settled. The teaching profession was outraged by this arbitrary approach, and 6,300 primary school principals and teachers signed a petition in 1995 against hasty implementation of the new arrangements. They were ignored. There were other initiatives (most notably, a drastic change in school management arrangements) that provoked less immediate resistance but which were to prove highly controversial in the following decade.[79]

Living in the past

Perhaps the biggest weakness of all was the refusal to recognise how Third World was the state of education in Hong Kong. By the end of the last century, for example, barely 40 per cent of the primary schools operated on a 'whole-day' basis.[80] The rest still split their pupils into morning and afternoon sessions just as they had done half a century earlier, an arrangement which had left many mothers free for shift or part-time work in the factories. By now, however, manufacturing had been relocated to the Mainland. Educational standards were also undermined by the lack of professionally trained and graduate staff throughout the system. The shortage of qualified teachers was not fully recognised as a severe handicap until the new century (and will be discussed in the next chapter).

The new policies were also abandoning recent reforms, which was to create new difficulties in the next century. Until the 1990s, the overriding educational priority for policy-makers had been basic schooling for all children. In 1991, the historical trend of Hong Kong education was reversed. As with public housing and other social services, officials in charge of education were anxious to expand the private sector and to encourage a business-related model among subsidised schools. The government, therefore, chose to favour middle-class aspirations for superior quality education through a 'Direct Subsidy Scheme' (DSS) which would make possible the quasi-privatisation of most of Hong Kong's best schools. The poor record of the private sector in the past was not seen as relevant, and DSS schools were to develop serious problems with corporate governance and contractual commitments after 2000 (as the next chapter will recount).

DSS schools were of special importance in the larger context of social issues. The initiative proved a 'pilot scheme' for the widening inequality of opportunity and the rationing of access to social services through increased fees and charges. Such measures were to become defining features of government policy in the next century. In 1991, almost overnight and in the face of considerable debate among educationalists and the wider community, education was about to become 'exclusive'. Yet, the DSS initiative aroused only limited public opposition and muted criticism from political groups. Even though the door was closing on the poorest families' access to high-quality education, the debate was remarkable for its moderation by comparison with Western countries.[81] Welfare advocacy was in decline for reasons that will be investigated in Chapter 7.

Welfare Comes in from the Cold

The Social Welfare Department aroused nothing but obstruction and contempt from the colonial administration's policy-makers for the first ten years after it was set up in 1958. From the very start, social workers were regarded as likely to plunge Hong Kong into bankruptcy because their demands for 'welfare' would quickly become uncontrollable. The senior official dealing with welfare spending at the time stated: 'There is a grave danger that this department will expand year by year to cover a field which is unlimited in scope.' The department remained miniscule in its operations for the next two years. Nevertheless, the same official expressed his anxiety in 1960 that we may 'find ourselves, before we can pull back, sliding irretrievably towards enormous and ever-mounting expenditure'.[82]

There was no possibility of any such cataclysm being allowed to occur. A culture existed among senior officials, the Director of the Social Welfare Department subsequently complained, that 'so often induces a negative, hyper-critical and "nit-picking" response to [the department's] proposals which are honestly designed to meet the social needs of Hong Kong'. The hostility to welfare was not just a matter of petty-mindedness. Deliberate sabotage was involved. One senior official later explained the steps taken to ensure that welfare's progress would be 'less vigorous' than the development of medical, educational or employment services. Financial officials and other policy-makers, he confessed, quite deliberately demanded 'monstrous-sized policies, plans and appreciations' from the Social Welfare Department. This tactic guaranteed an initial delay of at least two years in considering any welfare funding request.[83]

By 1962, the department had managed to put together a draft outline of the way ahead for welfare. This proposed blueprint became a target for vitriolic criticism, led by Cowperthwaite, the Financial Secretary. His indictment included allegations that the department was seeking to import unsuitable Western welfare models, undermining the Chinese family and leading Hong Kong towards bankruptcy.[84] To be fair to Cowperthwaite, he was not especially prejudiced against welfare: his language was equally offensive when defeating proposals to expand education and medical services.[85]

The contest between the Social Welfare Department and the senior echelons of the colonial administration was very uneven. Hong Kong had few professionally qualified social workers in the 1950s, and almost none who had experience of planning and managing large-scale programmes. The first priority for existing staff had been to launch as rapidly as possible the urgently needed services for the most vulnerable. These social workers were easily drowned by bureaucratic minutes and memoranda. The department, after toiling for seven years, published a preliminary policy document that obtained the legislature's approval in 1965.[86] But neither the director nor his senior staff were able to cope with the next level of hostilities. A detailed five-year plan describing the timetable, costing and outcome of future developments was supposed to be ready by 1967. Administrative incompetence within the department's directorate meant that the first compendious drafts could be ignored by the Government Secretariat, while the revised versions were treated contemptuously when submitted in 1971.[87]

The Governor to the rescue

The Social Welfare Department had one important ally in Sir David Trench, who was Governor from 1964 to 1971. He was not in favour of free education for all, it was noted earlier, but he was personally very anxious for the government to take greater responsibility for solving social problems.[88] When, in 1965, he informed the heads of departments responsible for public housing, social services and related activities of his intention, he discovered that they had no wish to discuss a reform agenda with him. In his determination to awaken a sense of social obligation among his senior officials, he presented a new request the following year in the humblest terms. 'An occasional exchange of views,' he pleaded, 'might freshen ideas all round,' adding that 'I do not think a meeting or two on these lines could do any harm, anyway, just to see if anything transpires.' Eventually, he was allowed to put tentative suggestions to a group of senior officials.

Trench's agenda for discussion turned out to be as menacing to the prevailing political culture of Hong Kong as the senior officials had suspected from the start. He wanted to talk about 'possible lines of attack on squatter problems generally', a minimum wage and shorter working hours for the labour force as a whole and more cultural activities. He also favoured social insurance.[89] Trench's difficulties in imposing his personal policies on the civil service provide compelling evidence of the anti-welfare and anti-social expenditure culture which prevailed among senior officials.

The outbreak of bombs, street violence and strikes in 1967 came as a boon to Trench's opponents. Officials were too busy with the security crisis to attend forums on social issues, they decided. In any case, that year's events gave the colonial administration some justification for feeling complacent about the public's tolerance of poor social conditions and extensive exploitation of the workforce.[90] Even commentators sympathetic to the case for better social services and worker protection conceded that these issues had little to do with the campaign against colonialism in 1967 (nor had they been a factor in the Star Ferry riots of the previous year).[91]

The Governor failed to achieve his plans for improved protection for industrial workers, for a public provident fund for retirement and for a social insurance scheme. On one issue, however, Trench proved more stubborn than the anti-welfare camp within the colonial administration. In 1966, he had formed a personal alliance with the Director of the Social Welfare Department to establish a social security system which would provide monetary benefits that would ensure a subsistence standard of living for those in serious need.[92] The department, predictably enough, allowed itself to be trapped for four years into an argument about the definition of subsistence and how many dollars a day were needed to stay alive.[93] At length, Trench broke through the endless bureaucratic correspondence with the announcement that 'an organized and wholly government sponsored system of public assistance' would be introduced. His firmness silenced potential business critics and convinced the community that a Public Assistance Scheme could be afforded.[94] It started to operate in 1971.

Another Governor tries again

By that year, the Social Welfare Department was shaking off its own Third World heritage, and welfare seemed at last to command a respectable priority on the official agenda. Its professional staff had grown in numbers over the previous decade. They now had the experience and the professional expertise to deal with the overlords of finance and policy on more equal terms. The most visible evidence of the department's newfound credentials was the production of workable policy documents and plans. In 1973, the long-delayed five-year plan appeared at last, together with the first of a series of White Papers and the first programme for elderly care. In 1977, Green Papers on the elderly and on social security were published, as well as recommendations for a new deal for the disabled.

The appointment of Sir Murray (later Lord) MacLehose as Governor in 1971 has been hailed by most commentators as the start of a new, caring era.[95] MacLehose had the advantage of being a much better public performer than most of his predecessors. His personal commitment to social reform is open to dispute, however.[96] Most notably, in response to demands from the British Prime Minister, he made a public pledge in 1975 that Hong Kong would 'achieve broad comparability of labour legislation and social welfare with other Asian countries, excluding Japan, by 1980'.[97] This deadline was essentially a conjuring trick. The colonial administration had already claimed to have met these Asian benchmarks, which were in any case ill-defined and undemanding.[98]

Overall, MacLehose's chances of improving on Trench's record were never promising. The new Governor was warned on his arrival that he would face stubborn opposition to social reform from business as well as the bureaucracy.[99] And so it turned out. MacLehose's most ambitious proposals were for social insurance and labour protection. Here, he was to suffer public humiliation at the hands of business leaders. In 1976, he proposed that the able-bodied unemployed should be eligible for public assistance benefits.[100] He had every reason to believe that this package would be endorsed by the business and professional elite.[101]

The following year, a blueprint for the introduction of a modern social insurance scheme was published. A Green Paper, 'Help for Those Least Able to Help Themselves', outlined 'a semi-voluntary contributory sickness, injury and death benefit scheme'. Business support promptly evaporated, and MacLehose announced that his reform proposals might be replaced by 'a counter-scheme to cover the same risks' put forward by 'a group of employers'.[102] In 1981, he finally withdrew the Green Paper's blueprint as 'too difficult to apply', including the proposed retirement benefits.[103] All that he managed to save was the extension to jobless workers in 1978 of Trench's 1971 Public Assistance Scheme.

These setbacks slowed but did not halt the modernisation of welfare programmes, both by the Social Welfare Department and the NGOs. By the 1980s, the professionals had become a considerable lobby which the government could no longer ignore. The community's awareness of social problems had improved, which forced a new level of accountability on the government. In 1991, welfare seemed to have won. A White Paper that year discarded the anti-social expenditure culture that had dominated official attitudes since the Social Welfare Department's establishment three decades earlier. 'Social welfare services should not be regarded as some form of charity, confined to the socially and financially disadvantaged,' this policy document laid down, '[t]he services are, and should be, available to all who need them.' This principle sounded like a statement of entitlement for those who in a modern society 'cannot cope without outside support'. The government retained an escape clause, nevertheless. The spectre of a 'dependency culture' was highlighted as a threat created by welfare 'that undermines the productive engine of the economy'.[104] That anxiety was to become the rationale for rejecting any suggestion of entitlement in the years ahead.

End of an era

In the meantime, Patten had taken over in 1992. Behind the scenes, the opposition to social expenditure was gathering new strength. The prevailing wisdom in Western nations was that government social services were expensive and poorly managed. The public would benefit from the greater choice and flexibility that the introduction of business practices and procedures would bring, it was argued. Earlier chapters indicated how the higher echelons of the Hong Kong civil service embraced this business-based model. As Conservative Party Chairman and a senior Cabinet Minister under Margaret Thatcher, Patten had been involved in promoting such views in the United Kingdom. In Hong Kong, he showed a sympathetic and often encouraging attitude towards reducing the government's role in the provision of housing and social services.

Yet, Patten possessed a strong personal commitment to those in need despite his Thatcherite background. On his arrival, he had quickly made himself familiar with the serious plight of Hong Kong's most vulnerable groups. He insisted that 'the deprived and the disabled' should be freed from 'any doubt about our determination to care for them properly in the years ahead'.[105] In 1992, he announced plans for a modern system of social security which would provide a wide range of cash benefits to ease the special financial burdens created by different forms of disability, disadvantage and deprivation. He responded with serious concern on discovering that 'those eligible for CSSA [the new social security scheme] were not coming forward' and discussed with the senior official responsible for welfare policy how to improve the take-up rate.[106] This refreshing level of social concern was to prove no blank cheque, however. Housing and social services did not dominate his agenda. They accounted for only 21 per cent of the 1,432 separate policy initiatives he introduced between 1992 and 1996.[107]

Consultants hired by the Social Welfare Department in 1995 recommended a drastic change in the subvention system. The department would no longer set the staffing standards which NGOs should meet, which, in practice, was an indirect but effective form of professional quality control. Instead, the department's responsibilities would be reduced to purchasing services from NGOs for a fixed price. A system to set average quality standards for services would be created. The opposition to the proposals was so intense that the colonial administration decided in 1996 not to proceed openly with the consultants' recommendations. Plans were laid, nevertheless, for a phased introduction of the recommendations from 1997 onwards.[108]

Conclusions

The picture that emerges from this chapter is of beleaguered professionals, in the health and welfare sectors especially, breaking through the financial and bureaucratic barriers erected by the colonial administration's senior officials. The more generous funding allocated to health, education and welfare in the 1990s was too little, nevertheless, to make up for earlier decades of under-spending. In the present century, health education and welfare services were to be badly handicapped by this legacy.

The future development of all three major social services was under serious threat as British rule was coming to an end. Opposition to social expenditure was gathering strength because of the growing prestige of the business model as the key to public sector efficiency. Within the health, education and welfare fields, the professionals were poorly placed to insist that their values and commitment should not be commercialised. In any case, the social reforms had come so late in the colonial era that they were easily reversed, as the next chapter will make clear.

Notes

1. *Report of the Commission . . . to Enquire into the Causes and Effects of the Present Trade Recession . . .* (Hong Kong: Noronha & Co., 1935), pp. 93–4.
2. Alfred H. Y. Lin, 'Warlord, Social Welfare and Philanthropy: The Case of Guangzhou under Chen Jitang, 1929–1936', *Modern China*, Vol. 30, No. 2 (April 2004), pp. 153, 192.
3. Sir Geoffry Northcote, Governor, *Hong Kong Hansard* (*HH*, hereafter), 13 October 1938, pp. 119–27.
4. Population data are derived from *Report on the Social & Economic Progress . . . for the Year 1938*, pp. 5, 7; *Report on the Social & Economic Progress . . . for the Year 1939*, p. 1.
5. Dr P. S. (later Sir Selwyn) Selwyn Clarke, Director of Medical Services, *HH*, 16 November 1939, pp. 219, 229.
6. *Taxation Committee Report* (Hong Kong: Noronha & Co., Ltd., 1939), p. 89; Northcote, *HH*, 13 October 1938, p. 116; Northcote, and Sydney (later Sir Sydney) Caine, Financial Secretary, *HH*, 16 November 1939, pp. 216, 219–20, 229. Business representatives were able, nevertheless, to keep the scope and level of taxation to much lower levels than was the norm in the United Kingdom and elsewhere in its colonial empire. Michael Littlewood, *Taxation without Representation: The History of Hong Kong's Troublingly Successful Tax System* (Hong Kong: Hong Kong University Press, 2010), Chapter 2.
7. Lo (later Sir) Man-kam, *HH*, 1 May 1947, pp. 139–40.
8. On the contrast between pre-and post-war social policies, see Leo F. Goodstadt, 'The Rise and Fall of Social, Economic and Political Reforms in Hong Kong, 1930–1955', *Journal of the Royal Asiatic Society Hong Kong Branch*, Vol. 44 (2004), pp. 57–81.
9. *Hong Kong Annual Report 1956* (Hong Kong: Government Printer, 1956), p. 6.
10. (1) DSW memo to CS, 'Social Welfare Planning', 13 November 1964. HKRS146–8-3–1 'Social Welfare Development Programme 1960–67'.
11. *Annual Report on Hong Kong for the Year 1946* (Hong Kong: Government of Hong Kong, 1947), pp. 4–5.
12. Population estimates for the early post-war years must be used with caution. The 1946 figure was based on registration for ration cards. The 1948 figure represented a respectable consensus of various departmental estimates. M. 6, 22 March 1946; M. 13 and M. 21 DSTI to Colonial Secretary, 29 January and 24 February 1947. HKRS170–2-1 'Census Estimate of Population'; 'Report on the Population of the Colony, Mid-Year 1949' (mimeo, Department of Statistics, 12 June 1949), pp. 2, 4, 13. HKRS259–6-1 'Report on the Population of the Colony, Mid-Year 1949'.

13. Leo F. Goodstadt, *Profits, Politics and Panics: Hong Kong's Banks and the Making of a Miracle Economy, 1935–1985* (Hong Kong: Hong Kong University Press, 2007), 'Table I: Domestic Exports and Total Exports, 1950–1960 (HKD millions)', p. 69.

14. The available statistics are far from ideal, but for 1951–2, they indicate that men found jobs easily, women less so. (26) Acting Government Statistician memo to Social Welfare Officer, 18 December 1951. HKRS22–1-73 'Social Welfare Squatters'; (124) [data from squatter survey in late 1952]. HKRS22–1-74 'Social Welfare Squatters'.

15. Hong Kong Government, *A Problem of People* (Hong Kong: Government Printer, n.d.), pp. 15–7.

16. With the exception of the 'May influx' in 1962, when Guangdong Province allowed a brief lifting of frontier controls.

17. David Podmore, 'The Population of Hong Kong', in Keith Hopkins (ed.), *Hong Kong: The Industrial Colony. A Political, Social and Economic Survey* (Hong Kong: Oxford University Press, 1971), p. 25.

18. Governor letter to Secretary of State, 9 February 1952, Sec. 0/2306/51. HKRS229–1-49 'United Kingdom Income Tax Act . . . '.

19. Sir John Cowperthwaite, Financial Secretary, *HH*, 26 February 1964, p. 51; 25 February 1965, p. 66; 24 February 1966, pp. 69, 73; 28 February 1968, pp. 58, 64, 66; 28 March 1968, p. 212. Sir Philip Haddon-Cave, Chief Secretary (former Financial Secretary), speech at Annual Banquet of the Overseas Bankers' Club (London), *Government Information Services* (*GIS* hereafter) (mimeo), 2 February 1982, p. 4.

20. Sir John Bremridge, Financial Secretary, *HH*, 24 February 1982, p. 428.

21. Data are from Census and Statistics Department, *2004 Gross Domestic Product* (Hong Kong: Government of the HKSAR, 2005), p. 20. Incomes were a different matter. Over much of this period, the distribution of incomes had become increasingly unequal despite a chronic shortage of labour. For a discussion of this issue, see Hon-Kwong Lui, *Income Inequality and Economic Development* (Hong Kong: City University of Hong Kong Press, 1997).

22. In addition, the capital costs, he claimed, would be equal to two years' expenditure on the resettlement housing programme. He also made an alarmist reference to United Kingdom tax rates. Cowperthwaite, *HH*, 26 February 1964, p. 52.

23. Haddon-Cave, Financial Secretary, *HH*, 1 March 1978, p. 542.

24. Ample examples can be found in HKRS146–8-3–1.

25. M. 29 M. D. A. Clinton, DCS, to PACS(S), 18 March 1971. HKRS146–8-3–1.

26. For example, a belief in the unique role of the 'Chinese family' among financial officials led to the informal exemption of Chinese 'native' banks from complying with the 1948 Banking Ordinance's requirements. The outcome was disastrous for depositors, and this sector of the financial services industry was decimated in the 1950s. Leo F. Goodstadt, 'Dangerous Business Models: Bankers, Bureaucrats & Hong Kong's Economic Transformation, 1948–86', *HKIMR Working Paper No. 8/2006*. June 2006, pp. 1, 6–9, 17–8.

27. *Hong Kong Departmental Report by the Social Welfare Officer for the Period 1948–54* (Hong Kong: Government Printer, n.d.), p. 1; CO1030/273 'Social Welfare Reports Hong Kong Covering 1954–57'.

28. *Hong Kong Annual Report of the Commissioner of Labour 1st April, 1948 to 31st March, 1949* (Hong Kong: n.p., n.d.), p. 24.

29. (4) 'Social Welfare Office Quarterly Report for . . . 1st April 1951 to 30th June 1951', p. 3. HKRS170-1-571-1 'Social Welfare Office Quarterly Progress Report'.

30. The example of breakdown cited was individuals disabled in industrial accidents. *Hong Kong Annual Departmental Report by the Commissioner of Labour . . . for the Financial Year 1956–57* (Hong Kong: Government Printer, n.d.), p. 73.

31. *Hong Kong Annual Departmental Report by the Commissioner of Labour for the Financial Year 1954–55* (Hong Kong: Government Printer, n.d.), p. 60.

32. M. 45 FS (J. J. Cowperthwaite), 11 May 1962. HKRS146-8-3-1.

33. See also Roger Bristow, *Hong Kong's New Towns: A Selective Review* (Hong Kong: Oxford University Press, 1989), pp. 40, 50.

34. David R. Phillips, *The Epidemiological Transition in Hong Kong: Changes in Health and Disease since the Nineteenth Century* (Hong Kong: Centre of Asian Studies, University of Hong Kong, 1988), pp. 18, 30.

35. For example, the superior child-health statistics for Hong Kong (and other better-off Chinese communities) by comparison with prosperous Western countries are still not fully understood according to Professor C. Y. Yeung, 'Health Problems in Chinese Children are Different', *Hong Kong Journal of Paediatrics*, Vol. 8, No. 2 (2003), p. 80.

36. Northcote, *HH*, 13 October 1938, pp. 119–27; Northcote and Selwyn Clarke, Director of Medical Services, *HH*, 16 November 1939, pp. 216, 219–20, 229.

37. (1) DMS secret memo to CS, 5 August 1946; Ag CS minute to Governor, 13 August 1946. HKRS163-1-280 'Tung Wah and Associated Hospitals. Proposals for the Government to take operation . . .'.

38. Although this term was not used. Governor minute 13 August 1946; SCA minute to CS, 26 March 1947. HKRS163-1-280.

39. Details of this bizarre event are preserved in HKRS163-1-828 'Tung Wah Eastern Hospital. Conversion of . . . into a teaching hospital'.

40. M. 63 A.C.O., 3 September 1959. HKRS306-1-142 'Abandoned Children'.

41. M. 1 AS2 to DCS, 11 April 1953. HKRS163-1-280.

42. (28)[A] 'Medical Development Plan Standing Committee Clinical Pathology Building Kwong Wah Hospital', Memo Paper No. 17/71, 19 October 1971. HKRS307-6-18 'Kwong Wah Hospital Future Development'.

43. (8)[1] 'Medical Development Programme Working Group Minutes . . . 8th February 1979', p. 1 and (12)[1] 'Medical Development Programme Working Group Minutes . . . 22nd February 1979', p. 1. HKRS146-12-20 'Medical Development Programme Working Group Minutes of Meeting and General'.

44. Catherine Jones, *Promoting Prosperity: The Hong Kong Way of Social Policy* (Hong Kong: Chinese University Press, 1990), pp. 177–8.

45. *The Further Development of Medical and Health Services in Hong Kong* (Hong Kong: Government Printer, 1974), p. v.

46. Leung Man-fuk, 'Medical and Health', in Choi Po-king and Ho Lok-sang (eds.), *The Other Hong Kong Report 1993* (Hong Kong: Chinese University Press, 1993), p. 232.

47. Victor C. W. Wong, 'Medical and Health', in Nyaw Mee-kau and Li Si-ming (eds.), *The Other Hong Kong Report 1996* (Hong Kong: Chinese University Press, 1996), p. 449.

48. (9) 'Medical Development Advisory Committee Review 1978/79', M.D.A.C. Joint Secretaries Paper No. 6 (March 1979 mimeo), p. 5. HKRS482–2-16–5 'Medical Development Advisory Committee'.

49. Yeung, 'Health Problems in Chinese Children are Different', pp. 70–86.

50. Joel W. Hay, *Health Care in Hong Kong: An Economic Policy Assessment* (Hong Kong: Chinese University Press, 1991), p. 31.

51 Yeung, 'Health Problems in Chinese Children Are Different', pp. 78–80.

52. Anthony Ng, 'Medical and Health', in T. L. Tsim and Bernard H. K. Luk (eds.), *The Other Hong Kong Report* (Hong Kong: Chinese University Press, 1989), pp. 189–90.

53. Leung, 'Medical and Health', p. 232; Robin Gauld and Derek Gould, *The Hong Kong Health Sector: Development and Change* (Hong Kong: Chinese University Press, 2002), pp. 56–7.

54. The major improvements are listed in C. Grant and P. Yuen, *The Hong Kong Health Care System* (Sydney: University of New South Wales, 1998), pp. 173–81. See also Peter P. Yuen, 'Dissatisfaction of Health Providers and Consumers: Health Care Reform Intransigence and SARS Outbreak Mismanagement', in Joseph Y. S. Cheng (ed.), *The July 1 Protest Rally: Interpreting a Historic Event* (Hong Kong: City University of Hong Kong Press, 2005), p. 448.

55. Hospital Authority, *Rising to the Challenge. Annual Plan 2000–2001* (Hong Kong: Hospital Authority, 2000), Vol. 1, p. 10.

56. P. C. Leung, 'Health and Medical Services', in Larry Chuen-ho Chow and Yiu-kwan Ho (eds.), *The Other Hong Kong Report 1998* (Hong Kong: Chinese University Press, 1999), pp. 285–6.

57. 'Note for Executive Council. Progress of Management Reforms by the Hospital Authority' (XCRI(96)21, 25 November 1996), pp. 3–4.

58. DPS/GH to SHW [Loose Minute of meeting with the Governor], 8 January 1997.

59. Lok Sang Ho, *Health Care Delivery and Financing in Hong Kong* (Hong Kong: City University of Hong Kong Press, 1997), pp. 9, 40.

60. Victor C. W. Wong, *The Political Economy of Health Care Development and Reforms in Hong Kong* (Aldershot: Ashgate, 1999), pp. 158–9, 171–4.

61. Ibid., pp. 204–12.

62. Two notable examples were: Harvard Team, *Improving Hong Kong's Health Care System: Why and For Whom?* (Hong Kong: Government Printer, 1999) and Health and Welfare Bureau, *Lifelong Investment in Health: Consultation Document on Health Care Reform* (Hong Kong: Government Secretariat, 2000).

63. The government was in no hurry to achieve this goal, nevertheless: 'This right is one we cannot fulfil now or next year, or I ventured to say, in ten years.' D. M. MacDougall, Colonial Secretary, *HH*, 8 September 1948, p. 253.

64. M. 92 DCS to CS, 9 June 1959; M. 93 FS to CS, 22 June 1959; M. 96 HE, 27 July 1959. HKRS457–2-5 'Financial Review of Educational Costs'.

65. Officials' attitudes towards unregistered schools are recorded in HKRS 8901–1-12 'Education/Social Welfare. 1 Facilities for Children of Primary School Age. 2 Unregistered Schools'.

66. Sir David Trench, Governor, *HH*, 26 February 1969, p. 68.

67. Special Committee on Housing, *Hong Kong Housing Survey 1957* (Hong Kong: 1958, mimeo), Vol. III and IV, Tables P 28A and P 29A; K. M. A. Barnett, *Hongkong: Report on the 1966 By-Census* (Hong Kong: Government Printer, n.d.), Vol. I, p. xi; Vol. II, pp. lxvii, 54, 57, 69; Census and Statistics Department, *Hong Kong Population and Housing Census 1971 Main Report* (Hong Kong: n.p., n.d.), p. 65; *Hong Kong By-Census 1976: Main Report. Volume 1: Analysis* (Hong Kong: Government Printer, 1979), p. 54.

68. In fairness, such a view has its contemporary supporters. An authoritative study of global experience since the 1960s found only a limited connection between economic success and the length and quality of education. There is 'only a weak correlation between economic growth and aggregate measures of improvements in educational attainment . . . even an optimistic valuation of the return to education would lead to only small differences in economic growth rates'. Barry P. Bosworth and Susan M. Collins, 'The Empirics of Growth: An Update', *Brookings Papers on Economic Activity*, Vol. 2003, No. 2 (2003), pp. 138–8, 140, 170. These findings were based on data covering 1960 to 2000, 84 countries, 95 per cent of gross world product and 84 per cent of the world's population.

69. Francis Yuan-hao Tien, *HH*, 30 March 1978, p. 696.

70. For details of the two departments' campaign and data on their success see HKRS1017–3-1 'Children Engaged in Industrial Employment in Hong Kong'.

71. Visiting Panel, *A Perspective on Education in Hong Kong November 1982* (Hong Kong: Government Printer, 1983), p. 49.

72. Ibid., p. 56.

73. T. L. Sun Pong, 'Caput Schools into Aided Schools: Perceptions of Hong Kong Principals on the Transition', M. Ed. Thesis (University of Hong Kong, 1983).

74. Tony Ng Shu-ming et al., 'Chapter 7 Education and Manpower Bureau: Planning and Provision of Public Secondary School Places' (Hong Kong: Audit Commission, 18 October 2003), pp. 29–34.

75. Kai-ming Cheng, 'Financing Education: An International Perspective', in Yue-ping Chung and Richard Yue-chim Wong (eds.), *The Economics and Financing of Hong Kong Education* (Hong Kong: Chinese University Press, 1992), p. 278.

76. Chris D. Godwin, Principal Assistant Secretary, Education and Manpower Branch, 'Pilot Study One: The School Education Programme: Redefining

the Relationship between Policy Branch and Department', in Jane C. Y. Lee and Anthony B. L. Cheung (eds.), *Public Sector Reform in Hong Kong: Key Concepts, Progress-to-Date and Future Directions* (Hong Kong: Chinese University Press, 1995), pp. 95, 96–7.

77. Note the caution, especially in relation to the impact of economic change, expressed by Anthony Sweeting in 'Education Policy and the 1997 Factor: The Art of the Possible Interacting with the Dismal Science', *Comparative Education*, Vol. 33, No. 2, Special Number (19) (June 1997), pp. 172, 176–7, 182.

78. Cheng Kai Ming, 'Educational Policymaking in Hong Kong: The Changing Legitimacy', in Gerard A. Postiglione (ed.), *Education and Society in Hong Kong: Toward One Country and Two Systems* (Armonk: M. E. Sharpe, Inc., 1991), p. 113.

79. Lee Wing-on and Mark Bray, 'Education: Evolving Patterns and Challenges', in Joseph Y. S. Cheng and Sonny S. H. Lo (eds.), *From Colony to SAR: Hong Kong's Challenges Ahead* (Hong Kong: Chinese University Press, 1995), pp. 370–2.

80. Tung Chee Hwa, Chief Executive, *GIS*, 13 August 2001.

81. Ching-kwan Lee and Tak-sing Cheung, 'Egalitarianism and Secondary School Places in Hong Kong', in Postiglione (ed.), *Education and Society in Hong Kong: Toward One Country and Two Systems*, p. 163.

82. M. 1 DFS to DSW, 11 October 1958; M. 19 DCS to CS, 22 December 1960. HKRS146–8-3-1.

83. M. 29 M. D. A. Clinton, DCS, to PACS(S), 18 March 1971. HKRS146–8-3-1.

84. M. 45 FS, 11 May 1962. HKRS146–8-3-1.

85. For example, Cowperthwaite, Financial Secretary, *HH*, 28 February 1962, p. 57; 25 February 1970, pp. 368–9; 24 February 1971, p. 419.

86. *Aims and Policy for Social Welfare in Hong Kong* (Hong Kong: Government Printer, 1964), pp. 9, 11–12; *Aims and Policy for Social Welfare in Hong Kong Revised* (Hong Kong: Government Printer, 1965), p. 11.

87. The record of administrative disasters is set out in HKRS146–8-3-4 'Policy on Social Welfare — Social Welfare Development 1960–67'.

88. He was also struggling to start serious discussion of how to take the first, tentative steps towards a social insurance system. M. 36 Governor, 10 November 1965. HKRS307–3-15 'Social Security in Hong Kong'.

89. (18)[1] Notes of GH Meeting, 28 November 1966. HKRS163–3-264 'Co-ordination of Social Service Policies'.

90. The key documents recording Trench's frustrations are in HKRS163–3-264.

91. A conspicuous example of this sort of analysis at the time was Derek G. Davies, 'Hongkong Affairs: A Position of Strength', *Far Eastern Economic Review*, 30 July/5 August 1967. The Star Ferry riots had a similar outcome. The same publication had initially identified the government's social deficiencies as crucial, but it treated the official report on the incident in highly patronising terms. See Editorial, 'Hongkong Affairs: Post Mortem', *Far Eastern Economic Review*, 2 March 1967.

92. (7) 'Notes of a meeting with the Governor [Sir David Trench] on 15th April 1966 by D. S. W.' HKRS890–2-31 'Correspondence with the Governor and notes of discussions with H. E.'.

93. Details of these developments are to be found in HKRS890–1-15 'Subsistence Level' and HKRS307–3-17 'Social Security in Hong Kong'.

94. Sir David Trench, *HH*, 26 February 1969, p. 61.

95. MacLehose, one scholar has stated, was specially selected by the United Kingdom government in the wake of political unrest in the 1960s because of his 'firm commitment to social reform'. That study then demonstrates that even MacLehose's much vaunted reforms to the public housing programme were continuations of Trench's initiatives. Christopher John Mackay, 'Housing Management and the Comprehensive Housing Model in Hong Kong: A Case Study of Colonial Influence', *Journal of Contemporary China*, Vol. 9, No. 25 (2000), p. 459, fn. 53.

96. But note the tributes recorded in Paul Wilding, 'Social Policy and Social Development in Hong Kong', *Public and Social Administration Working Paper Series 1996/3*, City University of Hong Kong, p. 13.

97. (3) Governor to Secretary for Home Affairs, 15 November 1973; (7)[1] 'Notes of a Discussion HE/C for L . . . 11 June 1977'; (27) 'Part of HE's "Brief" in May 1978 . . . ' HKRS1017–3-22 'Discussions with Comments by H. E. on Labour Matters'; MacLehose, *HH*, 6 October 1976, p. 20.

98. The British Parliament had already been told that standards of labour protection in Hong Kong 'compare very well with other countries in the area'. David Ennals, Secretary of State for Foreign and Commonwealth Affairs, *House of Commons Debates*, vol. 871, Col. 436, 27 March 1974. Significantly, claims of this sort had been criticised as misleading by London officials shortly before this ministerial statement. (50) 'Extract from Report by Overseas Labour Adviser Foreign and Commonwealth Office. Visit 9–21 Feb. 1974'. HKRS146–4-18 (10) 'International Labour Organisation Annual reports on Application of International Labour Conventions'.

99. Derek Davies, 'Hongkong: A Letter to the Governor', *Far Eastern Economic Review*, 27 November 1971.

100. MacLehose, *HH*, 6 October 1976, pp. 18–9.

101. According to industry's leading spokesman in the legislature, business support for MacLehose's reforms was overwhelming. Dr (later Sir Sze-yuen) Chung Sze-yuen, *HH*, 27 October 1976, pp. 79–80.

102. MacLehose, *HH*, 11 October 1978, p. 25.

103. MacLehose, *HH*, 7 October 1981, p. 21.

104. *Social Welfare into the 1990s and Beyond* (Hong Kong: Government Printer, 1991), p. 14.

105. Christopher Patten, Governor, *HH*, 7 October 1992, pp. 23–4.

106. The officials responsible agreed on an improved publicity campaign but as Patten was soon to depart, nothing was done in practice to raise the take-up rate. DPS/GH to SHW [Loose Minute of meeting with the Governor], 8 January 1997.

107. The misconceptions about Lord Patten and his agenda are further illustrated by the fact that less than 2 per cent of his initiatives related to political

issues. The data are derived from the annual *Policy Commitment* and *Progress Reports* for these years, together with 'Overview', *Progress Report. The 1997 Policy Address* (Hong Kong: Information Services Department, 1997).

108. For details of this affair, see 'Note for Executive Council: Review of the Social Welfare Subvention System' (XCCI(96)40, 26 September 1996) and Annexes. This paper was remarkable for an attack on the existing subvention system unsupported by any financial or other statistics to quantify the benefits that the proposed changes would generate.

5
Social Reforms: The New Poverty

No matter how stubbornly the government had resisted increased social expenditure and how firmly it had collaborated with the business and professional elite in rejecting social reforms until the 1970s, the development of health, education and welfare services could not be suppressed indefinitely. The government had eventually accepted responsibility for providing more and better public housing and social services. This commitment was not to last, however. In the new century, not only did the government seek to limit its social responsibilities but the reforms of the last two decades were deliberately reversed.

A dismantling got under way of the social service programmes. Some features of the 1990s system simply disappeared: the provision of virtually free hospital treatment for the entire community, for example, and access to the best government-subsidised schools regardless of family income. The quality of services was also under threat. The professionals were able to defend standards for some services more successfully than others. Hospital care in general withstood the destructive pressures of austerity better than post-secondary education, for example.

The situation was further complicated by government innovations which were supposed to offer more modern and efficient solutions to social problems, in particular the management of welfare services provided by non-governmental organisations (NGOs). In practice, waiting lists remained disgracefully long, regardless of the severity of the physical and mental distress of those in need of care. In reviewing this often chaotic and confusing process, this chapter can only seek to identify the most seriously harmful developments and to highlight some of the more glaring examples of the new poverty and the damage that government policies were inflicting on particularly vulnerable groups.

The retreat from the government's commitment to decent social services was all the more rapid because it had got under way — largely unnoticed by the community — even before the 1997–98 Asian financial crisis. Business leaders had fought vigorously against improvements in social programmes during the 1990s.[1] Senior officials mostly shared the business community's conviction that the public sector was inherently wasteful and less efficient than the commercial world. The colonial administration had embarked on schemes before 1997 to seek greater value for money in the housing field, for example, and to increase cost recovery in public hospitals.[2] The Social Welfare Department, the previous chapter explained, was supposed to adopt a private sector approach and transform the existing system for subsidising the welfare services into contractual undertakings with non-governmental organisations (NGOs). These had warned the government in 1995–96 that they would be unable to operate effectively under such an arrangement, which officials confessed was 'a genuine and justifiable concern'. Their reservations were disregarded, however, both before and after 1997.[3]

Without the consultancies and blueprints that were commissioned to promote a business culture within the public sector during the closing years of British rule, the retreat from the reform initiatives of the 1990s could not have taken place so quickly in the new century. As the economy went into recession during 1997–98, the momentum to dismantle past reforms gathered speed. The government faced no significant opposition to its claims that welfare had become unaffordable and that expansion of the social services was unsustainable. Fees and charges were raised, and cuts took place in the range of benefits provided through social security and by the social services in general.

Health: Painful Cuts

Hospitals were a prime target for cutbacks, partly because universal, low-cost public medicine looked like 'welfarism' at its worst, and the ruling elite wanted to boost the private sector. The modernisation of the hospital system in the 1990s, ironically, had made it easier for policymakers to undo its achievements. The Hospital Authority had become a free-standing statutory body, and the government's duty to allocate adequate funding in the annual Budget was thus obscured. Officials could now distance themselves from the supply of hospital services and from responsibility for their finances, creating the impression that it was the Authority's fault if it had cash problems which affected the quality of hospital care.

The separate status of the Hospital Authority also made it easier for the government to adopt the role of outside observer and to blame the victims for the unsatisfactory state of the health services. In 2005, the second Chief Executive, Donald Tsang Yam-kuen, provoked outrage by claiming that older people exaggerated their ailments. They queued at government clinics for several hours from dawn, he opined, as a pleasant prelude to a 'chat with their "buddies" [and] morning tea in a Chinese restaurant'.[4] This patronising comment reflected an attitude typical within the government. Subsequent official statements held the elderly directly responsible for the increased pressure on the available medical professionals and hospital facilities.[5]

The hospitals fight back

Unlike the rest of the public sector, the Hospital Authority did not surrender to financial cutbacks without a struggle. It challenged government claims that the social services were provided with ample funding, publishing statistics that showed spending on healthcare in Hong Kong was below the average for advanced economies.[6] But the pressure on the Authority's finances was unrelenting. Health services were not given adequate funding even after the SARS epidemic of 2003 which caused disruption to existing services, unforeseen additional expenditure and an urgent need for measures to raise standards.[7]

In 2005, Donald Tsang, who had been Financial Secretary when the budget constraints were first imposed, reassured the legislature that 'there has been no deterioration of service quality' in hospitals despite the financial cuts.[8] This claim had been already contradicted by the Hospital Authority and was to be challenged in its official statements during the years that followed.

- 2003: The Authority had warned that the government's new financial arrangements had cut the resources available of both money and staff, leading to longer waiting times and poorer services for patients.[9]
- 2005: The Authority explained that because of 'limitation of resources', treatment had to be rationed to those with 'more urgent conditions'; while 'quality started to be compromised' for other patients.[10]
- 2007: The Authority revealed that because of the inadequate annual budget, there was no alternative to 'limiting or refusing introduction of new technologies and pharmaceuticals, and delaying the replacement of equipment'.[11]
- 2008: The Authority admitted that waiting times had grown longer throughout the decade in all specialties, particularly surgical.[12]
- 2013: The Authority announced that by 2021, the total number of beds would rise by almost 10 per cent. The increase would be just sufficient to restore the number of beds to their level at the start of the austerity drive in 2000.[13]

Drugs denied

Quality of treatment — and medication especially — turned into a major battlefront in the government's drive to hold down its financial commitments to healthcare. The ruthlessness of the budgetary assault on the Hospital Authority became evident in 2001 when the official responsible for health policy revealed an extensive list of implants and drugs which would not be available to patients except at their own expense. The victims of this austerity were all patients with life-threatening diseases or in danger of severe disabilities. The charges for pacemakers seemed like outright extortion: what family would fail to go to desperate lengths to find the money to keep alive a relative with a damaged heart? Even children were given no special consideration. Among the drugs that patients had now to pay for were:

- growth hormone for children afflicted with growth retardation;
- interferon for hepatitis, leukaemia and multiple sclerosis;
- taxane, letrozole and anastrozole for breast cancer; and
- drugs for use following kidney transplants and during anti-cancer chemotherapy.[14]

What happened to patients who could not afford these 'self-financed items'? They could still expect 'effective treatment', officials claimed: 'the great majority of prescriptions' which patients would be given instead were 'drugs of proven efficacy'.[15] Hence, within the Hospital Authority, there was a catchphrase: patients get the right but not necessarily the best treatment.

By law, the government was not free to use higher fees and charges to ration hospital care. The health minister was empowered to set the scale of charges, but the Hospital Authority Ordinance also laid down 'that no person should be prevented, through lack of means, from obtaining adequate medical treatment'.[16] An equitable system of waivers for fees and charges that worked smoothly at the patient level proved impossible to devise, according to the government's own account.[17] Thus, to comply with the letter of the law, the government reinterpreted its statutory obligation not to allocate care on the basis of affordability. In 2006, the health minister explained how the government was able 'to ensure that no one will be denied treatment because of lack of means' thanks to the Samaritan Fund which was administered but not financed by the Hospital Authority.[18] This fund had been set up in 1950 when the colonial administration was rejecting any obligation for the immigrant community's social wellbeing. Its very name was a disclaimer of public responsibility for those in need and a denial of an obligation to provide assistance except on the part of individuals and institutions inspired by charitable ideals.

The bad Samaritan

Behind the budgetary rhetoric and bureaucratic sleight of hand, the sick continued to suffer unnecessarily because of the failure to provide the most up-to-date treatment. The 'Introduction' described the mistreatment of the mentally ill who, for years, continued to be prescribed outdated medication which had distressing side effects. The full range of patients with other illnesses denied modern medication is hard to calculate with any accuracy because of the obscurantism that surrounds the official data.

One dreadful indicator was provided by the Hospital Authority when introducing a fee-waiver scheme for patients whose cancers did not qualify for help from the Samaritan Fund. The new Community Care Fund would finance drugs to treat 'seven specific cancer diseases', the Authority announced in 2011: 'lung cancer, leukemia, colorectal cancer, renal cell carcinoma, gastrointestinal tumour, breast cancer and ovarian cancer'. A thousand patients were expected to benefit from the new arrangement in its first year.[19] They were the lucky ones. How many would remain on a waiting list and for how long was not revealed. Also undisclosed was the number of patients denied these drugs in the past, whose lives could have been improved or extended if modern medication had been made available to them in previous years. The new Fund and its programme also demonstrated that the Samaritan Fund was no guarantee that the government was meeting its legal duty 'to ensure that no one will be denied treatment because of lack of means'.

The government found a variety of excuses for not ending the misery caused by persistently under-funding the treatment of the seriously ill. Legislative Councillors expressed misgivings about the Samaritan Fund and asked the government in 2012 'to hammer out a long term funding arrangement' for the Fund. Officials responded with delaying tactics: this issue was to be dealt with in the larger context of healthcare financing and a forthcoming public consultation. In vain, too, did legislators call for an end to 'self-financed' medication and urge that patients have access at subsidised prices to all drugs 'proven to be of significant benefits'.[20]

Medical inflation and longevity

The health sector posed a unique challenge for the government's policymakers. Officials feared that they would be unable to resist the public's demands for excellence in healthcare. They felt overwhelmed by the pace at which medical science progresses. The spectre of what was called 'medical inflation caused by the availability of new drugs' was articulated by the health minister in 2010. He candidly confessed that he felt unable to support 'permanent assistance' — that is, a specific government commitment — for 'increasing resources for drugs and healthcare'. Science and technology were advancing too fast, he declared, and 'in the next few decades . . . more and more new drugs would come on stream'.[21] This statement amounted to an admission that the government found modern medicine too daunting for officials to manage.

If budgetary resources were as limited as officials claimed, a practical solution would have been to cover healthcare costs as part of a social insurance package. The previous chapter described how, before 1997, social insurance had long been anathema to the government and the business and professional elite. The colonial administration had first begun to contemplate such a scheme as long ago as 1957 but no progress had been made in the years that followed.[22] After the end of British rule, repeated consultation exercises were launched, each of which was marred by serious defects. There was a repeated failure to demonstrate leadership and present the government's own preferences. The consultation documents included proposals already known to be in conflict with the public's priorities, and they omitted initiatives that were likely to meet the community's aspirations. Most serious of all, nothing was done to reassure vulnerable groups and the middle class that they would not be worse off as a result of any changes that the government might introduce.[23]

Consultations were relaunched with a new blueprint in 2010, which was followed by five separate rounds of public opinion polls. The government then announced that firm proposals for a 'Health Protection Scheme' would be published by mid-2013 after which 'actual implementation of the proposals on healthcare, manpower planning and professional development' would commence, together with the preparation of the necessary legislation.[24] The government played up the traditional misgivings about social insurance and its allegedly pernicious consequences for Hong Kong. The health minister warned that 'public subsidies might aggravate moral hazards in using private health insurance and private healthcare services, hence contributing to medical inflation'. There was silence on the key issue of whether or not the government would provide a subsidy or offer tax incentives.[25] In 2013, a new health minister was willing to 'consider using financial incentives or government subsidies, including tax incentives, to encourage people to participate' in the new scheme. The details remained unclear, nevertheless, despite so many years of public consultations and government reviews.[26]

Hong Kong lagged far behind Singapore, Korea and Taiwan, which had all reformed their healthcare funding in the last century in order to ensure that access to these services would be both universal and financially sustainable.[27] Hong Kong's protracted delay in setting up arrangements to finance healthcare was all the more inexcusable because society

had already created on its own initiative the foundations for a comprehensive insurance system. Over 40 per cent of the total population had
some form of health cover by 2010, either as part of their employment
package or through a personal insurance policy.[28]

The third Chief Executive pledged to give special attention to healthcare. He declared that 'the basic premise of a medical and health policy
is that medical services should be accessible to everyone without regard
to the individual's social status or economic background'. He appeared
to believe that this goal had already been achieved — despite the shortcomings and shortfalls described earlier in this chapter — because the
government's recurrent spending on medical and health services was
'nearly HK$7,000 (US$870) per capita' a year. This level of spending, he
went on, 'in a city that is renowned for its low tax rates speaks volumes
about the government's commitment to healthcare'.[29] In terms of basic
policy, little seemed to change after Leung Chun-ying assumed office.
His health minister expressed much the same doubts as his predecessors
about the future affordability of public healthcare. His complaints about
the 'unfair' competition faced by the private sector were also similar:
the fees charged by the Hospital Authority were low but the quality of its
services was high.[30]

Promoting private profits

An important objective of the government's health policy was to expand
the private sector. The Hospital Authority's increased fees and charges
and the lengthening queues for treatment were all part of the effort to
drive patients away from the public sector, as was the 8 per cent reduction in the number of the authority's beds between 2000 and 2010
(which was not made up for by expansion in the private sector).

The long drawn-out consultation on health insurance was also
part of the same, go-private strategy. The 2011 announcement of the
proposed 'Health Protection Scheme' included a commitment to the
development of 'a competitive and transparent private sector providing
high quality service'. This goal faced serious obstacles. The first was the
lesson of recent history and the drawbacks of a business-based management culture in the hospital setting. The previous chapter recounted
the shortcomings of government-subsidised, charity hospitals run by
business people. In 1990, these institutions provided 40 per cent of total
hospital beds. But their management was heavily criticised, and 'their
standard of service was thought to be second-rate'.[31] These shortcomings
were quickly remedied after they had been incorporated into the new
Hospital Authority.[32]

Private sector hospitals did not flourish in the 1990s. They began with a 15 per cent share of the market which then collapsed to a mere 5 per cent, which the health minister later attributed to their poor treatment of patients and their exorbitant charges. None of this deterred him in 2005 from promoting an official policy of raising the Hospital Authority's fees to drive patients into the private sector.[33]

The first Chief Executive had claimed in 2003 that 'the private sector is able to offer more choice options on healthcare services to the community' when he applauded a project to entrust population-wide, cervical cancer screening to the private sector. His statement made it clear, however, that the initiative could not succeed without public sector support in providing publicity, logistical support, laboratory accreditation and even referral of patients.[34] His confidence proved misplaced about the private sector as a whole. Private hospitals were unable to match the Hospital Authority either in professional competence or efficient management of resources.[35]

The private sector continued to mistreat patients in much the same way as it had done in the 1990s. The government admitted in 2008 that 'lack of transparency of fees' meant that 'even middle-class patients . . . often choose public hospitals despite the long queues and the lack of choices'.[36] In 2012, the Director of Audit lambasted the government for negligent supervision of the private sector. He found that nothing was done after 'inspections in which serious irregularities were noted'. 'Cases involving the professionalism of doctors and nurses' were not referred to the statutory disciplinary bodies. No action was taken when private hospitals breached their obligation under the official Code of Practice to provide patients with clear information on fees and charges before services were provided.[37] The health sector provided another convincing case study of how the government and its austerity measures, combined with the adoption of business models, proved injurious. The most seriously ill suffered inferior care, while those driven into the private sector faced serious exploitation.

Education: Not a Social Service

Education was the darling of Hong Kong's first two chief executives. They sponsored programmes for a radical overhaul of the system in a drive to meet what they called the needs of a modern, Chinese, knowledge-based society. Education was to be viewed not as a social service but 'long-term investments that enhance the quality and productivity of our population'.[38]

This favouritism failed to arouse the public applause that was expected. Instead, education generated unremitting public complaints.

In political terms, much of the additional money spent on education in this century was counter-productive. In terms of its educational outcomes, the funding was inadequate to meet the new requirements which the first and second Chief Executives imposed on the system, still less to remedy the Third World deficiencies created by the low priority which education had commanded in the previous century.

Trouble with teachers

Education has provoked the most forthright recognition of the damage done by failing to overcome the Third World standards and systems adopted in earlier decades. As Chapter 4 pointed out, more than half of the children in primary schools still attended either a morning or an afternoon session instead of whole-day schooling in 2001. The failure to spend money in the past to transform the makeshift schooling arrangements of an era when education had been neither free nor compulsory could not be rectified overnight. An end to the shift system meant the number of classrooms would have to almost double, and additional premises took time to build.[39] Tung Chee Hwa could only promise that the last of the 400 schools operating two sessions a day would be converted to whole-day schooling in 2007.[40]

The historical neglect of education described in the previous chapter had led to decades of dependence on untrained staff. Even 20 years after the introduction of universal and compulsory primary and secondary education, a 1998 study found that the teaching profession was still far from fully qualified. In primary schools, the proportion of teachers with no professional qualifications had barely changed since 1978, although there had been a very substantial decline in unqualified teachers within the secondary sector. There had been a much faster improvement in the level of teachers with university degrees. But they still made up barely a quarter of the primary school staff in 1998, and only two-thirds of secondary school teachers (see Table 5.1).

Table 5.1
Teachers' qualifications, 1978–98[41]

| Sector | Primary Schools | | Secondary Schools | |
Year	1978	1998	1978	1998
Total number of teachers	17,900	21,200	15,300	23,900
No professional qualifications (per cent of total)	13	14	50	20
Qualified and university graduates (per cent of total)	3	24	43	65

As a result, the state of the teaching profession at the start of this century was unacceptable, according to the official then responsible for Hong Kong's education system. Her list of its serious handicaps made alarming reading.

> For historical reasons, teaching in Hong Kong can hardly be regarded as a "profession" . . . Teachers in Hong Kong do not yet share a common set of professional teaching standards and ethical commitments. Teacher preparation is uneven and not a pre-requisite for registration . . . The lack of specialisation and weak pedagogical content knowledge affect the efficacy of teaching, and contribute to the heavy reliance on the textbook.[42]

The government made an effort to raise teaching standards but the Third World legacy proved stubborn. A university degree was set as the minimum teaching qualification, and by 2010, 50 per cent of primary school teachers and 85 per cent of those in secondary schools were graduates. The government could claim that the unqualified teacher would soon become a thing of the past.[43] But further progress towards a fully graduate profession was not to be so quickly achieved. Funding was not the obstacle. The resistance came from older teachers. Schools were unable to dismiss out of hand their non-graduate staff who had been recruited in a previous era.[44]

Higher fees, lower standards

Despite the continuing shortfalls in school premises and the shortcomings of the teaching profession, an ambitious programme was launched in 2004 for the rapid transformation of education at the secondary and tertiary levels.[45] The government did not intend to cover all the funding required for this comprehensive restructuring. Although household incomes were now lower than they had been in 1997, parents would have to share the costs through paying higher fees.[46]

The government would lighten its own financial burden by cutting secondary schooling from seven years to six. This measure provided immediate relief from the chronic shortage of secondary school facilities, and it indirectly created new opportunities for introducing self-financed educational programmes. Hitherto, there had only been sufficient school places to offer two further years of education to half the 16-year-olds after their first public examination.[47] Abolition of Year 7 meant that the existing school places could accommodate all the 16-year-olds and, as a result, double to 60 per cent the proportion going on to post-secondary education.[48]

The lost year of secondary education would be made up by adding an extra year to the universities' undergraduate programmes, for which the fees would be much higher than they had been for a seventh year of secondary schooling.[49] The universities were supposed to foot the bill for switching from a three-to a four-year, first degree.[50] Tung Chee Hwa, complacently assumed that this new financial burden would not affect their 'core activities and the quality of education'.[51]

The shorter secondary school programme was also expected to provide an incentive for school leavers to improve their employment opportunities by studying for sub-degree qualifications, again incurring a higher level of fees than they would have paid if Year 7 of secondary schooling had not been abolished.[52] The supply of such courses could be increased most easily, it was decided, if market forces were mobilised through encouraging self-financing of the new post-secondary programmes.[53] These grew in number 'more than sixteen times' in the next seven years. In 2010, 65 per cent of the entire post-secondary student intake was enrolled in sub-degree courses, with 47 per cent of them self-financed.[54]

Thanks to the extensive privatisation of the post-secondary sector, Tung's original target was achieved. But market forces were unable to guarantee that the hurried creation of the new sub-degree products represented value for money. The media published frequent complaints about fees, the quality of the programmes and, most serious of all, the poor view of such qualifications taken by potential employers.[55] The shortcomings persisted, and a University Grants Committee report was scathing about the products in 2010. 'A general perception amongst students and parents (and employers)', it stated, was that 'Associate Degrees in particular were no more than "bridging qualifications on the path to first degrees"'. They did not fit students for 'immediate employment'. The report's overall verdict was brutal: 'This qualification has neither established a clear identity in the public mind nor much legitimacy as a stand-alone attainment.'[56] In response to the damning comments on the sub-degree programmes, the government made an unconvincing attempt to defend the status of such qualifications.[57]

The deficiencies in this sector were not just the outcome of hasty implementation aimed at maximising financial returns. The underlying policies were seriously flawed, according to the 2010 University Grants Committee document.

The overall supply of university places remained inadequate. The government had not increased the proportion of the relevant age group enrolled in first-year, first-degree places since 1994. Compared with other advanced economies, the report added, the supply of university education was low and under-funded.

Post-secondary education as a whole was far from satisfactory, according to the same report. The sector's rapid expansion had 'resulted in a fragmented and complex post-secondary education system with a degree of incoherence and duplication'.[58]

The government eventually responded to this indictment by setting up a Committee on Self-financing Post-secondary Education in 2012. Although it described itself as 'a pivotal platform', its priorities seemed to have little relevance to the grim realities of students paying high fees for diplomas that were of little market value. Its remedies seemed mainly cosmetic, and it defined its first goal as 'promoting transparency and good practices'. Its agenda for change in 2013 was leisurely and confined to 'an Information Framework' and 'a consultancy study . . . [to] pave the way for promoting good practices . . . in due course'.[59]

Help for the rich but no relief for the poor

As the sweeping changes in educational policy were being launched, the first Chief Executive was devoting considerable attention to 'inter-generational poverty', an issue about which his successor was also to express considerable concern. Both men believed that education was the solution. Tung promised to give children from 'needy families . . . ample opportunities to receive education' and to ensure 'that poverty is not an obstacle to further studies'.[60] Donald Tsang five years later promised to 'invest in education to combat inter-generational poverty'. He pledged to allocate 'substantial resources' to this goal. In practice, Tsang's 'investment' was confined to aid with 'the costs of textbooks and school-related expenses'.[61]

Little was done to free children from low-income families from the barriers to decent schooling which poverty creates. The first Commission on Poverty put forward limited proposals to ease the impact of poverty on schoolchildren. Initially, these measures were subject to such draconian criteria to qualify for financial assistance that they were unworkable.[62] In 2006, the government allocated the miniscule sum of HK$37 million to assist 234,000 students who could not afford the fees for extracurricular activities. The funding was subject to strict conditions and detailed monitoring, and the children who applied for help were not shielded from being identified and stigmatised.[63] In 2011, another 360,000 children and young persons — a third of the total student population — still needed government grants, fee remissions and other forms of help 'to ensure that their studies will not be affected by lack of financial means'.[64]

By contrast, there was open discrimination in favour of the better-off. They had privileged access to the best schools once these had been

allowed to levy substantial fees. As the previous chapter explained, education officials decided in 1991 to encourage a business-related model
among subsidised schools. Higher-income families would be able to
buy a superior quality of education through a 'Direct Subsidy Scheme'
(DSS).[65] This initiative amounted to privatisation through the back door.
Hong Kong's best-known schools were able to retain their government
subsidies while charging fees to finance more and better teachers and
more facilities and higher-quality amenities. The number of DSS schools
and the government subsidies they received rose sharply in this century:
from 40 schools each receiving an average subsidy of HK$23 million in
2003 to 84 schools each receiving an average HK$34 million in 2012.[66]

These establishments were required to ensure that 'students will not
be deprived of the chance to study at DSS schools solely because of their
inability to pay school fees'. These elite schools were obliged to allocate
a part of their fee income 'towards a fee remission/scholarship scheme'.
Suspicions grew that this concession to the underprivileged was not
being implemented and that the DSS sector was not free from other
malpractices. In 2009, the government set out to quash public concerns
and presented the legislature with a reassuring account of the measures
in place to oversee this sector.[67]

The following year, the Director of Audit took a very different view.
He uncovered cases in which the Education Bureau had supplied inaccurate and incomplete information to the Legislative and Executive
Councils. He also found financial irregularities and a lack of transparency. He reported that the government's monitoring of schools and
enforcement of regulations was slack. Its efforts to enforce the rules on
fee remission were at best half-hearted. Some 40 per cent of the schools
for which accounts were available did not comply with the requirement,
and a third of the schools spent less than half the funds nominally allocated to fee remission on this purpose.[68]

In response, the Education Bureau displayed a degree of impudent
indifference to the Director of Audit's findings. 'The majority of the
problems unearthed,' it claimed, 'are rather technical.' The Bureau's
working party response to the Director of Audit's revelations offered no
convincing solutions to the malpractices and delinquencies.[69]

Welfare: A Waste of Money

Hong Kong entered the 21st century with welfare programmes which
could be described as adequate although far from generous. The
Social Welfare Department was providing, subsidising and coordinat-
ing services on which depended not only the survival of the needy and
the vulnerable but the wellbeing of all who could not overcome the

challenges and tragedies of life through their own efforts. Poverty in the sense of not enough money to pay for food and shelter seemed manageable thanks to the start of the Comprehensive Social Security Scheme (CSSA) in 1993, as the previous chapter explained. In this century, however, 'welfare' was a political pariah. Nowhere was the government's determination to resist spending on the social services more intense than in the welfare field.

The case for austerity

In 2005, the second Chief Executive uttered the most sweeping government rejection of spending on social services in the modern history of Hong Kong.

> The Government must never try to assist the poor using its own resources for this is doomed to failure . . . just like pouring sand into the sea to reclaim land . . . or [by] increasing tax revenue for the specific purpose of assisting the poor.[70]

The new poor were very largely, he said, the product of immigration and the inevitable and universal price to be paid for prosperity by the world's financial centres.[71] Tsang tried to convince the public that poverty was unavoidable and incurable. 'In a free, open and mature capitalist economy, the wealth gap can hardly be eradicated,' he insisted.[72]

Henry Tang Ying-yen, who served both as Financial and as Chief Secretary and almost became the third Chief Executive, believed that the disadvantaged and deprived themselves shared his aversion to social spending.

> . . . helping the poor does not mean dishing out largesse . . . Besides, providing financial assistance is not the best way to lift people out of poverty. I believe that what the poor want most is an opportunity to improve their livelihood and that of their families through their own efforts.[73]

Senior officials demonised 'welfare' as a threat to a stable society and a flourishing economy.

> . . . in countries where welfarism is practised or a multitude of welfare services is provided . . . many problems have emerged, such as unemployment, especially youth unemployment, domestic violence, shortage of elderly service . . . Worse still, it will undermine the people's resilience against adversities, which is not conducive to the healthy development of the economy in the long run.[74]

Given the traditional hostility of the business and professional elite to social expenditure, it was inevitable that they would exploit the increased political leverage which the Basic Law had allocated to them to obstruct welfare proposals. At the corporate level, the prestigious Bank of China was sweeping in its denunciation of the reforms introduced in the final decade of British rule.

> Despite Hong Kong's claim of not being a welfare society, the free services it now provides can be regarded as among the best in the world. This . . . has brought about extremely unfavourable impacts. The most serious should be the rise of a dependency culture and the decline of self-initiative and self-reliance.[75]

Business representatives in the legislature lost little time in seeking to roll back history and to return to what they regarded as a golden age when social services — and welfare especially — had been virtually non-existent. This nostalgia for a world without welfare was eloquently expressed in 2000 by the import and export sector's representative in the legislature.

> There used to be no CSSA, no job referral service or Employees Retraining Scheme in Hong Kong, for the whole community attached importance to continuous self-improvement . . . Even if they became unemployed, Hong Kong people would try again in the belief that they could always make a living if they did not shrink from hardship. However, . . . Hong Kong people have got into the habit of blaming society and refusing to find out the cause in themselves. They have become passive and rely only on the Government instead of themselves.[76]

One prominent business leader and former chairman of the Hong Kong Council of Social Service complained that the public no longer believed as they had done in the 1950s and 1960s that 'to live in better conditions, all one could do was to work assiduously'. He complained that the community had developed 'many unrealistic expectations' about the role of the government.[77] Self-help was also recommended by another functional constituency legislator with a distinguished academic career. In 2009, he recalled how 'in the past, many poor and unemployed people would often become street hawkers'. He wanted this tradition to be revived to enable the less fortunate to keep themselves gainfully occupied through their own efforts.[78]

Business takeover

In 2000, the Social Welfare Department was providing financial support for almost a million elderly and disabled individuals — 13 per cent of the total population — through CSSA and through the non-means-tested old-age and disability allowances. The department also subsidised a comprehensive range of residential and day care, training and other services for 312,000 elderly, disabled and other vulnerable individuals. There were a further 51,000 families receiving counselling and support services.

These statistics demonstrated how heavily the wellbeing of the community as a whole had come to depend on the quality of the social services. The programmes, it must be emphasised, were barely adequate to meet the most urgent requirements of vulnerable groups, which included the sick and the elderly and children with disabilities and not just the able-bodied unemployed as was so often erroneously assumed.[79] The gaps between available supply and the community's needs were considerable, and services were to come under acute pressure in this century as households had to cope with the unaccustomed phenomenon of a shortage of jobs and the rising costs of housing, medical services and education.

Funding for the Social Welfare Department and the NGOs (through which the bulk of the social programmes were provided) was reduced by 9 per cent as the government pursued austerity between 2000 and 2003.[80] At the same time, a new system ('the lump sum grant') for subsidising the NGOs was introduced. Advocacy for the vulnerable had to give way to fund-raising once the government started to allocate its financial support through competitive tendering, a process designed to cut unit costs. Inevitably, the business manager took over within the NGO sector, and the qualified professional was sidelined in shaping social policies and programmes.[81] Special training schemes were set up so that NGOs could acquire such commercial skills as financial and human resource management (although participants found the courses of limited usefulness).[82]

'Management' issues replaced clients as the dominant item on NGOs' agendas. Harsh as this comment sounds, it is the inescapable conclusion to be drawn from a lengthy official review of the lump sum grant and its consequences. The Review Committee's 2008 report set out six principles for future developments: 'Partnership, Flexibility, Adequate Monitoring, Accountability and Communication, and above all, a Mindset for Change'. The clients were nowhere to be seen.[83] The principal management concern was finance, and cost-cutting in particular. In evaluating the outcome of the lump sum grant arrangement, the Review Committee rated it favourably. It declared that NGO services 'nowadays are, all in all, greater value for money', while quality was deemed acceptable in terms of 'satisfactory delivery as testified by service users'. No data were offered in support of these favourable ratings, nor was there any analysis of shortfalls.[84] Yet, NGOs had specifically complained to the Review Committee about the adverse impact of the reduction in the government subsidy between 2001 and 2006. 'The Government's financial pressures and the increasing complexity of social problems' meant that 'the quality and sustainability of welfare services' were at risk, they had asserted.[85]

Defenceless clients

Financial curbs and cutbacks caused serious shortfalls in welfare programmes for groups which were the most vulnerable physically as well as financially. They would not be left to starve. But many would die early or suffer prolonged and avoidable physical discomfort and mental anxiety, as the discussion of health services earlier in this chapter explained. When the age of austerity began, the welfare professionals and the NGOs could do little to protect the interests of the destitute and disadvantaged.

Within the government, the professionals tried briefly to shield these vulnerable groups against a rising tide of vilification of the unemployed and the socially disadvantaged as scroungers who preferred to live off CSSA instead of finding a job. A leading academic attacked the Social Welfare Department's staff for defending them on the grounds that the department and its professionals were out of touch with the labour market. [86] Their resistance continued until 2000.[87] A new Director of the department took over that year who regarded its performance with disquiet. She claimed that it had 'had grown into a bureaucracy' which needed 'delayering, streamlining and process re-engineering'. In fact, the staff had coped remarkably well with the surge in demand for the department's services after the 1997–98 Asian financial crisis despite their budget constraints.[88]

The NGOs fared no better. They delivered the bulk of the services and so were hard hit as social expenditure came under relentless attack in this century. In 2001, the new Director of Social Welfare expressed reservations about social expenditure because 'every dollar spent on welfare is at the expense of other policy areas'. She favoured a business culture. 'Private sector participation,' she claimed, 'through its enterprise and efficiency, can come up with more economical solutions to deliver a public service.' It sounded as if she believed that the hospitality industry could branch out and replace public sector social services in offering residential care for the elderly and the disabled. Professional social workers were denigrated. In 2004, the minister responsible for welfare attacked NGOs because they 'provided direct professional services to recipients instead of utilizing community resources'. They should change their role, he declared, 'to becoming a facilitator for helping the needy'.[89] There was no explanation of how a battered spouse, for example, or a frail elderly person would benefit if professional social workers were no longer involved in their care. Nor was it clear what would be the benefits from changing from 'provider' to 'facilitator'.

The superiority of the private sector continued to be preached. In 2012, the former Director of Social Welfare — now Chief Secretary — stated that her personal welfare goal was to establish greater consumer choice for elderly care products, especially residential care. 'Just like when we are getting into a hotel, we need to tell whether this is a five-star, four-star or three-star hotel,' she told a gerontologists' conference, '[w]e are talking about, really, value for money.'[90] But an elderly person in need of residential care was not a tourist who could pack up and leave if dissatisfied with room service. The elderly individual was often vulnerable, sometimes confused, frequently incapacitated and, increasingly, in need of special support services and medical care.

The Chief Secretary's assumption that market-driven forces would ensure an adequate supply of residential care was contradicted by a 2009 research report prepared for the government's Elderly Commission which had reached the opposite conclusion. Almost a third of the privately provided places were vacant, the study noted, while waiting times for subsidised places ranged from 22 to 40 months (according to the type of institution). Lower charges had been suggested as an important factor in the high demand for subsidised places, the report noted. A more likely explanation, it went on, was that 'the elderly (and probably their family members) have better confidence in the quality of subsidised [institutions]'.[91] Their misgivings about private homes were not evidence of miserliness on the family's part but sensible caution, it is reasonable to suggest: the private sector had been unable to guarantee the health and safety of vulnerable clients. Unacceptable standards of care have plagued elderly homes in foreign countries. After Hong Kong began to encounter what the legislature described as 'poor quality' private homes, drafting of legislation to regulate these institutions dragged on for some five years and was not finally enacted until 2011.[92] Families had good reason to feel nervous about the wellbeing of their elderly relatives if placed in the private sector's care.

Waiting to die

The Chief Secretary's business-based approach did not offer a solution for the most pressing welfare challenge: the serious shortfall in the supply of facilities for the most vulnerable members of the community. The elderly provided a striking example of this neglect. Officials routinely proclaimed their esteem for the aged. Yet, the government failed to expand the supply rapidly enough to meet increased demand, even though growth rates for demand for elderly services were relatively simple to forecast.

- 2001: the average waiting time for a nursing home place was 13 months and for a place in a care-and-attention home, 35 months.[93]
- 2007: average waiting times were: 42 months for nursing homes and 32 months for care-and-attention homes.[94]
- 2012: average waiting times were improving but still excessive: 37 months for nursing homes and 25 months for care-and-attention homes.[95]

These figures probably underestimated the true shortfall in supply. The government faced accusations in 2010 that the criteria used to assess an individual's need for residential care had been manipulated to suppress the actual level of demand and to cut down the numbers on the waiting lists. Suspicion was aroused by the government's remedy for the chronic shortfall, which has been to divert the elderly to 'enhanced home and community care services'. In these cases, it was explained, their applications for residential care 'would be suspended for the time being'. This stratagem deflated the numbers on the official waiting list but did not reduce the real shortfall.[96]

The tragic outcome was that almost 23,000 elderly men and women died between 2007 and 2011 while waiting for admission to the residential accommodation they needed. The annual total of these deaths had increased each year (see Table 5.2).

Table 5.2
Annual number of deaths among elderly on waiting lists for subsidised residential care[97]

Year	2007	2008	2009	2010	2011	Total
Deaths	4,068	4,403	4,538	4,794	5,147	22,950

The disabled left in distress

In 2010, the Financial Secretary proposed a special measure to assist those with severe disabilities. With 'this most vulnerable group,' it was stated, 'Government is mindful of their special caring needs and the immense pressure faced by their family carers in caring for them at home.' The implementation of this pledge proved painfully protracted. A pilot scheme was announced that would finance home care services for the equivalent of 20 per cent of those on the waiting lists until 2014. The scheme would provide 'personal care and escort service, occupational therapy/physiotherapy rehabilitation training service and nursing care service'. This list defined the quantum of care which the individual would require to achieve a reasonable quality of life in spite of severe disabilities.

Such a programme was far beyond the capability of any ordinary family to provide, and so daily life for the 80 per cent not covered by the scheme was grim.[98] In 2013, the government committed itself to extending the scheme to all those with severe disabilities who do not have residential care. At this stage, the scheme was still 15 per cent below target in terms of the numbers being assisted after two years in operation. No indication was offered of how long it would take to recruit and train the large numbers of qualified personnel needed to make possible the promised six-fold rise in those covered by the scheme.[99] There was also some indication that the decision to announce the scheme's expansion was inspired, in part, by a desire to divert criticism away from the government's failure to end the long waiting times for admission to residential care for this particularly vulnerable group.

Table 5.3 provides additional evidence of how cruel was the delay imposed on these unfortunate individuals and their families. The total numbers in this group who needed residential facilities were so small relatively that a phased solution by way of pilot schemes was indefensible by any standards of caring government. This table also highlights how the lack of long-term planning meant that waiting times for 'severely mentally handicapped persons' — the largest and most vulnerable group — improved only marginally between 2007 and 2012. The queues for places for other groups lengthened, and while actual waiting times fell, they still remained well over two years. Any delay in providing residential facilities to improve the quality of life for those with severe disabilities must be regarded as unconscionable.

Table 5.3
Persons with severe disabilities awaiting admission to residential facilities by category and average waiting times, 2007–12[100]

	Hostels for severely mentally handicapped persons		Hostels for severely physically handicapped persons		Care and attention homes for severely disabled persons	
Year	2007	2012	2007	2012	2007	2012
Number on waiting list	1,761	2,173	356	433	316	428
Waiting time (months)	83	82	78	37	40	31

Young children were not spared the damage and discomfort caused by shortfalls in essential services. A small group suffered from a variety of disabilities (autism, for example) which required special, pre-school programmes 'to ensure their physical, psychological and social developments'. These courses were crucial to improving their capacity to attend ordinary schools and participate in 'daily life activities' later on, as the welfare minister put it in 2012. The needs of these children were known but not met. The waiting times for admission to programmes for this vulnerable group deteriorated seriously from 2008 to 2012, and the proportion of the children in this group for whom there were no places rose from 36 per cent to 44 per cent (see Table 5.4).

Table 5.4
Children with disabilities aged 2 to 6 in need of early intervention through pre-school rehabilitation services, 2008–12[101]

Year	Total number of children with relevant disabilities	Percentage of total on waiting list	Average waiting time (months)
2008	5,200	36	9.8
2009	5,049	33	10.3
2010	5,602	39	10.6
2011	6,157	43	12.3
2012	6,472	44	14.4

Officials set no date by which all such children would be given places in the special programmes. The government's solution, as with the other shortfalls listed in this chapter, was an attempt to use 'home care' to make good the gap between demand and supply. Children from low-income families were to be given a grant to cover a weekly session of 'pre-school training and parent support services' under an ad hoc trial scheme. The poorer families were, unfortunately, the group least likely to have parents with the educational backgrounds or the space and privacy in their living accommodation which a 'home care' approach needed.[102]

No plans, no progress

The government was able to evade accountability for the shortfalls because it steadfastly refused to make planned commitments to the development of welfare services and the solution of the most acute deficiencies. Until 1998, five-year welfare plans had investigated the community's needs, quantified shortfalls, defined concrete targets for new services and identified the gaps between demand and supply that would remain at the end of the period. The planning exercises made the government's welfare performance open to professional scrutiny and public monitoring.[103] The decision to abolish all forward planning after 1998 left ministers and their officials with only nominal accountability.[104]

Welfare advocates allowed the government to win this strategic victory by default. The NGOs were taken in by new lump sum grant funding arrangements which promised greater autonomy and which included the pledge of 'an integrated and forward looking planning framework'. There was also a commitment to a joint exercise between the Social Welfare Department and NGOs which would produce 'long term Strategic Directions, Medium Term Plan for individual programme service areas' and annual plans.[105] The promise was broken. Too late, the Hong Kong Council of Social Service realised in 2000 that the abolition of the five-year plan exercise was a threat to all services that required longer-term commitments.[106]

Instead of forward planning based on adequate financial, management and social statistics, there would be 'new strategic directions to achieve the paradigm shifts from "service provision" to "social investment"', the welfare minister stated in 2004. The implication was that the government would spend money only on projects from which there would be some tangible returns. Furthermore, the welfare minister looked to partnership with the business sector as a replacement for public funding.[107]

In 2010, the government launched a campaign to counter the continuing criticism of its original decision to end long-term planning of social welfare programmes.[108] The prestigious government-appointed Social Work Advisory Committee was called on to publish a consultation paper on planning. This document presented an overview of Hong Kong society and the issues which the committee's members believed were the most relevant to welfare services. It made no mention of the 'disabled' or 'infirm'. The clients served by welfare agencies made no appearance in its pages (apart from a paragraph on young people with clinical depression — and here as a medical not a welfare problem). The term 'low-income' was used once, but not 'poor' or 'poverty'. As for the elderly, their needs were discussed solely in order to label them unaffordable given 'the low-tax environment'. When the Committee's final report appeared the following year, the welfare services' clients were still ignored although the 'poor' were allowed two passing mentions.[109]

The consultation paper depicted the welfare services in general as a threat to financial stability in very much the same terms as officials had used in the 1950s and 1960s (which the previous chapter recorded). What Hong Kong needed, the Committee's document claimed, was less rather than more public spending on welfare services.

> . . . many of the prevailing welfare services offered are remedial in nature and substantial resources are spent on providing immediate assistance and support to those facing imminent needs and hardship. There is a need . . . to build up the capacity of our people

and enhance the resilience of our society against adversities. Over time, the "empowered" individuals can also lend support to those in need and help them become self-reliant.[110]

Hong Kong is a community where high economic growth has been accompanied by an exceptionally unequal distribution of income (as Chapter 2 recounted). It had been deliberately denied social insurance in the past and belatedly provided with a compulsory retirement scheme, the Mandatory Provident Fund (MPF). Fees and charges for health and education services had risen. Against this background, how could the average family be expected to meet the challenges of disabilities, ill-health, old age and unemployment from their own resources, as the Committee proposed, when average household income was HKD18,000 a month, the same figure as in 2000?

Conclusions

This chapter has reviewed a catalogue of policy decisions which aggravated rather than relieved the physical and mental distress of those least able to care for themselves. In both the health and the welfare fields, individuals and their families, this chapter has shown, suffered from mistreatment that ranged from uncaring to callous. No matter how vulnerable or distressed the victims, no matter how old or how young, official policies displayed minimal compassion towards them. In education, the government made no effort to honour its commitment to ensure that children from low-income families had access to the best schools. At the post-secondary level, the 'self-financed' courses which catered mainly for students from a less privileged background had little credibility with potential employers and were condemned by educational experts.[111]

The government-business nexus was convinced that social expenditure was a luxury that threatened even the world's richest economies with ruin and which Hong Kong, therefore, could not afford. This dismissal of social responsibility was well illustrated by Professor Lau Siu-kai, a prominent sociologist turned political adviser, in an analysis of the gap between haves and have-nots. 'Poverty is only a relative problem,' he argued in 2004, '[t]here is no urgency in poverty elimination, and it does not require a high priority.' Furthermore, the need to avoid budget deficits meant that the government was not 'capable of appropriating sufficient funds for the elimination of poverty'. He warned that the business sector interpreted attempts to use the legislature or the courts to block government deals favouring commercial interests 'as evidence that Hong Kong people now focus more on the distribution than on the creation of wealth'. 'To avoid welfarism and dependence on government assistance,' he went on, 'the government's efforts to help the poor must not be overdone.'[112]

Nevertheless, the poverty created by Hong Kong's Third World legacy and the current shortfalls in social expenditure could not be dismissed indefinitely. In 2009, the government conceded that individuals had been made vulnerable because they had no access 'to essential services and opportunities such as housing, health care, education and employment, etc.'[113] They were the new poor. In some cases, the family was low-waged and could not afford the fees charged by schools. But the family might be middle-class with a comfortable income until suddenly faced with the crushing financial burdens that cancer can create. These were the hidden faces of a new financial vulnerability which was government-made, as this book documents throughout.

Notes

1. On the hostility towards improved social services and the dominant role of business leaders in framing post-colonial political arrangements, see Alvin Y. So, 'Hong Kong's Problematic Democratic Transition: Power Dependency or Business Hegemony?' *Journal of Asian Studies*, Vol. 59, No. 2 (May 2000), pp. 370, 373, 377.
2. James K. C. Lee, 'Balancing Collectivization and Individual Responsibility: Hong Kong Social Policy under the Chinese Regime', in Kwok-leung Tang (ed.), *Social Development in Asia* (Dordrecht: Kulwer Academic Publishers, 2000), pp. 30–1, 33.
3. 'Note for Executive Council: Review of the Social Welfare Subvention System' (XCCI(96)40, 26 September 1996), p. 2 and Annex B 'Main objections to the "unit grant" approach'.
4. Donald Tsang Yam-kuen, Chief Executive, *Hong Kong Hansard* (*HH* hereafter), 27 June 2005, p. 8942.
5. Food and Health Bureau, Health and Medical Development Advisory Committee, *Building a Healthy Tomorrow. Discussion Paper on the Future Service Delivery Model for our Healthcare System* (Hong Kong: Health, Welfare and Food Bureau, 2005), fn. 1. p. 8; Food and Health Bureau, *Your Health Your Life Healthcare Reform Consultation Document* (Hong Kong: SAR Government, 2008), pp. 14–5.
6. Hospital Authority, *Hospital Authority Annual Plan 2006–07* (Hong Kong: Hospital Authority, 2006), p. 4.
7. Hospital Authority, *Hospital Authority Annual Plan 2005–06* (Hong Kong: Hospital Authority, 2005), pp. 1–2.
8. Donald Tsang, Chief Executive, *HH*, 27 June 2005, p. 8943.
9. Hospital Authority, *Hospital Authority Annual Plan 2003–2004* (Hong Kong: Hospital Authority, 2003), pp. 34, 35, 53.
10. Hospital Authority, *Hospital Authority Annual Plan 2005–06*, p. 15.

11. Hospital Authority, *Hospital Authority Annual Plan 2007–08* (Hong Kong: Hospital Authority, 2007), p. 7.
12. Hospital Authority, *Hospital Authority Annual Plan 2008–09* (Hong Kong: Hospital Authority, 2008), p. 11.
13. Dr Leung Pak-yin, Hospital Authority Chief Executive, *Government Information Services* (*GIS*, hereafter), 15 May 2013; Hospital Authority, *Hospital Authority Annual Plan 2013–14: Keeping Healthcare in Sync*, 'Appendix 1 – Key Service Statistics', p. 96. Dr Leung did not make the comparison with 2000.
14. Dr Yeoh Eng-kiong, Secretary for Health and Welfare, *HH*, 9 May 2001, p. 5179. Financial restrictions on some of these drugs were lifted in later years (interferon in 2011 and 2012, for example). Details were provided in Angora Ngai (Food and Health Bureau) letter to Elyssa Wong (Clerk to Legislative Council Panel on Health Services), 17 May 2012, 'Annex', pp. 8–9. URL: www.legco.gov.hk/yr11-12/english/panels/hs/papers/hs0416cb2-2087-1-e.pdf
15. Legislative Council Secretariat, 'Grant for the Samaritan Fund' (CB(2)208/08-09(06), 7 November 2008), p. 2.
16. Hospital Authority Ordinance (cap. 113), s. 4(d).
17. The official transcript of the health minister's attempt to explain the waiver system was well-nigh incomprehensible. Yeoh, Secretary for Health, Welfare and Food, *GIS*, 8 November 2002.
18. The minister was quoting almost verbatim the statutory obligation set out in the Hospital Authority Ordinance (fn. 16 above). Dr York Chow Yat-ngok, Secretary for Health, Welfare and Food, *HH*, 8 November 2006, pp. 1649–50.
19. Hospital Authority, *GIS*, 27 July 2011.
20. Legislative Council Secretariat, 'The Samaritan Fund' (CB(2)1640/11-12(04), 10 April 2012), p. 4.
21. Chow, Secretary for Food and Health, *HH*, 20 October 2010, p. 282. Dr Chow had expressed similar sentiments in previous years; e.g., *HH*, 11 July 2007, p. 10270.
22. 'As time goes on, and as [health] costs continue to mount, the question is bound to come up in an acute form, whether a proper compulsory insurance scheme should be introduced, or whether the cost is to continue to be borne by the general taxpayer'. Arthur G. Clarke, Financial Secretary, *HH*, 27 March 1957, p. 114.
23. Peter P. Yuen, 'Dissatisfaction of Health Providers and Consumers: Health Care Reform Intransigence and SARS Outbreak Mismanagement', in Joseph Y. S. Cheng (ed.), *The July 1 Protest Rally: Interpreting a Historic Event* (Hong Kong: City University of Hong Kong Press, 2005), pp. 447, 452–3.
24. Chow, Secretary for Food and Health, *GIS*, 11 July 2011.
25. Dr Ko Wing-man, Secretary for Food and Health, *HH*, 31 October 2012, pp. 1107–9.
26. Ko, Secretary for Food and Health, *GIS*, 9 April 2013.
27. Yuen, 'Dissatisfaction of Health Providers and Consumers: Health Care Reform Intransigence and SARS Outbreak Mismanagement', p. 447.

28. Census and Statistics Department, 'Provision of Medical Benefits by Employers/Companies and Coverage of Medical Insurance Purchased by Individuals', *Thematic Household Survey Report No. 45* (Hong Kong: Census and Statistics Department, October 2010), p. 129.

29. He also emphasised his personal commitment to healthcare: 'During the election campaign, I spent more time discussing with the healthcare sector than any other sectors.' Leung Chun-ying, Chief Executive, *GIS*, 15 May 2013.

30. Ko, Secretary for Food and Health, *GIS*, 9 April 2013.

31. Anthony B. L. Cheung, 'Medical and Health', in Donald H. MacMillen and Man Si-wai (eds.), *The Other Hong Kong Report 1994* (Hong Kong: Chinese University Press, 1994), p. 354.

32. Yuen, 'Medical and Health Issues', p. 396.

33. Chow, Secretary for Health, Welfare and Food, *HH*, 27 January 2005, pp. 3968–9.

34. Tung, *GIS*, 28 November 2003.

35. Average bed occupancy rates in 2007 were 82 per cent for the public and 67 per cent for the private sector. *GIS*, 12 December 2007. The private sector shunned the more challenging conditions, psychiatric treatment for example. York, Secretary for Health and Welfare, *HH*, 25 May 2005, p. 7621.

36. York, Secretary for Food and Health, *GIS*, 5 May 2008. Private hospitals had claimed to have introduced a transparent system of fees as early as 2003. See Yeoh, Secretary for Health and Welfare, *HH*, 9 April 2003, pp. 5379–80.

37. Audit Commission, *Report No. 59* 'Chapter 3: Food and Health Bureau, Department of Health. Regulatory Control of Private Hospitals' (26 October 2012), pp. v, vi, 44–8.

38. John Tsang Chun-wah, Financial Secretary, *HH*, 27 February 2008, p. 4926.

39. Education and Manpower Bureau, 'LegCo Panel on Education Implementation of Whole-day Primary Schooling' (CB(2)2401/02-03(01), June 2003), pp. 2–3.

40. Joseph Wong Wing-ping, Secretary for Education and Manpower, *GIS*, 29 May 1999; Tung, *GIS*, 13 August 2001.

41. Government Secretariat, *Overall Review of the Hong Kong Education System: The Hong Kong Education System June 1981* (Hong Kong: Government Printer, 1982), 'Table (i): Number of teachers in day schools and colleges classified by qualification as at March 1980', p. 220; Wong, Secretary for Education and Manpower, *HH*, 17 November 1999, p. 1345.

42. The forum selected for the publication of this indictment was significant: Seminar on Teacher Development and Education Reform, Hong Kong Institute of Education. Law Fan Chiu-fun, Secretary for Education and Manpower, *GIS*, 9 November 2000.

43. Michael Suen Ming-yeung, Secretary for Education, *HH*, 14 April 2010, p. 6629.

44. Suen, Secretary for Education, *HH*, 23 November 2011, p. 2295.

45. For the background to this reform programme, see Education and Manpower Bureau, 'LegCo Panel on Education Reforming the Academic

Structure of Senior Secondary Education and Higher Education — Actions for Investing in the Future' (CB(2) 90/04-05(01), October 2004).

46. *Reforming the Academic Structure for Secondary Education and Higher Education — Actions for Investing in the Future* (Hong Kong: Education and Manpower Bureau, 2004), pp. 37, 40.

47. For an account of the annual struggle by students to find a school place after Form 5, see *Wen Wei Po*, 11 August 2005.

48. This goal had been adopted at the start of the decade. Tung, *HH*, 11 October 2000, p. 40. The potential impact of the lost year on the capacity of the system to cater to the post-16-year-olds was very clear from an Education and Manpower Bureau statement, *GIS*, 23 December 2004.

49. On this point, note the comments in Education Bureau, 'Item for Finance Committee' (FCR(2007-08)45, January 2008), p. 2.

50. Education Bureau, 'Item for Finance Committee' (FCR(2007-08)36, November 2007; Suen, Secretary for Education, *GIS*, 23 January 2008. Suen had earlier made clear the implications for the universities' capital costs dating back to 2006. *GIS*, 23 January 2008.

51. Tung, *GIS*, 6 December 2003. On the universities' financial constraints, see Arthur K. C. Li, Secretary for Education and Manpower, *GIS*, 18 June 2003; Fanny Law, Permanent Secretary for Education and Manpower, *GIS*, 12 November 2003.

52. Legislative Council Secretariat, 'Report of the Panel on Education for Submission to the Legislative Council' (CB(2)2417/07-08, 27 June 2008).

53. Li, Secretary for Education and Manpower, *HH*, 9 July 2003, pp. 8478, 8480.

54. University Grants Committee, *Aspirations for the Higher Education System in Hong Kong Report of the University Grants Committee* (Hong Kong, 2010), pp. 29–30.

55. For example, Editorial, *Ming Pao Daily*, 11 August and 31 October 2006; Teddy Ng, 'Aid Plan to Lift Associate Degree', *China Daily*, Hong Kong edition, 11 April 2008.

56. University Grants Committee, *Aspirations for the Higher Education System in Hong Kong*, pp. 29–31.

57. Education Bureau, 'Legislative Council Brief. Higher Education Review' (EDB(HE)CR 4/21/2041/89, November 2011), p. 4; Education Bureau, 'Progress report on the motion on "Improving further education and employment of sub-degree students" moved by Hon Cyd Ho at the Legislative Council meeting on 23 November 2011' (February 2012), pp. 7–9.

58. University Grants Committee, *Aspirations for the Higher Education System in Hong Kong*, pp. 1, 36.

59. Tim Lui Tim-leung, Committee on Self-financing Post-secondary Education Chairman, *GIS*, 26 April 2013.

60. Tung, *HH*, 12 January 2005, p. 3269; 13 January 2005, p. 3306.

61. Donald Tsang, *HH*, 13 October 2010, p. 22; 14 October 2010, p. 188.

62. Raymond Ngan and Mark Kin-yin Li, 'Responding to Poverty, Income Inequality and Social Welfare: The Neo-liberalist Government versus a Social Investment State', in Joseph Y. S. Cheng (ed.), *The Hong Kong Special*

Administrative Region in Its First Decade (Hong Kong: City University of Hong Kong Press, 2007), p. 554.

63. Commission on Poverty Task Force on Children and Youth, 'Implementation of the School-based After-school Learning and Support Programmes' (CoP TFCY Paper 5/2006, September 2006), p. 4. Schools had warned of the unfavourable labelling which this sort of scheme would create for participants. Education and Manpower Bureau, 'Legislative Council Panel on Education School-based After-school Learning and Support Programmes' (CB(2)1304/04-05(01), April 2005), p. 4.
64. John Tsang, Financial Secretary, 23 February 2011, *HH*, p. 5999.
65. Professor Chou Kee-lee, 'HKIEd Study: Disparity in Higher Education Attainment Is Widening between Rich and Poor', Hong Kong Institute of Education (31 January 2013).
66. Eddie Ng Hak-kim, Secretary for Education, *HH*, 27 February 2013, p. 7366.
67. Education Bureau, 'Legislative Council Panel on Education. Monitoring of Direct Subsidy Scheme (DSS) Schools' (CB(2)2073/08-09(01), June 2009), pp. 1–6.
68. Audit Commission, *Report No. 55,* 'Chapter 1 Education Bureau: Governance and Administration of Direct Subsidy Scheme schools' (25 October 2010), pp. 16–8, 23–6; *Report No. 55,* 'Chapter 1 Education Bureau: Administration of the Direct Subsidy Scheme' (25 October 2010), pp. 16–20, 26–7, 33–6, 41–4, 48.
69. Education Bureau, 'Report of the Working Group on Direct Subsidy Scheme' (December 2011), pp. 47, 51–2.
70. Donald Tsang, Chief Executive, *HH*, 27 June 2005, p. 8944.
71. Donald Tsang, Chief Executive, *HH*, 12 January 2006, p. 3881.
72. Donald Tsang, Chief Executive, *HH*, 12 October 2011, p. 29.
73. Henry Tang Ying-yen, Financial Secretary, *HH*, 16 March 2005, p. 5461.
74. Chow, Secretary for Health and Welfare, *HH*, 29 March 2006, p. 6103.
75. Economic Research Division Bank of China Group, 'An Assessment of the 2001/02 Budget', *Economic Review*, April 2001, p. 1.
76. Hui Cheung-ching, *HH*, 10 May 2000, pp. 6265–6.
77. Ho Sai-chu, *HH*, 10 May 2000, pp. 6260–1.
78. Professor Patrick Lau Sau-shing, *HH*, 29 October 2009, p. 970.
79. Considerable data were published in 1998 on the gaps between current and projected demand and supply for those in need of rehabilitation services and for the care of the elderly and disabled, as well as for welfare programmes generally, in Social Welfare Department, 'The Five Year Plan for Social Welfare Development in Hong Kong — Review 1998', pp. 103–6.
80. The reductions were made to recurrent expenditure. The actual cut in the subventions paid to NGOs was kept down to 6.5 per cent. Lump Sum Grant Independent Review Committee, 'Review Report on the Lump Sum Grant Subvention System' (December 2008), p. 5.
81. Ibid., p. viii.
82. Ivy Cheng, 'Impacts of the Lump Sum Grant Subvention System on the Subvented Welfare Sector: Information Note' (IN14/07-08, 8 May 2008), p. 4; Hong Kong Council of Social Service, 'Report on Training Needs Analysis

for NGOs 2009–2010', pp. 2, 9. The education sector underwent a similar experience. Education Bureau, 'Report of the Working Group on Direct Subsidy Scheme' (December 2011), p. 48.

83. Lump Sum Grant Independent Review Committee, 'Review Report on the Lump Sum Grant Subvention System', p. viii.

84. Ibid., p. 59.

85. Ibid., pp. 4–5, 12 and 'Table 1 Chronology of major events in relation to the introduction of LSGSS', p. 8.

86. Nelson Chow, 'Social Welfare', in Larry Chuen-ho Chow and Yiu-kwan Fan (eds.), *The Other Hong Kong Report 1998* (Hong Kong: Chinese University Press, 1999), pp. 267–8.

87. For the last stand on behalf of the Social Welfare Department's clients, see Health and Welfare Bureau, 'Legislative Council Panel on Welfare Services "Promoting Self-reliance Strategy"' (CB(2) 1943/99-00(03), May 2000), p. 1.

88. The discussion that follows of Mrs Carrie Lam Cheng Yuet-ngor's views, together with quotations, is based primarily on Carrie Lam, Director of Social Welfare, 'Role of Welfare in a Laissez-faire Society', Speech to the Hong Kong Democratic Foundation (18 April 2001). URL: www.hkdf.org/newsarticles.asp?show=newsarticles&newsarticle=120. She repeated these views at other public forums. See also Ngan and Li, 'The Dilemma and Crisis for Public Welfare Payments in Hong Kong', p. 418.

89. The minister admitted, however, that such a radical change in their operations might well be beyond their capacity. Chow, Secretary for Health, Welfare and Food, 'Minutes of the Social Welfare Advisory Committee (SWAC) Meeting Held on 21 December 2004' (Health, Welfare and Food Bureau, March 2005).

90. Carrie Lam, Chief Secretary, speech at the Hong Kong Association of Gerontology, *GIS*, 24 November 2012.

91. Ernest Chui Wing-tak et al., *Elderly Commission's Study on Residential Care Services for the Elderly Final Report* (Hong Kong: University of Hong Kong, December 2009), p. 15.

92. The background is recorded in Legislative Council Secretariat, 'Provision of Residential Care Places for Persons with Disabilities' (CB(2)1149/09-10(02), 23 March 2010), pp. 5–6.

93. Audit Commission, *Report No. 38* Chapter 5, 'Residential Services for the Elderly' (March 2002), pp. vi, 46.

94. Labour and Welfare Bureau, 'Legco Panel on Welfare Services. Subcommittee on Elderly Services Residential Care Services for the Elderly' (CB(2)835/07-08(01), January 2008), p. 2.

95. Labour and Welfare Bureau, 'Legislative Council Panel on Welfare Services. Provision of Subsidised Residential Care Services for the Elderly' (CB(2)2509/11-12(01), July 2012), Annex I.

96. Legislative Council Secretariat, 'Standardised Care Need Assessment Mechanism for the Elderly Services' (CB(2)2315/09-10(02), 30 September 2010), p. 3. Matthew Cheung Kin-chung, Secretary for Labour and Welfare, *HH*, 27 February 2013, p. 7345.

97. Cheung, Secretary for Labour and Welfare, *HH*, 'Annex', 25 April 2012, p. 8563.
98. The data and other details on this group are taken from Labour and Welfare Bureau, 'Legislative Council Panel on Welfare Services' (CB(2)1010/09-10(03), March 2010), pp. 4, 5; Legislative Council Secretariat, 'Provision of Subsidised Community Care Services for Persons with Disabilities' (CB(2)1618/09-10(02), 25 May 2010), p. 3.
99. Social Welfare Department, 'Joint Subcommittee on Long-term Care Policy Day Care and Community Support Services for Persons with Disabilities' (CB(2)992/12-13(01), April 2013), p. 2.
100. Social Welfare Department, 'Legislative Council Panel on Welfare Services Two New Integrated Rehabilitation Services Centres for Persons with Disabilities' (CB(2)254/07-08(04), November 2007), p. 2; Cheung, Secretary for Labour and Welfare, *HH*, 27 February 2013, pp. 7340-1.
101. The specific services were Special Child Care Centres and Integrated Programme in Kindergarten-cum-Child Care Centres. The table is calculated from the data released by Cheung, Secretary for Labour and Welfare, *HH*, 7 November 2012, 'Annex', p. 1510.
102. Ibid., 7 November 2012, pp. 1506, 1509.
103. See, for example, *The Five Year Plan for Social Welfare Development in Hong Kong — Review 1998*.
104. Gary Ma Fung-kwok, *HH*, 1 June 2000, p. 7161.
105. Lump Sum Grant Independent Review Committee, 'Review Report on the Lump Sum Grant Subvention System', pp. 91–2.
106. Task Force of Social Welfare Planning, 'Planning Mechanism and Protocol of Social Welfare Policy (Discussion Paper)' (Hong Kong Council of Social Service, 12 July 2000).
107. Yeoh, Secretary for Health and Welfare, *HH*, 5 February 2004, pp. 3097, 3098.
108. The public's criticism was summarised in Legislative Council Secretariat, 'Long-term Social Welfare Planning' (CB(2)1216/10-11(08), 8 March 2011), pp. 2–3.
109. The two references were inserted in deference to the Chief Executive, Donald Tsang and his desire 'to encourage the business sector's participation in helping the poor'. Social Welfare Advisory Committee, 'Report on Long-term Social Welfare Planning in Hong Kong' (July 2011), pp. 25, fn. 38, 42.
110. Social Welfare Advisory Committee, 'Long-term Social Welfare Planning in Hong Kong Consultation Paper' (April 2010), pp. 8, 11, 14, 16 in particular.
111. For the census evidence on the socio-economic characteristics of these students, see Chou, 'HKIEd Study: Disparity in Higher Education Attainment Is Widening between Rich and Poor'.
112. Professor Lau Siu-kai, Head Central Policy Unit, as reported approvingly in *Ta Kung Pao*, 14 December 2004.
113. Labour and Welfare Bureau, 'Legislative Council Panel on Welfare Services: Definition of Poverty' (CB(2)179/09-10(07), November 2009), pp. 4–5.

6
The Undeserving Poor

Comprehensive Social Security Assistance (CSSA) has become the key issue which defines the limits of the community's compassion. In this century, because families had shrunk in size and life expectancies had lengthened, CSSA had to fill the gap created by the repeated refusal in previous decades to set up a system of social insurance to protect the average family against the financial burdens of illness, disability, unemployment, retirement and old age. CSSA has been under constant attack since it was launched in 1993. The general conviction was that 'every poor person is poor because of a defect in his/her character', one review of Hong Kong's welfare history has observed, and 'there is no such thing as welfare right and entitlement'. Those seeking social security benefits were viewed as 'undeserving', and CSSA, therefore, should be 'punitive', limited in scope and 'made as unpleasant as possible'.[1] Its importance in easing the financial and social strains created by the 1997–98 Asian financial crisis went unrecognised. Indeed, during the economic recession that followed, government and business leaders repeatedly alleged that CSSA benefits were excessive and were undermining both the work ethic and traditional virtues of self-reliance and family support. These erroneous assertions were rarely challenged.

The public at large did not realise — and the government and business representatives were unwilling to admit — that a new poor had emerged. They had become destitute as a direct result of official policies adopted in the past. Their misfortunes were being aggravated by misguided and misinformed decisions in this century. They were also being victimised by a general consensus which was inspired by demeaning assertions first given a spurious credibility by an official report in 2000. This document claimed that elements in the workforce had been corrupted by the booming economy of the past. They had developed a 'get rich quick' mentality and 'a dependency culture' with 'unrealistic expectations' about what the government should do for them.[2]

The official statistics told the opposite story. Table 6.1 shows that CSSA remained an affordable safety net in this century, used by only a small minority of the community despite the increasing financial hardship suffered by many families (which earlier chapters described). CSSA was allocated a modest and declining share of total government revenue between 2001 and 2011, and the benefits received by the average recipient never rose above a third of the average employee's monthly earnings.

Table 6.1

CSSA: Recipients, payments and government revenue, 2001–11

Year	Total CSSA Recipients[3]	CSSA Recipients/ Total Population (per cent)	CSSA Expenditure/ Total Government Revenue (per cent)	Average monthly CSSA payment per recipient	Average monthly earnings (all employees)
2001	398,000	5.9	8.2	HK$3,000	HK$10,000
2006	522,000	7.6	6.1	HK$2,800	HK$10,000
2011	443,000	6.2	3.6	HK$3,700	HK$11,300

Nevertheless, CSSA and its beneficiaries were repeatedly smeared in public pronouncements by officials and business representatives. Such sentiments reflected a widespread conviction that, for the most part, the needy had only themselves to blame for their misery and that the government could do little or nothing to help except at excessive cost to the economy. A respected economist argued in 2006 that CSSA was a threat to Hong Kong's fiscal health, and he insisted that social security would make it impossible to maintain Hong Kong's low tax regime.[4] This prediction proved false. Since his forecast, profits tax has been cut from 17.5 to 16.5 per cent and salaries tax from 16 to 15 per cent.

The intense mistrust aroused by CSSA throughout the community had another dimension. It highlighted the contrast with most other advanced economies where rapid economic growth led to a high priority for social expenditure. In Hong Kong, the public has tolerated the absence of retirement and similar benefits which are taken for granted elsewhere. This chapter will explore the process by which an anti-welfare culture was created and the community was conditioned to accept the absence of social reforms as an essential feature of Hong Kong's continuing economic success.

This chapter starts with the statistical evidence which shows that two decades after the launch of CSSA, the needy and vulnerable in Hong Kong still showed no signs of a dependency mentality. And there was no significant repudiation of family responsibility for those in need.

The chapter then explains the shock to the community when the Asian financial crisis brought to an end more than four decades of unbroken annual GDP growth and ample work for all. It traces the government's campaign to deter the unemployed and the elderly from seeking social security. The chapter then investigates the colonial origins of the hostility to social insurance and social security and discusses the consequences for contemporary Hong Kong.

In Defence of the Poor

A prominent healthcare activist declared himself unable to discover any merit in the CSSA scheme. It was impossible for the government to provide this financial assistance, he went on, without encouraging a 'dependency habit'.[5] In reality, Hong Kong's social security did not offer an alternative lifestyle of idle comfort. CSSA benefits had been set initially at the minimum required for subsistence, according to a major academic review at the end of British rule. Even so, 'rates are so low that diets are still inadequate', the author concluded.[6]

The jobless in particular, were stigmatised mercilessly by officials and the business and professional elite. The first Commission on Poverty declared in 2005: 'There are strong financial incentives for lower-income groups in particular the larger households to receive CSSA payment instead of rejoining the workforce.'[7] This assertion was an unjustified slur. The proportion of the unemployed who received CSSA benefits averaged an annual 18 per cent for the period 1994 to 2012. In only six years during this period did the proportion of the unemployed population in receipt of CSSA exceed 20 per cent (see Table 6.2).

Earlier chapters have reviewed how hard-hit the average family was from 1998 and how little protection its members had against this change in its fortunes because of the lack of social insurance and the Third World state of much of its housing and social services. Ill-prepared as the community was, even its least fortunate members responded with impressive stoicism and astonishing self-reliance to loss of jobs and to retirement without pensions. The government consistently refused to recognise these facts. When an official advisory body complained in 2008 of the harm done by the stigma attached to CSSA, its recommendation for reducing the unwarranted humiliation went unheeded.[8]

Table 6.2

Ratio of 'unemployed individual CSSA recipients to total unemployed', 1994–2012[9]

Year	Total Unemployed	CSSA Unemployed/ Total Unemployed (per cent)	Year	Total Unemployed	CSSA Unemployed/ Total Unemployed (per cent)
1994	56,200	9	2004	239,400	19
1995	95,600	9	2005	197,300	21
1996	87,400	16	2006	171,100	22
1997	71,200	23	2007	145,300	23
1998	154,100	19	2008	128,000	24
1999	207,500	13	2009	192,600	18
2000	166,900	14	2010	157,200	20
2001	174,800	17	2011	126,700	22
2002	255,500	16	2012	123,100	20
2003	275,100	18			

The elderly, too, were subject to humiliating attacks. The number of the elderly and retired who sought CSSA was interpreted by a prominent member of the elite as evidence of children's selfishness. Hong Kong must 'promote filial piety', he declared, to 'prevent people from depending on the wider community to look after their elders'. The tightest possible stringency must be imposed on the level of CSSA benefits, he claimed, and families must be induced to accept their 'Confucian' obligations to vulnerable relatives.[10] Ignored were the official statistics that showed how, in this century, the proportion of the elderly population (i.e., those aged 60 and above) receiving CSSA benefits had remained well under 20 per cent and was declining (see Table 6.3).

Table 6.3
Elderly CSSA recipients as share of population aged 60 and over, 1999–2011[11]

Year	Population aged 60 and over receiving CSSA	Percentage of total population aged 60 and over receiving CSSA	Year	Population aged 60 and over receiving CSSA	Percentage of total population aged 60 and over receiving CSSA
1999	152,802	15.6	2006	187,776	16.7
2000	153,647	15.4	2007	187,295	16.0
2001	159,954	15.8	2008	185,043	15.3
2002	170,542	16.6	2009	187,875	14.8
2003	179,253	17.2	2010	188,283	14.2
2004	184,404	17.4	2011	187,099	13.5
2005	187,692	17.3			

Unemployment Is Good for Hong Kong

When the previously unbroken improvement of the community's living standards since the 1950s came to an abrupt halt in 1998, no one in the government — not the policy-makers nor the professionals in the departments dealing with health, welfare and labour issues — had any experience of how to respond to serious economic recession, a slump in the labour market and a fall in wages. Officials and the general public found it impossible to grasp how in the new economic environment, more extensive welfare spending to assist the growing number of people in need had become unavoidable. The rise in the funds allocated to CSSA caused consternation. There was an instinctive reluctance to recognise that economic independence was not an option for most CSSA beneficiaries who, on any test, were society's most deprived, disabled and disadvantaged. Instead, officials deemed it proper for CSSA applicants to encounter 'an extremely stigmatizing system' designed 'to meet only the most basic needs of the most deserving, in the direst need of financial assistance', a disgrace to the family only to be sought as a refuge of last resort.[12]

The disinclination to face the facts and deal objectively with the penury which vulnerable members of the community must endure was most marked when it came to the unemployed. Those who had lost their jobs were paying the price for their greed and inefficiency in the past, according to the first Chief Executive, Tung Chee Hwa. He alleged that 'high wage increases have created a bubble economy which needs to be adjusted if we are to remain competitive'.[13] Higher unemployment was good for Hong Kong, in his opinion. 'This is a necessary correction for us to move ahead and be competitive again and to regain our economic vitality,' he told the community in 1998.[14]

The Chief Executive was totally unaware, it seems, of the underlying efficiency of the workforce. Labour productivity had improved by 91 per cent between 1980 and 1996, faster than any advanced Western economy, according to the International Labour Office (ILO).[15] In this period, the labour market had operated with impressive smoothness in shifting the workforce out of the factories as Hong Kong switched from manufacturing to services.[16]

Lies, Deliberate Lies and CSSA Statistics

The opposition to CSSA did not start as an attempt to grapple with the unaccustomed emergency conditions created by the Asian financial crisis. It was already on the first Chief Executive's agenda when he came into office in 1997, and, almost immediately, an attack was launched on the CSSA scheme. The new administration claimed to be responding to 'growing public concern' and promised to reduce the number of unemployed persons receiving CSSA within a year. A steering group was set up whose official report was to provide the template for discrediting social security in years to come. Existing CSSA arrangements were denounced as 'worrying and unsustainable' because they could jeopardise Hong Kong's low tax base. In addition, it was claimed, spending on CSSA had 'taken up the lion's share of the public resources available from economic growth' which would otherwise have been available for 'new or improved' social services.[17] If a culprit were to be sought for adding new burdens to the Budget, the blame would have to fall on Tung himself and his ambitious housing plans. Public spending on housing had accounted for less than 11 per cent of the 1997 Budget but then rose sharply. It took almost 18 per cent of the 1999 Budget and returned to pre-1997 levels only in 2002 (as Chapter 1 explained).

The initial impression conveyed to the public had been that the CSSA steering group's target would be 'able-bodied recipients of working age', but its final recommendations included significant reductions in benefit levels for all groups. The bigger families were singled out for the largest cuts. The justification put forward was that, in the past, 'the calculation of CSSA benefits [did] not take account of the fact that it is easier for larger households to economize on their expenditures'. The approach sounded sensible enough. But the actual arithmetic took no account of the daily living conditions of the poor.

The steering group's remoteness from reality was highlighted by its calculation of the new, reduced payments scale. Its report presented examples of how households would be affected by its recommendations. Among them was the case of a five-person family with a teenage daughter still at school, her unemployed father and his wife, 'an elderly mother-in-law, and . . . a 21-year-old son who is suffering from carcinoma' [of the stomach]. The steering group proposed that such a family's monthly benefits should be reduced by almost 5 per cent.[18] There was no explanation of how the working group came to believe that a family in these circumstances would find it easier than smaller households to 'economize on their expenditures'.

At the heart of the campaign against CSSA were allegations that individuals gave up their jobs and lived on CSSA because they would be better off than workers who stayed in employment. This accusation was false. In 2000, there were still some officials in the health and welfare fields who found vilification of the poor too much to stomach (as the previous chapter pointed out). 'Most able-bodied CSSA recipients and people in other socially disadvantaged groups would like to work and become self-reliant,' a government document insisted, if they could 'overcome barriers to work and lead an independent life'.[19] And as Table 6.2 demonstrated earlier in this chapter, a majority of the unemployed did not receive CSSA.

Nevertheless, grossly misleading figures were produced in order to bring CSSA recipients into disrepute. A simple statistical trick was used to deceive the public. The government could — and should — have chosen to compare the total benefits received by a CSSA household with the monthly income of the average household. Instead, the government compared the average CSSA household's benefits with the individual worker's average monthly earnings. The deception lay in the fact that for the community as a whole, average household incomes were significantly higher than the individual worker's earnings (see Table 6.4).

Table 6.4
Average monthly household incomes and average monthly earnings per employee, 1997–2012 (HK$)

Year	Monthly household income	Monthly earnings per employee	Year	Monthly household income	Monthly earnings per employee
1997	19,000	10,000	2005	16,000	10,000
1998	18,000	10,000	2006	17,000	10,000
1999	17,500	10,000	2007	17,500	10,600
2000	18,000	10,000	2008	18,400	10,500
2001	18,000	10,000	2009	18,000	10,500
2002	16,500	10,000	2010	18,000	11,000
2003	16,000	10,000	2011	20,000	11,300
2004	16,000	9,800	2012	21,000	13,000

The steering group's report used this misleading comparison of CSSA payments with workers' wages to highlight 'a cause for concern as this may create inequities and disincentives to work'. 'The average monthly [CSSA] payment for a four-person household registered a real increase of 120% in the past ten years,' the official report claimed, 'whereas the median wage of workers in all industries grew only by 41% in real terms over the same period.'[20] (Ten years earlier, it should be noted, CSSA did not exist, which made the comparison dubious from the start.) How misleading was this comparison? In 1998, the average household monthly income according to the government's *Hong Kong Annual Digest of Statistics* was HK$18,000 — 80 per cent higher than the monthly CSSA benefits paid to a family of four.

This distortion technique proved highly successful in the official drive to promote fears that welfare was sapping the will to work. As a result, the impression became widespread that a family of four would be better off if it quit work and applied for CSSA. A prominent professional and academic, for example, confidently expressed this view at a Legislative Council meeting in 2002. A four-person family would qualify, he said, for 'slightly over HK$10,000 in CSSA payment on grounds of unemployment, together with rental allowance, and so on'. 'The median income for an individual is HK$10,000,' he went on.[21] What he did not say was that the median income for households that year was HK$16,500 (see Table 6.4).

Statistical manipulation was given a fresh lease of life when the first Commission on Poverty set out to reinforce the general belief that the level of CSSA benefits made it rewarding to abandon paid employment. The commission's key argument, constantly repeated ever since by the media and other commentators, was that a four-person household on CSSA received HK$9,005, which was 'close to the median wage' of HK$9,249 in 2004.[22] The analysis went on to highlight how much better off were CSSA recipients than employees in the 'the lower quartile of the overall wage distribution', whose average monthly wage was HK$6,756. And CSSA beneficiaries received other valuable rewards for being jobless, the document added. They had a right 'to a range of other benefits such as free public healthcare, public housing rental assistance and student financial assistance'.[23]

The mischief in this presentation was, once again, the inappropriate comparison between the total payments to a CSSA household and the monthly wages of the average individual employee. When this bias is removed, the alleged generosity of CSSA payments disappears, as the following analysis demonstrates.

- Table 6.4 shows that in 2004, the average household's monthly income was HK$16,000 — 78 per cent above the HK$9,005 paid to a four-person CSSA household. This enormous gap amply justified granting CSSA recipients' exemption from medical fees and helping them with public housing rents and school charges.
- The comparison based on the four-person household was grossly deceptive. The average monthly payment to all four-person CSSA households was HK$9,005 (as stated above). But for some CSSA groups, the benefits received were well below this sum. Thus, the average CSSA payment to an unemployed household was significantly lower: only HK$4,764 a month, according to the official figures.
- Average monthly benefits received by an unemployed individual were even lower. They amounted to only HK$2,186 — 68 per cent below the monthly wage of HK$6,756 earned by the average worker in the lowest group of wage-earners cited above.[24]

Resourceful and Self-reliant

These facts refute the accusations about the idle poor living in CSSA comfort made by the first Commission on Poverty. Its intention had been to make the case for the 'moral hazard' allegedly created by providing welfare payments for the unemployed. That is, the argument that availability of social security created a serious and, for some, an irresistible, temptation to abandon paid employment.

The suspicion that CSSA was abused by the unemployed has continued to thrive. The third Chief Executive promised in his first Policy Address that the CSSA scheme would be investigated — yet again — to see whether it had 'struck a proper balance between providing a safety net and encouraging people capable of working to join the workforce'. He did not distance himself from allegations of extensive fraud by the unemployed who sought CSSA when these were put to him by a business representative in the Legislative Council.[25] Like the rest of the government-business nexus, Leung had neglected to apply the proper test of whether Hong Kong suffered from 'welfare dependency': when workers became unemployed, how many of them received CSSA?

For the general public, finding the answer to that question was far from easy. The Census and Statistics Department routinely published CSSA data about those without work. But these statistics referred only to unemployed 'cases' (i.e., households), while unemployment rates referred to the individual worker without a job. The statistics on unemployed individuals receiving CSSA existed, but the government preferred not to publish them (though data on elderly beneficiaries were routinely

published in terms of individuals as well as 'cases'). These statistics generally were released only in response to the occasional Legislative Council
Question. They are presented in Table 6.2 which reveals the resourcefulness and self-reliance which the Hong Kong workforce has displayed in
avoiding the stigma of seeking CSSA despite the most adverse labour
market conditions experienced for half a century.

How the unemployed survive without CSSA has long been a mystery.
The struggle to borrow enough from friends, relatives and other sources
to cover their daily living costs was too embarrassing for them to disclose
in official surveys, the labour minister stated in 2003.[26] The government
later started to collect information on low-income households that did
not receive the CSSA payments for which they appeared to be qualified.
The statistics gathered were meagre and designed principally, it seems,
to demonstrate that poverty among the elderly was misunderstood.
Other categories of CSSA claimants were not analysed. The sole finding
of interest here was that of the 73,000 poor households not receiving
CSSA in 2012, some 61 per cent stated that they 'were not willing to
apply for CSSA'. No further explanation was sought from them, apparently, and how these families managed was not investigated.[27]

Poor Parents, Unfilial Offspring

The humiliation imposed by the CSSA system on the elderly was indirect
but no less painful than the denigration of the jobless who depended
on CSSA for their subsistence. The older applicant was not categorised
as 'undeserving' but as a failed parent. A core item in the anti-CSSA
rhetoric was the invocation of Chinese traditions. There was no pretence
that the goal was to foster these values for their own sake. The objective was to promote the message that those who advocated community
support for those in need were betraying their cultural heritage.

In the case of the elderly, who accounted for just over half of all CSSA
recipients, the government's goal was to suggest that those who had
filial children would not need to apply for social security. Thus, a prominent businesswoman and chairperson of the government's Women's
Commission, declared that 'if we can strengthen the promotion of the
traditional Chinese virtue of loving, respecting and taking care of the
elderly . . . we should be able to substantially reduce the pressure of
increasing social welfare expenditure'.[28] This view was shared by the government: 'We must make every effort to preserve this fine traditional
concept of family instead of shifting the responsibility of looking after
the elderly to society,' the welfare minister declared in 2006.[29]

As this chapter has already pointed out (Table 6.3), those aged 60 and
above receiving CSSA benefits had remained well under 20 per cent since

1999 even though, according to a 2012 government survey, the median personal income for the retired individual was only HK$2,000 a month (compared with HK$11,000 for individuals who had not yet retired).[30] This meagre sum on which the average elderly person had to subsist was shocking but hardly surprising. The survey revealed that only 8 per cent of this group had 'retirement fund/pensions'. Whom had they supposed would help finance their retirement? Some 27 per cent replied: 'raising children and expecting, in return, financial support from children in old age'. Only a small minority regarded the government as the main source of protection in old age: 13 per cent of the retired (and 8 per cent of those not retired).[31] These official statistics were persuasive evidence that allegations about a dependency mentality among the elderly and a desire to transfer responsibility from the family to the state were based on groundless preconceptions and ignorant prejudice.

One of the most important 'Confucian' measures adopted by the government was to promote 'ageing in the community'. The incentives offered included the promise of accelerated access to public housing for families with elderly members.[32] The policy had been destined to fail from the start, according to a report prepared for the government's Elderly Commission. A larger proportion of Hong Kong's elderly population look for residential care than in other modern cities. The explanation does not lie in any reluctance by Hong Kong families to care for their aged relatives, contrary to what is frequently alleged. The size of the average family is now too small to provide the care at home needed by victims of 'stroke, dementia, bone fracture', this report stated, and in any case, Hong Kong flats are too cramped to make homecare feasible.[33]

The government's offer of public housing as an incentive to share a home with an elderly relative was linked to the goal of reducing the numbers eligible for CSSA. Applicants for CSSA were assessed not just on their own financial means but on the earnings and assets of the entire household with whom they lived. Thus, the elderly person who took up residence with relatives forfeited the right to apply for CSSA on an individual basis.[34] This practice was justified officially first in terms of a family's duty to assist 'members who have no financial means' but also to prevent a transfer of 'the responsibility of supporting their family members to the taxpayers'. Family members who declined to provide financial help for relatives in need had to make a formal 'statement on non-provision of financial support'. In such cases, CSSA could be granted but only if specially authorised by the Director of the Social Welfare Department.[35]

This requirement came to be regarded as social blackmail. The welfare minister complained in 2011 that the document itself was 'commonly referred to in the community' as the 'bad [i.e., unfilial] son statement'.

This term, he lamented, could 'easily bring about the effect of labelling and cause misunderstanding'.[36] It continued to be used, nevertheless, because the media and the public believed this unflattering label to be an accurate description of what was intended.[37] As Table 6.3 suggests, this 'labelling' was highly successful. The proportion of the population aged 60 and over who obtained CSSA averaged annually a mere 16 per cent between 1999 and 2011.

Within the community, there was growing awareness that attitudes had to change, albeit gradually. 'Some people are saying that the social security system is breeding dependency and idleness,' lamented one academic specialist in elderly issues in 2005, '[i]n the past, our social security system relied on the civic ethic and the Confucian belief to sustain itself.'[38] In 2012, nevertheless, a government survey reported that only 22 per cent of the retired rejected the principle that 'children should be responsible for providing financial support for parents'. Expectations among those who had not retired were somewhat different, however. This group described themselves as having serious obligations to finance their own parents and grandparents after retirement. But only 13 per cent assumed that their own children and grandchildren would be 'the most responsible person for providing one's financial protection' after retirement. Instead, they saw themselves as relying on 'savings and investments' and 'purchase of insurance to cover possible medical and health care expenses for chronic illness in old age'.[39]

The 'bad son statement' had become a dangerous political liability by 2012, and when the third Chief Executive set about increasing the financial support offered to the elderly, he avoided the existing CSSA scheme. A flat-rate Old Age Living Allowance of HK$2,200 was launched, means-tested but not on a household basis.[40] The take-up rate was high because it was free from the CSSA stigma, and the over-65 population was actively encouraged to apply for the new allowance by a lengthy, government advertising campaign.[41] Among Leung's team, there was anxiety about this break with tradition. Once financial assistance for the elderly was freed from the constraints of 'Confucianism', why not those with disabilities, the low-waged and even the unemployed?

'Confucianism' was absent from official rhetoric in discussions of pensions for the elderly (which would remove the need for CSSA). To expect taxpayers to help finance retirement pensions would be a recipe for social unrest, the government argued, because the young would resent the demands of the old. Among the other serious drawbacks to 'a public-managed old-age pension scheme', according to the welfare minister, was that it was wrong in principle for 'the expenses of supporting the elderly [to] be shouldered by young people'.[42] Filial piety had its limits, apparently.

On the Mainland, the government displayed greater realism about the state of the urban family in this century. By 2004, less than 20 per cent of the income received by the elderly in Mainland cities came from their children.[43] In 2010, the *People's Daily* bade farewell to Confucianist aspirations.

> "Bringing up sons to provide for one's old age" has long been a deep-rooted concept for the Chinese. Any challenge to the concept is regarded as impiety. But now the concept has to change . . . a young couple have to support four aging parents and raise at least one child, [and] have started to challenge the traditional practice of family nursing.[44]

In 2013, the Mainland's 1996 Law on the Protection of the Rights and Interests of the Elderly was amended, transferring the main responsibility for the health and welfare of old people to the state (including the provision of pensions and health insurance). Although this break with Chinese traditional views on family obligations had encountered serious opposition as it went through the legislative process, the pace of urbanisation and the transfer of 250 million migrant workers to the cities meant that even in the rural areas, it was no longer possible for families to be the primary carers for the elderly.[45]

Capitalism's 'Ugly Face'

What made the denigration of CSSA beneficiaries particularly unfair was the considerable baggage which it preserved from its Third World origins. CSSA incorporated neither generosity nor dignity. It remained intended to provide the most desperate and deserving of the destitute with just sufficient for subsistence, two social scientists commented soon after CSSA had ben launched.

> The scheme deliberately had those features of the [19th century English] Poor Law that would make it a place of last resort. To apply for assistance was an admission of failure; for the application to succeed was a public statement of the greater failure of the family to provide.[46]

Chapter 4 described how a reforming Governor, Sir David Trench, found his proposals for social security, social insurance and labour protection vetoed by financial and departmental officials in the 1960s despite the political unrest of 1966 and 1967. His only victory was the introduction in 1971 of cash benefits at a bare subsistence level for the destitute in place of the traditional relief in kind. This Public Assistance Scheme (PAS) was an important advance but was, nevertheless, handicapped from the start by the anti-welfare prejudices of officials involved in designing the system. Among the key drafters was Kenneth J. Topley, who did not conceal his distaste for this social security assignment. He told Social Welfare Department staff, the official record noted, 'that he was unenthusiastic about talking with welfare people to whom he was "allergic"'.[47] (This contempt for the caring professions did not prevent him from subsequently being appointed Director of Social Welfare and then Director of Education.)

The next Governor, Sir Murray (later Lord) MacLehose, tried to introduce much the same range of social reforms as Trench had advocated. This time, it looked as if the government-business nexus would modify its opposition to welfare. In the 1970s, unemployment rose to record levels, reaching 6 per cent in 1973 and peaking at 9 per cent in 1975. (It did not return to its 1971 level until 1976.)[48] A senior legislator, Dr S. Y. (later Sir Sze-Yuen) Chung, explained the dismay he had felt during these years at the plight of those who had lost their jobs and who had no entitlement to welfare benefits. 'It was quite wrong, by today's social standards, that unemployed single men or couples without children had to live off their friends and relatives,' declared this prominent spokesman for manufacturing industry, 'or that some married men had to live off the public assistance granted to their children'.

Chung's statement was almost a direct quotation of the Governor's personal plea for jobless workers three weeks earlier. Chung urged the government to follow the practice of other high-growth Asian economies and introduce a modern provident system for the workforce which would provide both unemployment benefits and retirement pensions. He and MacLehose also supported a modern social insurance scheme offering 'a semi-voluntary contributory sickness, injury and death benefit scheme'.[49]

The business community rejected the proposal despite Chung's support for the Governor. MacLehose had completely misjudged the employers' goodwill, he later admitted.

> What is called 'the ugly face of capitalism' was notably absent in the recession of 1974–75 . . . and this was one of the reasons Hong Kong came through it so well. Now when the economy as a whole is doing comparatively well, and looks like continuing to do so, there are signs of this lesson being forgotten by some. It is all very well to say that in a free economy one must take the rough with the smooth; but those who take the rough are so seldom those who enjoyed the smooth. Our economy depends on the development of sound industry . . . based on a decently housed society whose elements observe mutual respect and restraint.[50]

MacLehose's defeat was not enough to satisfy the business community. The colonial administration was given notice that employers would not pay the costs of social or labour reforms. This ultimatum was delivered by Maria Tam Wai-chu. This young lawyer had just been appointed by MacLehose to the Legislative Council. She displayed a lack of gratitude towards him that was a powerful illustration of the strength of business resistance to social reform. 'The Government has been endeavouring to raise the living standard of the working class and to improve industrial safety [which] directly raised the cost of labour,' said this rising political star. 'Severance pay, workers' insurance, paid maternity leave, restrictions on night work and overtime of female workers etc.,' she grumbled, were 'all measures supported by the people, but all the responsibilities fall on the employers.'[51]

The Anti-welfare Alliance

Another important legacy from the past was the continuing resistance to social insurance that would help to finance retirement pensions, health insurance and unemployment benefits. Until late in the 20th century, an increasingly prosperous Hong Kong had repeatedly rejected proposals for a comprehensive, modern system of social security, Chapter 4 recounted, while social insurance continued to provoke intense hostility. This situation was in marked contrast to the pattern generally found in the world's advanced economies. By 1950, most of them had in place what have been termed 'the five basic welfare programs: worker's compensation; sickness and maternity benefits; old-age, invalidity, and death supports; family allowances; and unemployment insurance'.[52] The sole welfare entitlements in Hong Kong half a century later were worker's compensation and a retirement fund scheduled to start in 2000.

Basic welfare provisions were introduced elsewhere in the world, it has been argued, to provide protection against the poverty that individuals and their families would otherwise suffer when no longer able to earn a living. But employment had not been a problem for Hong Kong's workforce from its take-off as a major exporter of light industrial products in the early 1950s until the end of the century. Throughout this period, a chronic labour shortage prevailed (with rare exceptions) and wages were buoyant. As a result, individuals with health, physical, social or educational disabilities were not automatically excluded from the job market before the Asian financial crisis.

Social insurance has been blocked by the government-business nexus for half a century. The leading role was usually played by the senior officials in the colonial administration. Only when they were unable to defeat, delay or satisfactorily dilute reform proposals did business leaders have to flex their muscles. In 1967, the Financial Secretary, Sir John Cowperthwaite, killed off a blueprint for the introduction of social insurance, including a Mandatory Provident Fund (MPF) type fund, even though the proposals had been supported by the Governor. Cowperthwaite falsely alleged that the proposals were part of a plot against profits.[53] Retirement schemes were revisited and rejected by an official working party in 1975 and again in 1977. A third government study in 1986 produced a detailed rebuttal of all the arguments put forward not only for an MPF-type fund but for social insurance in general. The acting Financial Secretary argued that a retirement scheme of this sort would seriously disrupt Hong Kong's financial and labour markets and prove catastrophic for the economy as a whole. He also raised the spectre of higher taxation by portraying the 5 per cent contribution to be paid to the retirement fund by both employer and employee as equivalent to an increase in salaries and profits tax.[54]

In the 1990s, the government temporarily withdrew from its alliance with the business community and in 1992 put forward a new proposal for an MPF, which won no support. In 1994, an old age pension scheme was proposed but defeated by business and academic opposition.[55] The government subsequently rejoined the anti-welfare alliance and rejected further pleas for a pension scheme to provide financial support for those who would retire before adequate retirement incomes became available from the MPF (which was launched only in 2000).

The long-term damage from this sustained campaign was heavy, financially as well as socially. The numbers unable to maintain themselves have risen sharply in this century as a result of an ageing population, the loss of the former job opportunities for individuals with disabilities or limited schooling and increased unemployment. The government had become their only means of support. The average worker had had no realistic opportunity to provide for old age. Sickness remained uncovered, and health insurance was still under discussion when the third Chief Executive took office in 2012. The absence of social insurance meant that there was no universal and comprehensive scheme to which either the employer or the employee contributed to protect individuals against the normal as well as the unexpected contingencies of life. The unintended consequence was that the protection provided by social security, public housing and healthcare were financed entirely out of tax revenues.

Conclusions: An Unsatisfactory Alternative

The extent to which the current CSSA system added to the misery of the poor had a wider context. The insistence that 'low income' should be the criterion for subsidised medical treatment, no matter how life-threatening the illness, and that families should beggar themselves to pay for modern medication were extensions of the CSSA's 'principles'. Similarly, the humiliation of the 'bad son statement' inflicted on elderly applicants for social security was mirrored in the policy which required families to publicise their demeaning CSSA status in order for their children to qualify for other financial assistance towards the costs of their schooling.

In the absence of social insurance, Hong Kong was left with a social security scheme which was barely adequate for those in need. The system survived, it seems, because of the widespread — but mistaken — conviction that any relaxation of its stringency would create an incentive for hordes of workers to give up their jobs. Even academic specialists in the social services field declined to change their preconceptions. A Social Welfare Department statement that, as yet, there was no cause for 'too much concern' about welfare dependency was rejected as unconvincing by an eminent professor in 1998. The 'public impression was that CSSA now actually encourages dependency,' he asserted, because 'it is tempting for unemployed persons receiving CSSA to continue to rely on it . . . which is a more secure source of income than they could get from work.'[56] The facts presented in this chapter are ample proof that no such tendency existed in Hong Kong and that welfare dependency was a myth.

A decade later, the same distinguished academic was again making the case against CSSA, this time in a report commissioned by the government's Central Policy Unit. Now, his concern was social harmony. This professor argued that CSSA and 'other welfare programs' were to blame for 'new social conflicts'. They provided cash benefits that 'exceed individual earnings from the labor market, for people in the lower socio-economic classes', he said. The evidence for his assertion that social harmony was being undermined as a result? Focus groups had told researchers that 'availability of welfare programs . . . contributes to the increase in divorce rate'.[57]

Given the weight of respectable academic opinion in opposition to CSSA, there was little hope of convincing the public that social security was good for the community. In the Hong Kong Transition Project's 2006 survey, support was very low for improving welfare payments to the most vulnerable and disadvantaged groups in society whose survival depended on their CSSA benefits. Only 28 per cent of those surveyed were in favour of increasing CSSA payments, while 26 per cent believed they should be cut.[58] Support for more generous benefits fell still further in the years that followed, according to a 2011 Chinese University study. More than half the respondents were opposed to any increase in social security payments, while only 15 per cent supported such a move.[59]

These polling data were a tribute to the effectiveness of the government's continuing campaign to malign CSSA beneficiaries. Indeed, the demeaning content of official publicity about alleged fraud by CSSA applicants eventually proved too much for the community to stomach. Public indignation forced the hasty cancellation of this campaign in 2009. In that year, instances of fraud were very much in line with the past: a trivial '0.3% of all CSSA cases'.[60] Over 99 per cent were above suspicion.

Because the scheme lacks statistical transparency and accountability (as the gaps in the official data available for citation in this chapter illustrate), CSSA is likely to continue to be regarded as a scheme that rewards undeserving individuals with benefits that are unaffordable for Hong Kong under current economic conditions. The needy and the vulnerable have no protection against misleading and, frequently, malicious comment on their motives and behaviour during public discussions of CSSA by ministers and business representatives alike. The next chapter will endeavour to account for why this mistreatment has been tolerated by a society which is in other respects so compassionate.

Notes

1.   Jick-Joen Lee, *The Road to the Development of Social Welfare in Hong Kong: The Historical Key Issues* (Hong Kong: Hong Kong Institute of Asia-Pacific Studies, Chinese University of Hong Kong, 1996), pp. 26–7.
2.   Commission on Strategic Development, *Bringing the Vision to Life: Hong Kong's Long-Term Development Needs and Goals* (Hong Kong: Central Policy Unit, 2000), pp. 16–7.
3.   Census and Statistics Department, 'Statistics on Comprehensive Social Security Assistance Scheme, 2001 to 2011', *Hong Kong Monthly Digest of Statistics September 2012*, 'Table 2: Number of CSSA Recipients by Age Group, 2001 to 2011', p. FB6. The other figures are taken from the relevant issues of the *Hong Kong Annual Digest of Statistics*.
4.   Kui-Wai Li, *The Hong Kong Economy: Recovery and Restructuring* (Singapore: McGraw-Hill Education (Asia), 2006), pp. 188–9.
5.   Tim H. C. Pang of Patients' Rights Association, quoted in James T. H. Tang, 'Taking Care of the Deprived and the Elderly', in James T. H. Tang et al. (eds.), *Knowledge and Social Involvement* (Hong Kong: Faculty of Social Sciences, University of Hong Kong, 2005), p. 34.
6.   Chak-Kwan Chan, 'Welfare Policies and the Construction of Welfare Relations in a Residual Welfare State: The Case of Hong Kong', *Social Policy and Administration*, Vol. 32, No. 3 (September 1998), pp. 282–3.
7.   Commission on Poverty (CoP), 'Assisting the Unemployed: Welfare-to-Work', CoP Paper 19/2005 (Commission Secretariat, June 2005), p. 6.
8.   The Commission on Strategic Development recommended the introduction of special arrangements to assist the 'working poor' so that they could 'apply for assistance to supplement their meager incomes without being subject to the undesirable labelling effect'. 'An Overview of the Opportunities and Challenges of Hong Kong's Development' (CSD/6/2008, October 2008), p. 7. This advice was not taken. On the success of stigmatisation in deterring

applicants, see Chak Kwan Chan, *Social Security Policy in Hong Kong: From British Colony to China's Special Administrative Region* (Lanham: Lexington Books, 2011), pp. 168–9.

9. Data on individual CSSA recipients (rather than 'cases' which refer to households) are from Dr York Chow Yat-ngok, Secretary for Health, Welfare and Food, *Hong Kong Hansard* (*HH* hereafter), 29 June 2005, 'Table 10 Number of CSSA Recipients by Case Category, 1995 to 2004', p. 9069 and its explanatory notes in particular; Matthew Cheung Kin-chung, Secretary for Labour and Welfare, *HH*, 10 December 2008, Annexes 3 and 7, p. 2800 and *HH*, 30 January 2013, p. 5466. Data on total unemployed are from the relevant *Monthly* and *Annual Statistical Digests*. The 2012 figure refers to November.

10. Former President of the Law Society and chairman of the Hong Kong Progressive Alliance which in 2005 merged with the Democratic Alliance for the Betterment of Hong Kong (DAB), Ambrose Lau Hon-Chuen, *HH*, 10 May 2000, p. 6258.

11. Census and Statistics Department, 'Statistics on Comprehensive Social Security Assistance Scheme, 1999 to 2009', *Hong Kong Monthly Digest of Statistics September 2010*, p. FC6; 'Statistics on Comprehensive Social Security Assistance Scheme, 2001 to 2011', *Hong Kong Monthly Digest of Statistics September 2012*, p. FB6.

12. Chan, 'Welfare Policies and the Construction of Welfare Relations in a Residual Welfare State: The Case of Hong Kong', pp. 281, 282–3, 286–7; Brian Brewer and Stewart MacPherson, 'Poverty and Social Security', in Paul Wilding et al. (eds.), *Social Policy in Hong Kong* (Cheltenham: Edward Elgar, 1997), pp. 74, 76, 77.

13. Tung Chee Hwa, Chief Executive, *Government Information Service* (GIS hereafter), 29 May 1998.

14. Tung, *GIS*, 28 May 1998.

15. ILO Press Release, 'Americans work longest hours among industrialized countries, Japanese second longest etc.', 6 September 1999 (ILO/99/29).

16. This complex rebalancing is well tracked in John Dodsworth and Dubravko Mihaljek, *Hong Kong, China: Growth, Structural Change, and Economic Stability During the Transition* (Washington: International Monetary Fund, 1997), pp. 54–64.

17. Social Welfare Department, 'Report on Review of the Comprehensive Social Security Assistance Scheme' (December 1998), pp. 1, 3, 4.

18. Ibid., p. 27 and 'Example 4: A 5-person household comprising an elderly, a sick and 3 able-bodied recipients'.

19. Health and Welfare Bureau, 'Legislative Council Panel on Welfare Services "Promoting Self-reliance Strategy"' (CB(2) 1943/99-00(03), May 2000), p. 1.

20. Social Welfare Department, 'Report on Review of the Comprehensive Social Security Assistance Scheme', p. 14; Annex 4: 'Comparison of Estimated Average Monthly CSSA Payment with Average Monthly Household Income of the Lowest Income Groups (1993/94–1997/98)', p. 5.

21. Lau Ping-Cheung, *HH*, 10 April 2002, p. 5235.

188   *Poverty in the Midst of Affluence*

22. The final official estimate for the median wage that year was HK$9,800. See Table 6.4.
23. Commission on Poverty (CoP), 'Assisting the Unemployed: Welfare-to-Work', CoP Paper 19/2005 (Commission Secretariat, June 2005), p. 6.
24. These calculations are derived from Commission on Poverty data. It should be noted that for each CSSA 'case', entitlements were calculated on a household basis. The data also indicate that many 'cases' included more than one unemployed person. Commission on Poverty (CoP), 'Comprehensive Social Security Assistance Scheme (CSSA) Able-Bodied Caseload — Past Trend and 2014 Scenarios', Annex A 'Number of CSSA Cases by Nature of Case, 1994–2004', Annex B 'Number of CSSA Recipients by Nature of Case, 1994–2004' and Annex F 'CSSA Expenditure 1994/95–2004/05' (CoP Paper 20/2005, June 2005).
25. Leung Chun-ying, Chief Executive, *HH*, 16 January, 2013, p. 4923; 17 January 2013, pp. 4994–5.
26. Stephen Ip Shu-kwan, Secretary for Economic Development and Labour, *HH*, 12 February 2003, p. 3397.
27. Census and Statistics Department, 'Analysis of Low Income Households Not Receiving Comprehensive Social Security Assistance', *Hong Kong Monthly Digest of Statistics December 2012*, p. FA5. An official investigation of how retirement was financed was similarly uninformative and complained about problems in collecting accurate information on personal finances too serious to allow the figures to be published. Census and Statistics Department, 'Retirement Planning and the Financial Situation in Old Age', *Thematic Household Survey Report No. 52* (Hong Kong: Census and Statistics Department, 2013), p. 189.
28. Sophie Leung Lau Yau-fun, *HH*, 25 February 2004, p. 4031.
29. Chow, Secretary for Health and Welfare, *HH*, 26 April 2006, p. 6557.
30. Census and Statistics Department, 'Retirement Planning and the Financial Situation in Old Age', *Thematic Household Survey Report No. 52* (Hong Kong: Census and Statistics Department, 2013), p. 190.
31. Census and Statistics Department, 'Retirement Planning and the Financial Situation in Old Age', pp. 186, 190, 191; 'Table 9.6c: Current/future generation of retired persons aged 35 and over by person perceived as the most responsible person for providing one's financial protection after retirement/in old age', p. 206.
32. Transport and Housing Bureau, 'Legislative Council Panel on Housing: Housing-related Initiatives in the 2007–08 Policy Agenda' (CB(1)36/07-08(01), October 2007), 'Annex: The five enhanced public housing arrangements implemented since October 2007', p. 5. The background to this policy, which can be traced back to 1977, was summarised in Health, Welfare and Food Bureau, 'Progress Report on the Healthy Ageing Campaign' (CB(2)2280/03-04(03), May 2004), pp. 1–11.
33. Ernest Chui Wing-tak et al., *Elderly Commission's Study on Residential Care Services for the Elderly Final Report* (Hong Kong: University of Hong Kong, December 2009), pp. 9–11, 12.

34. Health and Welfare Bureau, 'Legislative Council Panel on Welfare Services: Issues Arising from Review of the Comprehensive Social Security Assistance (CSSA) Scheme' (CB(2)2256/99-00(12), June 2000), pp. 2–3.
35. Labour and Welfare Bureau and Social Welfare Department, 'Legco Panel on Welfare Services, Subcommittee on Poverty Alleviation: Government's Response to the Report of Subcommittee on Review of the Comprehensive Social Security Assistance Scheme' (CB(2)974/08-09(01), February 2009), pp. 4–5.
36. Cheung, Secretary for Labour and Welfare, *HH*, 8 June 2011, p. 11718.
37. The Mainland authorities employed a much narrower definition of 'unfilial' behaviour, which was confined to deliberate or physical abuse of the elderly. See, for example, the incidents reported in *New China News Agency*, 27 December 2012.
38. Dr Ernest W. T. Chui, quoted in Tang (ed.), 'Taking Care of the Deprived and the Elderly', p. 35.
39. Census and Statistics Department, 'Retirement planning and the financial situation in old age', p. 191; 'Table 9.6b: Current/future generation of retired persons aged 35 and over by views on whether children should be responsible for providing financial support for parents', p. 205; 'Table 9.6c: Current/future generation of retired persons aged 35 and over by person perceived as the most responsible person for providing one's financial protection after retirement/in old age', p. 206.
40. Patrick Nip Tak-kuen, Director of Social Work, *GIS*, 31 January 2013.
41. 'SWD proactively follows up applications for OALA', *GIS*, 30 March and 9 May 2013.
42. Chow, Secretary for Health, Welfare and Food, *HH*, 26 April 2006, pp. 6555, 6556.
43. *Renmin Ribao*, 26 September 2004.
44. 'Confucian filial piety evolves in changing society', *New China News Agency*, 19 April 2010.
45. The amendments and the issues involved were summarised in *New China News Agency*, 26 June and 29 December 2012.
46. The quotations are from Brewer and MacPherson, 'Poverty and Social Security', pp. 74, 76, 77.
47. M. 34 DSW to AD, 14 November 1967; M. 38 AD (Bain) to DSW, 20 February 1968. Hong Kong Public Records Office (HKRS hereafter) 890-1-15 'Subsistence Level'. Topley's assignment was to determine at what level subsistence should be fixed in terms of daily monetary costs.
48. *The 1975–76 Budget: Economic Background* (Hong Kong: Government Printer, 1977), p. 34; *The 1978–79 Budget: Economic Background* (Hong Kong: Government Printer, 1978), p. 32; Census and Statistics Department, *Hong Kong Annual Digest of Statistics 1984 Edition* (Hong Kong: Government Printer, 1985), p. 25. It should be noted that reliable and comprehensive data on the labour market were not available until the 1980s except for the Census exercises held every five years from 1961.

49. Sir Murray (later Lord) MacLehose, Governor, *HH*, 6 October 1976, pp. 18–9; 11 October 1978, p. 25; Dr (later Sir Sze-yuen) Chung Sze-yuen, *HH*, 27 October 1976, pp. 79–80.
50. MacLehose, *HH*, 7 October 1981, pp. 33–4.
51. She later became a major political personality in both Hong Kong and Beijing. Maria Tam Wai-chu, *HH*, 29 October 1981, p. 137.
52. The quotation and the subsequent comparisons with international experience are taken from Andrew Abbott and Stanley DeViney, 'The Welfare State as Transnational Event: Evidence from Sequences of Policy Adoption', *Social Science History*, Vol. 16, No. 2 (Summer 1992), especially pp. 247, 266–7 and 'Table 4: Orders of adoption of five major welfare programs', p. 262.
53. *A Report by the Inter-Departmental Working Party to Consider Certain Aspects of Social Security* (Hong Kong: Government Printer, 1967); M. 7 Governor to Financial Secretary, 22 June 1967; M. 24 Financial Secretary to Governor; (11) 'An Appreciation of the Report by the Inter-Departmental Working Party on Social Security', 10 October 1967. HKRS 163-9-486, 'Social Security — Implications of Change in HK Status-Quo . . . '.
54. For this document, see Education and Manpower Branch, 'Appendix: The Implications of Establishing a Central Provident Fund in Hong Kong' (October 1986), *HH*, 13 May 1987, pp. 1589–1607. For the Financial Secretary's arguments, see John F. Yaxley, Acting Financial Secretary, *HH*, 13 May 1987, pp. 1579–82.
55. Education and Manpower Branch, *Taking the Worry Out of Growing Old: A Consultation Paper on the Government's Proposals for an Old Age Pension Scheme, Hong Kong* (Hong Kong: Government Printer, 1994). The impact on public finances of this contributory, 'pay as you go' scheme was forecast to be very manageable. Ibid., pp. 12–3, Appendix VII.
56. Nelson Chow, 'Social Welfare', in Larry Chuen-ho Chow and Yiu-kwan Fan (eds.), *The Other Hong Kong Report 1998* (Hong Kong: Chinese University Press, 1999), pp. 267–8.
57. Nelson Chow and Terry Lum, 'Trends in Family Attitudes and Values in Hong Kong: Final Report', Department of Social Work and Social Administration, University of Hong Kong (Central Policy Unit, 22 August 2008), pp. 7, 19.
58. Hong Kong Transition Project, 'Parties, Policies and Political Reform in Hong Kong' (Hong Kong Transition Project and National Democratic Institute for International Affairs, May 2006), Table 59 'Which of these areas of government expenditure would you cut or increase spending on? FEB Ranked by Combined Increase', p. 48.
59. Hong Kong Institute of Asia-Pacific Studies in cooperation with the Hong Kong Professionals and Senior Executives Association, 'Disparity of Wealth Research Project Findings' (1 December 2011).
60. See Welfare Services Panel, 'Minutes of Special Meeting' (CB(2)2545/08-09, 29 July 2009).

7
An Absence of Advocates: How the 'Welfare' Lobby Lost Its Voice

The people of Hong Kong are 'more demanding, better organized, better resourced, and better able to articulate their interests' than ever before, a well-known political scientist has observed. Public hospital patients, public housing tenants, the elderly and the disabled all have organisations to lobby on their behalf and to protest against mistreatment and neglect by the government, he pointed out.[1] Yet, the political system has been able to evade the public's demands on social issues with almost total impunity.

No group in the legislature is in the business of promoting welfare for its own sake. The 'pan-democrats' are usually labelled by both officials and business leaders as the 'opposition', bent on preaching populism and welfarism. A majority of the group's members, however, are thoroughly pro-business. As one Democratic Party legislator proudly declared, foreign politicians 'tend to regard us as a right-wing political party in view of [our] objection to minimum wage and [our] support for "small government"'.[2] When the third Chief Executive, Leung Chun-ying, proposed a new monthly allowance of $2,200 for an estimated 400,000 elderly persons, it was taken for granted that none of the directly-elected legislators would oppose this measure for fear of a backlash from the electorate. But they were not to be intimidated by government 'populism', and the introduction of the allowance was delayed for months because of demands for fuller information about the proposal from labour activists and radicals, among others, in the legislature.[3]

Within the trade union movement, there has been a similar conservatism about welfare. For example, Chan Yuen-han, one of the most admired personalities in the pro-Mainland Federation of Trade Unions (FTU), has supported self-help as a solution for unemployment and pleaded for a return to Hong Kong's past through allowing the jobless to become street food vendors. This sort of initiative would give the unemployed their chance, she said, to go from hawker to entrepreneur.[4] As she was addressing the legislature in this vein, it was hard to recall that her trade union had ever had an interest in social reform, let alone political radicalism.

Public service unions had once been very ready to take industrial action to promote their members' interests, and between 1971 and 1982, a considerable number of work stoppages and other disputes occurred in the public sector. In 1981, it was confidently predicted that 'unionism, especially among government workers, will be the catalyst of social reform within the next decade'.[5] Although these unions were ready to campaign on specific social issues — notably, health and education — they refrained from becoming involved in policy-making. Their overwhelming priority remained pay and working conditions.[6] 'Following the start of Sino-British negotiations [in 1982] on the future of Hong Kong after 1997,' a leading unionist has said, 'civil servants' pressure on the Government in fighting for their rights subsided.'[7] Welfare had to take second place because political risk and its management had become the overriding concern for civil servants, as they were for the rest of the community.

Political Priorities

Political conservatism and the lack of agitation for social reforms and employees' rights did not mean that the community was either passive or powerless. Even in the absence of universal suffrage and the conventional democratic institutions of prosperous modern societies, the people of Hong Kong had the ability to force their rulers to bow to popular demand on issues the community considered non-negotiable. A particularly powerful illustration of the social and political factors at work was the contrast between the community's very different responses to two key educational controversies.

Passive resistance

The language of the classroom provided a striking example of how the community's initially passive reaction can mask patient but ultimately successful opposition. The proportion of secondary students taught through the medium of Chinese had fallen from over 90 per cent in 1960 to less than 10 per cent by 1980. The decline was caused by parents' preferences: they believed English had a high market value in an international economy like Hong Kong.[8] In 1998, the government decided to reverse this situation. It announced that only 112 secondary schools would be allowed to continue to use English.[9] Another 300 would be forced to switch to Chinese.[10] The new policy proved unpopular because it was seen as depriving the ordinary student of an opportunity to master

English, which parents regarded as essential for a decent career.[11] By 2008, continuing discontent among teachers and parents had persuaded the government that even non-elite schools should be given reasonable freedom to use English in the classroom.[12] It had taken ten years for public pressure to force the education authorities to give way. An official survey in 2013 demonstrated how well-founded the parent's insistence on English had been. This language was reported by employees in general to be of major importance, both in the workplace and as an educational goal, even by comparison with Putonghua.[13]

Protestors' power

Patriotic education provided a very different demonstration of the public's power to compel the government to back down. The government's efforts to introduce patriotic elements into school curricula had aroused more public mistrust than enthusiasm and a long-standing National Education campaign failed to overcome suspicions about political indoctrination.[14] In 2007, President Hu Jintao 'earnestly advised' Hong Kong's second Chief Executive, Donald Tsang Yam-kuen, to give patriotic education 'greater emphasis'.[15] Implementation of President Hu's request started cautiously, however, only in 2011.

When the third Chief Executive, Leung Chun-ying, took office the following year, he inherited a mounting controversy over a draft syllabus for National Education, its funding and its content. A petition against the proposed syllabus gathered 100,000 signatures followed by hunger strikes and repeated mass protests around the government's headquarters (Central Government Offices). A call from Beijing for Hong Kong people to enhance their 'patriotic sentiment' went unheeded.[16] Leung's administration lost its will to resist two months after the start of the protests. The deadline for the introduction of the National Education programme was abandoned. A month later, the offending draft syllabus was withdrawn.[17]

Declining welfare

The contrast between the two educational controversies highlights a striking feature of the political environment in this century. Social issues inspire restrained opposition, while Mainland-related controversies arouse immediate and intense reactions.

The government-business nexus faced minimal opposition when the sick, the elderly and those with disabilities were not spared the painful austerity programmes which the first Chief Executive, Tung Chee Hwa, introduced. He and the next Chief Executive were able to cut back the public housing programme and to deprive the social services of the resources to shorten waiting lists and to supply modern medication to cancer patients and the mentally ill. Ministers showed no hesitation in raising fees and charges for healthcare and education even though average earnings failed to improve in the first decade of this century and actually fell for the poorest and least skilled of the labour force, as previous chapters have recorded. The government had correctly calculated that the political costs of anti-welfare measures on this scale would be small.

This chapter will examine this mismatch. It will investigate why the advocates of social reform declined both in numbers and effectiveness over the past thirty years. It will explain how poverty became a secondary issue and why politics in its most fundamental form had to take precedence.[18] The presentation will trace the origins of the welfare lobby and how the caring professions were able to enlarge public housing and social service programmes in the 1960s and 1970s in the face of determined hostility to social expenditure from the colonial administration and its business collaborators. The chapter will review the rise of conventional political parties and why they, together with the pressure and interest groups from which they sprang, retreated from social issues and welfare advocacy except at the level of the individual constituent or client. Special attention will be given to the labour movement and its switch from protecting employees in the workplace to canvassing for their votes in elections.

In the background, the analysis will show, was a persistent sense of severe political risk to which families had to adjust successfully at all costs and which by the 1990s had reached almost unbearable levels. Survival of the Hong Kong way of life seemed to depend far more on the defence of political rights than on promoting social entitlement. The community has yet to lower its guard.

Unbearable Political Risk

This state of affairs was the direct outcome of a substantial yet subtle shift in the political environment of Hong Kong which got under way in the 1980s. This change unintentionally and unexpectedly reduced the importance attached to social policies so that they became rarely more than a marginal issue in electoral politics. At the first ever District Board elections in 1985, more than half the 237 directly elected seats were won by 'social workers, teachers, unionists, political activists, and even by "Trotskyists" and "pro-Taiwan" elements'. Less than 10 per cent could be classified as 'pro-Mainland'. Hong Kong itself, together with social and labour reform, topped the agenda. Within a year, it was plain that the political climate had changed. Almost 200 organisations and more than a thousand community activists held a public rally to establish the 'Joint Committee on the Promotion of Democratic Government'.[19] A single issue, political reform, was emerging as the overriding priority. 'Welfare' and its advocates were to be increasingly sidelined, and Hong Kong's political survival took over as the community's primary anxiety.

The events of June 4, 1989, strengthened the doomsayers' view of the future, and the community's main, almost overwhelming, apprehension was about its post-1997 political fate. Management of political risk became the dominant concern.[20] Professor Lau Siu-kai, who was to become a trusted adviser of both the first and second Chief Executives, blamed 'the 1997 issue' for smothering altruism as a civic virtue. The community's sense of 'their collective powerlessness' led to the abiding conviction that the most dangerous threat to Hong Kong's survival was political. 'Hong Kong people are using every means to safeguard the future of themselves and their families including illegal, illicit or shady methods,' he complained, '[s]elf-seeking overrides mundane moral concerns. Self-interest drives out concern for others.'[21]

There followed, Lau said, 'an exodus of people, prominent among whom are the better educated and those with professional and managerial skills', who, in 'eschewing their social responsibilities by their alacrity to abandon Hong Kong', deprived the community of leaders who added an essential moral dimension to public life.[22] Thus began the disappearance of individuals who previously had been heavily engaged in campaigning for social reforms. Seen through the eyes of individual families, however, this disengagement from society did not look so culpable.

> . . . people in [Hong Kong could] no longer escape from the ubiquitous, noisy, and haunting messages of the issue of Hong Kong's future, the construction of Daya Bay nuclear power plant, the drafting of Basic Law, the exodus of migrants, the debate on political reform, and the outcry for democracy in the June 4th Incident. Consistently, each event involved the conflict of interests between Hong Kong people and the Beijing regime and each event saw local interest succumb to the interest of the Chinese government.[23]

Business Mismanagement

The traditional advocates of welfare had lost their role much earlier, however. In the first decade after World War II, there was considerable business participation in 'charitable' organisations which tried to remedy the shortage of social services at the district level especially. But this traditional system did not survive Hong Kong's economic takeoff. The Kaifongs and the smaller benevolent associations suffered from a decline in the numbers of well-meaning individuals who had the personal wealth to supply local welfare services.[24] By the 1960s, a new generation of business leaders had emerged which did not have their fathers' loyalties to clan and dialect groups or their traditional values of personal philanthropy. Sons and daughters of the affluent no longer viewed the community as their personal concern. The concept of the business firm as an extended family was in decline, and the workforce was seen as a cost centre that had to be rigidly controlled. By the 1980s and the start of District and Legislative Council elections, social expenditure seemed menacing to the business community as a whole. Elected politicians, it was believed, would be unable to resist the temptation to buy electoral support through welfare schemes financed by higher taxation.[25]

The community's expectations also altered with the general improvement in living standards, and the public started to look for professional standards of social services. The traditional 'charitable' sector found it hard to meet this challenge. The problems were highlighted by the Po Leung Kuk which had a long history of providing care for orphaned and abandoned children and of protecting women and children in need. This charitable organisation was a leading partner in the government-business nexus, and its board members acquired both social prestige and political influence. They had privileged access to the colonial administration and rose to the defence of official social polices when they came under public attack.[26]

Po Leung Kuk's own performance was deeply flawed, however, and its shortcomings help to explain why the traditional 'charitable' organisations lost their role in the community. A 1968 in-depth review of the organisation and the people who ran it included the following observations.

- Membership [of the managing committee] is frankly admitted to be the key stepping stone to social (and in Hongkong this means political) advancement . . . the efficiency of the Po Leung Kuk would be considerably increased if the drive for personal prestige were not so prominent a feature of the institution. There seems to be a concentration on seeking the right kind of publicity rather than creating a more efficiently-run organisation.
- The low salaries offered by the Kuk make it difficult to find suitably qualified people . . . The lack of staff can have distressing consequences. One Kuk orphan . . . spent two years in hospital, during which time she was visited by the Kuk only twice. No attempt was made to keep up her education, and the Kuk made no effort to inspire her with the feeling that the institution cared about her and was anxious about her welfare.
- The Kuk authorities seem infuriatingly reluctant to improve the lot of the average inmate. Most of the children attend the

> Kuk's primary school. When it comes to secondary education, only the top three children in the primary-six class are allowed to continue their studies. No one seems able to explain satisfactorily why the bulk of the Kuk's wards are denied the chance of a full education, thus condemning them to jobs at the bottom of the employment ladder when they are discharged.[27]

A year later, the Po Leung Kuk was publicly shamed in the Legislative Council after it refused to accept government funding to expand care for children with mental disabilities. The Director of Medical and Health Services was asked by a legislator 'whether or not the Directors of the Po Leung Kuk . . . welcome taking care of children of this type'. The government's reply was damning: 'They would like to get rid of these children.'[28]

The Rise of the Professionals

Almost unperceived, the care of those with disabilities had got under way from the start of the post-war period. To a considerable extent, 'the present social service network was built primarily before the 1960s by the non-governmental Western-style social agencies, many with a religious background', it has been pointed out. These non-governmental organisations (NGOs) were determined to fill the vacuum left by the colonial administration's 'passive and minimal' policies.[29]

They had to battle against intimidating Third World conditions. Public health facilities in private sector slums and squatter areas were primitive, as Chapter 3 explained. Welfare services were equally rudimentary until the 1960s. Progress was made, nevertheless, mainly because the early NGO programmes had the personal support of a group of medical doctors. Their experiences during the Japanese invasion and the enemy occupation of Hong Kong had given them a resilience and a talent for improvisation in the face of a collapse of all normal public services.[30] They were not deterred by a lack of support from the colonial administration or the hostility of individual officials.

But as post-war life returned to normal, new obstacles were encountered. Child health services provide a good illustration. In the 1950s, qualified personnel were few, and the demand for their services was so high that the available specialists were inevitably attracted away from public and university hospitals into the private sector. The result was to reduce the numbers of those with the interest and the expertise to mount campaigns to upgrade medical policy and programmes. Improvements started modestly in the 1960s, driven very much by individual medical professionals in collaboration with voluntary agencies, usually with 'informal' cooperation from government professionals.

Although progress gathered speed in the 1970s and 1980s, it was not until the 1990s that standards became adequate.[31]

The government could not stifle the medical profession but it was determined to hinder the takeoff of the social work profession. Officials were especially sceptical about whether there was any need for social workers to have professional qualifications. Thus, 'apart from a handful of outspoken expatriates', the early architects of modern social services consisted of a small group with mixed credentials and little credibility with the government.[32] They were, nevertheless, the vital building block in laying the foundations for almost all the more complex services for those with disabilities and in need of special facilities.

An informal conspiracy grew up between doctors, teachers and social workers in the NGOs and the public sector, and they became adept in mobilising resources and circumventing official restrictions in order to launch programmes for adults with disabilities and for children with special needs.[33] They had infiltrated the bureaucracy and were able to circumvent the barriers created by such official policies as the restriction of rehabilitation services to those who could be returned to the workforce. Even before 1965, when the first government social welfare programme was adopted, a basic network of facilities and programmes had been created for the most challenging groups of vulnerable individuals.[34]

Among the government's professionals, there were 'activists' who were already aware that the young, hardy immigrants would eventually turn into an elderly population. In January 1966, the Housing Authority agreed that it should make 'special provision for the infirm, the handicapped and the aged', and the Commissioner for Housing proposed to start with a partnership with the Social Welfare Department to care for the elderly.[35] Specially designed public housing became available in 1969 with the opening of the first hostel and sheltered accommodation for the elderly. A public drive began to highlight the urgency of the ageing challenge. Sir Yuet-keung Kan, an Executive Councillor with extensive involvement in social affairs, was recruited to deliver what in retrospect proved to be an accurate prediction of what lay ahead.

> The aged have, it is true, not posed a serious problem for us so far. We are a community in which the young predominate, and in which traditions of family solidarity have minimised the need for organised assistance for the old. Not only will the passing years increase the proportion of old people among us, however, but it seems also certain that the weakening of old traditions will confront us with a growing need for organised help for them.[36]

Medical and health planners joined the informal campaign on ageing issues in the 1970s. They began to review how Hong Kong might cope with an ageing population's special requirements. Hospital bed ratios should be increased by 30 per cent, it was recommended in 1974, 'to improve psychiatric services, expand geriatric services and handle more patients in the light of the changing age structure of the population'.[37] Nevertheless, the professionals within the colonial administration were unable to overcome the general complacency of the rest of the government and the community at large about what would happen as Hong Kong aged.

Pressures Groups and Political Activists

In the 1960s and 1970s, the expansion of public housing, hospital services and education and social welfare programmes altered the balance within Hong Kong society.[38] For the first time, the middle class was not totally dependent on clients or employers in the business world, whose profit and market-driven imperatives it was obliged to share. The social services were creating a new professional group, which had very different goals and a very different clientele. The new professionals were developing facilities and services on the basis of what an individual or family needed rather than what they could afford.[39] In the 1970s, the ideal of social justice began to attract the attention of 'a new brand of young intellectuals, who had been brought up and educated in Hong Kong and were more Western in their outlook'. They believed, it was said, that economic success meant that resources were 'readily available for guaranteeing everyone a living above the subsistence level'. All that was lacking in their view was government commitment to such a goal, and they were prepared to challenge officialdom.[40]

Modern NGOs were not as easily co-opted into the ranks of government supporters as traditional bodies had been — notably, the Kaifongs, the Tung Wah Hospital Group and the Po Leung Kuk — with the promise of political access, social status and the chance to advance within the colonial power system. The NGOs employed professionally trained social workers and full-time administrative and support staff whose motivation included a strong element of anti-colonialism, which provoked official hostility at a very high level.

- In 1970, Sir David Trench, the Governor, publicly denounced religious bodies (which were major providers of social services) for their critical attitude towards the government's endeavours. Their 'hearts are so full of love', he said, 'that it unfortunately impairs their judgment in practical situations'.[41]
- In 1984, Sir John Bremridge, Swire taipan turned Financial Secretary, claimed, 'that the proclivities of decent men and women

to spend hugely on social and other measures can be restrained only by tough budgetary policies'. He was especially suspicious of imported standards of service: 'Those who compare our programmes with those of presently far richer countries in the West do so at their — indeed our — peril.'[42]

At lower levels within the colonial administration, there was more tolerance of critics and reformers because of the informal working partnerships between government professionals and their NGO colleagues. The Social Welfare Department, for example, felt perturbed about the implications of government-subsidised agencies presenting themselves to the public as in conflict with official policies. But the department's social workers accepted that NGOs who used confrontation tactics to embarrass the government could not be condemned if their protests helped to solve social problems and improve the community's welfare.[43]

The growing numbers of qualified social workers provided the backbone of well-organised groups demanding adequate housing and social programmes. Their aggressive lobbying on social issues through pressure groups and collective protests, became a regular feature of the political landscape in the 1970s. Social workers won a reputation for their 'vanguard role in catalysing political participation'.[44] From their ranks emerged several of the leading figures in the political parties that were forming after the introduction of Legislative Council elections in 1985.

The End of Advocacy

But the era of advocacy was coming to an end. By the 1990s, social work professionals had become disenchanted with political action, a study showed. They were less active politically than their counterparts in Australia and New Zealand, for example, and were reported to have largely relinquished the role of advocate and lobbyist for their clients.[45] So too had the rest of the new professional class that had so recently emerged. Mainland officials had not wooed this group as assiduously as they had the business community, and the professionals' anxieties about their post-1997 future remained unallayed. Their formal qualifications made them attractive immigrants, particularly in British Commonwealth countries where many of them had trained. In the run-up to 1997, some 800,000 individuals were estimated to have emigrated from Hong Kong, a significant proportion of whom would have been from the caring professions.[46]

The rising middle class had grown 'cynical and retreatist in orientation' by this date, according to a distinguished Hong Kong sociologist.

> They either stay aloof from politics or submit to an institutional environment from which they feel increasingly estranged. They

> maintain their distance from political matters . . . Whether they
> are returnees, applicants for foreign passports, or people who have
> never thought of leaving, they do not constitute a bourgeois social
> force which has the commitment and vision to defend a liberal
> social and political order.[47]

The wilting of effective advocacy in the 1990s was all the more striking because the level of information about the causes and consequences of poverty reached new heights between 1995 and 1999, thanks to a surge in academic and NGO research.[48] These reports and their statistical findings attracted considerable media coverage but were largely ignored by policy-makers.[49] In any case, poverty could not compete for headlines for very long against the political controversies between the colonial administration and China's leaders over political reform in the closing years of British rule.

Chapter 5 described the silencing of the caring professionals in the public service in this century. The government's social work professionals had been able to resist the denigration of CSSA recipients until 2000 despite serious attacks on the Social Welfare Department from opponents of social security. After which the department fell into line with the rest of the government. The Hospital Authority had continued to openly contradict the government's claims that budget cuts were not undermining the quality of care available to patients until 2008.

As for the NGOs, they continued to provide the bulk of the education and welfare services in the current century but were treated as mere contractors. They were no longer consulted by the government on social policy in the way that they had been in the past. They offered little protest. The political balance had changed, as the NGOs understood very well according to a 2007 government-sponsored survey, and there was little they or their former allies among the professionals in the government could do to resist the new measures being introduced, no matter how flawed.[50] The changed relationship between the government and NGOs was very damaging to the interests of the disabled and disadvantaged. The NGOs' staff were the professionals in close and constant contact with every sort of disability and deprivation. For their voices to be silent and their expertise to go unheeded seriously weakened efforts to promote social reform and to preserve existing standards.

Under Tung Chee Hwa, 'the HKSAR government put economic rationalism above social welfare,' one academic study noted. The government was the dominant purchaser of welfare services and could control 'the various producers (the NGOs, the private sector) as agents'. The NGOs could no longer afford to dispute official priorities or to highlight shortcomings in official programmes, and the average NGO board member had a powerful disincentive to avoid giving offence to officials. This situation, an impressive academic study suggested, 'invites suspicion' that the government's reorganisation of social welfare pro- grammes and their funding in this century has not been 'committed to the best interests of the public'.[51] In retrospect, the failure of NGOs and pressure groups to take their case to the public at large and to develop mass support for social reforms was a fatal misjudgment. They were left with no significant political leverage. They had let themselves be labelled as naive do-gooders, which made them vulnerable to official pressures and easily sidelined.

Never Mind the Workers

Nowhere was the subordination of social policies to political priorities more evident than in the employment field. In 1990, a leading labour specialist warned that Hong Kong's 'political milieu, especially that vis- à-vis China was (and is) the overriding factor, as compared to economic and institutional variables, in influencing society, trade unions and indus- trial relations in Hong Kong'.[52] Thus, before 1997, Hong Kong's labour movement had become largely irrelevant to campaigns and controversies about social reform. After 1997, most trade union representatives in the legislature showed no more enthusiasm about government intervention in social affairs than other legislators. In the aftermath of the 1997–98 Asian financial crisis, the labour movement proved unable to protect low-skilled workers as they fell victim to rising unemployment and falling wages in the economic recession. The government's retreat from welfare commitments after 2000 went ahead largely unresisted by the workforce, while union leaders seemed powerless to prevent the grossly unfair treat- ment of the labour force recorded in earlier chapters.[53]

In the second half of the last century, protection of wages and working conditions only occasionally commanded a high priority among the general public. An absence of industrial unrest was a deeply embedded feature of Hong Kong society and was not easily discarded, it has been widely assumed, because of 'the characteristic aversion of the Chinese to open collective confrontations'.[54] High-speed, sustained economic growth had encouraged a special form of 'self-reliance' among the labour force, it has been frequently observed. Virtually unbroken full employ- ment from the 1950s until the end of the century had provided a simple remedy for aggrieved workers. They could almost always find a compa- rable job virtually next door, 'an oblique yet an easy way to vent their anger towards their employer', who would be penalised by a tight labour market in seeking to replace them.[55] Public pressure on the colonial administration to increase its role in matters of employment was small, and even labour experts were sceptical about both the merits and the affordability of government intervention to protect the labour force.[56]

In the last resort, however, the real obstacle to the emergence of an independent and influential labour movement was Hong Kong's peculiar political circumstances, and the trade unions offer a particularly striking illustration of how politics were able to displace social reforms. Before World War II, the United Kingdom government had adopted measures to improve protection for workers and their rights throughout the British Empire, and after World War II, trade unions in most colonies acquired considerable power. Hong Kong proved the exception because the colonial administration declined to comply with the United Kingdom's post-war directives to safeguard the rights of the workforce.

The trade unions themselves were unable to force the colonial administration to adopt a more progressive attitude because after Hong Kong's industrial takeoff in the early 1950s, the labour movement did not develop either the structure or the strategy needed to operate effectively.[57] Unions were excluded from all but token involvement in labour affairs. This isolation was aggravated by the Federation of Trade Unions, the largest labour organisation, whose loyalty to the Chinese Communist Party led it to withdraw from formal contacts with the colonial administration between 1950 and 1981.[58]

Labour militancy was discredited among the community at large by the political disturbances that broke out in 1967 at the height of Mao Zedong's Cultural Revolution (1966–76). Although an industrial dispute triggered the first clashes between workers and police, subsequent violence took place mainly on the streets and was almost completely absent from the work place.[59] Much has been made of the 1967 bombs, riots and strikes as the catalyst in forcing urgently needed social reforms on reluctant officials.[60] The reality was that strikes and direct action were about respect for Maoism rather than workers' rights or social reform.[61]

The confrontation with the colonial administration failed despite the often passionate ideological commitment of the unionists involved. The strikers' principal targets were public utilities and the government departments responsible for transport and communications (including the port and ferry services), which traditionally had been recruiting grounds for the FTU. But the campaign was poorly coordinated, not surprisingly because the FTU and its leadership had had little experience of organising large-scale strikes after 1950.[62] The consequences were catastrophic for the participants who had worked for government departments, public utilities and large British and Shanghainese firms: they forfeited their retirement funds, health, housing and other benefits.[63]

The bungled attempt to use industrial action to achieve political ends in 1967 was detrimental to the long-term interests of the labour force. Officials and business leaders alike had less incentive than ever to regard conditions in the workplace as of any great importance to the general public. As a result, new employment legislation enacted in 1968 which was hailed as 'the Hong Kong charter' proved little more than tokenism.[64] Its proposals had been under negotiation with employers since 1960, and the improved protection now offered to the workforce fell short of the commitments originally made by the colonial administration to British ministers in 1958.[65]

After 1967, Mainland organisations made an almost total exit from political and social reform campaigns in Hong Kong, which was illustrated with particular clarity by their programmes for Hong Kong's young people. These concentrated on organising groups to visit the Mainland and to begin to see Hong Kong's future in terms of the Mainland. The programme organisers steered clear of the student movement in the 1970s from which the first social pressure groups and political parties were to grow. The Mainland's activists and supporters declined to cooperate with other student groups in 'combating the injustices in colonial capitalist Hong Kong' and did not participate, for example, in student protests against government corruption before the Independent Commission Against Corruption (ICAC) was set up in 1974.[66]

The Ballot Box Comes First

The Chinese Communist Party ended the FTU's exclusion from public affairs in 1981, but this decision did not lead to increased labour activism. The FTU's workplace role was publicly downgraded in 1984, the year in which the Sino-British Joint Declaration launched the transition to the resumption of Chinese sovereignty in 1997. FTU Chairman, Cheng Yiu-tong, explained that his organisation now had four functions:

- to participate in social affairs and to promote political democratization . . . a new subject;
- to participate actively in the drafting of the Basic Law;
- to build up good relations with every sector on a new basis . . . the transformation [to Chinese rule] needs to be founded on prosperity and stability; and, lastly,
- to fight for legitimate rights for the workers and to seek greater welfare . . . the establishment of a fund for protection of wages on insolvency, a long service gratuity, and a central provident fund.[67]

The FTU was thus transformed into a political organisation whose residual agenda for the defence of the workforce's interests was narrowly defined and expressed in very moderate terms. The rest of the labour movement followed suit, unable to resist the temptation to see elections to district bodies and the legislature as the best way to protect the wider interests of the labour force.[68]

The result was to make political activism the FTU's paramount concern for the longer term. Its potential political muscle was considerable. It was a long-established, well-organised mass movement, with over 200,000 members. Although it had become more of a benevolent society after 1967 than an aggressive guardian of workers' rights, its members included substantial numbers of highly motivated and well-trained activists, loyal to the Chinese Communist Party and well-versed in 'agitation-propaganda'. Its internal discipline was impressive, and it was better organised than rival unions and political organisations. When a conventional, pro-Mainland political party, the Democratic Alliance for the Betterment of Hong Kong (DAB), was set up in 1992, the FTU was able to ensure that canvassers and other electoral workers for pro-Mainland candidates vastly outnumbered their pro-democracy rivals.[69]

After 1997, the FTU's transformation reached a new stage, and its goal has been described as 'evolving and developing "community unionism"'. 'In its membership maintenance and liaison work', it shifted its attention 'away from the workplace level to that of the residential neighbourhood'. In place of militant protection of workers' rights, it has been stated, the FTU's principal goal became to ensure victory in elections to the Legislative and District Councils for its candidates.[70] To all intents and purposes, the FTU became another political party. While it was able to capitalise on its radical past which left it with a pro-labour image, in practice, the FTU was too integrated into the business-dominated, post-colonial political arrangements to function as a countervailing force to the employers' lobby.

The FTU's history is a striking illustration of the process by which social reform and the very notion of welfare came to command such a low political priority and to retain so few advocates. The FTU's leadership put political activism before workers' welfare, in much the same way as the rest of the traditional supporters of social reforms did. Individual FTU leaders have admitted that they did so with regret. Very soon after the end of British rule, the redoubtable Chan Yuen-han lamented publicly that the labour force was getting no more attention from the new administration of Tung Chee Hwa and his team than from their colonial predecessors. On such issues as 'high property prices, poor working environment, uncertain employment prospects, poor retirement protection for the elderly and difficult livelihood for the general public', she stated, Special Administrative Region officials offered the same unsympathetic responses as the unions had got before 1997.[71]

This complaint was for the record only. The FTU's hands were tied by an understanding reached with the Chinese Manufacturers Association in 1994 to avoid industrial disputes. When public confidence in Tung Chee Wah's administration was evaporating in 1998, the FTU publicised

its 1994 pact with employers to maintain harmonious labour relations, a gesture to reassure market sentiment because it demonstrated
the strength of the FTU's collaboration with the government-business
nexus.[72] The workforce was left in no doubt that militancy to protect
itself against wage cuts and layoffs would not be supported by Hong
Kong's biggest union.

But the FTU was not able to maintain this collaboration indefinitely.
In a well-known television encounter in 2012, Chan made much the same
complaint as she had done in 1998 about the way in which the labour
force and its interests had been neglected by the government since 1997
which gave priority to business. On this occasion, however, her audience
heard her describe post-1997 officials as less open to trade unions than
the colonial administration had been. Before 1997, she asserted, the
government had been willing to listen to the workers' representatives.[73]

Chan was preparing to take action on behalf of the workforce. Her
open criticism in 2013 of the third Chief Executive's Policy Address indicated how passivity and patience were wearing thin in her camp. She
accused Leung Chun-ying of applying 'double standards' in his treatment of workers and their case for protection from unfair employment
conditions. She suggested that he had 'been forced by the commercial
sector to act in collusion with them'. She warned him that her union
members were demanding that she be 'more belligerent' in dealing with
his administration.[74] The FTU, apparently, had given up hope that wages
and working conditions would improve sufficiently to compensate for
the decline in their quality of life in this century so long as business
interests continued to dominate the government's agenda.

Conclusions: Going 'Green'

This chapter has shown how the community came to give overriding
priority to the preservation of Hong Kong's unique combination of
personal freedom, social stability and open and honest government.
In the process, the deprived, disadvantaged and disabled lost their
traditional defenders, and the advocates of social reform declined in
numbers and influence. Yet, there was still a collective conscience at
work in Hong Kong, whose indignation at revelations of mistreatment
of victims of life's tragedies was usually prompt and politically too overwhelming for officials to ignore.

A striking example was the public outrage when a mother and her
two daughters were stabbed to death in 2004 after her unsuccessful
appeals both to the police and to social workers for protection from
her husband's violence. The community understood very well that this
family's tragic circumstances had been compounded by the inadequate

provision of social services in a new public housing project. As a result, the government was compelled to expand the social programmes for this and similar estates and to increase the allocation of resources to them over several years.[75]

There was an impressive social awareness and activism in other fields. It was striking how effective environmental and heritage campaigners were in forcing reforms on reluctant officials in this century. Welfare advocates were nothing like as successful even though the supply, standards and charges for public housing and social services, together with the protection of wages and working conditions, were what determined the quality of life for the average family. Furthermore, the environmental reforms put forward were highly technical, well beyond the ability of the average member of the community to comprehend, it might have been assumed. The heritage initiatives might also have seemed remote from the community's concerns and of no material benefit to the public at large.[76] Yet, while officials were free to retreat from the public sector's 'welfare' responsibilities and to raise the fees paid by their users, environment and heritage forced their way on to the political agenda and compelled the government to give them considerable priority.

The special advantage that environmental and heritage campaigners enjoyed was that official policies had previously been so minimalist that the lobbyists were creating from scratch an infrastructure to protect public health and preserve society's cultural legacy (in its broadest sense) as a virtual 'green field' operation. The government had great difficulty in discrediting the solutions advocated by pressure groups and other concerned bodies because the environment and heritage campaigners had considerable technical expertise and were far more adept at communicating with the general public. The environmental experts involved in these campaigns had close ties with the government's own professionals (which paralleled the development of medical and welfare services in the 1950s and 1960s discussed earlier in this chapter).

The needy and vulnerable groups in society, by contrast, were far less able to communicate their case to the public for reasons explained in the 'Introduction'. The physical distress, the mental strain and the financial burden that poverty, illness and disability impose, not only on the immediate victims but on their families as well, are largely hidden from the general public. The poor, the infirm and the disabled constituted a minority of the population. And as a minority, they were easily overlooked and their sufferings misunderstood.

Pollution and environmental degradation, by contrast, were daily experiences for every member of society. The destruction of the remaining heritage was also very visible. The government could not escape its responsibilities for safeguarding the public from pollution and preserving its past. But officials and political commentators felt free to denounce older and ill-educated workers as workshy when they became virtually unemployable in the post-industrial economy and had to turn to CSSA, as the previous chapter recounted.

It was also significant that business was willing to take part of the responsibility for halting pollution and the destruction of heritage. For example, 'the Business Environment Council, which was established in 1989 by 17 big corporations, had grown into a network of over 20,000 companies' by 2006, one study noted.[77] Nothing comparable was created to agitate for urgent efforts to alleviate, let alone eradicate, the widespread poverty that was prevalent in Hong Kong. Indeed, the business community consistently opposed remedial measures such as social insurance as a threat to their interests. This situation highlights the high price paid by the needy and vulnerable for the disappearance of welfare advocacy.

Notes

1. John P. Burns, *Government Capacity and the Hong Kong Civil Service* (Hong Kong: Oxford University Press, 2004), pp. 34–6.
2. Sin Chung-kai, *Hong Kong Hansard* (*HH* hereafter), 10 July 2004, p. 9467. Note how limited was the Democratic Party leadership's commitment to minimum wage legislation when forced by public opinion to express some support for the measure: 'We are in favour of introducing it in some trades as a start instead of adopting an across-the-board approach.' Albert Ho, *HH*, 15 February 2006, p. 4590.
3. Legislative Council Secretariat, 'Finance Committee of the Legislative Council: Minutes of the 5th Meeting Held . . . on Tuesday, 30 October 2012' (FC77/12-13, 20 December 2012).
4. Chan Yuen-han, Federation of Trade Unions, *HH*, 16 November 2005, p. 2059.
5. John F. Jones, 'Introduction: Social Services at a Glance', in John F. Jones (ed.), *The Common Welfare: Hong Kong's Social Services* (Hong Kong: Chinese University Press, 1981), p. xi.
6. David A. Levin and Stephen Wing Kai Chu, 'Bureaucratic Insurgency: The Public Sector Labour Movement', in Stephen Wing Kai Chiu and Tai Lok Lui (eds.), *The Dynamics of Social Movement in Hong Kong* (Hong Kong: Hong Kong University Press, 2000), especially pp. 171–2; Raymond K. H. Chan, *Welfare in Newly-Industrialised Society: The Construction of the Welfare State in Hong Kong* (Aldershot: Avebury, 1996).*ong Kong* (Aldershot: Avebury, 1996), pp. 117–8, 167–8.
7. Wong Wai-hung, Federation of Hong Kong Civil Service Unions Chairman, 'Staff Relations in the Civil Service and the Trade Union Response: Review and Prospects, 1971–1985', in Y. C. Jao et al. (eds.), *Labour Movement in a Changing Society* (Hong Kong: Centre of Asian Studies, University of Hong Kong, 1988), pp. 152–4.

8. Education Commission, *Report No. 6 Enhancing Language Proficiency: A Comprehensive Strategy Part 2 (Annexes)* (Hong Kong: 1995), p. 8; Fong-ying Yu, 'Tradition and Change in Chinese Education', and Daniel W. C. So, 'Searching for a Bilingual Exit', in Robert Lord and Helen N. L. Cheng (eds.), *Language Education in Hong Kong* (Hong Kong: Chinese University Press, 1987), pp. 224–9, 250.

9. The Education Department had promoted priority for Chinese in schools before 1997, with limited success. The background is summarised in Education Department, 'Panel on Education. Information Paper Mother Tongue Teaching' (18 April 1997). Nevertheless, the 1998 measure seemed a hastily drafted programme. (This conclusion is based on Legislative Council Secretariat, 'Panel on Education . . . Medium of Instruction for Secondary Schools' (CB(2)623/08-09(07), 8 July 2009.)

10. On the paradoxical rise in the public status of Chinese while parents' increasing economic preference was for English, see Anthony E. Sweeting, 'Hong Kong Education within Historical Processes', in Gerald A. Postiglione (ed.), *Education and Society in Hong Kong: Toward One Country and Two Systems* (Armonk: M. E. Sharpe, 1991), p. 63.

11. Reporting by the Chinese language press became sceptical about the merits of the new language policy, e.g., *Sing Tao Daily*, 7 March 2008.

12. Michael Suen Ming-yeung, Secretary for Education, 'Symposium on Medium of Instruction', 16 March 2008. URL: www.edb.gov.hk/index.aspx?nodeID=133&langno=1&UID=102909

13. Census and Statistics Department, 'Use of Language in Hong Kong', *Thematic Household Survey Report No. 51* (Hong Kong: Census and Statistics Department, 2013), pp. 4–5, 23, 24, 27–8.

14. For example, see the reporting on efforts by the Committee on the Promotion of Civic Education and the Commission on Youth to promote this subject in *Ming Pao Daily*, 23 March 2004.

15. Donald Tsang Yam-kuen, Chief Executive, *HH*, 10 October 2012, pp. 42–3.

16. Jia Qinglin, Politburo Standing Committee Member, quoted in *New China News Agency*, 12 September 2012.

17. Leung Chun-ying, Chief Executive, *Government Information Service* (*GIS* hereafter), 8 September 2012; Committee on the Initiation of Moral and National Education Subject, *GIS*, 8 October 2012.

18. Joan Y. H. Leung, 'Political Parties: Public Perceptions and Implications for Change', in Ian Scott (ed.), *Institutional Change and the Political Transition in Hong Kong* (London: Macmillan, 1998), pp. 102–9.

19. Fred Y. L. Chiu, 'Politics and the Body Social in Colonial Hong Kong', in Tani E. Barlow (ed.), *Formations of Colonial Modernity in East Asia* (Durham: Duke University Press, 1997), pp. 315–6.

20. The extent to which political reform ousted social justice among interest and pressure groups of every kind is neatly illustrated in Suzanne Pepper, *Keeping Democracy at Bay: Hong Kong and the Challenge of Chinese Political; Reform* (Lanham: Rowman & Littlefield, 2008), p. 208.

21. Lau Siu-kai, 'The Fraying of the Socio-economic Fabric of Hong Kong', *Pacific Review*, Vol. 10, No. 3 (1999), p. 429.

22. Ibid., p. 430.

23. Leung Sai-wing, 'The 'China Factor' in the 1991 Legislative Council Election: The June 4th Incident and Anti-Communist China Syndrome', in Lau Siu-kai and Louie Kin-sheun (eds.), *Hong Kong Tried Democracy: The 1991 Elections in Hong Kong* (Hong Kong: Hong Kong Institute of Asia-Pacific Studies, Chinese University of Hong Kong, 1993), p. 192.

24. Lau Siu-kai and Kuan Hsin-chi, *The Ethos of the Hong Kong Chinese* (Hong Kong: Chinese University Press, 1988), p. 105. But note that the Kaifongs are described as having a continuing role as a supplier of welfare services for at least another decade in Chak Kwan Chan, *Social Security Policy in Hong Kong: From British Colony to China's Special Administrative Region* (Lanham: Lexington Books, 2011), pp. 93–8.

25. Joseph Y. S. Cheng, 'Introduction', in Joseph Y. S. Cheng (ed.), *Hong Kong in Transition* (Hong Kong: Oxford University Press, 1986), p. 21; Siu-kai Lau, *Society and Politics in Hong Kong* (Hong Kong: Chinese University Press, 1982), pp. 130–42.

26. See Peter P. F. Chan, former Po Leung Kuk Chairman, 'Letters to the Editor: Social Welfare', *Far Eastern Economic Review*, 8 September 1966.

27. Andrew K. N. Li, 'Girls without Love', *Far Eastern Economic Review*, 22–28 September 1968. These charges were disputed but not refuted by Chan, the former Po Leung Kuk Chairman, in 'Case for the Defence', *Far Eastern Economic Review*, 13–19 October 1968.

28. Kan Yuet-keung (later Sir Yuet-keung) and Dr Teng Pin-hui, *HH*, 13 August 1969, pp. 484–5; Jung yen, 'Hongkong Look-See', *Far Eastern Economic Review*, 17–23 August 1969.

29. Jick-Joen Lee, *The Road to the Development of Social Welfare in Hong Kong: The Historical Key Issues* (Hong Kong: Hong Kong Institute of Asia-Pacific Studies, Chinese University of Hong Kong, 1996), p. 3.

30. Personal memoirs of the first, post-war student generation illustrate the importance of the Japanese hostilities in shaping attitudes. S. F. Lam and Nina Lam, *HKU Undergraduates of '46: Their Untold Stories* (Hong Kong: n.d., n.p.).

31. C. Y. Yeung, 'Evolution of Child Health Care in Hong Kong', *Hong Kong Journal of Paediatrics*, Vol. 6, No. 1 (2001), pp. 66–71.

32. Catherine Jones, *Promoting Prosperity: The Hong Kong Way of Social Policy* (Hong Kong: Chinese University Press, 1990), pp. 169–74.

33. Impressive examples of this process can be found in Hong Kong Society for Rehabilitation, *The Rebirth of the Phoenix: Fifty Years in Serving People with Disabilities* (Hong Kong: Hong Kong Society for Rehabilitation, 2010), pp. 22–6.

34. Historical developments were summarised in an unpublished Social Welfare Department document, 'Brief History of Rehabilitation Division of SWD' (mimeo, 1976).

35. See enclosures (1), (2) and (6). HKRS306-1-217A 'Housing for the Elderly, the Infirm and the Handicapped'. The Commissioner for Housing's response was in marked contrast to his failure to join the Director of Social Welfare in actively collaborating with Sir David Trench's abortive campaign

to persuade senior officials to accept greater social responsibility in this decade (discussed in Chapter 4).

36. (91)[3] 'Hon Y. K. Kan's Speech at the Opening of the Wah Hong Hostel 9 May 1969'. HKRS306-1-217A.

37. (74) 'Note of the 32nd Meeting of the Ad Hoc Working Group of the Medical Development Advisory Committee Report held on 23rd April 1974 . . . ', p. 1. HKRS163-9-932 'Ad Hoc Working Group of the Medical Development Advisory Committee'.

38. Nelson W. S. Chow, 'Review of Social Policies', in Alex Y. H. Kwan and David K. K. Chan (eds.), *Hong Kong Society: A Reader* (Hong Kong: Writers' and Publishers' Cooperative, 1986), pp. 158–9.

39. An excellent evaluation of the issues involved is Benjamin K. P. Leung, *Perspectives on Hong Kong Society* (Hong Kong: Oxford University Press, 1996), pp. 36–9.

40. Nelson Chow, 'Social Welfare and the Challenges of a New Era', in Wong Siu-lun and Toyojiro Maruya (eds.), *Hong Kong Economy and Society: Challenges in the New Era* (Hong Kong: Centre of Asian Studies, University of Hong Kong, 1998), pp. 138–42.

41. David Baird, 'Thy Will Be Done', *Far Eastern Economic Review*, 29 January 1970.

42. Sir John Bremridge, Financial Secretary, *HH,* 29 February 1984, p. 592.

43. The conflict between social progress and its political costs was explained in a very straightforward way in Social Welfare Department, '"Conflict" approach in community development adopted by some voluntary agencies', CDSG Paper No. 5 (mimeo, 11 September 1973). HKRS794-1-2 'Steering Group on Community Development'.

44. Jones, *Promoting Prosperity: The Hong Kong Way of Social Policy*, pp. 222–5; Tai-lok Lui, 'Pressure Group Politics in Hong Kong', in Joseph Y. S. Cheng, (ed.), *Political Participation in Hong Kong: Theoretical Issues and Historical Legacy* (Hong Kong: City University of Hong Kong Press, 1999), pp. 150–3.

45. Ernest Chui and Mel Gray, 'The Political Activities of Social Workers in the Context of Changing Roles and Political Transition in Hong Kong', *International Journal of Social Welfare*, Vol. 13 (2004), pp. 170, 171–2, 175–7.

46. Nan M. Sussman, 'Identity Shifts as a Consequence of Crossing Cultures: Hong Kong Chinese Migrants Return Home', in Chan Kwok-bun et al., (eds.), *East-West Identities: Globalization, Localization, and Hybridization* (Leiden: Brill, 2007), p. 6.

47. Tai-lok Lui, 'The Hong Kong New Middle Class on the Eve of 1997', in Joseph Y. S. Cheng (ed.), *The Other Hong Kong Report 1997* (Hong Kong: Chinese University Press, 1997), pp. 224, 225.

48. Of the 27 major articles on poverty issues listed in a literature review prepared by the Legislative Council Secretariat in 2005, only one had appeared before 1990, while 16 had been published between 1995 and 1999. Simon Li, 'Information Note. Causes of Poverty in Hong Kong: A Literature Review' (Legislative Council Secretariat, IN16/04-05, 10 January 2005), pp. 5–7.

49. The most important of these research projects were: Lui Tai Lok and Wong Hung, *Disempowerment and Empowerment: An Exploratory Study on Low-income Households in Hong Kong* (Hong Kong: Oxfam, 1995); Wong Hung and Chua Hoi Wai, *Research on Expenditure Pattern of Low Expenditure Households in Hong Kong* (Hong Kong: Hong Kong Council of Social Service, 1996); Stewart MacPherson and Oi Yu Lo, *A Measure of Poverty*, Department of Public and Social Administration (1997), City University of Hong Kong, Working Paper Series 1997/2.

50. This discussion is based on the very balanced analysis presented by Elaine Y. M. Chan, 'Civil Society', in Lam Wai-man et al. (eds.), *Contemporary Hong Kong Government and Politics* (Hong Kong: Hong Kong University Press, 2012), second edition, p. 192.

51. The most thoughtful and objective review of these developments remains Kenneth L. Chau and Chack-kie Wong, 'The Social Welfare Reform: A Way to Reduce Public Burden', in Lau Siu-kai (ed.), *The First Tung Chee-hwa Administration: The First Five Years of the Hong Kong Special Administrative Region* (Hong Kong: Chinese University Press, 2003), pp. 215–27.

52. Ng Sek-hong, 'The Development of Labour Relations in Hong Kong and Some Implications for the Future', in Ian Nish et al. (eds.), *Work and Society: Labour and Human Resources in East Asia* (Hong Kong: Hong Kong University Press, 1996), p. 298.

53. See Zhao Xiaobin et al., 'Income Inequalities under Economic Restructuring in Hong Kong', *Asian Survey*, Vol. 44, No. 3 (May/June 2004), pp. 462–3.

54. Ian Nish, Gordon Redding, and Ng Sek-hong, 'Industrial Harmony, the Trade Union Movement and Labour Administration in Hong Kong', in Ian Nish et al. (eds.), *Work and Society: Labour and Human Resources in East Asia*, pp. 272, 285. Numerous large-scale exceptions to this preference for non-confrontation by the labour force can be cited from both Hong Kong and Mainland history.

55. Ibid., p. 272.

56. Ng Sek-hong, 'Hong Kong Labour Law in Retrospect', in Lee Pui-tak (ed.), *Hong Kong Reintegrating with China: Political, Cultural and Social Dimensions* (Hong Kong: Hong Kong University Press, 2001), pp. 130–1, 140–1, 150–1.

57. The obstacles faced by the trade union movement and its handicaps in mobilising support from the industrial labour force were summed up in L. F. Goodstadt, 'Labour Pains', *Far Eastern Economic Review*, 22 June 1967.

58. Norman Miners, 'The Representation and Participation of Trade Unions in the Hong Kong Government', in Jao et al. (eds.), *Labour Movement in a Changing Society*, pp. 42–5.

59. J. L. Hillard, Essential Services Corps Commissioner, 'Survey of Strikes — June 1967' (mimeo, ESC 90/67, 15 September 1967), para. 16.

60. Note the tentative view of such a conclusion taken by Alan Smart and Tai-kok Lui, 'Learning from Civil Unrest: State/Society Relations in Hong Kong Before and After the 1967 Disturbances', in Robert Bickers and Ray Yep (eds.), *May Days in Hong Kong: Riot and Emergency in 1967* (Hong Kong: Hong Kong University Press, 2009), pp. 152–3, 159.

61. Data on the strikes and their impact are summarised in Gary Ka-wai Cheung, *Hong Kong's Watershed: The 1967 Riots* (Hong Kong: Hong Kong University Press, 2009), pp. 62–6.

62. Trade union activism was at its height in the years 1946–49 and again in 1953–54, as the official data on days lost through industrial disputes demonstrate. Otherwise, strikes were limited in scale and incidence. For the historical background and statistics, see Joe England and John Rear, *Industrial Relations and Law in Hong Kong* (Hong Kong: Oxford University Press, 1981), pp. 134, 312–5; Ed Snape and Andy Chan, 'Hong Kong Trade Unions: In Search of a Role', in Patricia Fosh et al., *Hong Kong Management and Labour: Change and Continuity* (London: Routledge, 1999), pp. 260–3.

63. 'Probably one-third of the [striking] workers finally dismissed fell into the category of long-service employees with 15 or more years of service and considerable . . . provident funds accruing to them'. Hillard, 'Survey of Strikes — June 1967', paras 15, 261.

64. L. F. Goodstadt, 'Into the C19th — 10 Years Later', *Far Eastern Economic Review*, 18–24 February 1968.

65. Minutes of the 16th Meeting, 6 April 1961, pp. 1–2; Minutes of the Thirty-first Meeting of the General Committee of the Federation, 17 November 1961, p. 2. HKRS270-5-39 'Federation of Hong Kong Industries, Minutes of Meetings of the General Committee'; Minutes of 84th Meeting, 11 September 1964, p. 2; Minutes of the 105th Meeting, 10 December 1965, pp. 2–3. HKRS163-1-118 'Federation of Hong Kong Industries, Minutes of the Meetings of the . . . '; (33). Secretary of State Telegram to Governor, No. 718, 15 August 1958. HKRS1017-4-4 'General Conditions of Employment Legislation re . . . '.

66. Benjamin K. P. Leung, 'The Student Movement in Hong Kong: Transition to a Democratizing Society', in Chiu and Lui (eds.), *The Dynamics of Social Movement in Hong Kong*, pp. 213–7.

67. Cheng Yiu-tong, FTU Chairman, 'The Role of a Trade Union Centre in a Changing Society: The Case of the Hong Kong Federation of Trade Unions', in Jao et al. (eds.), *Labour Movement in a Changing Society*, pp. 114–5.

68. The switch to electoral activities by both the FTU and the labour movement as a whole are well described in Ming K. Chan, 'Under China's Shadow: Realpolitik of Hong Kong Labour Unionism toward 1997', in Charles Burton (ed.), *Politics and Society in Hong Kong towards 1997* (Toronto: Joint Centre for Asia Pacific Studies, 1992), pp. 16–8, 25–8.

69. Ivan Chi-keung Choy, 'Political Parties and Political Participation in Hong Kong', Joseph Y. S. Cheng, (ed.), *Political Participation in Hong Kong: Theoretical Issues and Historical Legacy* (Hong Kong: City University of Hong Kong Press, 1999), pp. 139–40.

70. This summary of the FTU's activities is based on a highly sympathetic analysis by Sek-hong Ng and Olivia Ip, 'Labour and Society', in Joseph Y. S. Cheng (ed.), *The Hong Kong Special Administrative Region in Its First Decade* (Hong Kong: City University of Hong Kong Press, 2007), pp. 469, 474–7.

71. 'Nothing but old wine in a new bottle . . . regrettably, we still get the same conclusion in this Council' as in the colonial legislature. Chan Yuen-han, *HH*, 8 April 1998, pp. 499–500.

72. Cheng, FTU Chairman, *HH*, 8 April 1998, p. 425.

73. Chan, FTU, interviewed on 《把酒當歌：陳婉嫻》, ATV, 16 March 2012. URLs: www.youtube.com/watch?v=PTSbrydsxmc; www.youtube.com/watch?v=j30UUXinSA4

74. Chan, FTU, *HH*, 17 January 2013, pp. 4989–90.

75. 'Review Panel on Family Services in Tin Shui Wai', *GIS*, 20 April 2004; 'Home Affairs Launches "Tin Shui Wai Neighbourhood Mutual Help" Scheme', *GIS*, 13 December 2007; 'Housing Advisory and Service Team to Assist Public Housing Tenants in Tin Shui Wai', *GIS*, 31 January 2008; Legislative Council Secretariat. 'Panel on Welfare Services. Minutes of Meeting Held on Monday, 14 January 2008 . . . ' (CB(2)976/07-08, 13 February 2008), pp. 5–11.

76. Convenient summaries of developments in the environmental and heritage fields are provided by Mee Kam Ng, 'Outmoded Planning in the Face of New Politics' and Ho Kin-chung, 'The Environment after 1997', in Joseph Y. S. Cheng (ed.), *The Hong Kong Special Administrative Region in Its First Decade.*

77. This report also highlights how much less successful welfare NGOs had been by comparison with the environmental lobby in mobilising business engagement. CIVICUS, 'The Hong Kong Special Administrative Region: A Vibrant but Loosely Organised Civil Society. Civil Society Index Report for the Hong Kong Special Administrative Region, PRC' (2006), pp. 54, 55–6, 58.

Conclusions: History Repeats Itself

This book has described a severe decline in the wellbeing of the community and the rise of a new form of poverty. The defining feature of poverty in contemporary Hong Kong is that it cannot be blamed on economic recession, currency collapse, trade protectionism overseas, loss of competitiveness, political unrest or industrial or social strife. Hong Kong has escaped all such threats to its prosperity, chapter after chapter have demonstrated. This society has remained a model of political maturity and social discipline even though social reforms introduced in earlier decades have been dismantled as the government retreated from its responsibilities not only towards the needy and the vulnerable but towards the community as a whole.

Who Are the New Poor?

Contemporary Hong Kong has continued to flourish economically and to enjoy social stability. The welfare minister proudly declared in mid-2013 that 'our city has all the necessary prerequisites to provide social protection and satisfy the basic needs of everyone in the community'. This statement was not open to challenge. He then asserted that 'by whatever yardstick, the Hong Kong SAR Government has not dodged and will never shy away from finding the best possible solutions to help the poor'.[1] This book has shown how tragically short of this standard the government has consistently fallen. The emergence in this century of a new poor has been traced in previous chapters, which have identified who these unfortunates are and how they are the victims of misguided official policies.

- *Those suffering from the conventional causes of poverty: destitution caused by unemployment, low wages and no savings.* In Hong Kong, their numbers ought to be minimal because the truly destitute are eligible for social security regardless of residence and the other restrictions that normally apply to applicants for Comprehensive Social Security Assistance (CSSA). Yet, as previous chapters have shown, the gaps in this safety net are serious.

- *Patients suffering from serious illnesses, the infirm and those with disabilities.* The health and welfare programmes are supposed to ensure that these groups get the treatment and facilities they need even if they cannot afford the Hospital Authority's fees and charges. There is supposed to be no discrimination against those who lack money. The government's commitments and legal obligations have not been honoured.

- *Children and students denied equal access to good quality education because of their families' limited finances.* The costs of education have been raised so that lower-income families have to make a painful decision. They can go into debt and impoverish themselves in order to give their sons and daughters the best possible schooling or condemn them to the lower levels of the labour market.

    Very similar are the young people who are truly caring. They refuse to apply for education loans or to let their parents borrow money to pay the fees. These youngsters believe their earnings are needed to relieve the immediate financial strain on their parents, to pay for a sick relative's treatment or for another child's schooling. Or they feel they could not repay the loans without serious hardship to the family.

- *The large numbers of the elderly and unemployed who meet the criteria for CSSA but do not receive it.* They choose poverty because the application process is so demeaning and the stigma which the government has created around CSSA beneficiaries is too humiliating.

    They include the heroic parent (or grandparent) who refuses to impose an extra burden on the younger generation through bowing to the CSSA's insistence on getting a financial contribution from family members.

- *Individuals and families who have adequate earnings and a decent standard of living but are confronted by serious illness or some similar emergency.* Often, the government insists that their medical treatment must be self-financed. Frequently, too, waiting times for diagnosis, treatment or care for the loved one in public hospitals seem so distressingly long that the family beggar themselves in the private sector.

To these should be added the victims of past policy decisions that have left them in miserable conditions which they could not be expected to overcome through their own efforts.

- *The elderly and unemployed who suffer the 'disgrace' of relying on CSSA.* These are the victims of decades of refusal by the government-business nexus to ensure that the workforce was enabled to buy protection against retirement, illness and unemployment through social insurance schemes.

- *Tenants in buildings which should be classified as unfit for human habitation.* Their health and safety are at risk because of the shortage of public rental housing to which they can be transferred.

Who's to Blame?

This new poverty can be attributed to government decisions. The most crucial have been about management of the economy and public finances. As Chapter 1 reported, the first Chief Executive, Tung Chee Hwa, admitted publicly that he could have halted the recession which followed the 1997–98 Asian financial crisis. He knew that the result of his refusal to do so would be severe and prolonged pain for most families. His decision, that chapter recounted, was based on an entirely mistaken analysis of the economy. Tung chose austerity. Investor and consumer confidence plummeted, and the downturn worsened.

For the management of public finances, Tung adopted a budget programme which included redundancies, privatisation and sub-contracting to reduce the size of the public service. The social consequences were malignant because these measures exposed the less-skilled individuals to exploitation. Workers were supplied to the government by private contractors who flouted labour laws and their contractual obligations. Officials proved reluctant to end these abuses. For the employee, the result was impoverishment. The second Chief Executive promised to introduce minimum wage legislation and a competition law, both of which had become crucial to protect the community against malpractices. The government then bowed to business pressures and delayed repeatedly the introduction of the necessary legislation.

Economic recovery was not to prove the salvation of the new poor because most of them could never be made financially self-supporting. A high proportion of CSSA beneficiaries, for example, have no capacity to earn their own living. The elderly accounted for almost 60 per cent of the total CSSA caseload in 2012, and age had removed them permanently from the labour market. (By contrast, the unemployed accounted for less than 10 per cent of all CSSA cases.)

As a result, the regular invocation by officials of economic growth as the solution to poverty made sense only as a very broad generalisation. Economic growth did not automatically lead to jobs for all in contemporary Hong Kong, and certainly not the elderly. Experience in this century showed that earnings lagged badly behind the rise in GDP and improvements in labour productivity. The faster the growth of GDP, the more revenue the government would have at its disposal to expand social expenditure. But sustained superior performance of the economy did not induce policy-makers to make the financial commitments to housing and the major social services (health, education and welfare) which were needed to overcome a Third World legacy of under-spending in the past and to achieve standards which matched Hong Kong's economic achievements.

Business Favouritism

Business interests have swayed government policy alarmingly in this century. Tung Chee Hwa abandoned his ambitious plans to end Hong Kong's recurrent housing crisis when confronted by opposition from developers. The Housing Authority withdrew from the property market, and developers were given a free hand. The supply of new flats slumped, and prices rose. The infrastructure for producing public housing was so thoroughly dismantled that the third Chief Executive's plan for the Housing Authority to resume a substantial role in the property market faced a five-year delay.

The first two Chief Executives could have resisted the developers' demands. Property was the one sector whose assets could not be liquidated and removed from Hong Kong. No matter what tycoons might threaten about withdrawing their investments, the land and buildings could not be relocated to Shanghai, Singapore, London or New York.[2] Furthermore, the property sector's profits depended heavily on government goodwill because they were vulnerable to changes in taxation and town planning policies, and to the introduction of rent control and tenancy protection legislation, as the recent history of Hong Kong showed. Developers, nevertheless, generally had the upper hand. They rightly assumed that the community did not want to see the property market disrupted or property prices to tumble. But the indulgence shown to property interests throughout the first decade of this century eventually passed beyond the levels of public tolerance, and Tsang Yam-kuen was forced to take the first tentative steps towards reviving the public housing programme in 2010.

In allocating financial support between business and social services, the government applied double standards. Most notorious was the favouritism shown to small and medium-sized enterprises (SMEs) which were offered a large and seemingly endless supply of loan guarantees whose justification was seriously challenged from the start and whose benefits to the economy officials were unable to describe except in the vaguest of terms.

Funding for the social services, however, was tightly policed because of the widespread conviction within the government that all public services were inherently wasteful and inefficient and should make way for the private sector. The consequences for the quality of social services were dire. The Hospital Authority, for example, publicly refuted official claims that budget cuts were not affecting the standard of treatment. Medication was so tightly rationed that inferior and obsolescent drugs were prescribed for seriously ill patients in public hospitals who could not afford the charges for the most appropriate medicine. In the welfare field, neither the elderly nor children with special needs were spared. The queues for residential and other care facilities remained scandalously long. Officials declined to set targets for ending the shortfalls.

Official parsimony was also conspicuous in dealing with victims of industrial accidents when employers failed to meet their legal compensation obligations. After the statutory Employees Compensation Assistance Fund had run into 'financial difficulty' in the late 1990s, the official solution included imposing a new limit on the assistance provided by the Fund. This result, the labour minister claimed in 2013, 'aptly balanced the interests of injured employees, employers and the Board' even though the casualties of unsafe working conditions were left worse off.[3]

Moral Exits

There were also attempts to distract attention from the government's shortcomings. A notable example was the promotion of 'social enterprises' and similar business-based programmes. Their aims were edifying, and the idealism and enthusiasm of their participants were impressive. To some extent, they repackaged a long-standing strategy to subsidise work programmes for individuals whose disabilities barred them from 'open' employment. The first sheltered workshop was established in 1949 in the government's North Point Relief Camp. With financial support from the government, the late 1950s saw workshops set up for the blind, and facilities for the mentally ill followed a decade later. By 1988, sheltered workshops were catering for almost 60 per cent of the disabled population of working age.[4]

In this century, the government's espousal of business-based initiatives was inspired mainly by expediency. Promotion of 'corporate social responsibility' initiatives, for example, was acknowledged from the start to be a useful defence against the rise of anti-business sentiment.[5] Officials embraced social enterprises with no clear understanding of what was involved. The Financial Secretary in 2006 confessed his own uncertainties. 'So what is "social enterprise"?' he asked, 'While there is no common definition, I think it is, first and foremost, a business.' 'Like any other business firms, meeting the bottom-line is key to survival,' he added.[6] Among the community at large, social enterprises were of little interest.[7] The gains for the government, however, were clear enough, particularly when large business conglomerates could be induced to join the programme. Social enterprises helped to shift welfare from income-support measures to profit-making ventures, and business participation allowed the government to disengage from responsibility for social wellbeing.[8]

The social enterprise programme itself suffered from an in-built conflict for which there was no obvious solution. A government-sponsored investigation of social enterprises and their potential pointed out that they have a 'double-bottom line, that is, social goals and economic goals'. In theory, this report went on, 'with the help of businessmen and entrepreneurs, NGOs should be able to run a business without marginalising their social goals'. Nevertheless, there remained a clash of interests, which was ethical as well as commercial. 'The initial mentality of NGOs is serving their clients (usually the vulnerable groups)', which was in direct conflict, this report warned, with 'the mentality of running a business (cost containment, profit making, and cost-effectiveness)'. Social workers and their agencies were thus 'trapped between social missions and economic goals'. By personal vocation and professional training, they could not put profits first. In running a business, they could not hope to succeed unless they did so.[9]

Social enterprises were also part of a broader strategy intended to provide a large number of small-scale or district-level activities which would allow Chief Executives and their ministers to demonstrate their concern for particular groups of 'clients'. These projects were frequently little more than window-dressing which, in budgetary terms, involved relatively little additional spending. For example, the Partnership Fund for the Disadvantaged was established in 2005 as 'a tripartite partnership' of NGOs, business and government with the aim of 'creating a cohesive, harmonious and caring society'. Its 410,000 potential beneficiaries included 'survivors of domestic violence, youth, people with disabilities, ex-offenders, elderly, low income families and pregnant teenagers'. But its funding averaged less than HK$180 per potential client in 2005–08, which could do little either to relieve poverty or to provide the intensive social work support that much of its caseload appeared to need.[10] Other programmes were better funded. The much vaunted 'Enhancing Self-Reliance Through District Partnership Programme' was officially described as producing 'shop assistants, planters, female garment workers, beauticians and massotherapists'. By 2012, after six years in operation, it had created only 2,300 new jobs at a cost of HK$65,000 per additional employee (equivalent to the average wage for half a year).[11] Such schemes were short-term commitments and often linked to a moral exit from government involvement through being partnered with businesses or NGOs. In the meantime, as this book has shown, the government was firmly opposed to increased social expenditure as a matter of principle, regardless of whether the economy boomed or how buoyant was public revenue. The government-business nexus was convinced that the market should prevail and that the public sector should make way for private enterprise. In the process, subsidies for social services should be drastically reduced. Lip service was paid to the principle that the poor should not be totally deprived of housing, health, education and welfare services. But earlier chapters have displayed ample evidence of how the poor suffered physical pain, mental distress and even reduced life expectancy through the harshness of the price-rationing and means-testing they faced.

The Search for Solutions

The levels of government funding in this century were far from adequate, but it was toxic policies that wreaked the most serious havoc in terms of personal suffering, both for ordinary families and for the needy. The solution to the new poverty that afflicted Hong Kong has an obvious starting point: the reversal of policies and programmes which could be shown to have increased the financial and physical distress of the community. For example, the insistence that the social services should adopt private sector models could end and be replaced by a return to a commitment to supply services and facilities on the basis of what the vulnerable need rather than on what they could afford to pay for.

A reversal of pernicious policies would require the government to accept responsibility for the community's wellbeing through adequate provision of housing, healthcare, education and welfare services. The last (1991) White Paper published on social welfare set out a definition of what such an obligation involved.

> Most societies, and Hong Kong is no exception, accept an obligation to assist their members to overcome personal and social problems and to fulfil their role in life to the optimum extent in accordance with the particular social and cultural development of their society. In particular, they recognize a responsibility to help their disadvantaged members to attain an acceptable standard of living.[12]

The caring professionals in both public sector and the NGOs would have no difficulty today in restructuring existing programmes and practices to implement these principles and to achieve these goals. Much of the explanation for Hong Kong's extraordinary economic success and its surging labour productivity regardless of static wages and deteriorating working conditions has been the determination to upgrade personal performance. This outlook also flourished in the public sector among the caring professions. A particularly impressive case has been the Hospital Authority. For several years in this century, it battled in vain for the financial resources to maintain the quality of services to its patients. Although the funding devoted to health by comparison with other advanced economies was unsatisfactory, Hong Kong still managed to achieve a life expectancy well above their average.[13]

While welfare advocacy has weakened over the past three decades, Chapter 7 reported, and the role of caring professionals in policy-making declined, they continued to exploit whatever opportunities were available to remedy misguided government policies. A striking example was the teaching profession's response to the official adoption in 2004 of the 'New Academic Structure' programme for the secondary and post-secondary systems. Its implementation was set to commence in 2009 and required drastic changes in the organisation of both secondary schools and universities. Syllabuses, subjects, teaching methods and public examinations were to be totally transformed.

The training organised for the teaching of totally new subjects was minimal. The attention given to the requirements of students with special needs was both belated and limited. There was a complacent insistence that any student could and should be taught the new liberal studies programme without textbooks. Teachers faced mounting pressure and confusion, but official response to their professional anxieties was generally little more than bland reassurances.[14] The burdens were passed on to the teaching profession with barely an acknowledgement from the education authorities.[15] A typical example of patronising indifference from officials was the government's admission in 2012 that 'there are still great concerns about workload, allocation of lesson time and how to cater for student diversity'. The Education Bureau's initial solution was empty rhetoric in the form of an offer to 'continue to enhance support measures for schools and teachers, disseminate good practices to schools to facilitate learning and teaching'.[16] The following year, the reform programme finally began to unravel. Despite the teachers' best endeavours, schools could not overcome the inherent defects of the new system. The strains imposed on teachers had reached breaking point, and the third Chief Executive's team accepted that classroom and examination workloads had to be eased.[17]

A search for solutions to toxic policies would face practical obstacles. Because the government-business nexus has regarded 'welfare' as a malign influence on society, objective review of social programmes has been deterred. An important example has been the failure to restructure programmes to protect employees in a post-industrial economy. Exploitation of the labour force reached alarming levels in this century, Chapter 1 explained, and serious breaches of the law went undetected or unpunished. Part of the explanation appears to be the way that the Labour Department continued to operate as if it were factory workers who were most at risk despite the transfer of the bulk of Hong Kong's manufacturing capacity to Guangdong Province by the early 1990s. Although the department reduced the manufacturing sector's share of total workplace inspections in this century, the attention given to industrial workers remained far in excess of their share of total employment. The department's coverage of white collar employees was much less generous.[18]

Another bizarre feature of policy-making in contemporary Hong Kong has been the lack of statistical information to justify government initiatives and innovations. Decisions about social services, for example, were nearly always presented in a bald package which described no more than the number of additional clients to be served or the facilities to be expanded. Almost never were these related to the existing supply or to potential demand. Rarely, if ever, did the official document give an indication of how soon an overall shortfall would be overcome or when service quality would be raised to the prescribed standard. The Hospital Authority, for example, tried to explain in 2010 the rationale for additional spending on the modernisation of its equipment. 'Modern healthcare is heavily technology driven,' it declared, 'advancement in medical technology contributes to better patient care through faster and more accurate diagnosis.' Its briefing document for the legislature referred to the importance of 'imaging and cancer' and 'molecular testing and genetic' services. No information was provided on relative priorities or target dates. Or why the same amount of money was allocated to a modern 'telephone system' as to new surgical equipment.[19] All this information was available to officials, and limited data were supplied eventually to legislators but in a form which did not make it easy to assess the merits of this modernisation programme.[20]

History Repeats Itself

In evaluating the performance of the first three Chief Executives and their teams, it would be unfair to treat them as if they were entirely free agents. They inherited a legacy of past neglect because of the colonial administration's hostility towards social expenditure. This colonial background is poorly understood, not surprisingly, because under British rule, 'government' seemed to take place in an alien environment and to be conducted by foreigners in a foreign language in accordance with unfamiliar laws and customs imported from the United Kingdom. Nevertheless, a disregard for history is an obstacle to understanding the major challenges of the present. Although a dramatic transformation of Hong Kong's identity took place in 1997, a prominent Hong Kong academic has pointed out, policy-making is carried out 'in cultural contexts which are deep-rooted in society and reflect the political culture of the society'. 'Governments may change,' he added, 'but the political culture may remain unchanged for a much longer period.'[21]

Indeed, a striking feature of governance in Hong Kong has been the reluctance of rulers in this century to tackle the Third World deficiencies they had inherited and which continued to handicap the housing sector, as well as the quality of health, education and welfare services. Ministers remained locked into the same flawed strategy adopted under British rule: unless a social issue posed an imminent threat of disaster, public funds need not be spent on its solution. The continuing mistrust of social insurance among officials, business leaders and the wider community was the most notable example of how past decisions caused long-term financial and social burdens. Chapter 6 showed that throughout the previous century, the colonial administration argued that the economy would be ruined if business profits and low taxation were not maintained. This outlook led to stubborn opposition to social insurance. In consequence, the workforce will have to rely on means-tested, tax-funded, social security to finance its old age for at least another two decades before Mandatory Provident Fund accounts are large enough to provide adequate retirement incomes.

Similarly, Financial Secretary John Tsang Chun-wah followed a colonial-era strategy in evading decisions about services for the elderly. In 2008, he declared that 'an ageing population will lower our standard of living and undermine economic vitality and competitiveness'. It would also put 'immense pressure on public finances' because 'medical, long-term care expenses and social security payments, will increase substantially'.[22] In 2013, he used the same doomsday scenario to justify holding down government spending — social expenditure especially — in order to avoid a rise in taxation (just as his colonial predecessors had been shown to argue in Chapter 4).

> With an increase in the number of the elderly, a shrinking working population, reduction in the number of taxpayers and decelerated economic growth, I expect that the growth of government revenue will drop substantially if our tax regime remains unchanged. Meanwhile, expenditure on welfare and healthcare will soar. We may not be able to make ends meet.[23]

An obvious solution for the problems Tsang listed would be to introduce social insurance instead of continuing to rely on tax revenue to finance social security and health and welfare services. In any case, social expenditure could be increased significantly without making Hong Kong tax rates 'uncompetitive' because the effective rate of tax on the highest-income groups is so low and the taxation system itself is carefully constructed to avoid imposing social responsibilities on the affluent (as Chapter 2 explained). In fact, tax is not the issue, nor have financial resources ever been a serious obstacle to better public housing and modern social services, the historical and contemporary evidence presented in this book makes clear.

Neither the Financial Secretary nor other government leaders have recognised another, far larger potential burden on public finances which cannot be postponed indefinitely. In comments on CSSA throughout this century, Chief Executives and their teams consistently refused to see how cost-effective the scheme was in financing retirement, health-care and unemployment for the lower-income groups. Instead, there was constant denigration of the scheme and of the beneficiaries whom it saved from destitution. Chapter 6 highlighted the astonishing levels of self-reliance among both the elderly and the unemployed, most of whom did not turn to CSSA for relief.

But this self-restraint cannot last forever. The numbers applying for CSSA are likely to increase in the future, if only because of the long-term effects of the decline in the size of the average family, which in this century numbered less than three members. And stagnant earnings and incomes will have a similar effect. The trend in this century has been for wages to lag behind productivity, and actually to fall for the low-earning groups. Thus, the capacity to save will be lower than in the past, which will reduce the ability of families to finance members in need and to pay higher fees for medical treatment and schooling. Financial Secretaries have left it to their successors to defuse this fiscal bomb.

The unelected Special Administrative Region government has shown a marked tendency to adopt measures, which ironically will create much the same sort of Third World legacy for future decades as the colonial administration's under-spending on schooling did in the past. Chapter 5 drew attention to the alarming treatment of those unable to enter the better schools and regular degree programmes. Entry to superior quality secondary schools, which receive full government subsidies, is being confined very largely to students whose parents could afford the high fees charged. Society has been disinclined to judge the social justice of this situation. But the loss to the economy ought not to be ignored: not all society's highly talented individuals are being given the education that would maximise their productive abilities. (The offspring of the affluent are not necessarily endowed with high IQs.)

The problem has been even more acute at the post-secondary level for students who did not qualify for university programmes. In a drive to placate parents worried about their children's careers when a year was chopped off their secondary schooling, the government chose a private sector model to supply a new market for employment qualifications with associate degrees. The results were horrifying. Parents discovered that the fees were wasted because these diplomas had little credibility with employers. Senior officials showed no enthusiasm for cleaning up the mess which their policies had created.

Hong Kong was thus in danger of recreating the shortcomings that arose in the 1980s after secondary education for all had finally been made free and compulsory. Those in charge of policy at that time assumed that this policy decision was all that was required of them. The lack of trained teachers and decent school buildings was of no interest. Indeed, Chapter 4 cited evidence which suggested that education officials had chosen deliberately to make no effort to upgrade the school system. By the end of the century, Third World standards had still not been eliminated. Today, youngsters attending many of the non-elite secondary school or enrolled for many sub-degree programmes face the risk of being handicapped throughout their careers, while for the community as a whole, there will be a substantial bill for replacing low-quality educational arrangements at a later date.

Housing seems to be the most intractable crisis, and once again, Hong Kong seems unable to escape from Third World situations. The government can overcome the supply crisis if it spends enough money and resists pressures from developers. But emergency building programmes do not offer a solution. On the contrary, experience in the last century showed (in Chapter 3) that when crisis measures are taken to accelerate supply, control over contractors is lost. Corruption and substandard construction get tolerated as long as buildings are finished in record time, leaving a stock of shoddy buildings to be rebuilt at the tax-payers' expense in years to come.

Future quality is more difficult to manage. In the public sector, there were complaints in 2013 within the Housing Authority that 'the standards we now achieve are too good and we should be building less sophisticated Public Rental Housing'. A senior housing official responded by asking 'Why are we being challenged because we provide decent housing for those most in need?'[24] Quality homes for Hong Kong people still cannot be taken for granted.

It is not clear that the government will be resolute enough to enforce the higher standards of management and maintenance needed to halt the alarming rate of dilapidation predicted for the current stock of private housing, as Chapter 3 noted. Repairs and renovation need to be policed far more effectively than in the past. Essential is a building code which incorporates standards that will guarantee safe, comfortable homes which are designed to last much longer than 50 years. Quality also depends on a recognition that leaving maintenance to the market is an invitation for owners to allow buildings to deteriorate into slums. Officials do not seem to realise that slum property is a paying investment, while management and maintenance cost money.

Political Priorities

Chapter 7 analysed the rise and fall of 'welfare' advocacy in Hong Kong. A tempting conclusion is that Hong Kong has ended up with the level of public housing and social services that it deserves. The community decided that its survival depended on a political struggle that left little room for campaigns to protect the needy and the vulnerable. Thus, society as a whole accepted with little resistance the unsatisfactory state of the social services on which ordinary families depended, while the distress and the deprivation of the new poor provoked little public anger. On Mainland issues, the record was entirely different. The community displayed a robust determination to block measures which the people of Hong Kong believed might imperil their unique way of life. The general conviction that Hong Kong's values must come first was expressed with special eloquence by Donald Tsang Yam-kuen during a visit to the United States in 2003.

> . . . the protest march in Hong Kong on July 1 . . . was a defining moment for us. In steaming temperatures, cheek by jowl, 500,000 of our residents took to the streets in a protest against the government . . . As someone born and bred in Hong Kong, as the son of a Policeman, I was moved by the calm, peaceful and rational manner in which Hong Kong people conducted themselves that day. Despite the uncomfortable conditions, tempers did not overheat. There were no angry scenes in the streets. No destroying of public or private property. No baton charges by police, or water cannons fired into the crowd. Hong Kong people cared enough about the future of their society — about the values that they hold dear — to take to the streets in defence of them.[25]

What made the Tsang's defence of the July 1 protest all the more impressive was that he did not hesitate to deliver this message before another American audience which included two Chinese ambassadors.[26] At that time, he was still not sure that the Central People's Government would promote him to the post of Chief Executive when Tung Chee Hwa stepped down.

In response to Hong Kong's zeal in defence of its own values, there has been a barrage of criticism from the Mainland of the public's lack of docility. There has also been considerable censure by the government-business nexus of the community's alleged ignorance of Mainland affairs which was said to obstruct the fostering of patriotic sentiment. In all this, little attention has been paid to Hong Kong's Mainland achievements. On the eve of Deng Xiaoping's 1978 initiatives to modernise China's economy, Liao Chengzhi, the nation's leading authority on Hong Kong, denounced the persecution inflicted in the past on anyone with Hong Kong or other external connections. They had been vilified together with 'landlords, rich peasants, counter-revolutionaries . . . enemy agents'. In 1970, he went on, special measures had been introduced to compel cadres to break off connections with their Hong Kong relatives.[27]

Deng's reforms should have eradicated such hostility because they were accompanied by the leadership's open endorsement of economic cooperation between Guangdong Province and Hong Kong. Shortly after the reforms were officially adopted, the Foreign Trade Minister, Li Qiang, visited Hong Kong and acknowledged the way that a flood of Mainland officials in search of expertise and resources had already been welcomed by the Hong Kong business community.[28] The message that Hong Kong had a major contribution to make to the nation's economic takeoff was widely publicised thereafter by the Mainland authorities.[29]

But just over two years later, Guangdong's leaders denounced Hong Kong in contemptuous terms. 'Our spiritual civilization is higher than Hong Kong's', a provincial vice-governor boasted in 1981, which he castigated for its low moral standards.[30] Resistance to taking Hong Kong as a model intensified with the increase in cross-border business, and the province was urged in 1982 to 'erect a great iron wall against capitalist corrosion of the minds of cadres and the masses'.[31] In 1985, an official publication reported that some Mainland staff posted to joint ventures were treating their Hong Kong partners with the same hostility as when the state was taking control of China's capitalist activities in the 1950s.[32]

Nevertheless, Hong Kong industrialists and investors persisted in cooperating with national policy to create a modern industrial base in Guangdong. 'Without Hong Kong, the Chinese mainland could not have accessed the global market' in the two decades following the adoption of Deng Xiaoping's 'open door' policies, a Chinese leader declared in 2000.[33] Hong Kong became the Mainland's largest source of foreign direct investment (FDI), supplying over 40 per cent of the total inflow.[34] There could be no doubt about the strenuous efforts made by

Hong Kong to collaborate with the Mainland in its drive to modernise the nation.

The relationship at the financial level became stronger than ever in this century, but manufacturers were forced to suffer the loss of the incentives and exemptions which they had been granted initially on the Mainland. As Chapter 1 suggested, this recent Mainland experience deepened the business community's conviction that social and labour reforms were a direct threat to their profitability and hardened their resistance to 'welfare' initiatives in Hong Kong. The business community also discovered how ineffective the government was when it came to protecting Hong Kong commercial interests against adverse changes in Mainland policies. In recent years, the financial as well as the manufacturing sectors suffered from the government's poor management of relations with Mainland authorities, as Chapter 2 discussed.

The political environment entered a new phase during the 2012 Chief Executive elections, and the priority of social issues started to rise. There was growing comprehension within the general community that the global and Mainland economies no longer offered the most lucrative markets for local firms to exploit. The biggest profit opportunities were to be found in Hong Kong itself. In response, the government faced growing pressure for measures to safeguard the consumer and the labour force against business malpractices, and it became increasingly difficult for ministers to resist and delay such reforms. As Chapter 7 noted, the Federation of Trade Unions (FTU), the largest trade union and hitherto a pillar of political support for the government, had begun to protest in 2012 at the failure to protect the employment rights and livelihood of the workforce. There was thus a possibility that Chief Executives and their ministers would no longer be able to rely on their partnership with business representatives and on the collaboration of the largest trade union's leaders to ensure a majority for the administration's proposals in the legislature. Even without the introduction of universal suffrage, the government may have to make the wellbeing of the community rather than the interests of business its primary concern.

The Mainland Has the Final Say

The Mainland could prove the most powerful factor of all in compelling the government to accept greater responsibility for the social wellbeing of the community. As Chapter 2 noted, China's leaders became deeply suspicious from 1991 of the colonial administration's social programmes, which they believed were unaffordable and thus a danger to the financial wellbeing of the future Special Administrative Region. At the end of British rule, welfare spending was still under attack from senior Mainland officials, creating a strong impression that expenditure in this area would be reined in by the new government (which indeed took place under Tung Chee Hwa).[35]

Mainland belief in the overwhelming importance to be given to economic growth has since modified. In 2011, the nation's 12th Five-Year Plan abandoned the 'business-first' development model, and Premier Wen Jiabao called for 'a complete change of GDP-obsessed mentality'. The 2011–15 target for annual average GDP growth was cut to 7 per cent (compared with the 10.7 per cent annual average achieved from 2002). Disposable incomes would rise by an annual average of no less than 7 per cent during the new Five-Year Plan, while the minimum wage level would be increased each year by 'at least 13 per cent'. Old-age pension systems would cover the entire rural population and all 'non-working urban residents'.[36]

Chapter 1 recorded Tsang Yam-kuen's efforts to persuade China's leadership to have Hong Kong included in the national plan on the grounds that considerable opportunities for economic growth would follow. The implications for social policy attracted limited attention. Nevertheless, they were formally discussed when the Special Administrative Region's Commission on Strategic Development organised a forum to review how Hong Kong should respond to the plan. Little time was devoted specifically to social issues, but it was significant that some participants complained about Hong Kong's failure to upgrade its social services and to tackle the widening gap between rich and poor as the Mainland was doing.[37] As far as the government itself was concerned, the national five-year plan raised only one serious social policy issue: Hong Kong's working poor and how to assist those families in which earnings were below the subsistence (i.e., CSSA) level.[38] There was no significant follow-up action on this subject, however.

Otherwise, the widening social responsibilities accepted by the Central People's Government had little impact on Hong Kong policy-makers. At the end of 2012, the Mainland claimed that 'medical services have become more affordable and accessible; and fewer and fewer people are becoming poor or return to poverty because of illness'.[39] The Hong Kong Special Administrative Region had adopted policies which, as this book has reported extensively, made medical and other social services more expensive and inaccessible and which allowed serious illnesses to aggravate the financial hardship of patients and their families.

In 2016, the 13th Five-Year Plan will embrace Hong Kong more comprehensively, Leung Chun-ying has declared, and Hong Kong will have to view itself 'as a part of the nation, the family and its polity'.[40] Will it be possible in 2016 for the Special Administrative Region government to pick and choose from the next national plan, embracing the economic opportunities and rejecting the social obligations? The economic integration with the Mainland pursued by all three Chief Executives may well have the unintended consequence of raising the priority of social wellbeing at the expense of the traditional principle of 'business first' because growth at any cost had become politically incorrect on the Mainland.

Notes

1. Matthew Cheung Kin-chung, Secretary for Labour and Welfare, *Government Information Services* (*GIS* hereafter), 21 June 2013.
2. On such threats, see, for example, Bruce Gilley, 'Li Besieged', *Far Eastern Economic Review*, 28 January 1999.
3. Cheung, Secretary for Labour and Welfare, *Hong Kong Hansard* (*HH* hereafter), 17 April 2013.
4. Marianne Savage, 'Sheltered Workshops: The Extent to Which Business Practices Can or Should Be Applied to Sheltered Workshops', MBA dissertation, University of Hong Kong (September 1988), pp. 8–9 and Appendix 1: 'Data on Disabled Persons in Hong Kong 1987', p. 93, f.n. #. There is a tendency to underestimate these past endeavours. See Po-ying Amy Ho, 'The Incubation of Social Entrepreneurship in Hong Kong', 2010 International Conference on Social Enterprises in Eastern Asia: Dynamic and Variations, Taipei (14 June 2010), pp. 7–8; Tang Kwong Leung et al., 'Social Enterprises in Hong Kong: Toward a Conceptual Model. Final Report' (Central Policy Unit, April 2008), p. 69.
5. The political advantages for the governments of Singapore and Japan were described in the government-commissioned report, Hong Kong Policy Research Institute Ltd, 'A Study on Tripartite Partnership: Benchmarking Study from an International Perspective: Final Report' (Central Policy Unit, October 2005), pp. 6, 35–6, 38.
6. Henry Tang Ying-yen, Financial Secretary, *GIS*, 6 April 2006.
7. 'There is a lack of public understanding and receptivity to SEs.' Tang et al., 'Social Enterprises in Hong Kong: Toward a Conceptual Model. Final Report', p. 65.
8. Ibid., pp. 7–10.
9. Ibid., pp. 50, 51, 53, 60.
10. Ann Hon, Assistant Director of Social Welfare (Subventions), *GIS*, 22 May 2008.
11. Tsang Tak-sing, Secretary for Home Affairs, *HH*, 31 October 2007, pp. 1121–2, A1–2; Cheung, Secretary for Labour and Welfare, *HH*, 14 November 2012, p. 2129.
12. *Social Welfare into the 1990s and Beyond* (Hong Kong: Government Printer, 1991), p. 13.
13. Hospital Authority, *Hospital Authority Annual Plan 2007–08* (Hong Kong: Hospital Authority, 2007), p. 9; Dr Ko Wing-man, Secretary for Food and Health, World Health Summit Regional Meeting, *GIS*, 9 April 2013.

14. For summaries of the government's responses on key issues (and how consistent they were over time), see Legislative Council Secretariat, 'Panel on Education. Implementation of the New Academic Structure' (CB(2)1996/09-10(02), 8 July 2010), pp. 3, 4, 6; 'Panel on Education. Implementation of the New Academic Structure' (CB(2)1694/11-12(05), 17 April 2012), pp. 3–5, 9–11.

15. The serious difficulties encountered in implementing the new system were set out in a report by the Joint Committee of Hong Kong Secondary School Councils and Secondary School Principals' Associations of 18 Districts, 'Executive Summary of Report on Survey of the New Academic System' (CB(2)622/11-12(02), 11 November 2011), pp. 1–6.

16. Education Bureau, 'Legislative Council Panel on Education Progress on the Implementation of the New Academic Structure' (CB(2)1694/11-12(04), April 2012), p. 2.

17. Dr Catherine K. K. Chan, Deputy Education Secretary, *GIS*, 18 April 2013. On the public and professional dissatisfaction with the new secondary school system which led to the government concessions, see editorial, *Ming Pao Daily*, 19 April 2013.

18. See the inspection data in 'Figure 6.2: Number of Inspections Made in . . . by Major Economic Sector' in the on-line *Report of the Commissioner for Labour, 2002* and *Labour Department Annual Reports*, 2003 to 2010.

19. Hospital Authority, 'Modernization of Medical Equipment in the Hospital Authority' (CB(2)865/09-10(05), February 2010).

20. See Kirk Yip (Food and Health Bureau) letter to Mary So (Panel on Health services), 'Modernization of Medical Equipment in the Hospital Authority', FH/H/1/5, 9 April 2010.

21. Kai Ming Cheng, 'The Policy Making Process', in Gerard A. Postiglione and Wing On Lee (eds.), *Schooling in Hong Kong: Organization, Teaching and Social Context* (Hong Kong: Hong Kong University Press, 1997), p. 65.

22. John Tsang Chun-wah, Financial Secretary, *HH*, 27 February 2008, p. 4991.

23. John Tsang, Financial Secretary, *HH*, 27 February 2013, p. 7426.

24. D. W. Pescod, Director of Housing, *GIS*, 27 June 2013.

25. Donald Tsang, Chief Secretary, speech at the Center for Strategic and International Studies, Washington, *GIS*, 19 September 2003.

26. The Chinese diplomats were Ambassadors Wang Guangya and Liu Biwei. Donald Tsang, Chief Secretary, *GIS*, 18 September 2003.

27. Liao Chengzhi, Overseas Chinese Affairs Office Director, 'Refuting the reactionary errors of the "Gang of Four" about so-called "overseas relationships"', *Renmin Ribao*, 4 January 1978.

28. For his speech, see *Ta Kung Pao*, 21 December 1978.

29. For example, Xi Zhingxun, Provincial First Party Secretary, *Nanfang Ribao*, 12 August 1979; Liu Nianzhi, All-China Federation of Industry and Commerce Vice Chairman, *New China News Agency*, 30 November 1979.

30. Reported in *Wen Wei Po*, 1 March 1981.

31. Pan Weiwen, 'A talk about the advantages and disadvantages of being neighbours to Hong Kong and Macao', *Yangcheng Wanbao*, 17 March 1982.

32. Yang Qinquan and Jiang Zhiyuan, Guangzhou Party Propaganda Department, 'Analysis of the results of Guangzhou's foreign economic cooperation and future strategy', *Guangzhou Yanjiu*, No. 5 (September–October 1985), pp. 35–7.
33. Li Ruihan, Chinese People's Political Consultative Conference Chairman, *China Daily*, 7 November 2000.
34. This claim was made in the presence of the then Vice-Premier Li Keqiang. Donald Tsang Yam-kuen, Chief Executive, *GIS*, 17 August 2011.
35. This prospect was recognised very perceptively by Professor Tang Shu-hung, 'The Hong Kong Fiscal Policy: Continuity or Redirection?', in Li Pang-kwong (ed.), *Political Order and Power Transition in Hong Kong* (Hong Kong: Chinese University Press, 1997), pp. 187–8, 227–8.
36. The quotations and statistics are from *New China News Agency* reporting Premier Wen Jiabao, 27 February and 14 March 2011, 5 March and 11 September 2012; and Yin Weimin, Minister of Human Resources and Social Security, 8 March 2011.
37. Commission on Strategic Development, 'Summary of Views Expressed at the Seventh Meeting of the Commission on Strategic Development Held on 12 May 2011', p. 6.
38. Commission on Strategic Development, 'An Overview of the Opportunities and Challenges of Hong Kong's Development' (CSD/6/2008, October 2008), pp. 6–7.
39. For this quotation and a detailed overview of Mainland policy in the health sector, see 'Medical and Health Services in China', *New China News Agency*, 26 December 2012.
40. Leung Chun-ying, Chief Executive, *GIS*, 6 December 2012.

Bibliography

Unpublished Sources

Hillard, J. L., Essential Services Corps Commissioner, 'Survey of Strikes — June 1967' (mimeo, ESC 90/67, 15 September 1967).

Hong Kong Housing Authority, HD (CR) 1/247 XII, HD/SAO/A 37.

Hong Kong Housing Authority, Memorandum HA 31/99, 'Management Enhancement Programme: Next Steps for Corporate Reform' (HD(CR) MEP/8, 30 April 1999).

'Note for Executive Council. Progress of Management Reforms by the Hospital Authority' (XCRI (96) 21, 25 November 1996).

'Note for Executive Council. Review of the Social Welfare Subvention System' (XCCI (96) 40, 26 September 1996).

Social Welfare Department, 'Brief History of Rehabilitation Division of SWD' (mimeo, 1976).

Special Committee on Housing, *Hong Kong Housing Survey 1957* (mimeo, 1958), Vols. III and IV.

Public Records Office Hong Kong

CO1030/273 'Social Welfare Reports Hong Kong Covering 1954–57'

HKRS22-1-73/4 'Social Welfare Squatters'

HKRS41-1-1233 'Taxation General Policy regarding . . . in the Colony'

HKRS41-1-2769(1) 'Inland Revenue Ordinance 1. General question of imposing etc . . .'

HKRS54-10-1(406) 'Documents handed in by Mr Turnbull of Messrs Deacon & Co'

HKRS70-3-13 'Building Control. Peony House — Failing by completion'

HKRS146-4-18 (10) 'International Labour Organisation Annual Reports on Application of International Labour Conventions'

HKRS146-8-3-1 'Social Welfare Development Programme 1960–1967'

HKRS146-8-3-4 'Policy on Social Welfare — Social Welfare Development 1960–67'

HKRS146-12-20 'Medical Development Programme Working Group Minutes of Meeting and General'

HKRS156-3-95 'Squatters on Land not Required for Development'

HKRS163-1-118 'Federation of Hong Kong Industries Minutes of the Meetings of the . . .'

HKRS163-1-280 'Tung Wah and Associated Hospitals. Proposals for the Government to take operation . . .'

HKRS163-1-828 'Tung Wah Eastern Hospital. Conversion of . . . into a teaching hospital'

HKRS163-1-1007 'Finance Estimated Capital Investment in Hong Kong'

HKRS163-3-64 'Squatter Clearance and Resettlement 1. General Questions of . . . 2. Programmes of . . . '

HKRS163-3-219 'Working Party on Squatters, Resettlement and Government Low Cost Housing'

HKRS163-3-264 'Co-ordination of Social Service Policies'

HKRS163-9-486 'Social Security — Implications of Change in HK Status-Quo . . .'

HKRS163-9-932 'Ad Hoc Working Group of the Medical Development Advisory Committee'

HKRS170-1-571-1 'Social Welfare Office Quarterly Progress Report'

HKRS170-2-1 'Census Estimate of Population'

HKRS229-1-49 'United Kingdom Income Tax Act . . .'

HKRS259-6-1 'Report on the Population of the Colony, Mid-Year 1949'

HKRS270-5-39 'Federation of Hong Kong Industries Minutes of Meetings of the General Committee'

HKRS270-5-56 'Cotton Advisory Board. Minutes of Meeting'

HKRS306-1-142 'Abandoned Children'

HKRS306-1-217A 'Housing for the Elderly, the Infirm and the Handicapped'

HKRS307-3-15 'Social Security in Hong Kong'

HKRS307-3-17 'Social Security in Hong Kong'

HKRS307-6-18 'Kwong Wah Hospital Future Development'

HKRS394-20-8 'Resettlement Policy Committee'

HKRS457-2-5 'Financial Review of Educational Costs'

HKRS482-2-16-5 'Medical Development Advisory Committee'

HKRS794-1-2 'Steering Group on Community Development'

HKRS8901-1-12 'Education/Social Welfare. 1 Facilities for Children of Primary School Age. 2 Unregistered Schools'

HKRS890-1-15 'Subsistence Level'

HKRS934-940 'Working Party on Housing'

HKRS1017-2-6 'Committee to Review the Unemployment Situation in the Colony'

HKRS1017-3-1 'Children Engaged in Industrial Employment in Hong Kong'

HKRS1017-3-4 'Unemployment Relief'

HKRS1017-3-22 'Discussions with Comments by H.E. on Labour Matters'

HKRS1017-4-4 'General Conditions of Employment Legislation re . . .'

Government Publications

Aims and Policy for Social Welfare in Hong Kong (Hong Kong: Government Printer, 1964).

Aims and Policy for Social Welfare in Hong Kong Revised (Hong Kong: Government Printer, 1965).

Annual Report on Hong Kong for the Year 1946 (Hong Kong: Government of Hong Kong, 1947).

Homes for Hong Kong People into the 21st Century. A White Paper on Long Term Housing Strategy in Hong Kong February 1998 (Hong Kong: SARG, 1998).

Hong Kong Annual Departmental Report by the Commissioner of Labour for the Financial Year 1954–55 (Hong Kong: Government Printer, n.d.).

Hong Kong Annual Departmental Report by the Commissioner of Labour for the Financial Year 1956–57 (Hong Kong: Government Printer, n.d.).

Hong Kong Annual Departmental Report by the Registrar General 1959–60 (Hong Kong: Government Printer, n.d.).

Hong Kong Annual Report 1951 (Hong Kong: Government of Hong Kong, 1952).

Hong Kong Annual Report of the Commissioner of Labour 1st April, 1948 to 31st March, 1949 (Hong Kong: n.p., n.d.).

Hong Kong Departmental Report by the Social Welfare Officer for the Period 1948–54 (Hong Kong: Government Printer, n.d.).

'Minutes of the Social Welfare Advisory Committee (SWAC) Meeting Held on 21 December 2004' (Health, Welfare and Food Bureau, March 2005). URL: www.lwb.gov.hk/download/committees/swac/minutes041221_e.pdf

Progress Report. The 1997 Policy Address (Hong Kong: Information Services Department, 1997).

'Public Consultation on Tax Reform, Final Report' (June 2007). URL: www.taxreform.gov.hk/eng/pdf/finalreport.pdf

'Reforming Hong Kong's Tax System, Consultation Document' (2006). URL: www.taxreform.gov.hk/eng/document.htm

Reforming the Academic Structure for Secondary Education and Higher Education — Actions for Investing in the Future (Hong Kong: Education and Manpower Bureau, 2004). URL: www.edb.gov.hk/FileManager/EN/Content_2174/consultation%20document291004.pdf

Report by the Inter-Departmental Working Party to Consider Certain Aspects of Social Security (Hong Kong: Government Printer, 1967).

'Report of Investigation Task Force on Statistical Data Quality Assurance' (March 2013). URL: www.gov.hk/en/residents/government/policy/government_reports/reports/docs/DQA.pdf

Report of the Commission . . . to Enquire into the Causes and Effects of the Present Trade Recession . . . (Hong Kong: Noronha & Co., 1935).

Report on the Social & Economic Progress . . . for the Year 1938 (Hong Kong: n.p., n.d.).

Report on the Social & Economic Progress . . . for the Year 1939 (Hong Kong: n.p., n.d.).

Review of Policies for Squatter Control, Resettlement and Government Low-Cost Housing 1964 (Hong Kong: Government Printer, 1964).

Review of the Institutional Framework for Public Housing: The Report June 2002 (Hong Kong: SAR Government, 2002). URL: www.cityu.edu.hk/hkhousing/pdoc/pdoc2002(eng).pdf

Social Welfare into the 1990s and Beyond (Hong Kong: Government Printer, 1991).

Taxation Committee Report (Hong Kong: Noronha & Co., Ltd., 1939).

The 1975–76 Budget: Economic Background (Hong Kong: Government Printer, 1977).

The 1978–79 Budget: Economic Background (Hong Kong: Government Printer, 1978).

The Five Year Plan for Social Welfare Development in Hong Kong — Review 1998 (Hong Kong: Social Welfare Department, 1998).

The Further Development of Medical and Health Services in Hong Kong (Hong Kong: Government Printer, 1974).

Audit Commission, *Report No. 38*, 'Chapter 5: Residential Services for the Elderly' (Hong Kong, March 2002). URL: www.aud.gov.hk/pdf_e/e38ch05[1].pdf

———, *Report No. 39*, 'Chapter 5: Special Finance Scheme for Small and Medium Enterprises' (Hong Kong, 15 October 2002). URL: www.aud.gov.hk/pdf_e/e39ch05.pdf

———, *Report No. 47*, 'Chapter 4: Four Small and Medium Enterprise Funding Schemes' (Hong Kong, 23 October 2006). URL: www.aud.gov.hk/pdf_e/e47ch04.pdf

———, *Report No. 55*, 'Chapter 1: Education Bureau: Administration of the Direct Subsidy Scheme' (Hong Kong, 25 October 2010). URL: www.aud.gov.hk/pdf_e/e55ch01.pdf

———, *Report No. 59*, 'Chapter 3: Food and Health Bureau, Department of Health. Regulatory Control of Private Hospitals' (Hong Kong, 26 October 2012). URL: www.aud.gov.hk/pdf_e/e59ch03.pdf

———, *Report No. 59*, 'Chapter 4: Food and Health Bureau, Department of Health, Lands Department. Land grants for private hospital development' (Hong Kong, 26 October 2012). URL: www.aud.gov.hk/pdf_e/e59ch04.pdf

———, *Report No. 59*, 'Chapter 5: Create Hong Kong. Government's Financial Support to Film Industry' (26 October 2012). URL: www.aud.gov.hk/pdf_e/e59ch05.pdf

Barnett, K. M. A., *Hongkong. Report on the 1966 By-Census*, Vol. I (Hong Kong: Government Printer, n.d.).

Census and Statistics Department, *2004 Gross Domestic Product* (Hong Kong: HKSAR Government, 2005).

———, *2006 Population By-Census: Thematic Report: Household Income Distribution in Hong Kong* (Hong Kong: Census and Statistics Department, 2006).

———, 'Analysis of Low Income Households not Receiving Comprehensive Social Security Assistance', *Hong Kong Monthly Digest of Statistics, December 2012* (Hong Kong: Census and Statistics Department, 2012).

———, *Hong Kong By-Census 1976. Main Report. Volume 1: Analysis* (Hong Kong: Government Printer, 1979).

———, *Hong Kong Population and Housing Census 1971 Main Report* (Hong Kong: n.p., n.d.)

———, *Population Census. Thematic Report Household Income Distribution in Hong Kong* (Hong Kong: Census and Statistics Department, 2012).

———, 'Provision of Medical Benefits by Employers/Companies and Coverage of Medical Insurance Purchased by Individuals', *Thematic Household Survey Report No. 45* (Hong Kong: Census and Statistics Department, 2010).

————, 'Retirement Planning and the Financial Situation in Old Age', *Thematic Household Survey Report No. 52* (Hong Kong: Census and Statistics Department, 2013).

————, 'Statistics on Comprehensive Social Security Assistance Scheme, 1996 to 2006', *Hong Kong Monthly Digest of Statistics July 2007* (Hong Kong: Census and Statistics Department, 2007).

————, 'Statistics on Comprehensive Social Security Assistance Scheme, 1999 to 2009', *Hong Kong Monthly Digest of Statistics September 2010* (Hong Kong: Census and Statistics Department, 2010).

————, 'Statistics on Comprehensive Social Security Assistance Scheme, 2001 to 2011', *Hong Kong Monthly Digest of Statistics, September 2012* (Hong Kong: Census and Statistics Department, 2012).

————, 'The Cultural and Creative Industries in Hong Kong, 2011', *Hong Kong Monthly Digest of Statistics May 2013* (Hong Kong: Census and Statistics Department, 2013)

————, 'The Situation of the Six Industries in Hong Kong in 2010', *Hong Kong Monthly Digest of Statistics, March 2012* (Hong Kong: Census and Statistics Department, 2011).

Cheng, Ivy, 'Impacts of the Lump Sum Grant Subvention System on the Subvented Welfare Sector: Information Note' (IN14/07-08, 8 May 2008). URL: www.legco.gov.hk/yr07-08/english/sec/library/0708in14-e.pdf

Cheung Chun-yuen, Barry, Urban Renewal Authority Chairman, *Urban Renewal Authority: New Strategy New Focus for Urban Renewal. Annual Report 2010–11.* URL: www.ura.org.hk/en/download-centre/publications/annual-report/ura-annual-report/2010-2011.aspx

Cheung, Matthew Kin-chung, Secretary for Labour and Welfare, 'Poverty in Hong Kong: Our Challenges and Responses', speech to Hong Kong Democratic Foundation, 22 September 2010. URL: www.hkdf.org/newsarticles.asp?show=newsarticles&newsarticle=282

Civil Service Bureau, *Civil Service Reform: Consultation Document* (March 1999). URL: www.info.gov.hk/archive/consult/1999/reforme.pdf

Commerce and Economic Development Bureau, *Item for Finance Committee*, HEAD 152 Subhead 700, 'New Item "SME Financing Guarantee Scheme — Special Concessionary Measures"' (FCR(2012–13)12, April 2012). URL: www.legco.gov.hk/yr11-12/english/fc/fc/papers/f12-12e.pdf

————, 'Legislative Council Panel on Commerce and Industry. Progress Update on the Support Measures for Small and Medium Enterprises' (CB(1)389/10-11(06), November 2010). URL: www.legco.gov.hk/yr10-11/english/panels/ci/papers/ci1116cb1-389-6-e.pdf

Commission on Poverty (CoP), 'Assisting the Unemployed: Welfare-to-Work', CoP Paper 19/2005 (Commission Secretariat, June 2005). URL: www.cop.gov.hk/eng/pdf/CoP%20Paper%2019.2005%28e%29.pdf.

————, 'Comprehensive Social Security Assistance Scheme (CSSA) Able-Bodied Caseload — Past Trend and 2014 Scenarios' (CoP Paper 20/2005, June 2005). URL: www.cop.gov.hk/eng/pdf/CoP%20Paper%2020.2005%28e%29.pdf

————, Task Force on Children and Youth, 'Implementation of the School-based After-school Learning and Support Programmes' (CoP TFCY Paper 5/2006, September 2006).

Commission on Strategic Development, 'An Overview of the Opportunities and Challenges of Hong Kong's Development' (CSD/6/2008, October 2008). URL: www.cpu.gov.hk/english/documents/csd/csd_6_2008.pdf

————, *Bringing the Vision to Life: Hong Kong's Long-Term Development Needs and Goals* (Hong Kong: Central Policy Unit, 2000).

————, 'Summary of Views Expressed at the Seventh Meeting of the Commission on Strategic Development Held on 12 May 2011'. URL: www.cpu.gov.hk/doc/en/commission_strategic_development/csd_summary_7_2009.pdf

Communications and Technology Branch, *Public Consultation Paper on 2004 Digital 21 Strategy* (Hong Kong: CITB, 2003). URL: www.legco.gov.hk/yr03-04/english/panels/itb/papers/itbcb1-65-1e.pdf

Description of Flats on Sale Sub-committee, *Local Completed Residential Properties: Sales Descriptions and Pre-contractual Matters* (Hong Kong: Law Reform Commission, 2001).

Development Bureau, 'Legislative Council Panel on Development Subcommittee on Building Safety and Related Issues: Measures to Enhance Building Safety in Hong Kong' (CB(1)681/10-11(01), December 2010). URL: www.legco.gov.hk/yr11-12/english/panels/dev/dev_bs/papers/dev_bs0611cb1-2099-2-e.pdf

————, 'Panel on Development Subcommittee on Building Safety and Related Issues: Consolidation of Financial Assistance Schemes for Building Maintenance and Repair' (CB(1)2087/10-11(02), May 2011). URL: www.legco.gov.hk/yr10-11/english/panels/dev/dev_bs/papers/dev_bs0511cb1-2087-2-e.pdf

Economic Analysis and Business Facilitation Unit, 'Legislative Council Subcommittee to Study the Subject of Combating Poverty. Indicators of Poverty—An Update for 2005' (CB(2) 2727/05-06(03), July 2006). URL: www.legco.gov.hk/yr04-05/english/hc/sub_com/hs51/papers/hs510718cb2-2727-03-e.pdf

Economic Analysis Division, *First Quarter Economic Report 2012* (May 2012). URL: www.hkeconomy.gov.hk/en/pdf/er_12q1.pdf

————, *Half-Yearly Economic Report 2012* (Hong Kong: SAR Government, 2012). URL: www.hkeconomy.gov.hk/en/pdf/box-12q2-5-2.pdf

Economic Services Bureau, *Legislative Council Panel on Economic Services. Development and Competitiveness of the Hong Kong Container Port* (November 1998).

Education and Manpower Branch, *Taking the Worry Out of Growing Old: A Consultation Paper on the Government's Proposals for an Old Age Pension Scheme, Hong Kong* (Hong Kong: Government Printer, 1994).

Education and Manpower Bureau, 'LegCo Panel on Education Implementation of Whole-day Primary Schooling' (CB(2)2401/02-03(01), June 2003). URL: www.legco.gov.hk/yr02-03/english/panels/ed/papers/ed0616cb2-2401-1e.pdf

————, 'LegCo Panel on Education Reforming the Academic Structure of Senior Secondary Education and Higher Education — Actions for Investing in the Future' (CB(2) 90/04-05(01), October 2004). URL: www 07-08/english/panels/ed/papers/ed1018cb2-44-1-e.pdf

————, 'LegislativeCouncilPanelonEducationSchool-basedAfter-schoolLearning and Support Programmes' (CB(2)1304/04-05(01), April 2005). URL: www.legco.gov.hk/yr04-05/english/panels/ed/papers/edcb2-1304-1e[1].pdf

Education Bureau, 'Item for Finance Committee' (FCR(2007-08)36, November 2007). URL: www.legco.gov.hk/yr07-08/english/fc/fc/papers/f07-36e[1].pdf

————, 'Item for Finance Committee' (FCR(2007-08)45, January 2008). URL: www.ugc.edu.hk/eng/doc/ugc/publication/other/2008/f07-45e[1].pdf

————, 'Legislative Council Brief. Higher Education Review' (EDB(HE)CR 4/21/2041/89, November 2011). URL: www.legco.gov.hk/yr11-12/english/panels/ed/papers/ed1114-edbhecr421204189-e.pdf

————, 'Legislative Council Panel on Education. Monitoring of Direct Subsidy Scheme (DSS) Schools' (CB(2)2073/08-09(01), June 2009). URL: www.legco.gov.hk/yr08-09/english/panels/ed/papers/ed0706cb2-2073-1-e.pdf

————, 'Legislative Council Panel on Education. Progress on the Implementation of the New Academic Structure' (CB(2)1694/11-12(04), April 2012). URL: www.legco.gov.hk/yr11-12/english/panels/ed/papers/ed0420cb2-1694-4-e.pdf

————, 'Progress Report on the Motion on "Improving Further Education and Employment of Sub-degree Students" Moved by Hon Cyd Ho at the Legislative Council Meeting on 23 November 2011' (February 2012). URL: www.legco.gov.hk/yr11-12/english/counmtg/motion/cm1123-m3-prpt-e.pdf

————, 'Report of the Working Group on Direct Subsidy Scheme' (December 2011). URL: www.edb.gov.hk/FileManager/EN/Content_175/dss%20report_full.pdf

Education Commission, *Report No. 6 Enhancing Language Proficiency: A Comprehensive Strategy Part 2 (Annexes)* (Hong Kong: 1995).

Education Department, 'Panel on Education. Information Paper Mother Tongue Teaching' (18 April 1997). URL: www.legco.gov.hk/yr96-97/english/panels/ed/papers/ed18043a.htm

Efficiency Unit, *Paper for Briefing to LegCo Panel on Public Services Second Phase of the Enhanced Productivity Programme* (CB(2)902/98-99(0), December 1998). URL: www.legco.gov.hk/yr98-99/english/panels/ps/papers/ps2112_3.htm

————, 'Survey on Outsourcing of Government Activities in 2004'. URL: www.eu.gov.hk/attachments/english/psi_out_sg/survey2004.pdf

Finance Bureau, *Information Note for Legislative Council Panel on Public Finance. Short Term Phase of the Enhanced Productivity Programme* (CB(2)902/98-99(03), December 1998). URL: www.legco.gov.hk/yr98-99/english/panels/ps/papers/ps2112_4.htm

————, *Profits Tax Review Consultation Document* (Hong Kong: Government Secretariat, July 1997).

Financial Services and the Treasury Bureau, *Enhanced Productivity Programme 2002–03* (Hong Kong: Hong Kong SAR Government, 2003). URLs: www.fstb.gov.hk/tb/epp/report/2002-03/pdf/english/epp_swd.pdf; www.fstb.gov.hk/tb/epp/report/2002-03/pdf/english/epp_health.pdf

Food and Health Bureau, 'Legislative Council Panel on Health Services. Grant for the Samaritan Fund' (CB(2) 208/08-09(05), November 2008). URL: www.legco.gov.hk/yr08-09/english/panels/hs/papers/hs1110cb2-208-5-e.pdf

——, 'Legislative Council Panel on Health Services. Samaritan Fund' (CB(2)1640/11-12(03), April 2012). URL: www.legco.gov.hk/yr11-12/english/panels/hs/papers/hs0416cb2-1640-3-e.pdf

Food and Health Bureau, Health and Medical Development Advisory Committee, *Building a Healthy Tomorrow. Discussion Paper on the Future Service Delivery Model for our Healthcare System* (Hong Kong: SAR Government, 2005).

——, *Your Health Your Life: Healthcare Reform Consultation Document* (Hong Kong: SAR Government, 2008).

Government Secretariat, *Overall Review of the Hong Kong Education System: The Hong Kong Education System June 1981* (Hong Kong: Government Printer, 1982).

Harvard Team, *Improving Hong Kong's Health Care System: Why and For Whom?* (Hong Kong: Government Printer, 1999).

Health and Welfare Bureau, 'Legislative Council Panel on Welfare Services: Issues Arising from Review of the Comprehensive Social Security Assistance (CSSA) Scheme' (CB(2)2256/99-00(12), June 2000). URL: www.legco.gov.hk/yr99-00/english/panels/ws/papers/b2256e12[1].pdf

——, 'Legislative Council Panel on Welfare Services. "Promoting Self-reliance Strategy"' (CB(2) 1943/99-00(03), May 2000). URL: www.legco.gov.hk/yr99-00/english/panels/ws/papers/b1943e03.pdf

——, *Lifelong Investment in Health: Consultation Document on Healthcare* (Hong Kong: SAR Government, 2001). URL: www.fhb.gov.hk/en/press_and_publications/consultation/HCR1.HTM

Health, Welfare and Food Bureau, 'Progress Report on the Healthy Ageing Campaign' (CB(2)2280/03-04(03), May 2004). URL: www.legco.gov.hk/yr03-04/english/panels/ws/papers/ws0510cb2-2280-3e.pdf

Hong Kong Government, *A Problem of People* (Hong Kong: Government Printer, n.d.).

Hospital Authority, *Hospital Authority Annual Plan 2005–06*. URL: www.ha.org.hk/visitor/ha_view_content.asp?Parent_ID=300&Content_ID=126698&Lang=ENG

——, *Hospital Authority Annual Plan 2006–07*. URL: www.ha.org.hk/visitor/ha_view_content.asp?Parent_ID=300&Content_ID=131918&Lang=ENG

——, *Hospital Authority Annual Plan 2007–08*. URL: www.ha.org.hk/hesd/v2/AHA/ANP0708/HAAP0708_E_final.pdf

——, *Hospital Authority Annual Plan 2008–09*. URL: www.ha.org.hk/visitor/ha_visitor_index.asp?Parent_ID=100&Content_ID=300&Dimension=100&Lang=ENG

————, *Hospital Authority Annual Plan 2013–14: Keeping Healthcare in Sync.* URL: www.ha.org.hk/upload/publication_12/451.pdf

————, *Hospital Authority Statistical Report 1999–00.* URL: www.ha.org.hk/upload/publication_15/114.pdf

————, 'Mental Health Service Plan for Adults 2010–2015'. URL: www21.ha.org. hk/files/PDF/mental%20health%20platform/MentalHealthServicePlan_Pamphlet_ENG_Final.pdf

————, 'Modernization of Medical Equipment in the Hospital Authority' (CB(2)865/09-10(05), February 2010). URL: www.legco.gov.hk/yr09-10/english/panels/hs/papers/hs0208cb2-865-5-e.pdf

————, *Rising to the Challenge. Annual Plan 2000–2001* (Hong Kong: Hospital Authority, 2000), Vol. 1.

Housing Branch, *Homes for Hong Kong People: The Way Forward. Long Term Housing Strategy Review Document January 1997* (Hong Kong: Government Printer, 1997).

Housing Department, 'Information Paper for the Legislative Council Panel on Housing: Greater Private Sector Involvement in Housing Authority's Estate Management and Maintenance Services. 4th Report on the Progress of Implementation (November 2001 to April 2002)' (CB(1) 1947/01-02, May 2002). URL: www.legco.gov.hk/yr01-02/english/panels/hg/papers/hgcb1-1947-e.pdf

————, 'Panel on Housing: Greater Private Sector Involvement in Housing Authority Estate Management and Maintenance Services. Final Report on the Progress of Implementation (November 2002 to April 2003)' (CB(1) 1877/02-03, May 2003). URL: www.legco.gov.hk/yr02-03/english/panels/hg/papers/hgcb1-1877-e.pdf

ICAC, 'Landmark Cases: 26 Public Housing Blocks Case'. URL: www.icac.org.hk/new_icac/eng/cases/26p/26p.htm

Labour and Welfare Bureau, 'LegCo Panel on Welfare Services Subcommittee on Elderly Services Residential Care Services for the Elderly' (CB(2)835/07-08(01), January 2008). URL: www.legco.gov.hk/yr07-08/english/panels/ws/ws_els/papers/ws_els0122cb2-835-1-e.pdf

————, 'Legislative Council Panel on Welfare Services: Definition of Poverty' (CB(2)179/09-10(07), November 2009). URL: www.legco.gov.hk/yr09-10/english/panels/ws/papers/ws1109cb2-179-7-e.pdf

————, 'Legislative Council Panel on Welfare Services. Pilot Scheme on Home Care Services for Frail Elders' (CB(2)1010/09-10(03), March 2010). URL: www.legco.gov.hk/yr09-10/english/panels/ws/papers/ws0308cb2-1010-3-e.pdf

————, 'Legislative Council Panel on Welfare Services. Provision of Subsidised Residential Care Services for the Elderly' (CB(2)2509/11-12(01), July 2012). URL: www.legco.gov.hk/yr11-12/english/panels/ws/papers/ws0710cb2-2509-1-e.pdf

Labour and Welfare Bureau and Social Welfare Department, 'Legco Panel on Welfare Services, Subcommittee on Poverty Alleviation. Government's Response to the Report of Subcommittee on Review of the Comprehensive Social Security Assistance Scheme' (CB(2)974/08-09(01), February 2009).

URL: www.legco.gov.hk/yr08-09/english/panels/ws/ws_pa/papers/ws_pa 0305cb2-974-1-e.pdf

Lam Cheng Yuet-ngor, Carrie, Director of Social Welfare, 'Role of Welfare in a Laissez-faire Society', speech to the Hong Kong Democratic Foundation (18 April 2001). URL: www.hkdf.org/newsarticles.asp?show=newsarticles&news article=120

LegCo Panel on Housing, 'Minutes of Meeting . . . 17 October 2000' (CB(1) 121/00-01, 4 November 2000). URL: www.legco.gov.hk/yr00-01/english/ panels/hg/minutes/hg171000.pdf

———, 'Updated Background Brief on Land Supply for Housing (Position as at 25 July 2011)' (CB(1) 2805/10-11(01), 25 July 2011). URL: www.legco.gov. hk/yr10-11/english/panels/hg/papers/hg0726cb1-2805-1-e.pdf

———, 'Updated Background Brief on Regulation of Sales of First-hand Private Residential Properties (Position as at 29 March 2011)' (CB(1) 1738/10-11(04), 29 March 2011). URL: www.legco.gov.hk/yr10-11/english/panels/ hg/papers/hg0404cb1-1738-4-e.pdf

Subcommittee on Long Term Housing Strategy Review, 'Minutes of Meeting . . . 20 February 1997' (CB(1) 1317/96-97, 17 April 1997). URL: www.legco.gov.hk/yr96-97/english/panels/hg/lthsr/minutes/lt200297 .htm

———, 'Minutes of Meeting . . . 9 April 1997' (CB(1) 1518/96-97, 9 May 1997). URL: www.legco.gov.hk/yr96-97/english/panels/hg/lthsr/minutes/lt090497 .htm#E10E1

———, 'Minutes of Meeting . . . 22 April 1997' (CB1/PS/10/95/1, 11 June 1997). URL: www.legco.gov.hk/yr96-97/english/panels/hg/lthsr/minutes/ lt220497.htm

———, 'Minutes of Meeting . . . 24 April 1997' (CB(1) 1519/96-97, 9 May 1997). URL: www.legco.gov.hk/yr96-97/english/panels/hg/lthsr/minutes/ lt240497.htm

———, 'Minutes of Meeting . . . 13 May 1997' (CB(1) 1830/96-97, 11 June 1997). URL: www.legco.gov.hk/yr96-97/english/panels/hg/lthsr/minutes/ lt130597.htm

Legislative Council Panel on Development, 'Subcommittee on Building Safety and Related Issues: Measures to Enhance Building Safety in Hong Kong' (Development Bureau, CB(1)681/10-11(01) December 2010), 1–3. URL: www.legco.gov.hk/yr10-11/english/panels/dev/dev_bs/papers/dev_ bs0113cb1-681-1-e.pdf

———, 'Minutes of Special Meeting . . . 14 October 2011' (CB(1)798/11-12, 12 January 2012). URL: www.legco.gov.hk/yr11-12/english/panels/dev/ minutes/dev20111014.pdf

Legislative Council Secretariat, 'Background Brief on Funding Schemes for Small and Medium Enterprises' (CB(1)1873/06-07(03), 11 June 2007). URL: www. legco.gov.hk/yr06-07/english/panels/ci/papers/ci0612cb1-1873-3-e.pdf

———, 'Finance Committee of the Legislative Council: Minutes of the 5th Meeting . . . 30 October 2012' (FC77/12-13, 20 December 2012). URL: www.legco.gov.hk/yr12-13/english/fc/fc/minutes/fc20121030.pdf

————, 'Finance Committee of the Legislative Council Minutes of the 7th Meeting . . . 16 December 2011 (FC70/11-12, 16 March 2012). URL: http://www.legco.gov.hk/yr11-12/english/fc/fc/minutes/fc20111216.pdf

————, 'Grant for the Samaritan Fund' (CB(2)208/08-09(06), 7 November 2008). URL: www.legco.gov.hk/yr08-09/english/panels/hs/papers/hs1110cb2-20 8-6-e.pdf

————, 'Long-term Social Welfare Planning' (CB(2)1216/10-11(08), 8 March 2011). URL: www.legco.gov.hk/yr10-11/english/panels/ws/papers/ws0314 cb2-1216-8-e.pdf

————, 'Panel on Education. Implementation of the New Academic Structure' (CB(2)1694/11-12(05), 17 April 2012). URL: www.legco.gov.hk/yr11-12/english/panels/ed/papers/ed0420cb2-1694-5-e.pdf

————, 'Panel on Welfare Services. Minutes of Meeting Held on Monday, 14 January 2008 . . . ' (CB(2)976/07-08, 13 February 2008). URL: www.legco.gov.hk/yr07-08/english/panels/ws/minutes/ws080114.pdf

————, 'Pilot Scheme on Home Care Services for Persons with Severe Disabilities' (CB(2)1986/09-10(03), 7 July 2010). URL: www.legco.gov.hk/yr09-10/english/panels/ws/ws_rccs/papers/ws_rccs0713cb2-1986-3-e.pdf

————, 'Provision of Residential Care Places for Persons with Disabilities' (CB(2)1149/09-10(02), 23 March 2010). URL: www.legco.gov.hk/yr09-10/english/panels/ws/ws_rccs/papers/ws_rccs0329cb2-1149-2-e.pdf

————, 'Provision of Subsidised Community Care Services for Persons with Disabilities' (CB(2)1618/09-10(02), 25 May 2010). URL: www.legco.gov.hk/yr09-10/english/panels/ws/ws_rccs/papers/ws_rccs0531cb2-1618-2-e.pdf

————, 'Report of the Panel on Education for Submission to the Legislative Council' (CB(2)2417/07-08, 27 June 2008). URL: www.legco.gov.hk/yr07-08/english/panels/ed/papers/ed_ppr.htm

————, 'Report of the Panel on Welfare Services for submission to the Legislative Council' (CB(2)2468/11-12, 4 July 2012). URL: http://www.legco.gov.hk/yr11-12/english/panels/ws/reports/ws0711cb2-2468-e.pdf

————, 'Short-term Food Assistance' (CB(2)248/11-12(04), 8 November 2011). URL: www.legco.gov.hk/yr11-12/english/panels/ws/papers/ws1114cb2-24 8-4-e.pdf

————, 'The Samaritan Fund' (CB(2)1640/11-12(04), 10 April 2012). URL: www.legco.gov.hk/yr11-12/english/panels/hs/papers/hs0416cb2-1640-4-e. pdf

————, 'Updated Background Brief . . . Medium of Instruction for Secondary Schools' (CB(2)623/08-09(07), 8 July 2009). URL: www.legco.gov.hk/yr08-09/english/panels/ed/papers/ed0711cb2-2122-7-e.pdf

————, 'Welfare Services Panel. Minutes of Special Meeting' (CB(2)2545/08-09, 29 July 2009). URL: http://legco.gov.hk/yr08-09/english/panels/ws/minutes/ws20090729.pdf

————, 'Youth Hostel Scheme' (CB(2)612/12-13(07), 7 February 2013). URL: www.legco.gov.hk/yr12-13/english/panels/ha/papers/ha0218cb2-612-7-e. pdf

Leung Chun-ying, 'Seek Change Maintain Stability Serve the People with Pragmatism. Report on the Work of the Current-term Government in its

First Year June 2013.' URL: http://www.ceo.gov.hk/eng/report-yearone/files/Year1_Full.pdf

Li, Simon, 'Information Note. Causes of Poverty in Hong Kong: A Literature Review' (Research and Library Services Division, IN16/04-05, 10 January 2005). URL: www.legco.gov.hk/yr04-05/english/sec/library/0405in16e.pdf

Liu, Eva et al., *Supply of Flats* (Research and Library Services Division, RP09/96-97, 3 April 1997), URL: www.legco.gov.hk/yr97-98/english/sec/library/967rp09.pdf

Lump Sum Grant Independent Review Committee, 'Review Report on the Lump Sum Grant Subvention System December 2008' URL: www.swd.gov.hk/doc/ngo/(5)-Report%20eng.pdf

Market Research Division, 'Survey of the Financing Situation of Small and Medium-Sized Enterprises', *Hong Kong Monetary Authority Quarterly Report* (October 2000), 33–8.

MDR, 'Survey of Housing Aspirations of Households (1999) Prepared for Planning Department. Executive Summary' (Hong Kong: 1999).

Miller, Tony, Director of Housing, 'Becoming Stakeholders of Hong Kong: Home Ownership', speech to the Hong Kong Institute of Real Estate Administration (19 February 1997). URL: www.housingauthority.gov.hk/en/about-us/news-centre/speeches/1435.html

NDRC, *The Outline of the Plan for the Reform and Development of the Pearl River Delta (2008–2020)*. URL: http://en.ndrc.gov.cn/policyrelease/P020090120342179907030.doc

Ng, Shu-ming, Tony, et al., 'Chapter 7: Education and Manpower Bureau: Planning and Provision of Public Secondary School Places' (Hong Kong: Audit Commission, 18 October 2003). URL: www.aud.gov.hk/pdf_e/e41ch07.pdf

OFTA, *Report on the Effectiveness of Competition in Hong Kong's Telecommunications Market: An International Comparison June 2003* (Hong Kong: Spectrum Strategy Consultants, 2003). URL: http://tel_archives.ofca.gov.hk/en/report-paper-guide/report/rp20030620.pdf

Planning and Lands Bureau, *People First — A Caring Approach to Urban Renewal. Urban Renewal Strategy* (Consultation Paper, July 2001). URL: www.devb.gov.hk/en/publications_and_press_releases/press/index_id_1600.htm

Planning, Environment and Lands Branch, *Report of the Task Force on Land Supply and Property Prices* (June 1994).

Rating and Valuation Department, 'Property Market Statistics Private Domestic — Average Prices by Class (from 1982)'. URL: www.rvd.gov.hk/en/doc/statistics/his_data_2.xls

Security Bureau, 'Proposals to Implement Article 23 of the Basic Law. Consultation Document' (Hong Kong, September 2002). URL: www.info.gov.hk/archive/consult/2002/bl23-e.pdf

Select Committee on Building Problems of Public Housing Units, *First Report January 2003: Volume I Main Report* (Hong Kong: Legislative Council, 2003).

Social Welfare Advisory Committee, 'Long-term Social Welfare Planning in Hong Kong Consultation Paper' (April 2010). URL: www.swac.org.hk/documents/SWAC%20Consultation%20Paper%20%28Eng%29.pdf

————, 'Report on Long-term Social Welfare Planning in Hong Kong' (July 2011). http://www.lwb.gov.hk/download/committees/swac/SWAC_consultation_report_Eng.pdf

Social Welfare Department, 'Joint Subcommittee on Long-term Care Policy Day Care and Community Support Services for Persons with Disabilities' (CB(2)992/12-13(01), April 2013). URL: www.legco.gov.hk/yr12-13/english/panels/ltcp/papers/ltcp0423cb2-992-1-e.pdf

————, 'Legislative Council Panel on Welfare Services Two New Integrated Rehabilitation Services Centres for Persons with Disabilities' (CB(2)254/07-08(04), November 2007). URL: www.legco.gov.hk/yr07-08/english/panels/ws/papers/ws1112cb2-254-4-e.pdf

————, 'Report on Review of the Comprehensive Social Security Assistance Scheme' (December 1998). URL: www.swd.gov.hk/doc/pubctn_en/sfsr.doc

————, 'The Five Year Plan for Social Welfare Development in Hong Kong — Review 1998'. URL: www.swd.gov.hk/doc/pubctn_ch/e5yrplan.pdf

Steering Committee on Review of the Urban Renewal Strategy, 'Report on the Building Conditions Survey' (SC Paper No. 18/2009, 30 June 2009). URL: www.ursreview.gov.hk/eng/doc/SC paper 18-2009 Progress Report on Building Conditions ENG.pdf

Task Force of Social Welfare Planning, 'Planning Mechanism and Protocol of Social Welfare Policy (Discussion Paper)' (Hong Kong Council of Social Service, 12 July 2000). URL: www.hkcss.org.hk/er/SvcPlan.doc

Trade and Industry Bureau, *Government Response to Consumer Council's Report Entitled "Competition Policy: The Key to Hong Kong's Future Economic Success"* (November 1997).

Transport and Housing Bureau, 'Legislative Council Panel on Housing: Housing-related Initiatives in the 2007–08 Policy Agenda' (CB(1)36/07-08(01), October 2007). URL: www.legco.gov.hk/yr07-08/english/panels/hg/papers/hg1022cb1-36-1-e[1].pdf.

————, 'Panel on Housing, Subcommittee on the Long Term Housing Strategy. Measures to Maximize the Rational Use of Public Rental Housing Resources' (CB(1)600/12-13(03), February 2013). URL: www.legco.gov.hk/yr12-13/english/panels/hg/hg_lths/papers/hg_lths0227cb1-600-3-e.pd

————, 'Report on Public Consultation on Subsidising Home Ownership' (October 2010). URL: www.thb.gov.hk/eng/policy/housing/policy/consultation/con_report1005.pdf

University Grants Committee, *Aspirations for the Higher Education System in Hong Kong Report of the University Grants Committee* (Hong Kong, 2010). URL: www.ugc.edu.hk/eng/doc/ugc/publication/report/her2010/her2010-rpt.pdf

Visiting Panel, *A Perspective on Education in Hong Kong November 1982* (Hong Kong: Government Printer, 1983).

Williams, Gertrude, *Report on the Feasibility of a Survey into Social Welfare Provisions and Allied Topics in Hong Kong* (Hong Kong: Government Printer, n.d.).

Wong, Diana, 'Subdivided Flats in Hong Kong: Information Note' (IN22/12-13, 28 May 2013). URL: www.legco.gov.hk/yr12-13/english/sec/library/1213in22-e.pdf

Wong, Dominic Shing-wah, Secretary for Housing, 'LegCo Panel on Housing. Minutes of Meeting . . . 17 October 2000' (CB(1) 121/00-01, 4 November 2000). URL: www.legco.gov.hk/yr00-01/english/panels/hg/minutes/ hg171000.pdf

Yang, Qinquan, and Jiang Zhiyuan, Guangzhou Party Propaganda Department, 'Analysis of the Results of Guangzhou's Foreign Economic Cooperation and Future Strategy', *Guangzhou Yanjiu*, No. 5 (September–October 1985), 35–7.

Yip, Kirk (Food and Health Bureau), Letter to Mary So (Panel on Health services), 'Modernization of Medical Equipment in the Hospital Authority', FH/H/1/5, 9 April 2010. URL: www.legco.gov.hk/yr09-10/english/panels/ hs/papers/hs0208cb2-1282-1-e.pdf

Government-Sponsored Research Publications

Chow, Nelson, and Terry Lum, 'Trends in Family Attitudes and Values in Hong Kong: Final Report', Department of Social Work and Social Administration, University of Hong Kong (Central Policy Unit, 22 August 2008). URL: www. cpu.gov.hk/english/documents/new/press/20080822%20Trends%20 in%20family%20attitudes%20and%20values%20in%20Hong%20Kong.pdf

Chui, Ernest Wing-tak, et al., *Elderly Commission's Study on Residential Care Services for the Elderly Final Report* (Hong Kong: University of Hong Kong, December 2009). URL: www.legco.gov.hk/yr09-10/english/panels/ws/papers/ws0111cb2-66 8-3-e.pdf

Hong Kong Policy Research Institute Ltd, 'A Study on Tripartite Partnership: Benchmarking Study from an International Perspective: Final Report' (Central Policy Unit, October 2005). URL: www.cpu.gov.hk/english/docu- ments/new/press/Benchmarking%20study%20%28English%29.pdf

Public Policy Research Centre, *Low-Wage Workers in Hong Kong: Final Report*. Hong Kong Institute of Asia-Pacific Studies, Chinese University of Hong Kong (Central Policy Unit, September 2008) URL:URL: www.cpu.gov.hk/ english/documents/new/press/20080901%20Low-wage%20worker%20 in%20Hong%20Kong.pdf

Tang, Kwong Leung, et al., 'Social Enterprises in Hong Kong: Toward a Conceptual Model. Final Report' (Central Policy Unit, April 2008). URL: www.cpu.gov.hk/english/documents/new/press/20080421%20Social%20 Enterprises%20in%20Hong%20Kong.pdf

Wu, Xiaogang, 'Hong Kong's Post 80s Generation: Profiles and Predicaments. A CPU Commissioned Report', Centre for Applied Social and Economic Research, Hong Kong University of Science and Technology (Central Policy Unit, May 2010). URL: www.cpu.gov.hk/english/documents/new/press/ HK%27s%20Post%2080s%20Generation%20-%20Profiles%20and%20 Predicaments.pdf

Books and Monographs

Bristow, Roger, *Hong Kong's New Towns: A Selective Review* (Hong Kong: Oxford University Press, 1989).

Burns, John P., *Government Capacity and the Hong Kong Civil Service* (Hong Kong: Oxford University Press, 2004).

Castells, M., et al., *The Shek Kip Mei Syndrome: Economic Development and Public Housing in Hong Kong and Singapore* (London: Pion Limited, 1990).

Chan, Chak Kwan, *Social Security Policy in Hong Kong: From British Colony to China's Special Administrative Region* (Lanham: Lexington Books, 2011).

Chan, Raymond K. H., *Welfare in Newly-Industrialised Society: The Construction of the Welfare State in Hong Kong* (Aldershot: Avebury, 1996).

Chaney, David C., and David B. L. Podmore, *Young Adults in Hong Kong: Attitudes in a Modernizing Society* (Hong Kong: Centre of Asian Studies, University of Hong Kong, 1973).

Cheung, Anthony Bing-leung, and Kin-sheun Louie, *Social Conflicts in Hong Kong, 1975–1986: Trends and Implications* (Hong Kong: Hong Kong Institute of Asia-Pacific Studies, Chinese University of Hong Kong, 1991).

Cheung, Gary Ka-wai, *Hong Kong's Watershed: The 1967 Riots* (Hong Kong: Hong Kong University Press, 2009).

Consumer Council, *Competition Policy: The Key to Hong Kong's Future Economic Success* (Hong Kong: Consumer Council, 1996).

———, *How Competitive Is the Private Residential Property Market?* (Hong Kong: Consumer Council, 1996).

Dodsworth, John, and Dubravko Mihaljek, *Hong Kong, China: Growth, Structural Change, and Economic Stability During the Transition* (Washington: International Monetary Fund, 1997).

Emmons, Charles F., *Hong Kong Prepares for 1997: Politics and Emigration in 1997* (Hong Kong: Centre of Asian Studies, University of Hong Kong, 1988).

England, Joe, and John Rear, *Industrial Relations and Law in Hong Kong* (Hong Kong: Oxford University Press, 1981).

Enright, Michael J., et al., *The Hong Kong Advantage* (Hong Kong: Oxford University Press, 1997).

Gauld, Robin, and Derek Gould, *The Hong Kong Health Sector: Development and Change* (Hong Kong: Chinese University Press, 2002).

Ghai, Yash, *Hong Kong's New Constitutional Order: The Resumption of Chinese Sovereignty and the Basic Law* (Hong Kong: Hong Kong University Press, 1997).

Goodhart, Charles, and Lu Dai, *Intervention to Save Hong Kong: Counter-Speculation in Financial Markets* (Oxford: Oxford University Press, 2003).

Goodstadt, Leo F., *Profits, Politics and Panics: Hong Kong's Banks and the Making of a Miracle Economy, 1935–1985* (Hong Kong: Hong Kong University Press, 2007).

———, *Uneasy Partners: The Conflict between Public Interest and Private Profit in Hong Kong* (Hong Kong: Hong Kong University Press, 2009), second edition.

Grant, C., and P. Yuen, *The Hong Kong Health Care System* (Sydney: University of New South Wales, 1998).

Hay, Joel W., *Health Care in Hong Kong: An Economic Policy Assessment* (Hong Kong: Chinese University Press, 1991).

Hayek, F. A., *New Studies in Philosophy, Politics, Economics and the History of Ideas* (London: Routledge and Kegan Paul, 1985).

Heilbroner, Robert, *Twenty-First Century Capitalism* (London: UCL Press, 1993).

Ho, Lok Sang, *Health Care Delivery and Financing in Hong Kong* (Hong Kong: City University of Hong Kong Press, 1997).

Hong Kong Society for Rehabilitation, *The Rebirth of the Phoenix: Fifty Years in Serving People with Disabilities* (Hong Kong: Hong Kong Society for Rehabilitation, 2010).

Huque, Ahmed Shafiqul, et al., *The Civil Service in Hong Kong: Continuity and Change* (Hong Kong: Hong Kong University Press, 1998).

Jones, Catherine, *Promoting Prosperity: The Hong Kong Way of Social Policy* (Hong Kong: Chinese University Press, 1990).

Lam, S. F., and Nina Lam, *HKU Undergraduates of '46: Their Untold Stories* (Hong Kong: n.p., n.d.).

Lau, Chi Kuen, *Hong Kong's Colonial Legacy* (Hong Kong: Chinese University Press, 1997).

Lau, Siu-kai, *Society and Politics in Hong Kong* (Hong Kong: Chinese University Press, 1982).

Lau, Siu-kai, and Kuan Hsin-chi, *The Ethos of the Hong Kong Chinese* (Hong Kong: Chinese University Press, 1988).

Lau, Siu-kai, and Wan Po-san, *Social Conflicts in Hong Kong 1987–1995* (Hong Kong: Hong Kong Institute of Asia-Pacific Studies, Chinese University of Hong Kong, 1997).

Lee, Jick-Joen, *The Road to the Development of Social Welfare in Hong Kong: The Historical Key Issues* (Hong Kong: Hong Kong Institute of Asia-Pacific Studies, Chinese University of Hong Kong, 1996).

Leung, Benjamin K. P., *Perspectives on Hong Kong Society* (Hong Kong: Oxford University Press, 1996).

Li, Kui-Wai, *The Hong Kong Economy: Recovery and Restructuring* (Singapore: McGraw-Hill Education (Asia), 2006).

Littlewood, Michael, *Taxation without Representation: The History of Hong Kong's Troublingly Successful Tax System* (Hong Kong: Hong Kong University Press, 2010).

Lo, Sonny Shiu-Hing, *The Dynamics of Beijing-Hong Kong Relations: A Model for Taiwan?* (Hong Kong: Hong Kong University Press, 2008).

Lui, Hon-Kwong, *Income Inequality and Economic Development* (Hong Kong: City University of Hong Kong Press, 1997).

Lui, Tai Lok, and Wong Hung, *Disempowerment and Empowerment: An Exploratory Study on Low-income Households in Hong Kong* (Hong Kong: Oxfam, 1995).

Ma, Ronald, and Edward F. Szczepanik, *The National Income of Hong Kong 1947–1950* (Hong Kong: Hong Kong University Press, 1955).

McGuinness, Paul B., *A Guide to the Equity Markets of Hong Kong* (Hong Kong: Oxford University Press, 1999).

Mihaljek, Dubravko, et al., *People's Republic of China — Hong Kong Special Administrative Region: Recent Economic Developments* (Washington: International Monetary Fund, 1998).

Pepper, Suzanne, *Keeping Democracy at Bay: Hong Kong and the Challenge of Chinese Political Reform* (Lanham: Rowman & Littlefield Publishers, Inc., 2008).

Phillips, David R., *The Epidemiological Transition in Hong Kong: Changes in Health and Disease since the Nineteenth Century* (Hong Kong: Centre of Asian Studies, University of Hong Kong, 1988).

Shao, Wenguang, *China, Britain and Businessmen: Political and Commercial Relations, 1949–57* (Basingstoke: Macmillan, 1991).

Snape, Ed, and Andy Chan, 'Hong Kong Trade Unions: In Search of a Role', in Patricia Fosh et al., *Hong Kong Management and Labour: Change and continuity* (London: Routledge, 1999).

UN-Habitat, *The State of the World's Cities Report 2006/2007: 30 Years of Shaping the Habitat Agenda* (London: Earthscan, 2006).

———, *State of the World's Cities 2008/2009 Harmonious Cities* (London: Earthscan, 2008).

Wong, Hung, and Chua Hoi Wai, *Research on Expenditure Pattern of Low Expenditure Households in Hong Kong* (Hong Kong: Hong Kong Council of Social Service, 1996).

Wong, Victor C. W., *The Political Economy of Health Care Development and Reforms in Hong Kong* (Aldershot: Ashgate, 1999).

Yeung, Henry Wai-chung, *Transnational Corporations and Business Networks: Hong Kong Firms in the Asian Region* (London: Routledge, 1998).

Articles, Essays and Working Papers

Abbott, Andrew, and Stanley DeViney, 'The Welfare State as Transnational Event: Evidence from Sequences of Policy Adoption', *Social Science History*, Vol. 16, No. 2 (Summer 1992), 245–74.

Barnett, K. M. A., Census Commissioner, 'Introduction', in W. F. Maunder, *Hong Kong Urban Rents and Housing* (Hong Kong: Hong Kong University Press, 1969).

Bibby, Andrew, 'Responsible Contracting: An Approach Aimed at Improving Social and Labour Practices in the Property Services Sector', Working Paper No. 282 (Geneva: International Labour Office, 2011). URL: www.ilo.org/wcmsp5/groups/public/ed_dialogue/sector/documents/publication/wcms_172950.pdf

Bosworth, Barry P., and Susan M. Collins, 'The Empirics of Growth: An Update', *Brookings Papers on Economic Activity*, Vol. 2003, No. 2 (2003).

Brewer, Brian, and Stewart MacPherson, 'Poverty and Social Security', in Paul Wilding et al. (eds.), *Social Policy in Hong Kong* (Cheltenham: Edward Elgar, 1997).

Burns, John P., 'Civil Service Systems in Transition: Hong Kong, China and 1997', in Ming K. Chan (ed.), *The Challenge of Hong Kong's Reintegration With China* (Hong Kong: Hong Kong University Press, 1997).

Cain, Frank M., 'Exporting the Cold War: British Responses to the USA's Establishment of COCOM, 1947–51', *Journal of Contemporary History*, Vol. 29, No. 3 (July 1994), 501–22.

Chan, Chak-Kwan, 'Welfare Policies and the Construction of Welfare Relations in a Residual Welfare State: The Case of Hong Kong', *Social Policy & Administration*, Vol. 32, No. 3 (September 1998), 278–91.

Chan, Chris King-chi, 'Labour Policies under Hu-Wen's Regime: Transformation and Challenges', in Joseph Y. S. Cheng (ed.), *China: A New Stage of Development for an Emerging Superpower* (Hong Kong: City University of Hong Kong Press, 2012).

Chan, Elaine Y. M., 'Civil Society', in Lam Wai-man et al. (eds.), *Contemporary Hong Kong Government and Politics* (Hong Kong: Hong Kong University Press, 2012), second edition.

Chan, Ming K., 'Under China's Shadow: Realpolitik of Hong Kong Labour Unionism toward 1997', in Charles Burton (ed.), *Politics and Society in Hong Kong towards 1997* (Toronto: Joint Centre for Asia Pacific Studies, 1992).

Chao, Kang, 'Industrialization and Urban Housing in Communist China', *Journal of Asian Studies*, Vol. 25, No. 3 (May 1966), 381–96.

Chau, Kenneth L., and Chack-kie Wong, 'The Social Welfare Reform: A Way to Reduce Public Burden', in Lau Siu-kai (ed.), *The First Tung Chee-hwa Administration: The First Five Years of the Hong Kong Special Administrative Region* (Hong Kong: Chinese University Press, 2003).

Cheng, Chak Hung J., and Michael K. Salemi, 'Feast and Famine: Explaining Big Swings in the Hong Kong Economy between 1981 and 2007', *HKIMR Working Paper No. 37/2009* (December 2009).

Cheng, Joseph Y. S., 'Goals of Government Expenditure in a Laissez-Faire Economy: Hong Kong in the 1970s', *Asian Survey*, Vol. 19, No. 7 (July 1979), 695–706.

———, 'Introduction', in Joseph Y. S. Cheng (ed.), *Hong Kong in Transition* (Hong Kong: Oxford University Press, 1986).

———, 'Towards the Establishment of a New Order', in Beatrice Leung and Joseph Cheng (eds.), *Hong Kong SAR: In Pursuit of Domestic and International Order* (Hong Kong: Chinese University Press, 1997).

Cheng, Kai Ming, 'Educational Policymaking in Hong Kong: The Changing Legitimacy', in Gerard A. Postiglione (ed.), *Education and Society in Hong Kong: Toward One Country and Two Systems* (Armonk: M. E. Sharpe, Inc., 1991).

———, 'Financing Education: An International Perspective', in Yue-ping Chung and Richard Yu-chim Wong (eds.), *The Economics and Financing of Hong Kong Education* (Hong Kong: Chinese University Press, 1992).

———, 'The Policy Making Process', in Gerard A. Postiglione and Wing On Lee (eds.), *Schooling in Hong Kong: Organization, Teaching and Social Context* (Hong Kong: Hong University Press, 1997).

Cheng, Leonard K., 'Strategies for Rapid Economic Development: The Case of Hong Kong', *Contemporary Economic Policy*, Vol. 13. No. 1 (January, 1995), 28–37.

Cheng Yiu-tong, 'The Role of a Trade Union Centre in a Changing Society: The Case of the Hong Kong Federation of Trade Unions', in Y. C. Jao et al. (eds.), *Labour Movement in a Changing Society* (Hong Kong: Centre of Asian Studies, University of Hong Kong, 1988).

Cheung, Anthony B. L., 'Civil Service Reform in Post-1997 Hong Kong: Political Challenges, Managerial Responses?', *International Journal of Public Administration*, Vol. 24, Issue 9 (2001), 929–50.

———, 'Medical and Health', in Donald H. MacMillen and Man Si-wai (eds.), *The Other Hong Kong Report 1994* (Hong Kong: Chinese University Press, 1994).

Cheung, Anthony B. L., and Kin-sheun Louie, 'Social Conflicts in Hong Kong: 1975–1986', in Lau Siu-kai (ed.), *Social Development and Political Change in Hong Kong* (Hong Kong: Chinese University Press, 2000).

Chiu, Fred Y. L., 'Politics and the Body Social in Colonial Hong Kong', in Tani E. Barlow (ed.), *Formations of Colonial Modernity in East Asia* (Durham: Duke University Press, 1997).

Chiu, Sammy W. S., 'Social Welfare', in Nyaw Mee-kau and Li Si-ming (eds.), *The Other Hong Kong Report 1996* (Hong Kong: Chinese University Press, 1996).

Chou, Kee-lee, 'HKIEd Study: Disparity in Higher Education Attainment Is Widening between Rich and Poor', Hong Kong Institute of Education (31 January 2013). URL: www.ied.edu.hk/media/news.php?id=20130131

Chow, Nelson W. S., 'Review of Social Policies', in Alex Y. H. Kwan and David K. K. Chan (eds.), *Hong Kong Society: A Reader* (Hong Kong Writers' and Publishers' Cooperative, 1986).

———, 'Social Welfare and the Challenges of a New Era', in Wong Siu-lun and Toyojiro Maruya (eds.), *Hong Kong Economy and Society: Challenges in the New Era* (Hong Kong: Centre of Asian Studies, University of Hong Kong, 1998).

———, 'Social Welfare', in Larry Chuen-ho Chow and Yiu-kwan Fan (eds.), *The Other Hong Kong Report 1998* (Hong Kong: Chinese University Press, 1999).

Choy, Ivan Chi-keung, 'Political Parties and Political Participation in Hong Kong', in Joseph Y. S. Cheng (ed.), *Political Participation in Hong Kong: Theoretical Issues and Historical Legacy* (Hong Kong: City University of Hong Kong Press, 1999).

Chui, Ernest Wing-tak, 'The 1995 Legislative Council Election: Inefficacious Opposition Characterized by Fragmentation', in Kuan Hsin-chi et al. (eds.), *The 1995 Legislative Council Elections in Hong Kong* (Hong Kong: Hong Kong Institute of Asia-Pacific Studies, Chinese University of Hong Kong, 1996).

Chui, Ernest, and Mel Gray, 'The Political Activities of Social Workers in the Context of Changing Roles and Political Transition in Hong Kong', *International Journal of Social Welfare*, Vol. 13 (2004), 170–80.

CIVICUS, 'The Hong Kong Special Administrative Region: A Vibrant but Loosely Organised Civil Society. Civil Society Index Report for the Hong Kong Special Administrative Region, PRC' (2006). URL: www.civicus.org/new/media/CSI_HongKong_Country_Report.pdf

Claessens, Stijin, and Simeon Djankov, 'Publicly-Listed East Asian Corporates: Growth, Financing and Risks', paper presented to the Regional Conference on Asian Corporate Recovery: Corporate Governance, Government Policy (World Bank, 15 March 1999).

DeGolyer, Michael E., and Janet Lee Scott, 'The Myth of Political Apathy in Hong Kong', *Annals*, Volume 547 (September 1996), 68–78.

Federation of Hong Kong Industry, 'Hong Kong Enterprises in the Pearl River Delta: Current Situation and Future Prospects' (《珠三角港資企業現況與前景 問卷調查報告》), Survey Report, 2012. URL: www.industryhk.org/english/fp/fp_res/files/Current%20Situation%20and%20Prospect%20of%20HK%20Manufacturing%20Companies%20in%20the%20PRD%20_2012.pdf

———, 'The Pearl River Delta: Hong Kong business Executives' Current Drive to Transform and Upgrade' (《珠三角港商轉型升級已是大勢所趨》), press release, 23 May 2012. URL: www.industryhk.org/english/news/news_press/pr_120523_015.php

Godwin, Chris D., Principal Assistant Secretary, Education and Manpower Branch, 'Pilot Study One: The School Education Programme: Redefining the Relationship between Policy Branch and Department', in Jane C. Y. Lee and Anthony B. L. Cheung (eds.), *Public Sector Reform in Hong Kong: Key Concepts, Progress-to-Date and Future Directions* (Hong Kong: Chinese University Press, 1995).

Goodstadt, Leo F., 'Crisis and Challenge: The Changing Role of the Hongkong & Shanghai Bank, 1950–2000', *HKIMR Working Paper No.13/2005*, July 2005.

———, 'Dangerous Business Models: Bankers, Bureaucrats and Hong Kong's Economic Transformation, 1948–86', *HKIMR Working Paper No.8/2006*, June 2006.

———, 'Painful Transitions: The Impact of Economic Growth and Government Policies on Hong Kong's "Chinese" Banks, 1945–70', *HKIMR Working Paper No. 16/2006*, November 2006.

———, 'The Rise and Fall of Social, Economic and Political Reforms in Hong Kong, 1930–1955', *Journal of the Royal Asiatic Society Hong Kong Branch*, Vol. 44 (2004), 57–81.

———, 'Urban Housing in Hong Kong, 1945–63', in in I. C. Jarvie (ed.), *Hong Kong: A Society in Transition* (London: Routlege and Kegan Paul, 1969).

Ho, Kin-chung, 'The Environment after 1997', in Joseph Y. S. Cheng (ed.), *The Hong Kong Special Administrative Region in Its First Decade* (Hong Kong: City University of Hong Kong Press, 2007).

Ho, Lok-sang, 'Housing as a Mover of the Domestic Economy', in Joseph Y. S. Cheng (ed.), *The July 1 Protest Rally: Interpreting a Historic Event* (Hong Kong: City University of Hong Kong Press, 2005).

———, 'Policy Blunder of the Century Threatens Hong Kong's Economic Future', in Lau Siu-kai (ed.), *The Tung Chee-hwa Administration: The First Five Years of the Hong Kong Special Administrative Region* (Hong Kong: Chinese University Press, 2003).

Ho, Po-ying Amy, 'The Incubation of Social Entrepreneurship in Hong Kong', 2010 International Conference on Social Enterprises in Eastern Asia: Dynamic and Variations, Taipei (14 June 2010). URL: www.parc-jp.org/

solidarityeconomy/about/taiwan20100614/Po-ying%20Amy%20HO,%20
The%20Incubation%20of%20Entrepreneurship%20in%20Hong%20K.pdf
Hong Kong Council of Social Service, 'Report on Training Needs Analysis
for NGOs 2009–2010'. URL: www.hkcss.org.hk/institute/download/
TNA_20092010.pdf
——, 'Response to SWAC's 2nd Stage Consultation Exercise on Long Term
Social Welfare Planning in Hong Kong'. URL: www.hkcss.org.hk/ltwp/
download/HKCSS_LTSW_Planning_2nd_consult%20final.pdf
Hong Kong Institute of Asia-Pacific Studies, 'Summary of Survey of Hong Kong
People's Views on "Real Estate Hegemony"', 10 August 2011. URL: www.
cuhk.edu.hk/hkiaps/tellab/pdf/telepress/11/Press_Release20110810.pdf
Hong Kong Institute of Asia-Pacific Studies in Cooperation with the Hong
Kong Professionals and Senior Executives Association, 'Disparity of Wealth
Research Project Findings' (1 December 2011). URL: www.cuhk.edu.hk/
hkiaps/tellab/pdf/telepress/11/2011_12_01_Press_Conf.pdf
Hong Kong Trade Development Council Research, 'Economists' Pick', 5
September 2008. URL: www.hktdc.com/business-news/article/Economic-
Forum/Beyond-Cheap-Labour-Building-a-Competitive-Edge-through-
Adding-Value/ef/en/1/1X000000/1X0041HG.htm
Hong Kong Transition Project, 'Calm after the Storm? Hong Kong People
Respond to Reform' (Hong Kong Transition Project and National
Democratic Institute for International Affairs, October 2010). URL: www.
hktp.org/list/calm_after_the_storm_ndi_20.pdf
——, 'Parties, Policies and Political Reform in Hong Kong' (Hong Kong
Transition Project and National Democratic Institute for International
Affairs, May 2006). URL: www.hkbu.edu.hk/~hktp/NDI/NDIReport.pdf
——, 'Will the People Speak? And What Will They Say? Preparing to Go to the
Polls for the First SAR election' (May 1998). URL: http://hktp.hkbu.edu.
hk/may98/598brief.html
——, *Winter of Despair. Confidence and legitimacy in crisis in the Hong Kong SAR
(December 2001)* (Hong Kong: Hong Kong Baptist University, 2002).
Hu, Yueh, 'The Problem of the Hong Kong Refugees', *Asian Survey*, Vol. 2, No.
1 (March 1962), 28–37.
Huque, Ahmed Shafiqul, 'Understanding Hong Kong', in Paul Wilding et al.
(eds.), *Social Policy in Hong Kong* (Cheltenham: Edward Elgar, 1997).
Joint Committee of Hong Kong Secondary School Councils and Secondary
School Principals' Associations of 18 Districts, 'Executive Summary of
Report on Survey of the New Academic System' (CB(2)622/11-12(02), 11
November 2011). URL: www.legco.gov.hk/yr11-12/english/panels/ed/
papers/edcb2-622-2-e.pdf
Jones, John F., 'Introduction: Social Services at a Glance', in John F. Jones
(ed.), *The Common Welfare: Hong Kong's Social Services* (Hong Kong: Chinese
University Press, 1981).
Kearney, A. T., '2012 Global Cities Index and Emerging Cities Outlook' (2 April
2012). URL: www.atkearney.com/images/global/pdf/2012_Global_Cities_
Index_and_Emerging_Cities_Outlook-FINAL3.pdf

King, Ambrose Yeo-chi, 'Administrative Absorption of Politics in Hong Kong: Emphasis on the Grass Roots Level', in Ambrose Y. C. King and Rance P. L. Lee (eds.), *Social Life and Development in Hong Kong* (Hong Kong: Chinese University Press, 1981).

Kregel, J. A., 'Derivatives and Global Capital Flows: Applications to Asia', *Cambridge Journal of Economics*, Vol. 22, No. 6 (November 1998), 677–92.

La Grange, Adrienne, 'Housing (1997–2007)', in Joseph Y. S. Cheng (ed.), *The Hong Kong Special Administrative Region in Its First Decade* (Hong Kong: City University of Hong Kong Press, 2007).

Lam, Jermain T. M., 'Enhanced Productivity Program in Hong Kong: A Critical Appraisal', *Public Performance & Management Review*, Vol. 27, No. 1 (September, 2003), 53–70.

Lau, Siu-kai, 'Government and Political Change in the Hong Kong Special Administrative Region', in James C. Hsiung (ed.), *Hong Kong the Super Paradox: Life after Return to China* (London: Macmillan, 2000).

——, 'Political Reform and Political Development in Hong Kong: Dilemmas and Choices', in Y. C. Jao et al. (eds.), *Hong Kong and 1997: Strategies for the Future* (Hong Kong: Centre of Asian Studies, University of Hong Kong, 1985).

——, 'The Fraying of the Socio-economic Fabric of Hong Kong', *Pacific Review*, Vol. 10, No. 3 (1999), 426–41.

Lau, Siu-kai, and Wan Po-san, 'Social Conflicts in Hong Kong: 1987–1995', in Lau Siu-kai (ed.), *Social Development and Political Change in Hong Kong* (Hong Kong: Chinese University Press, 2000).

Lee, Ching-kwan, and Tak-sing Cheung, 'Egalitarianism and Secondary School Places in Hong Kong', in Gerard A. Postiglione (ed.), *Education and Society in Hong Kong: Toward One Country and Two Systems* (Armonk: M. E. Sharpe, Inc., 1991).

Lee, Eliza W. Y., 'Governing Post-Colonial Hong Kong: Institutional Incongruity, Governance Crisis, and Authoritarianism', *Asian Survey*, Vol. 39, No. 6 (November–December 1999), 940–59.

——, 'The Renegotiation of the Social Pact in Hong Kong: Economic Globalisation, Socio-economic Change, and Local Politics', *Journal of Social Policy*, Vol. 34, Part 2 (April 2005), 293–310. doi:10.1017/S0047279404008591

Lee, James K. C., 'Balancing Collectivization and Individual Responsibility: Hong Kong Social Policy under the Chinese Regime', in Kwok-leung Tang (ed.), *Social Development in Asia* (Dordrecht: Kulwer Academic Publishers, 2000).

Lee, Wing-on, and Mark Bray, 'Education: Evolving Patterns and Challenges', in Joseph Y. S. Cheng and Sonny S. H. Lo (eds.), *From Colony to SAR: Hong Kong's Challenges Ahead* (Hong Kong: Chinese University Press, 1995).

Leung, Benjamin K. P., 'The Student Movement in Hong Kong: Transition to a Democratizing Society', in Stephen Wing Kai Chiu and Tai Lok Lui (eds.), *The Dynamics of Social Movement in Hong Kong* (Hong Kong: Hong Kong University Press, 2000).

Leung, Joan Y. H., 'Political Parties: Public Perceptions and Implications for Change', in Ian Scott (ed.), *Institutional Change and the Political Transition in Hong Kong* (London: Macmillan, 1998).

Leung, Man-fuk, 'Medical and Health', in Choi Po-king and Ho Lok-sang (eds.), *The Other Hong Kong Report 1993* (Hong Kong: Chinese University Press, 1993).

Leung, P. C., 'Health and Medical Services', in Larry Chuen-ho Chow and Yiu-kwan Ho (eds.), *The Other Hong Kong Report 1998* (Hong Kong: Chinese University Press, 1999).

Leung, Sai-wing, 'The "China Factor" in the 1991 Legislative Council Election: The June 4th Incident and Anti-Communist China Syndrome', in Lau Siu-kai and Louie Kin-sheun (eds.), *Hong Kong Tried Democracy: The 1991 Elections in Hong Kong* (Hong Kong: Hong Kong Institute of Asia-Pacific Studies, Chinese University of Hong Kong, 1993).

Levin, David A., and Stephen Wing Kai Chu, 'Bureaucratic Insurgency: The Public Sector Labour Movement', in Stephen Wing Kai Chiu and Tai Lok Lui (eds.), *The Dynamics of Social Movement in Hong Kong* (Hong Kong: Hong Kong University Press, 2000).

Lin, Alfred H. Y., 'Warlord, Social Welfare and Philanthropy: The Case of Guangzhou under Chen Jitang, 1929–1936', *Modern China*, Vol. 30, No. 2 (April 2004), 151–98.

Lo, Wai-chung, 'A Review of the Housing Policy', in Joseph Y. S. Cheng (ed.), *The July 1 Protest Rally: Interpreting a Historic Event* (Hong Kong: City University of Hong Kong Press, 2005).

Lui, Tai-lok, 'How a Fragmented Business-Government Alliance Has Helped Change Hong Kong's Political Order', *Hong Kong Journal*, No. 10 (April 2008). URL: www.hkjournal.org/PDF/2008_summer/5.pdf

———, 'Pressure Group Politics in Hong Kong', in Joseph Y. S. Cheng (ed.), *Political Participation in Hong Kong: Theoretical Issues and Historical Legacy* (Hong Kong: City University of Hong Kong Press, 1999).

———, 'The Hong Kong New Middle Class on the Eve of 1997', in Joseph Y. S. Cheng (ed.), *The Other Hong Kong Report 1997* (Hong Kong: Chinese University Press, 1997).

Mackay, Christopher John, 'Housing Management and the Comprehensive Housing Model in Hong Kong: A Case Study of Colonial Influence', *Journal of Contemporary China*, Vol. 9, No. 25 (November 2000), 449–66.

MacPherson, Stewart, and Oi Yu Lo, *A Measure of Poverty*, Department of Public and Social Administration (1997), City University of Hong Kong, Working Paper Series, 1997/2.

Miller, Tony, 'Management Enhancement Programme in the Housing Department', in Anthony B. L. Cheung and Jane C. Y. Lee (eds.), *Public Sector Reform in Hong Kong: Into the 21st Century* (Hong Kong: Chinese University Press, 2001).

Miners, Norman, 'The Representation and Participation of Trade Unions in the Hong Kong Government', in Y. C. Jao et al. (eds.), *Labour Movement in a Changing Society* (Hong Kong: Centre of Asian Studies, University of Hong Kong, 1988).

Mole, David, 'Introduction', in David Mole (ed.), *Managing the New Hong Kong Economy* (Hong Kong: Oxford University Press, 1996).

Ng, Anthony, 'Medical and Health', in T. L. Tsim and Bernard H. K. Luk (eds.), *The Other Hong Kong Report 1989* (Hong Kong: Chinese University Press, 1989).

Ng, Mee Kam, 'Outmoded Planning in the Face of New Politics', in Joseph Y. S. Cheng (ed.), *The Hong Kong Special Administrative Region in Its First Decade* (Hong Kong: City University of Hong Kong Press, 2007).

Ng, Sek-hong, 'Hong Kong Labour Law in Retrospect', in Lee Pui-tak (ed.), *Hong Kong Reintegrating with China: Political, Cultural and Social Dimensions* (Hong Kong: Hong Kong University Press, 2001).

———, 'The Development of Labour Relations in Hong Kong and Some Implications for the Future', in Ian Nish et al. (eds.), *Work and Society: Labour and Human Resources in East Asia* (Hong Kong: Hong Kong University Press, 1996).

Ng, Sek-hong, and Olivia Ip, 'Labour and Society', in Joseph Y. S. Cheng (ed.), *The Hong Kong Special Administrative Region in Its First Decade* (Hong Kong: City University of Hong Kong Press, 2007).

Ngan, Raymond M. H., 'Responding to Poverty, Income Inequality and Social Welfare: The Neo-liberalist Government versus a Social Investment State', in Joseph Y. S. Cheng (ed.), *The Hong Kong Special Administrative Region in Its First decade* (Hong Kong: City University of Hong Kong Press, 2007).

Ngan, Raymond M. H., and Mark Y. K. Li, 'The Dilemma and Crisis for Public Welfare Payments in Hong Kong', in Joseph Y. S. Cheng (ed.), *The July 1 Protest Rally: Interpreting a Historic Event* (Hong Kong: City University of Hong Kong Press, 2005).

Nish, Ian, Gordon Redding, and Ng Sek-hong, 'Industrial Harmony, the Trade Union Movement and Labour Administration in Hong Kong', in Ian Nish et al. (eds.), *Work and Society: Labour and Human Resources in East Asia* (Hong Kong: Hong Kong University Press, 1996).

Owen, Nicholas C., 'Economic Policy', in Keith Hopkins (ed.), *Hong Kong: The Industrial Colony. A Political, Social and Economic Survey* (Hong Kong: Oxford University Press, 1971).

Podmore, David, 'The Population of Hong Kong', in Keith Hopkins (ed.), *Hong Kong: The Industrial Colony. A Political, Social and Economic Survey* (Hong Kong: Oxford University Press, 1971).

Pong, T. L. Sun, 'Caput Schools into Aided Schools: Perceptions of Hong Kong Principals on the Transition', M. Ed. Thesis (University of Hong Kong, 1983).

Redding, Gordon, 'Culture and Business in Hong Kong', in Wang Gangwu and Wong Siu Lun (eds.), *Dynamic Hong Kong: Business and Culture* (Hong Kong: Centre of Asian Studies, University of Hong Kong, 1997).

Savage, Marianne, 'Sheltered Workshops: The Extent to Which Business Practices Can or Should Be Applied to Sheltered Workshops', MBA dissertation, University of Hong Kong (September 1988).

Smart, Alan, and Tai-kok Lui, 'Learning from Civil Unrest: State/Society Relations in Hong Kong before and after the 1967 Disturbances', in Robert

Bickers and Ray Yep (eds.), *May Days in Hong Kong: Riot and Emergency in 1967* (Hong Kong: Hong Kong University Press, 2009).

So, Alvin Y., 'Hong Kong's Problematic Democratic Transition: Power Dependency or Business Hegemony?', *Journal of Asian Studies*, Vol. 59, No. 2 (May 2000), 359–81.

———, 'New Labour Law and Its Implication for the Human Rights Regime in China', in Joseph Y. S. Cheng (ed.), *China: A New Stage of Development for an Emerging Superpower* (Hong Kong: City University of Hong Kong Press, 2012).

So, Daniel W. C., 'Searching for a Bilingual Exit', in Robert Lord and Helen N. L. Cheng (eds.), *Language Education in Hong Kong* (Hong Kong: Chinese University Press, 1987).

Sussman, Nan M., 'Identity Shifts as a Consequence of Crossing Cultures: Hong Kong Chinese Migrants Return Home', in Chan Kwok-bun et al. (eds.), *East-West Identities: Globalization, Localization, and Hybridization* (Leiden: Brill, 2007).

Sweeting, Anthony, 'Education Policy and the 1997 Factor: The Art of the Possible Interacting with the Dismal Science', *Comparative Education*, Vol. 33, No. 2, Special Number (19) (June 1997), 171–85.

———, 'Hong Kong Education within Historical Processes', in Gerald A. Postiglione (ed.), *Education and Society in Hong Kong: Towards One Country and Two Systems* (Armonk: M. E. Sharpe, 1991).

Tai, Benny Yiu-ting, 'The Development of Constitutionalism in Hong Kong', in Raymond Wacks (ed.), *The New Legal Order in Hong Kong* (Hong Kong: Hong Kong University Press, 1999).

Tang, James T. H., 'Taking Care of the Deprived and the Elderly', in James T. H. Tang et al. (eds.), *Knowledge and Social Involvement* (Hong Kong: Faculty of Social Sciences, University of Hong Kong, 2005).

Tang, Shu-hung, 'The Hong Kong Fiscal Policy: Continuity or Redirection?', in Li Pang-kwong (ed.), *Political Order and Power Transition in Hong Kong* (Hong Kong: Chinese University Press, 1997).

Tomlinson, B. R., 'What Was the Third World?', *Journal of Contemporary History*, Vol. 38, No. 2 (April, 2003), 307–21.

Tsang, Jasper Yok-sing, 'Can the LegCo-ExCo Relationship Be Improved?', speech to Hong Kong Democratic Foundation, 5 February 2010. URL: www.hkdf.org/newsarticles.asp?show=newsarticles&newsarticle=263

"Vision for Hong Kong" Study Group, *To Be the Services Metropolis of the Pearl River Delta: A Blueprint for Hong Kong* (Hong Kong: Hong Kong General Chamber of Commerce and Hong Kong Coalition of Service Industries, 2002). URL: www.hkcsi.org.hk/reports/prd_blueprint/blue_print_report.pdf

Wang, Chunxin, Senior Economist, *Economic Review Monthly* (Bank of China (HK) Ltd, May 2003).

Weng, Byron S. J., 'The Hong Kong Model of "One Country, Two Systems": Promises and Problems', in Peter Wesley-Smith and Albert Chen (eds.), *The Basic Law and Hong Kong's Future* (Hong Kong: Butterworths, 1988).

Wilding, Paul, 'Social Policy and Social Development in Hong Kong', *Asian Journal of Public Administration* Vol. 19, No. 2 (December 1997), 244–75.

————, 'Social Policy and Social Development in Hong Kong', *Public and Social Administration Working Paper Series 1996/3*, City University of Hong Kong.

Wong, Chack Kie, 'Squaring the Welfare Circle in Hong Kong: Lessons for Governance in Social Policy', *Asian Survey*, Vol. 48, No. 2 (March–April 2008), 323–42.

Wong, Hung, 'Misled Intervention by a Misplaced Diagnosis: The Hong Kong SAR Government's Policies for Alleviating Poverty and Social Exclusion', *China Review*, Vol. 7, No. 2 (Autumn, 2007), 123–47.

Wong, Siu-lun, and Shirley Yue, 'Satisfaction in Various Life Domains', in Lau Siu-kai et al. (eds.), *Indicators of Social Development Hong Kong 1988* (Hong Kong: Hong Kong Institute of Asia-Pacific Studies, Chinese University of Hong Kong, 1991).

Wong, Victor C. W., 'Medical and Health', in Nyaw Mee-kau and Li Si-ming (eds.), *The Other Hong Kong Report 1996* (Hong Kong: Chinese University Press, 1996).

Wong, Wai-hung, 'Staff Relations in the Civil Service and the Trade Union Response: Review and Prospects, 1971–1985', in Y. C. Jao et al. (eds.), *Labour Movement in a Changing Society* (Hong Kong: Centre of Asian Studies, University of Hong Kong, 1988).

Yeung, C. Y., 'Evolution of Child Health Care in Hong Kong', *Hong Kong Journal of Paediatrics*, Vol. 6, No. 1 (2001), 66–71.

————, 'Health Problems in Chinese Children Are Different', *Hong Kong Journal of Paediatrics*, Vol. 8. No. 2 (2003), 70–86.

Yu, Fong-ying, 'Tradition and Change in Chinese Education', in Robert Lord and Helen N. L. Cheng (eds.), *Language Education in Hong Kong* (Hong Kong: Chinese University Press, 1987).

Yuen, Peter P., 'Dissatisfaction of Health Providers and Consumers: Health Care Reform Intransigence and SARS Outbreak Mismanagement', in Joseph Y. S. Cheng (ed.), *The July 1 Protest Rally: Interpreting a Historic Event* (Hong Kong: City University of Hong Kong Press, 2005).

————, 'Medical and Health Issues', in Joseph Y. S. Cheng, *The Other Hong Kong Report 1997* (Hong Kong: Chinese University Press, 1997).

Zhao Xiaobin et al., 'Income Inequalities under Economic Restructuring in Hong Kong', *Asian Survey*, Vol. 44, No. 3 (May–June, 2004), 442–73.

Index